NIETZSCHE AND PHENOMEN

NIETZSCHE AND PHENOMENOLOGY

Power, Life, Subjectivity

Edited by Élodie Boublil and Christine Daigle

Indiana University Press

Bloomington and Indianapolis

This book is a publication of

Indiana University Press
Office of Scholarly Publishing
Herman B Wells Library 350
1320 E. 10th Street
Bloomington, Indiana 47405–3907 USA

iupress.indiana.edu

Telephone orders	800–842–6796
Fax orders	812–855–7931

© 2013 by Indiana University Press

Manufactured in the United States of America

Library of Congress Cataloging-in-Publication Data

Nietzsche and phenomenology : power, life, subjectivity / edited by Élodie Boublil and Christine Daigle.
  pages cm — (Studies in Continental thought)
  Includes bibliographical references and index.
  ISBN 978-0-253-00925-8 (cloth : alk. paper) — ISBN 978-0-253-00932-6 (pbk. : alk. paper) — ISBN 978-0-253-00944-9 (ebook) 1. Nietzsche, Friedrich Wilhelm, 1844-1900. 2. Phenomenology. I. Daigle, Christine, [date]
  B3317.N486 2013
  193—dc23

                                        2013000400

1 2 3 4 5 18 17 16 15 14 13

Contents

vi | *Contents*

Part III. Subjectivity in the World

Acknowledgments

W<small>E WOULD LIKE</small> to thank our contributors for their enthusiastic response to our invitation to write on the very important topic this volume explores. Without the quality of their individual investigations, this book would not have been possible. We also wish to thank Dee Mortensen, Sarah Eileen Jacobi, and Tim Roberts at Indiana University Press, and the copyeditor, Judith Hoover, for their support and invaluable help on this project. Further, we would like to thank John Sallis for seeing enough value in our manuscript to include it in this prestigious series. Thanks are due to Christopher R. Wood for his work as research assistant on this project; as always, we could count on him for excellent work. Thanks are also due to Bettina Bergo, who translated Didier Franck's contributions, and to Ron Ross for his translations of Françoise Bonardel's and Françoise Dastur's essays. Alina Vaisfeld is to be thanked for her help finalizing the translation of Rudolf Boehm's essay. We are grateful to Rudolf Boehm and Didier Franck for trusting us with the translations of their essays for inclusion in this volume, as well as Kluwer and Presses Universitaires de France for granting us the rights to those essays.

More personal thanks are also due.

Élodie Boublil would like to thank Christine for giving her the chance to work on this project. Christine has been a wonderful coeditor, and Élodie has learned a lot from her experience and *joyful* science. Élodie also acknowledges the support of the Canadian Centre for German and European Studies, which sponsored a research trip to Germany. More personally, Élodie would like to thank her parents, friends, and professors for their support, trust, and inspiring dedication.

Christine Daigle would like to thank Élodie for having set this whole enterprise in motion. Élodie has been a great coeditor, and working with her has been a wonderful experience. Her professionalism, expertise, and hard work have improved this manuscript and made it the valuable book it is now. For that Christine is very thankful. Christine also acknowledges the support of the Canadian Social Sciences and Humanities Research Council, which has, in part, supported this project through a Standard Research Grant. More personally, Christine would like to thank her partner, Eric Gignac, for everything.

NIETZSCHE AND PHENOMENOLOGY

Introduction

Élodie Boublil and Christine Daigle

Against the shortsighted.—Do you think this work must be fragmentary because I
give it to you (and have to give it to you) in fragments?
—*Human, All Too Human* II, "Assorted Opinions and Maxims," §128

Putting *Nietzsche* and *phenomenology* together in the same sentence might be
startling to some, even unpalatable to others. Nietzsche's writing style along with his
rejection of the *Spirit of Gravity*[1] would seem to oppose the very goal of the phenomenological project as well as its foundational and scientific ambition. To Nietzsche
scholars, his philosophy would be irreducible to any kind of philosophical school or
movement and would need to be treated on its own if one wants to respect the claim
for singularity conveyed by his philosophy. To would-be phenomenologists, the so-
called nihilistic enterprise led by Nietzsche should not be the last word addressed to
modernity before its unavoidable decay: another method—another pathway—should
be implemented in order to ultimately uncover some common ontological and ethical
grounds upon which humanity could dwell.

Husserl's phenomenological project uncovers the foundational nature of transcendental subjectivity from a scientific as well as a practical point of view. As Husserl
claimed at the end of the *Vienna Lecture (May 1935)*, the intentional and teleological structure of transcendental subjectivity guarantees its universality and allows it to
overcome the value-relativism and theoretical positivism to which previous critiques
of metaphysics have led:

> The "crisis" could then become clear as the "seeming collapse of rationalism." Still,
> as we said, the reason for the downfall of a rational culture does not lie in the essence
> of rationalism itself but only in its exteriorization, its absorption in "naturalism"
> and "objectivism." The crisis of European existence can end in only one of two ways:
> in the ruin of a Europe alienated from its rational sense of life, fallen into a bar-
> barian hatred of spirit; or in the rebirth of Europe from the spirit of philosophy,
> through a heroism of reason that will definitively overcome naturalism.[2]

Heidegger's view seems to take up this same task while emphasizing its ontological rather than epistemic sense. The call of Being would seem to replace any metaphysical ground insofar as it would allow *Dasein* to comprehend the very possibility of its own existence and to achieve it authentically. In Merleau-Ponty, notions of perception and institution would probably help get rid of the objectivistic connotations associated with the notion of foundation—and, ultimately, the overcoming of Cartesian ontology—while granting individuals as well as communities some power to perpetuate and flourish through their own expressions and instantiations. Even roughly and briefly summarized, these three phenomenological approaches seem to show that there is a positivity at stake in phenomenology that would go beyond the destructive process implemented by Nietzsche's philosophy. Why, then, explore the historical and philosophical relations between Nietzsche and phenomenology? Could phenomenology actually qualify as a *fröhliche Wissenschaft*?[3]

The topic of our volume is one that ought to have been explored for a long time. Scholars hinted at the connection, pointed in its direction, even suggested how potentially rich such a reading would be, and yet, possibly due to the aforementioned reasons, there is still only one book-length inquiry into the topic.[4] Boehm's "Husserl und Nietzsche" (1968)[5] constituted the first attempt to draw a comparison between Husserl's phenomenology and Nietzsche's thought. Boehm notably put the emphasis on their common approach to life as a meaning-making process and on the fact that there seems to be a precedence of the life-world (*Lebenswelt*) over theoretical and scientific constructions in both philosophies. Why has this similarity been left unexplored until rather recently when, it is our conviction, such an inquiry into the connection between Nietzsche and phenomenology can yield very interesting results? It may be time to go beyond the detrimental dichotomy that has characterized the relations between Nietzsche's and phenomenology's respective projects up to this point, and to leave aside the shortsighted views conveyed by a historical approach that would conceive of philosophy as fragmentary. Before exposing why this encounter would be philosophically fruitful, we would first like to explain why ceasing to see both Nietzsche's works and phenomenological works *fragmentarily* calls for a new form of comparativism that would avoid hasty assimilations, irreducible dividing lines, or anachronistic evaluations.

If it is true that any philosophy is liable to be misinterpreted, one such as Nietzsche's—with its peculiar style and manner of expression—is all the more vulnerable to being misread.[6] The history of scholarship on Nietzsche abounds with examples of misconceptions. Nietzsche has been variously conceived of as an anti-Semite, a misogynist, an apolitical thinker, and a thinker whose politics could be used to support a specific agenda (be it democratic, aristocratic, or fascist). He has been understood to be an amoralist, an immoralist, or a moralist after all. He is conceived of as an existentialist or as a materialist. An existentialist or a postmodern par excellence.[7] He is read as a philosopher determined to sound idols with his hammer,[8] using extensive and acerbic criticism, all the while being influenced by past philosophers from the pre-Socratics to even Kant—often perceived to be his archenemy.[9] Some interpreters have focused on Nietzsche's critical and nihilistic moment to such an extent that they forget or can no longer see that he was a great builder. These interpreters have entirely missed the constructive moment in his thought. Contrary to them, we wish to take Nietzsche seriously when he asserts, "We negate and must negate because something in us wants to live and affirm" (*The Gay Science* §307; hereafter GS). We want to consider Nietzsche's affirmative contribution to philosophy and examine what he offers as a result of his rejection of some philosophical views. Our volume will not consist in offering purely historical analyses dealing with the reception and influence of Nietzsche's works. Rather, it aims to uncover, phenomenologically, some common enterprise shared by these philosophers, given their acknowledgment of the necessity to define again subjectivity, and examine how it is informed by its relation to life and power. Doing so will allow us to shed new light on phenomenology's project and perspective.

While the "shortsightedness" of many interpreters may explain the lack of treatment of our topic, another reason may well have been at work. Comparative work in philosophy is problematic in many ways. Indeed comparative work is what we do when we inquire into the possibility of reading Nietzsche as a phenomenologist. But there are different ways and methods to approach comparativism itself. In this volume, contributors examine various ties between Nietzsche's philosophy and that of Husserl, Fink, Heidegger, and Merleau-Ponty, among others. This is problematic methodologically as there is no apparent unity within phenomenology, no single iteration of phenomenology that encompasses all individual instances. Thus we lack a monolithic phenomenology to contrast and compare Nietzsche's philosophy to. Likewise there is no agreement among scholars as to how to interpret Nietzsche, as we hinted at above. Thus there is not *one* Nietzsche confronting *one* phenomenology. Ought the project to be abandoned, then, since we seem to be standing on less than firm terrain? We do not think so. In fact we think that there is a more fundamental unity to be uncovered through careful analysis. We see Nietzsche and phenomenologists of any inclination to be engaged in an understanding and deciphering of the world and the human being therein in terms of subjectivity, life forces, and power.

Thus our aim is not to state some identity between the content of Nietzsche's philosophy and that of these phenomenologists. In other words, we are not looking for strictly identical views and treatments of philosophical concepts. If we are going to claim that Nietzsche was a phenomenologist avant la lettre, then we would rather engage in a particular kind of comparative work in which we would examine what concepts and philosophical tenets he may share with proclaimed phenomenologists, while retaining a genealogical approach of these perspectives by evaluating how they would enrich, in a similar way, our relation to the natural as well as the social worlds.

Nietzschean perspectivism is precisely what allows us to undertake our project. While perspectivism does not validate just any interpretation of a philosophy, it allows the scholar to enter its pathways through various angles and see where these lead. In Nietzsche, there are no *Holzwege*; all paths lead somewhere.[10] This is both helpful and dangerous since Nietzsche and his readers are led to take risks by suggesting new interpretations. It is in this spirit, while taking the necessary methodological precautions, that both we and our contributors approach the questions that this collection poses: Are there concepts in Nietzsche that stand as phenomenological concepts? Are there concepts in phenomenology that have their origin in Nietzschean proposals? Is the Nietzschean philosophical method akin to that of phenomenologists? What type of phenomenology, if any, stands closer to Nietzsche, and what is it in that phenomenology and in Nietzsche's philosophy that allows us to bring them together? In a Nietzschean vein, we ourselves have adopted certain phenomenological perspectives toward our set of questions. Thus we are not aiming at scientific truth or certainty but at some interpretative suggestions that can feed contemporary thought and renew some debates in phenomenology and the history of philosophy.

By showing the connections between Nietzsche's philosophy and the phenomenological movement, this volume sheds new light on the history of nineteenth- and twentieth-century philosophy. However, it also has intrinsic philosophical value and aims to go beyond the strict study of Nietzsche's historical reception by phenomenologists. Indeed bringing Nietzsche and phenomenology together is likely to yield interesting results with regard to a better understanding of human consciousness as intertwined with its world and with others.

The exploration of the notions of intentionality, intersubjectivity, consciousness and life-world, embodiment, and values, as they are dealt with by Nietzsche and phenomenologists from both an ontological and an epistemological perspective will shed light on crucial contemporary philosophical problems. Philosophers are still struggling with founding ethics and values in a world that is now secular and devoid of its past transcendent realm of certainty, and therefore have trouble finding criteria to arbitrate between mundane, political, and religious worldviews. We are indeed still working out the implications of the death of God, famously proclaimed in Nietzsche's *The Gay Science*:

> Who gave us the sponge to wipe away the entire horizon? What were we doing when we unchained this earth from its sun? Where is it moving to now? Where are we moving to? Away from all suns? Are we not continually falling? And backwards, sidewards, forwards, in all directions? Is there still an up and a down? Aren't we straying as though through an infinite nothing? . . . How can we console ourselves, the murderers of all murderers? . . . There was never a greater deed—and whoever is born after us will on account of this deed belong to a higher history than all history up to now! (GS §125)

The ethical problem that ensues from the death of God necessitates that we reconceive of ourselves and our relation both to and with the world and others. Understanding ourselves in phenomenological terms as intentional consciousnesses may have great ethical—and, by extension, political—implications. Some of our contributors will delve into these and show that the interrogations of the madman have haunted European philosophy throughout the twentieth century and that the phenomenological method is in some sense an attempt to overcome nihilism by trying to recover the meaningfulness of the human experience and of the things themselves and reopening multiple horizons. Our volume will inevitably leave some questions unanswered. In fact asking the question of "Nietzsche and phenomenology" is an opening of the inquiry. We hope to settle a number of issues and indeed demonstrate that this undertaking is valid and fruitful both historically and philosophically. Readers will be convinced, as we are, that our question(s), rather than being *Holzwege*, in fact open(s) up rich pathways that must be explored. The following contributions take us on some of these.

Summary of Contributions

This volume is divided into three parts, following the core philosophical issues that seem to be at stake in tackling the question of the relation between Nietzsche and phenomenology: life, power, and subjectivity. The first part of the book explores from both a historical and a comparative perspective the connections between Nietzsche's approach to life and the way phenomenologists conceived of the life-world with regard to subjectivity's mundane experiences. Boehm's "Husserl and Nietzsche" opens the inquiry by exploring the relations between life and reason in the works of the two thinkers. Boehm concludes that, far from being irreducibly opposed, Nietzsche's thought as well as phenomenology both draw on Leibnizian ontology and introduce an interpretation of life that overcomes metaphysical and representational thinking. They do so while assigning a new foundational task to modern subjectivity in order to answer the crisis of European nihilism. By exploring the connections between consciousness, individuation, and the world, both Nietzsche and Husserl propose a description of intentionality that renews the philosophical conception of the phenomenal realm and therefore helps rebuild the origin and goal of meaning-making processes despite subjectivity's finitude (see Daigle). The structure of subjective experience in suffering (see Geniusas) and moral judgments (see Golden) is further questioned in this section in order to see how we might reconcile Husserl's teleology and Nietzsche's genealogy. Even if their respective dynamics seem to go in opposite directions, both Husserl and Nietzsche show the impossibility of reducing subjective life to psychological mechanisms and call for a new task of interpretation in order to free subjectivity from its natural—in the sense of the "natural attitude"—and moral bonds. The next two essays examine the ontological and historical foundations of the transcendental nature and creativity of life uncovered by such inquiries. For instance, Nishitani's reception of Nietzsche challenges Heidegger's interpretation, according to which he would have been the last metaphysician and the achiever of nihilism—showing therefore strong connections between Nietzsche's conception of transvaluation and the kind of *lived* phenomenology initiated by the Kyoto School (see Bonardel). On the other hand,

Fink's philosophy, with its emphasis on play and creativity, also demonstrates a fruitful interplay between Nietzsche and phenomenology by conceiving the latter as the "herald" of a new "ontological experience" (see Dastur). Indeed Nietzsche's conception of creative life would have anticipated the idea of a "cosmological difference" within the world itself—a sort of primordial dehiscence within the subject and the world which intrinsically inhabits the movement of life.

The second part of the book focuses on the notion of power, on the possibilities opened up by such a conception of life, and on the ontological, aesthetic, and historical expressions and forces conveyed by Nietzschean and phenomenological interpretations of the life-world. The phenomenological importance of embodiment and style in phenomenology echoes Nietzsche's dramatic and philological approach to existence (see Babich). Both methods point to new epistemological practices which consider life as performance and rely on the embodied experiences of human mind in order to *read* worldly phenomena in light of their own perspectival perceptions. By escaping metaphysical and representational thinking, Nietzsche's thought—as well as phenomenology in its three main moments (Husserl, Heidegger, Merleau-Ponty)—draws on a particular kind of vision which cannot be dissociated from the enigma of subjectivity and the riddles that the latter faces (see Boublil). Interpreting the phenomenological gaze in terms of pure *presencing* would miss the enigma and dynamism its forces try to preserve and keep alive, whether we call it "will to power," "intentional consciousness," *Ereignis,* or the "flesh." It is important, then, to question the ontological structures and features of these forces that sustain subjectivity's intentional relation to the world. Beyond their different motives and conclusions, Husserl's and Nietzsche's interests in biology demonstrate a common will to account for the forces and dynamism that characterize, from a phenomenological point of view, the life of subjectivity and the perception of the world (see Bergo). Such an enterprise has anticipated and influenced later philosophical (Merleau-Ponty) and epistemological (Andrieu, Varela) works that attempt to overcome Cartesian dualistic ontology in order to better express the reality and unity of subjectivity's life and forces. Nietzsche and Merleau-Ponty's genealogical and archaeological conceptions of activity and passivity also show a similar will to overcome Cartesian and metaphysical dichotomies (see Chouraqui). Both approaches point toward an indirect ontology that nonetheless insists on the fundamental dynamics of forces and desires that keep on feeding an originary differentiation involved in subjective and mundane processes. This ontological power is also an aesthetic one since it cannot be dissociated from its expressions. The case of the work of art also helps illustrate and delve into such connections. By exploring the meaning of Transfiguration through Nietzsche's analysis of Raphael's painting in *The Birth of Tragedy* and Merleau-Ponty's understanding of the meaning of the Transfiguration of the flesh (see Johnson), it is possible to reconsider the links between transcendence and incarnation and therefore offer a phenomenological notion of expression capable of conveying truth and profundity without leaving aside subjectivity's bodily engagement with the world.

The third section of this volume aims to grasp and assess the ethical, political, and ontological consequences of reading Nietzsche alongside phenomenology by exploring and delineating a concept of subjectivity divested of its metaphysical residues or postmodern condemnations while still remaining tied to the issues of life and power that motivated them. For instance, in *Dawn*, Nietzsche has carried out a series of phenomenological analyses that anticipate the challenges the phenomenological method faces once the vanity of any Cartesian epistemological way of thinking is acknowledged (see Ansell-Pearson). This perspectivism calls for a new mode of life sustained by cheerfulness (*Heiterkeit*) before the infinite task of world-interpretation. Becoming what we are thus involves the fashioning of possibilities of life through a shared commitment to life experiences and "experimental" philosophy. Therefore one can see in Nietzsche the premise of a phenomenology of values where human life is focused on the issues of the appearance of meaning and value and their consistency despite the historical and cultural power relations they are intertwined with (see Hatab). Such an ethics of life could answer some of phenomenology's original concerns regarding the life-world and intersubjective relations. Sharing with phenomenology a similar lack of metaphysical grounds upon which moral systems could be justified, Nietzschean ethics would nonetheless escape moral relativism by understanding subjectivity's relation to the world in terms of contention and commitment. It thus seems necessary to reshape the notions of intentionality and subjectivity by taking into account both their embodied structure and their life and expressions. The last two chapters therefore reveal drive intentionality and embodied experience as the proper object of phenomenology but also the source of its ultimate and unresolved questions (see Franck). A confrontation between Nietzsche and phenomenology thus indicates what remains to be addressed by philosophy as well as the ontological—and thereby ethical—limits of contemporary thought.

Notes

1. In *Thus Spoke Zarathustra*, Nietzsche flayed what he calls the "Spirit of Gravity," which refers to the seriousness and profoundness of theories developed by theologians and philosophers and which approach life from a moral perspective. Thinking in terms of "good" and "evil" prevents one from "flying" and being creative in the sense that it refers to some predefined and illusory meaning granted to existence. This expression also targets any willing to look for objective truth and may also be applied to any modern scientific method that has a foundational goal.

2. Husserl, "Philosophy and the Crisis of European Man," 191–92.

3. The title of Nietzsche's 1882 book, *Die fröhliche Wissenschaft*, translates as "The Gay Science." As Walter Kaufmann has pointed out in his introduction to his translation of the work, Nietzsche has opted for "gay," *fröhlich*, rather than "cheerful," *heiter*, for a good reason: "'Gay science,' unlike 'cheerful science,' has overtones of a light-hearted defiance of conventions: it suggests Nietzsche's 'immoralism' and his 'reevaluation of values'" (Kaufmann, "Translator's Introduction," 5). As we will see, Nietzsche's method, as well as the phenomenological method, are critical and nihilistic but with the aim of reconstructing and offering new grounds for valuing. A "science" that would be merely nihilistic would be anything but gay.

4. The collection of essays titled *Nietzsche and Phenomenology* (Cambridge Scholars Publishing) is a conference proceedings of a meeting held by the British Society for Phenomenology in the spring of 2009 on the theme "Nietzsche and Phenomenology."

5. See our translation in chapter 1 of this volume. Boehm's essay first appeared in French as "Husserl et Nietzsche" in 1962.

6. Nietzsche's aphoristic style makes him vulnerable to misinterpretations. However, it plays an important methodological—and dare we say "phenomenological"—role in his philosophy. Nietzschean aphorisms are not definitions in the strict sense of the word (the Greek *aphorismos* means "determination" and is derived from the verb *aphorizo*, which means "to mark off with boundaries"). While aphorisms in Nietzsche do circumscribe a certain theme or topic, they are also open to a multiplicity of interpretations. Jill Marsden has suggested that they reflect the spontaneity of thought. Taken together they do not present a neatly organized and systematic discourse, but "[they are] only fragmentary to the extent that [they fragment] expectations. By failing to supply the 'connective tissue' that would impose a semblance of unity on the text, Nietzsche compels his readers to be active in their reception of his ideas" ("Nietzsche and the Art of the Aphorism," 30). Considering the impact of this methodological choice, Blondel proposed that Nietzsche's aphoristic discourse is "subversive" (*Nietzsche*, 28ff.). Indeed it is the right method for a philosophy that aims to go beyond the metaphysical all the while critiquing language. This is in agreement with Giorgio Colli's judgment, according to which the aphoristic style is revealing of Nietzsche's distrust of logical proofs and argumentative series (see Nachwort, 708–9). For more on the aphoristic style, see Marsden, "Nietzsche and the Art of the Aphorism." For an argument as to why the aphoristic style is appropriate for a phenomenological approach, see Daigle, "Nietzsche's Notion of Embodied Self," 228. For a discussion of the aphoristic style as it pertains specifically to *Dawn*, see Keith Ansell-Pearson's essay in this volume.

7. Conducting a bibliographical search on Nietzsche and any of these keywords—*politics, ethics, existentialism, materialism, naturalism*—yields a wealth of sources with divergent readings of his philosophy. Divergence in interpretation is certainly not peculiar to Nietzsche's philosophy, but we contend that it has been—and continues to be—much more marked in his case than in the cases of other, even controversial philosophers.

8. This is a reference to Nietzsche's explanation of the task of *Twilight of the Idols*, which has as a subtitle "How to Philosophize with a Hammer." In the foreword of the work he says, "This little book is a *grand declaration of war*; and as regards the sounding-out of idols, this time they are not idols of the age but *eternal* idols which are here touched with the hammer as with a tuning fork" (*Twilight of the Idols* 32).

9. This is a mistaken view, as Hill, among others, has convincingly shown in his *Nietzsche's Critiques*. Hill's study and Nietzsche's relation to Kant is briefly discussed by Daigle in chapter 2 of this volume.

10. This is, of course, a reference to Heidegger's famous collection of essays titled *Holzwege*. *Holzwege* are literally paths in the woods that do not lead anywhere.

Bibliography

Blondel, Eric. *Nietzsche: Le corps et la culture*. Paris: PUF, 1986.

Colli, Giorgio. Nachwort [Afterword] to *Menschliches, Allzumenshliches I und II*, by Friedrich Nietzsche. In *Kritische Studienausgabe*. Edited by Giorgio Colli and Mazzino Montinari. München: Walter de Gruyter, 1999.

Daigle, Christine. "Nietzsche's Notion of Embodied Self: Proto-Phenomenology at Work?" *Nietzsche-Studien* 40 (2011): 226–43.

Hill, R. Kevin. *Nietzsche's Critiques: The Kantian Foundations of his Thought*. Oxford: Clarendon Press, 2003.

Husserl, Edmund. "Philosophy and the Crisis of European Man." In *Phenomenology and the Crisis of Philosophy,* translated by Quentin Lauer. New York: Harper & Row, 1965.

Kaufmann, Walter. "Translator's Introduction." In *The Gay Science*, by Friedrich Nietzsche, translated by Walter Kaufmann. New York: Vintage, 1974.

Marsden, Jill. "Nietzsche and the Art of the Aphorism." In *A Companion to Nietzsche*, edited by Keith Ansell-Pearson. Oxford: Blackwell, 2006.

Nietzsche, Friedrich. *Human, All Too Human: A Book for Free Spirits*. Translated by R. J. Hollingdale. Introduction by R. Schacht. Cambridge: Cambridge University Press, 1996.

———. *The Gay Science*. Translated by W. Kaufmann. New York: Vintage Books, 1974.

———. *Twilight of the Idols/The Anti-Christ*. Translated by R. J. Hollingdale. London: Penguin Books, 1990.

Rehberg, Andrea, ed. *Nietzsche and Phenomenology*. Newcastle upon Tyne: Cambridge Scholars Publishing, 2011.

PART I

LIFE AND INTENTIONALITY

1 Husserl and Nietzsche

Rudolf Boehm

Just as the same city viewed from different directions appears entirely different and, as it were, multiplied perspectively, in just the same way it happens that, because of the infinite multitude of simple substances, there are, as it were, just as many different universes, which are, nevertheless, only perspectives on a single one, corresponding to the different points of view of each monad.

—Leibniz, *Monadology*

EACH POINT OF view limits our view.[1] However, a point of view is needed in order to see anything at all. "All life is taking a position," said Husserl[2]; it is "an engaging."

Philosophers' lives do not seem exempt from this rule. In the end, philosophers are able to reach such a point of view—which is essential for them to see anything at all—only when they "engage," when they "take a position."[3] Nevertheless a philosopher's point of view—as little as any other—does not essentially concern itself with what is uncovered by her gaze, since, although indispensable for seeing, points of views rather indicate the limits within which philosophers are able to grasp what they see.

As clear and lucid as this reflection may seem, it shall here be given a more detailed explanation: to elucidate it is almost my only intention in the following account. As my example, I choose *Husserl* and *Nietzsche*. The latter took a position for the right and the power of life—against the insolence of a reason, which is, secretly or openly, an enemy to life, to its right, and to its power. The former advocated a new kind of rationalism, which alone, so he thought, would be able to restore life's meaning. In light of what is raised by such an opposition, there is presumably no other choice but to take a stand for one side or for the other—to take "life's side" or "Reason's side"—if, in the end, one wishes to reach a standpoint or insight on this level. Yet the affirmation still holds that whatever becomes open to view does so only despite the boundaries that are proper to these two opposite points of view. This will become more perspicuous not when we manage to overcome these two divergent points of view (which would mean, at best, adopting a third one) but rather when we intercept the path that links the two viewpoints together at this level. It becomes essential, then, in the following pages, to attempt to delineate, albeit provisionally, the path that links together the two—unarguably opposed—points of view of Nietzsche and Husserl.[4]

However, before we explore this path, let us note that it is always such a "change in position" or such an "entering of a path" that endows a philosopher with a plurality of viewpoints.[5] But this does nothing to change the problem.[6] Let us note also that with precisely such a "change in position" a philosopher exposes herself usually to objections and criticisms from those who take a philosopher's commitment to be the essence of philosophy. Such critique forgets that the fundamental is not what is essential, and that the essential is not the fundamental.[7] The requirement to have gained a viewpoint is fundamental in order to see, yet what is essential is to see.

I

It seems surprising that the far-reaching analogy—if not the agreement between Husserl's analysis of the crisis of European rationalism, especially in the treatise on *The Crisis of European Sciences and Transcendental Phenomenology*[8] and the one developed by Nietzsche in *Twilight of the Idols*,[9] for instance—has been barely noticed.[10] For Husserl, as well as for Nietzsche, what is ultimately at stake in this crisis is the Socratic-Platonic ideal of philosophy and the knowledge inherited and renewed from the modern era by the West. For both Husserl and Nietzsche, this ideal has proven to be abstract and unrealizable; the attempts that have been undertaken—since the beginning of the modern world (defined precisely by these attempts)—to realize this ideal have, on the one hand, engendered merely grandiose constructs, the meaning of which grows more and more distant from a meaning that real life would require. On the other hand, these attempts have brought to light facts and situations that, as seemed evident, would resist all attempts at being subjected to the reign of reason and the relevance of which would in fact make the ideal of rationalism itself appear doubtful, questionable, and even suspicious.

It is to nothing else but the "life-world" (Husserl's concept of *Lebenswelt*) that any rationalism remains abstract and ultimately blind; that is precisely the world in which rationalism should take its roots in order to implement itself. For both Husserl and Nietzsche, this life-world is the "only real world."[11] However, since the life-world constitutes a unique system of subjective relativities, it will never be able to conform to an actual rationalization nor to serve as ground for the merely theoretical construction of a truly rigorous science or philosophy. What is real in this life-world is so not depending on whether it is more or less "true" or "false"; in this world, everything is expression, realization, and effectivity. What truly causes effects in this life-world is that which gains access to the motivations of this world's life. What in particular—if one can here speak of something merely particular—determines the effective course of events in the domain of the history of ideas is not the "objective" meaning, objectively "true" meaning, of any fact or situation, but rather it is the conception, analysis, or interpretation of a fact or situation that will successfully establish itself independently of its "truth" or "falsity." On this plane of the real history of life, it is completely useless to ask oneself, for instance, whether or not the dominant Renaissance conception of the meaning of Antiquity really and objectively expressed the "true" and "genuine" meaning of Antiquity itself. Insofar as the meaning of Antiquity is indeed still determined for us by the image of Antiquity, which the Renaissance conveyed, Antiquity *acquires* its meaning from it: it *is* that meaning.[12]

One can say in general that the historical life-world, the only real world, is the world of *absolute meaning* if one understands by "absolute" meaning one that is simply and entirely independent from any "objective" ground, since, as a matter of fact, every meaning escapes *as such* the reign of the principle of noncontradiction and therefore escapes being grasped by genuine knowledge. Indeed nothing satisfies the demand of signifying and *not signifying* the same thing at the same time and in the same respect if one does not add: for someone, for us Europeans, for our time, and so on. But such an addendum precisely reduces the principle of noncontradiction—as Husserl showed like no one else[13]—into a merely empirical judgment about psychical facts.

However, it is well known that for Nietzsche the crisis of rationalism, which breaks out when the latter is confronted with the realities of the life-world, is more than a mere crisis: it is the definitive ruin of this ideal. For Husserl, on the other hand, the contemporary crisis of traditional rationalism can and must initiate a reflection from which a renewed rationalism would have to emerge, at last truly absolute, truly all-encompassing, and really concrete. According to Husserl, this new rationalism will have to give up on settling on the ground of the life-world itself, which has shown itself to be simply unable to support the construction of absolute knowledge—and must rather be founded on a basis that it would first have to make for itself: namely, the basis of *absolute subjectivity*, upon which the relativities of the life-world must be traced as phenomena of relative subjectivity.

Here an opposition between the perspectives of Husserl and Nietzsche already opens up, one that seems insurmountable. But as soon as we attend to a reflection offered by Nietzsche in *Twilight of the Idols*, this impression fades away. Nietzsche ends the famous passage where he recounts the "History of an error" and which is entitled "How the 'True World' Finally Became a Fable" by asking the following question: "The true world—we have abolished. What world has remained? The apparent one perhaps?" To which he answers: "But no! With the true world we have also abolished the apparent one."[14] For Nietzsche, this conclusion means—as he continues within brackets—"Noon; moment of the briefest shadow; end of the longest error; high point of humanity; INCIPIT ZARATHUSTRA."[15] What does this mean for us?

It is obvious that when Nietzsche talks here about the *Abschaffen* (Abolishing) of the *wahren Welt* (true world) and of the *scheinbaren Welt* (apparent world), he means something different each time with the same word *abschaffen*. Yet indeed, if the "true world" of the Reason of the old rationalism is to be disposed of as an illusion, since the apparently, or perhaps assumed "apparent" world proves to be the "only real world" (Husserl), then no "rational ground" will any longer justify referring to the life-world as the "apparent" world. Dismissing the illusory idea of a "true world" of which rationalism dreamed, one has thereby also dismissed the illusion of thinking of our life-world as merely an "apparent" world. Our life-world is throughout and absolutely constituted by what the rationalist notion of truth forces us to take as "mere appearances," but it is therefore not an apparent world. Rather, these appearances themselves and their life-world-constitutive system are the whole reality and, consequently, in this sense of reality, the entire truth even if the latter is quite different from the one imagined by traditional rationalism: if the truths of the life-world are no longer to be measured according to their degree of correspondence to the truth of a "true world" (because this exemplary world proves to be inexistent), then truth and appearance—and incidentally appearance and phenomenon (*Schein und Erscheinung*)—cease to stand against each other and instead merge into each other.

Was the task of the "transvaluation of all values" (*Umwertung aller Werte*) that Nietzsche posited at the end of his intellectual journey—and the solution of which was supposed to be provided by his major work—not precisely the task that, evidently, emerged because of the lucid reflection with which he concludes in *Twilight of the Idols* the story of the "longest" error of humanity: "With the true world we have also abolished the apparent one"? We must content ourselves here with posing this question. In any case, as is well known, Nietzsche was not able to finish this work and, moreover, left behind only outlines of a draft for a transvaluation of the truth-value of the "apparent world." The task, if indeed it was Nietzsche's task, was enormous, as we can now concretely assess in light of the dimensions of Husserl's work, which become slowly perceivable while remaining utterly impossible to take in with one glance.[16] We should demonstrate indeed that the Husserlian conception of a new rationalism grounded upon a reference back to absolute subjectivity—the Husserlian conception of a new "first philosophy" that would not be metaphysics anymore but "transcendental phenomenology"[17]—corresponds, in its essentials, exactly with the task of the transvaluation, as we have indicated it following Nietzsche's conclusion to the history of the "longest error" of mankind. For Husserl, the point is to grasp and ground the Absolute implied by the life-world's system of relativities; it is as such that subjectivity concerns him. Or, put differently, Husserl needs to "make true" (*wahrmachen*) what skepticism has so far objected to and opposed to the rationalist ideal of truth:[18] to force antirationalist skepticism, by leading it back to its ultimate consequences, to admit and to reveal what must be "true" about antirationalist skepticism itself. This is even one of the definitions Husserl gives for the method of "phenomenological reduction"—which he considers "the most fundamental of all methods"—and for "the original Cartesian motif,"[19] which guides this method.

As we know, this method is supposed to bring to light the constitutive intentionality of consciousness and thereby the sense of everything and everyone that can be constituted for us as an object. This ambition stands in analogy to the task that emerges in the realm of propositions and that requires an analysis of the sense of the terms of each proposition before making any judgment. It essentially aims at freeing our questions and problems from all abstract criteria stemming from preconceived ideas about "truth," "objectivity," or "being" ("in-itself")—criteria and ideas that are merely ungrounded postulates and cannot consequently pretend to serve as measures for what is genuinely a phenomenon. Let us recall here only one of the most famous examples of Husserl's procedure: his analysis of the apparent or so-called problem of knowledge in the *Cartesian Meditations*.[20]

II

One still wonders today about the very meaning of this Husserlian notion of "constitution" of an object "through" "transcendental" consciousness.[21] For instance, is the constitution of a *thing* through consciousness, in the Husserlian sense, the same as the "creation" of that thing? Or is it only its "unveiling"? The answer is that none of those describes the constitution of a thing. The being of a thing cannot have any other meaning for us; or more precisely, what we call the being of a thing can *very simply* have no other meaning than the one it derives from the way we constitute, and can generally constitute, this "concept" of being-a-thing (*Dingseins*). First and fundamentally, the problem of constitution concerns only the constitution of a thing—and of anything generally—*as an object* for us. Although every question, which would relate to the ontic genesis of what we are able to recognize and approach as an object only thanks to this constitution, can receive a verifiable meaning only from this very constitution, it does not follow that this genesis is equivalent to the becoming of the *thing* itself that we consider an object. Nevertheless the constitution of objects, which interests phenomenological research, is not to be reduced to a pure epistemological problem, which would concern only the "unveiling" of things that "are" already "there," simply awaiting to be "unveiled." Formally, every constitution is, in the phenomenological sense, an *interpretation* insofar as every constitution is—in accordance with the common use of the term—a constitution *of* "something" *as* "something."[22] We know that the Husserlian theory of phenomenological constitution is originally founded upon a distinction between *hylē* and *morphē*, between "sensuous content [*Inhalt*]" and "intellective form" or "noetic apprehension [*Auffassung*]."[23] This distinction goes back in turn to the one to be made, according to Husserl, between "sensation" and "perception" in general, since one and the same "sensation" can awaken many different "perceptions," whereas many different "sensations" can be grasped by one single "perception."[24] When introducing this distinction (which Husserl did not invent himself) in the *Logical Investigations*, he talks about a "surplus" of "interpretation" and "meaning" that the perception has over the sensation.[25] This phenomenon of interpreting sensuous content by and through perception is at the core of Husserl's problem of the constitution of objects. But, precisely, an interpretation is neither a simple "unveiling" nor a simple "creation" of something in the objective sense of the word. It is a shedding of light, but not of a thing that would be already there or given as revealed by the interpretation. It is creation not of the object that it presents but of its meaning.

It is true that in the works following the *Logical Investigations* and *The Phenomenology of Internal Time Consciousness*,[26] Husserl avoids the use of the word *interpretation* when talking about problems of phenomenological constitution even if he continues to speak of "apprehension" (*Auffassung*) and "presentation" (*Darstellung*).[27] But we should specify now that it is only *initially*, as we said before, that Husserl's theory of constitution is founded upon this distinction between "matter" and "form," which only seems to be truly radical. Even if Husserl continues to use the "content-apprehension" schema for propaedeutic reasons,[28] he gives up and overcomes the latter in principle as early as his first inquiries into the structure of the fundamental constitution of "immanent" time.[29] It seems that, for Husserl, using the word *interpretation* with regard to the phenomenon of constitution was too closely tied up with that original schema. However, giving up and overcoming the "content-apprehension" schema merely amounts to the recognition that on the fundamental level of the constitution of "immanent" time—and therefore ultimately—there is no "object" of interpretation that could have been considered as pregiven "matters" or "contents." Every "matter" and every "content" are themselves the outcomes of previous "apprehensions" of pregiven "matters" or "contents," which were themselves the outcome of previous accomplishments of apprehension and so on ad infinitum.[30] What is "first" here are not the elements, pregiven in whatever form of "in-itself," but the perpetually moving interweaving of pure perspectives, which, as perpetually flowing, makes itself, constitutes itself, and undoes itself independently from any active interference of our consciousness. And that is precisely what *Time* ultimately is: the fundamental proof of a perspectivism that is and moves only of itself and in itself.[31] Here the *truth* is finally revealed, which lies hidden in that whose evidence would have us doubt the possibility of (objective) "truth" as such. And insofar as the sense of "interpretation"—which is peculiar to the constitution—deepens and refines itself, it links itself to the "absolute meaning," which we mentioned earlier.

Let us attempt to circumscribe more precisely this sense with the help of our previous reflections. First of all, the point is not to measure these constitutive interpretations against a vague and preconceived idea of "objective" truth. Once this phenomenological principle is established, these constitutive interpretations remain interpretations for sure, but their truth is no longer dependent upon their relation to a presumed objective content of what is taken as the object of interpretation. The problem of their truth is no longer a matter of adequacy to some "content" or "object" but merely and solely a matter of evidence—or, as Husserl puts it, of original *presence*.[32] Or, if you wish, the problem of truth is only that of the actuality of what is constituted as an object by—and only by—the interpretation. Every question regarding truth must orient itself first and ultimately exclusively toward this sole actuality and toward the measure *it* prescribes.

But it is sufficient to have shown here in what sense phenomenological constitution—the problem that Husserl has posited—is essentially interpretation. Now it must be shown in what sense the "interpretation," of which Nietzsche speaks, is, for its part, constitution. Thus we return again to the Husserlian problematic just sketched.

III

One must admit that, once more, our enterprise faces a difficulty here which initially appears to be insurmountable; this difficulty ensues from the central place that the concept of "will to power" occupies in Nietzsche's philosophy. What precedes might have shown the possibility of inscribing Husserl's perspectives within Nietzsche's perspectivism, but the point of view of the will to power in Nietzsche's thought appears to change the situation completely, so much so that any continued attempt to directly confront Nietzsche's and Husserl's ideas must appear to be useless, indeed impossible. In any case, the doctrine of the will to power appears to be incompatible with any form of rationalism, be it phenomenologically construed or not. Here we come upon the core of our question.

Thus let us first inquire into the meaning of this doctrine of the will to power. Let us first voice our conviction that one must embrace Heidegger's thesis according to which this doctrine is essentially *metaphysical;*[33] let us add to this that one must speak of metaphysics here in a sense that is analogous to Husserl's idea of the discipline not as "first philosophy" (first philosophy is, in reality, transcendental phenomenology) but rather as the "last philosophy."[34] Further, let us refer to Heidegger's additional indication regarding the meaning to be ascribed to Nietzsche's doctrine: one ought to try to understand and interpret it together with Leibniz's *Monadology,* Hegel's *Phenomenology of Spirit,* and Schelling's essay *Philosophical Inquiries into the Essence of Human Freedom.*[35] Indeed in the new edition of Nietzsche's annotations, on which was based the compilation of the posthumous publication *The Will to Power,* which gives us a glimpse of the original connection between some of the most important manuscripts of Nietzsche,[36] we must clearly distinguish the "monadological" and Leibnizian reminiscences, references, and implications that are characteristic of Nietzsche's attempt to think metaphysically what lastly and actually *is,* namely, will to power.[37]

Let us attempt to sketch in general terms how Nietzsche's metaphysical idea presents itself to us. As he says, the world is composed of a determined number of "centers of force" (*Kraftzentren*).[38] Each of these beings (*Seiende*) or "forces" is nothing but, first and abstractly, pure "power" in the traditional sense of *potentia* (*dynamis*). In this first sense, such a force is something that would not only remain inexistent if it did not receive a determination of its being from another force. More, it could not be—as pure "power" (*potentia*)—for an instant without receiving a determination of being through the mere fact that this other force already *exists* and did not remain in a state of pure "power." Indeed the "centers of force" (monads) are not only "potential" beings in the sense given above, but rather, precisely, centers of *force*; this force must have always already found expression, application, flourishing, that is to say, its existence. Since only such forces exist, all force must, in order to come to its realization, receive its realization from an other force, which is superior to it, or it must impose itself upon a force inferior to itself.

In a certain sense, this doctrine is a mere "variation" on the more "classical" ontological theories according to which a "substance" is substance insofar as it is through self-determination, and it is "subject"[39] insofar as it is determined (in the form of "accidents") by something else (by another substance) and could not do without this determination by something else in order to exist. What Nietzsche adds is the following: if the absolute (albeit abstract) primacy of the state of "subject," that is, of a pure potential "force," is posited, then every "self-determination" (self-domination) necessarily takes the form of a "determination through something other" (an expansive domination), in such a way that every act of self-determination must turn against a determination already received from another "center of force" and must thereby subject the expansion of the force of the other center of force to its own power; that is, it must subject this force itself and, to that extent, the existence of the other center of force. Thus every form of determination and domination of a being over itself supposes, implies, and necessitates a determination and domination of this being over another (and its reduction to the state of "subject"), and every absence of power over the other being brings about one's submissiveness to the power of that other being.

This allows us to define more precisely the character and measure of the "force" of these centers of force of which the Nietzschean world is composed; these forces exist only insofar as they unfold, and their unfolding allows the center, of which they are the forces, only then to be "for itself," "self-sufficient" and "independent" ("substance"), if the unfolding has the shape of an expansion of its realm of power within which it dominates other forces. Consequently, these forces are forces of being only insofar as they manifest an expansive tendency of the center, from which they emanate, that is to say insofar as they are in this sense "will" to "power," that is, will to superiority, primitive will to domination and expansion.

It is undisputable that all images that this Nietzschean idea of actuality provokes refer to the moral realm or to realms related to morality and that the implications of this doctrine must seem unsettling. It is also Nietzsche's conviction that the mere fact that this doctrine should concern and disturb a certain idea of morality has previously prevented a glimpse into the actuality that he wishes to describe. The moral implications of the Nietzschean doctrine of the role of will to power provide concrete examples for its explanation. Thus it follows from this doctrine that "freedom" exists only as superiority and domination, that there is no escape whatsoever from the alternative of being a "master" or a "slave." However, this does not mean that relations between human beings are in fact that simple. All that is said is that, insofar as one is free in relation to an other, this other is necessarily and, in this same relation, dependent on one; it is a relation that does not in any way foreclose the possibility that a relation between these two individuals can be the opposite in a different regard. Above all it must be reiterated that all these moral implications of the doctrine of will to power remain only implications: the doctrine itself is *primarily* metaphysical.[40] And we must also add—and thereby return to the problem we announced earlier—that Nietzsche was brought to this monadological concept, prefigured in Leibniz, through considerations that pertain to a "theory of knowledge," to which he turned because of the dissolution of traditional rationalism of which we spoke earlier. We also thereby return to Husserlian problems.

Let us consider the "constitution" of a thing as thing from the Nietzschean point of view:

> "Thingness" was first created by us. The question is whether there could not be many other ways of creating such an apparent world [41]—and whether this creating, logicizing, adapting, falsifying is not itself the best-guaranteed reality; in short, whether that which "posits things" is not the sole reality; and whether the "effect of the external world upon us" is also not only the result of such active subjects[42]—the other "entities" act upon us; our adapted apparent world is an adaptation and overpowering of their actions; a kind of defensive measure. The subject alone is demonstrable; hypothesis that only subjects exist—that "object" is only a kind of effect produced by a subject upon a subject—a *modus of the subject*.[43]

Without insisting any further on its evident Leibnizian and monadological resonance nor on the no less evident divergences between these two monadologies, we must first retain from this Nietzschean note[44] that it returns to a conception of the actual being (*wirklich Seiende*) as a willful center of force—thereby relying precisely upon the problem that Husserl describes as the problem of "phenomenological constitution." If this constitution, in particular the constitution of the "thingness of a thing" is an interpretation or, as Nietzsche often expresses it here and elsewhere, an adapting of an "apparent" world, then the problem for Nietzsche is to know the causes and motives of this adapting, which evidently are to be found outside of the realm of "objective knowledge" of the "reality [*Wirklichkeit*] of things"—the realm of "logic" and "truth" in the classical sense—since precisely this realm is the object of the question. Nietzsche gives the answer: the constitution of something as a thing is to be understood as a "defensive measure" of a "subject," in virtue of which it opposes the influence of another subject to which it is exposed and which seeks to reduce the subject itself to the status of an available thing and of a mere object. The "thingness" (*Dingheit*) is but the status of an actuality (which is in the end also that of a "subject") reduced to dependence and availability for another actuality (another "subject" and "center of force"). "Things" are "subjects" on which a more powerful subject has been able to impose its domination. For clarity's sake, let us add here that this relation in no way excludes a certain reversibility: a "subject" can always, in some respects, dispose of an other as a thing and be, in other respects, subjected as a thing to the domination of this other "subject."

The metaphysical conception of the actual being (*wirklich Seienden*) as center of force—and this force as will to power—serves as a foundation for Nietzsche's interpretation of the phenomenon of constitution of what offers itself to us as an object. This conception itself is a development of Leibniz's monadological metaphysics. But Husserl too saw the necessity of a last recourse to a metaphysics of a Leibnizian monadological type in the pursuit of his transcendental-phenomenological studies.[45] If it is surprising to find in Nietzsche a reference to a "rationalist" system like Leibniz's, it must be noted that it is after all no less astonishing to find the same reference in Husserl, whose position on the crisis of classical rationalism does initially not differ from Nietzsche's, as we saw.[46]

For Husserl, the "matter" upon which the interpretive activity of a Subject acts is, in the end, the absolute flux of time; yet also for him, this absolute flux of time is nothing but the absolute subjectivity in a state of pure potentiality (*Potenz*) and not without further ado the subjectivity of an "I," but rather that of an absolute *life* on the basis of which an "I-Subject" must constitute *itself*, resisting, so to speak, the current of this flux, as "person" and as "concrete monad."[47] This self-constitution of an "I" is accomplished in the form of "acts of positioning" (actively constituting "thetic" acts),[48] which are not grounded on "absolute facts" and, to this extent, are thus arbitrary and "falsifying" positions. It is precisely for this reason that their positive results must be eliminated from the phenomenological reduction. This reduction, as *epochē*, opposes itself to the necessary tendency of "all life" to "always take a position"[49] without always—or almost never—being able to rely upon absolute facts that could found these acts of positioning; according to Husserl, the necessity of this tendency is ultimately that of a "defensive measure" against the impulse and the urgency of time as the all-encompassing expression of the misery of a mortal life.

IV

Here we must touch upon the question that may arise from the fact that, for Nietzsche, all of this process is that of an "eternal return" of all of its stages, whereas Husserl connects this process to a "teleology of history" of an eschatological style. However, Nietzsche's idea of the "eternal return" is also not free from any tie to a certain eschatological interpretation of history, which he cannot escape, as Karl Löwith in particular has shown[50] and as the above indicates. On the other hand, although Husserl certainly remained beholden to this idea of an absolute teleology of history, he himself occasionally considered it with the greatest amount of skepticism and referred to it as "myth," "poetry," or even "novel."[51] Would the true meaning of this "novel" be comparable to the meaning that Nietzsche himself grants to poetry and art in general—and which is thus at the heart of philosophy itself?

We must break off here. Do our remarks suffice to ground the question of which will to power lies hidden in the ideal, or in the "myth," of European reason and Europe's claim to reason—and of which heir to the reason of Europe and mankind lies hidden in the metaphysics of the will to power? It should suffice to point out the possibility of interpreting Nietzsche's "morphology of the will to power" in terms of a phenomenological philosophy and Husserl's phenomenological philosophy in terms of a philosophy of "irrational" perspectives of a "certain kind of life." However, this would mean that Nietzsche's philosophy is not essentially an "irrationalism" and that Husserl's philosophy is not essentially a "rationalism." They would be merely points of view, to be grasped in the metaphysical sense of the Leibnizian monadology and located on a "plane" on which neither one nor the other would be able to dominate in an absolute sense.

Notes

This essay was translated by Élodie Boublil and Christine Daigle from "Husserl und Nietzsche," published in 1968. The essay was first written and published in French in 1962 as "Deux points de vue: Husserl et Nietzsche."

1. If we get rid of the possibility of an "absolute point of view," we must also get rid here of the perpetual efforts made by philosophers—especially Husserl—to reach such a standpoint. This essay does not aim—even implicitly—to deal with the problem of the possibility of such a point of view.

2. Husserl, "Philosophy as Rigorous Science" 140. Originally published as "Philosophie als strenge Wissenschaft," 336.

3. Gadamer, *Truth and Method*, 266, 251n1. Regarding the history of the meaning of the word *understand* ("Importance of understanding history"), Gadamer wrote, "The original meaning seems to have been the legal sense of the word, i.e., representing a case before a court. That the word then developed an intellectual sense is obviously due to the fact that to represent a case in court involves understanding it, i.e., mastering it to such an extent that one can cope with all the possible moves of the opposing party and assert one's own legal standpoint."

According to this, to represent means to understand, since it is not possible—nor can it be effective—to represent something without understanding it. What would happen, though, if it were the contrary? If the "commitment," the fact of getting involved in a cause, of adopting a standpoint, was the first condition to account for and to understand something—would the history of the meaning of the word *understand* be clarified? One can ultimately rely on or commit oneself to something without understanding it, but one would surely not understand a thing without getting involved in it and adopting some standpoint. In the end, this seems to be Gadamer's genuine opinion, though it is not explicit in the given point.

4. It would require some work in the beginning of a book in order to carry out such an attempt with a compelling and persuasive force. It would thus be presumptuous not to compel ourselves to an extreme succinctness in the following pages. On the other hand, one can ask which absolutely decisive proof of the connection that is asserted, or just glimpsed at here, would be able to contribute to the problematic we are concerned with.

5. We are far from being opposed to the thesis Strasser came up with in his study "Intuition und Dialektik in der Philosophie Edmund Husserls," 148 ff. See also his book *Phenomenology and the Human Sciences*.

6. See Boehm, "Pensée et Technique."

7. See Boehm, *Das Grundlege und das Wesentliche*, and also the general formulation of a "principle of differentiating reason" in his preface to the German translation of Merleau-Ponty's *Phenomenology of Perception (Phänomenologie der Wahrnehmung)*, in particular xii–xvii. [In the latter, Boehm refers to Leibniz's principle of sufficient reason and explains how it has been appropriated by

phenomenology within a philosophy of finitude and transformed in light of an idea of primordial differentiation.—Trans.]

8. Husserl, *Crisis*. See Boehm, "Das Fragment einer kritische Studie zu diesem Werk Husserls," 169–72.

9. Nietzsche, *Twilight of the Idols*, 486 (hereafter TI). See in particular the chapter "'Reason' in Philosophy," 479–84.

10. Every discussion about the objective correctness of Nietzsche's and Husserl's judgments on the destiny of European Rationalism and on the contemporary situation of philosophy should be set aside here. However, let us note that Husserl did not get the analogy between Nietzsche's views and his own theory, but no doubt he considered Nietzsche's thought as a mere expression of this crisis of Rationalism; and if Nietzsche on his part would have known Husserl's work, he would have had just the same look at Husserl's philosophy (as he would have known partly about it, had he lived until the end with intellectual clarity; only fifteen years in age separate Nietzsche from Husserl).

11. "The only real world, the one that is actually given through perception, that is ever experienced and experienceable—our everyday life-world" (Husserl, *Crisis*, 48–49).

12. According to Gadamer (*Truth and Method*, 299), it is considered a "principle of history of effect" (as he has called it on other occasions): "A hermeneutics adequate to the subject matter would have to demonstrate the reality and efficacy of history within understanding itself. I shall refer to this as 'history of effect.' *Understanding is, essentially, a historically effected event.*"

13. At least implicitly; see paragraphs 25 and 26 of the first volume of *Logical Investigations*, 111–17.

14. Nietzsche, TI 486.

15. Ibid.

16. The Louvain edition of Husserl's works, while now at eleven volumes, is still only in its beginning. What posthumous material has been published so far can be considered only fragmentary with regard to the material scope and concrete range of Husserl's posthumous notes. The editors themselves are not in a position to always oversee the whole of posthumous works. The most difficult task awaits them still.

17. See, in particular, Husserl, *Erste Philosophie (1923/1924)*, *Husserliana VII* (hereafter Hua VII), editor's introduction, xviii; there are important quotes collected together in the introduction by the editor.

18. "The more profound sense of the contemporary philosophy lies in making true (in the higher sense) the radical subjectivism of the skeptical tradition" (Hua VII, II, §9, 61). To "make true" (*wahrmachen*) does not mean here only to "take seriously," "to concretize," but rather *literally* (emphasis added) to "make *true*."

19. Husserl, Hua VII, 234, and *Crisis*, 77 and 133.

20. See in particular §41 of *Cartesian Meditations*, 84 (hereafter CM). Nothing is as characteristic of Husserl's "style of thinking" as this question about the theses or postulates implied in some of the questions or inquiries that he himself is inclined to pursue. So he asks himself sometimes, in the posthumous notes, "How is it that you are so wise?" See *Zur Phänomenologie des inneren Bewusstseins (1893–1917)*, 195 (hereafter Hua X); *On the Phenomenology of the Consciousness of Internal Time*, 202.

21. After the beautiful article by Walter Biemel, "Die entscheidenden Phasen der Entfaltung von Husserls Philosophie," the Husserlian problem of constitution has received its most comprehensive and coherent presentation in Robert Sokolowski's book *The Formation of Husserl's Concept of Constitution*.

22. A group of persons constitute a committee; an elected house of deputies constitutes itself as a legislative body; and a nation constitutes itself as a republic.

23. Husserl, *Ideas I*, §85, 246–51; Husserl himself refers here to his first work, *Philosophie der Arithmetik*, 69 (hereafter Hua XII); *Philosophy of Arithmetic*, 72, and to his *Logical Investigations*, II, section 7, §58, 812–15. I refer further to the important section 14 of the fifth investigation (563–69).

24. *Logical Investigations*, II, 5, §14 (563–69).

25. Ibid.

26. The Lectures *On the Phenomenology of the Consciousness of Internal Time*, as Husserl had written and held them in his draft from 1905; the 1917 text as further developed by Edith Stein and the 1928 edited version by Heidegger contain significant parts—and that, not only in the supplements—that were first written later, namely by 1917. See Hua X.

27. Further, that something will indeed be "conceived as" or "represents itself as" means that it "represents itself as this or that" in an everyday use of language, in a pre-phenomenological use of language. It does not mean that it thus will be "conceived" or "present itself" or "be" itself. Further, Husserl talks of "manifestation" (*Bekundung*), a concept that he seems to be using as synonymous with "constitution." See Husserl, *On the Phenomenology of the Consciousness of Internal Time*, §18, 185, Hua X, 179.

28. What Husserl himself says about this, in particular in sections 81 and 85 of *Ideas I* (234–39, 246–51) and 107 of *Formal and Transcendental Logic* (283–90) has been too little noted.

29. Husserl takes a decisive step in 1907–8. It finds its clearest expression in the remark, "Not all kinds of constitution have the Scheme *Auffassungsinhalt—Auffassung*" (Hua X, 7).

30. See in particular the whole concluding paragraph 107 of *Formal and Transcendental Logic*.

31. I refer to the "passive" character of the most fundamental constitution of "time"; see *Ideas I* §98 (Hua III, 246), 286–90; *Formal and Transcendental Logic*, Appendix II, §3, 319–22; *Cartesian Meditations*, §§37–39, 75–81. I know of no interpretation of the fundamental problem of phenomenology in which one would take into account in a determining fashion this fundamental passivity of the transcendental subjectivity in Husserl's sense. For such an account, see Boehm, *Das Grundlegende und das Wesentliche*, 220–22.

32. See De Waelhens, *Phénoménologie et vérité*.

33. See in particular Heidegger, "Nietzsche's Word 'God Is dead,'" 189.

34. Husserl, Hua VII, 385 (text of 1908).

35. Heidegger, "Nietzsche's Word 'God Is dead,'" 189. It makes almost no difference that, with regard to Nietzsche, Heidegger refers here to *Thus Spoke Zarathustra* rather than to *Will to Power*. [In the French article, Boehm includes the title *Will to Power* in the list of works to be interpreted together. This is left out in the German version. However, it is clear that it is to the book *Will to Power*, and not the doctrine, that he refers to in the next sentence. —Trans.]

36. One finds in the third volume of Karl Schlechta's edition of Nietzsche, *Werke in drei Bänden* a new presentation of the text "Will to power" with the title "From the notes of the 1880s." Most of the positive or negative judgments that have been passed since then appear to me to be insufficiently grounded. The form Schlechta chose for the edition of the text, which can be considered suitable for Nietzsche's plan for the Will to Power, can be truly appreciated only where he has made his intentions clear and rendered Nietzsche's notes for a specific—and an at least approximately complete—manuscript in full and in a way that is true to the manuscript.

In these cases Schlechta's editorial principle proves to be very instructive. Precisely for this reason, Schlechta is to be reproached for having realized his project of rendering the text in the context of the original manuscript only in a few instances (though possibly the most important ones). Admittedly he was guided by the negative goal of destroying the "myth" of "the Will to Power." Even if a purely negative goal such as his was permissible as an editorial principle, this goal could be fulfilled precisely only with a complete edition. Only a "positive" goal can justify the edition of selected texts. See, for instance, my detailed study "Le problème du 'Wille zur Macht,'" 402–34.

37. I refer here to the Nietzschean manuscript W II 1 (from the year 1887), which is almost completely reproduced in the original order by M. Schlechta in volume 3 of *Werke in Drei Bänden*, 507–62. It is this manuscript that contains the essence of Nietzsche's notes relevant to his conception of a "metaphysics of the will to power" (Heidegger). With the first notes of this manuscript, Nietzsche attempts to renew the spirit of the seventeenth century, which he opposes to the decadence of the

centuries that follow. He quotes with respect Descartes (510) and Leibniz (511). Of course, my following remarks are not grounded on this fact, which is in itself negligible.

38. Nietzsche, *Werke in drei Bänden*, 3:704.

39. I am using here a primitive and a "classical" notion of "subject" which has strangely fallen into oblivion since the beginning of the nineteenth century. For Aquinas, "*pati, recipere, subjectum esse*" belong together. See Boehm, *Das Grundlegende und das Wesentliche*, 219 ff., as well as my article "Het wijsgerig mensbeeld in de filosofie der XIXe eeuw," 565 ff.

40. Already in 1876, in "Richard Wagner in Bayreuth," Nietzsche wrote, "To me . . . the most vital of questions for philosophy appears to be to what extent the character of the world is unalterable: so as, once this question has been answered, to set about *improving that part of it recognized as alterable* with the most ruthless of courage" (*Untimely Meditations*, 207–8).

41. This is about the same "apparent world" of which the characteristic of being "apparent" has been shown to be an "appearance" itself.

42. The Nietzschean notion of "Subject" is not the one I used previously (see note 7 above), rather a common (vulgar) contemporary notion. It is not possible to determine here to what extent the notion as it appears in Nietzsche's thought comes close to the one I discussed earlier (and which is similar to the one to be found in Husserl).

43. Nietzsche, *The Will to Power*, book 3, §569, 307.

44. It is merely a "note" and not an "aphorism," the term that, out of bad habit, is used to refer to just any text written by Nietzsche.

45. See Husserl, *Cartesian Meditations* (hereafter CM), in particular §60 (139ff.). And *Erste Philosophie*, Hua VIII, 54th lesson. In these, Husserl's monadological speculations go back to 1907–8. [In the French article, Boehm indicates 1907–9 as the time period.—Trans.]

46. Husserl says, "Phenomenology leads to the monadology that Leibniz anticipated with an *aperçu* of a genius." This is the last sentence of the lectures in *Erste Philosophie* (Hua VIII, 190). On this, compare also the studies on Husserl's opinion on classical idealism and rationalism [references to 18ff and in particular 49ff. of Boehm's own book, *Von Gesichtpunkt der Phänomenologie*—Trans.].

47. See CM, in particular §33, 67.

48. See CM, §38, 77–80.

49. See the first paragraph of this essay, as well as paragraph 13, 17–18.

50. Löwith has revisited this point many times; see, for instance, "Nietzsche's Revival of the Doctrine of Eternal Recurrence," 214–22.

51. See, for example, Husserl, *Crisis*, end of §68, 234, and Appendix to §73, 397–400 (Hua VI, 508–13).

Bibliography

Biemel, Walter. "Die entscheidenden Phasen der Entfaltung von Husserl's Philosophie." *Zeitschrift für philosophische Forschung*, no. 12 (1959): 187–213.

Boehm, Rudolf. "Das Fragment einer kritische Studie zu diesem Werk Husserls." *Archivio di Filosofia*, no. 2 (1954): 169–72.

———. *Das Grundlege und das Wesentliche*. Den Haag: Nijhoff, 1965.

———. "Deux points de vue: Husserl et Nietzsche." *Archivio di Filosofia*, no. 3 (1962): 167–81.

———. "Het wijsgerig mensbeeld in de filosofie der XIXe eeuw." *Dietsche Warande en Belfort*, no. 106 (1961): 565.

———. "Husserl und Nietzsche." In *Von Gesichtpunkt der Phänomenologie: Husserl Studien*. Den Haag: Nijhoff, 1968.

———. "Le problème du 'Wille zur Macht,' oeuvre posthume de Nietzsche." *Revue philosophique de Louvain*, no. 71 (1963): 402–34.

———. "Pensée et Technique." *Revue internationale de philosophie*, no. 52 (1960): 194–220.

De Waelhens, Alphonse. *Phénoménologie et vérité*. Paris: Gallimard, 1953.

Gadamer, Hans-Georg. *Truth and Method*. Translated by Joel Weinsheimer and Donald G. Marshall. New York: Continuum, 1989.

Heidegger, Martin. "Nietzsche's Word 'God Is Dead.'" In *Off the Beaten Track*, translated by Julian Young and Kenneth Haynes. Cambridge: Cambridge University Press, 2002.

Husserl, Edmund. *Cartesian Meditations*. Translated by Dorion Cairns. The Hague: Nijhoff, 1960.

———. *The Crisis of European Sciences and Transcendental Phenomenology*. Translated by David Carr. Evanston, IL: Northwestern University Press, 1970.

———. *Erste Philosophie (1923/1924)*. *Husserliana VII*. Edited by Rudolf Boehm. Den Haag: Nijhoff, 1956.

———. *Erste Philosophie (1923/1924)*. *Husserliana VIII*. Edited by Rudolf Boehm. Den Haag: Nijhoff, 1959.

———. *Formal and Transcendental Logic*. Translated by Dorion Cairns. Den Haag: Nijhoff, 1969.

———. *Ideas I*. Translated by W. R. Boyce Gibson. New York: Macmillan, 1958.

———. *Logical Investigations*. Translated by N. Findlay. New York: Humanities Press, 1970.

———. *On the Phenomenology of the Consciousness of Internal Time*. Translated by John Barnett Brough. Dordrecht: Kluwer Academic, 1991.

———. "Philosophie als strenge Wissenschaft." *Logos* 1 (1910–11): 289–341.

———. *Philosophie der Arithmetik*. *Husserliana XII*. Edited by Lothar Eley. Den Haag: Nijhoff, 1970.

———. "Philosophy as Rigorous Science." In *Phenomenology and the Crisis of Philosophy*, translated by Quentin Lauer. New York: Harper and Row, 1965.

———. *Philosophy of Arithmetic*. Translated by Dallas Willard. Dordrecht: Kluwer Academic, 2003.

———. *Zur Phänomenologie des inneren Bewusstseins (1893–1917)*. *Husserliana X*. Edited by Rudolf Boehm. Den Haag: Nijhoff, 1966.

Löwith, Karl. "Nietzsche's Revival of the Doctrine of Eternal Recurrence." In *Meaning and History*. Chicago: University of Chicago Press, 1949.

Merleau-Ponty, Maurice. *Phänomenologie der Wahrnehmung*. Translated by Rudolf Boehm. Berlin: de Gruyter, 1966.

Nietzsche, Friedrich. *Twilight of the Idols*. In *The Portable Nietzsche*. Edited by Walter Kaufmann. New York: Penguin Books, 1982.

———. *Untimely Meditations*. Edited by Daniel Breazeale. Translated by R. J Hollingdale. Cambridge: Cambridge University Press, 1997.

———. *Werke in Drei Bänden*. 3 vols. Edited by Karl Schlechta. München: Hanser, 1954–56.

———. *The Will to Power*. Translated by Walter Kaufmann and R. J. Hollingdale. New York: Vintage Books, 1967.

Sokolowski, Robert. *The Formation of Husserl's Concept of Constitution*. Den Haag: Nijhoff, 1964.

Strasser, Stephan. "Intuition und Dialektik in der Philosophie Edmund Husserls." In *Edmund Husserl 1859–1959*. Den Haag: Nijhoff, 1959.

———. *Phenomenology and the Human Sciences*. Pittsburgh: Duquesne University Press, 1963.

2 The Intentional Encounter with "the World"

Christine Daigle

In *HUMAN, ALL Too Human*, Nietzsche begins his investigation by considering the human encounter with objects in the world.[1] His approach to the problem is initially conducted via a critique of Kant's philosophy in the first chapter, "Of First and Last Things." The book, written for the free spirit—the one that is freed from all alienating metaphysical illusions—was written in the spirit of the Enlightenment and was dedicated to Voltaire, "one of the greatest liberators of the spirit."[2] However, being a liberating book and one for the free spirit (or one for the spirit to be freed) does not make *Human, All Too Human* a rejection of the quest for truth. Quite the contrary: the task for Nietzsche is to reject everything that, up until now, has passed as truth in order to uncover the true nature of the human, his place in the world, and the relation between the human being and the world. Nietzsche thus puts to work Kant's call, "Sapere Aude!"—Dare to know—that Enlightenment call for the human being to stop relying on authority and to seek knowledge for oneself, using the power of one's spirit. This appetite for knowledge, paired with the courage that is necessary for it, implies a critique and a questioning of the philosophical tradition.[3]

This is a problem that Nietzsche begins to tackle rather early. Already in the essay "Truth and Lies in a Nonmoral Sense" from 1873, he calls into question the notion of truth and of the reality of the thing in-itself.[4] According to him, the latter is "pure truth, apart from any of its consequences," and it is posited as out of our reach and "the least worth striving for" (TL 116). The task of the philosopher is to aim at a critical knowledge that will demonstrate that what passes for truth is a "movable host of metaphors, metonymies, and anthropomorphisms: in short, a sum of human relations which have been poetically and rhetorically intensified, transferred, and embellished, and which, after long usage, seem to a people to be fixed, canonical, and binding. Truths are illusions which we have forgotten are illusions" (TL 117). In this early essay, Nietzsche sows the seeds of his future thinking on metaphysics and on the problem of truth. *Human, All Too Human* revisits this and opens with the chapter "Of First and Last Things." The interlocutor is Kant, and the philosophy that is taking shape is a phenomenology.[5]

In *Human, All Too Human*, Nietzsche's reflections are articulated by taking into account and examining the encounter between the human being and objects of the world as well as the world itself. His approach to the problem is grounded in a critique of Kant's philosophy. The first chapter contains this critique and sets the foundations for a Nietzschean phenomenology. In it, we see Nietzsche's interest in Kant quickly evolve into a phenomenological approach. While he may initially find the distinction between the phenomenal and the noumenal appealing, he does not follow Kant's move toward a more idealist understanding of noumena. His phenomenological views form his response to—and his overcoming of—Kant. Indeed the thing in-itself that may lie behind the phenomenal realm is regarded as insignificant, precisely because it is outside of our reach. This is not the case in Kant.

Nietzsche's critique of Kant goes hand in hand with his rejection of earlier rationalistic accounts of the self. This rejection makes room for his own view of an intentional consciousness at work in its encounter with the world.[6] The phenomenological concept of intentionality is one that Nietzsche uses, albeit without naming it. A close analysis of his writings reveals that he conceives of the human being as a multifaceted and labyrinthic being that constructs itself via its intentional experience of the world. The human subject is a "subjective multiplicity" (*Beyond Good and Evil* §12; hereafter BGE). Nietzschean perspectivism, which is tied to this notion of the individual, understands our experience of the world in terms of a multifaceted embodied experience. He posits the human as the colorist of the world. The goal becomes to operate a "phenomenological reduction" (Nietzsche does not use this term, but the method he proposes is the same) to go back to the things we have "colored." This is especially difficult, however, since, for Nietzsche, "We behold all things through the human head and cannot cut off this head" (HTH I §9).

To explore these questions, I will discuss Nietzsche's relation to Kant, which is much more complex than has been acknowledged. I will examine how the relation to Kant's philosophy is at the heart of the phenomenological turn as we find it in the first chapter of *Human, All Too Human*. Then I will consider the relation between consciousness and the world in Husserl in an attempt to shed light on this relation in Nietzsche. Following this, I will analyze the Nietzschean notion of the individual and will show how this individual is to be conceived as an intentional consciousness that one can bring very close to what is delineated in Husserl's *Cartesian Meditations*.[7]

In a recent article, Keith Ansell-Pearson argues that an encounter between Nietzsche and Husserl is potentially fruitful if one considers the right set of problems. While it is important not to minimize the differences between the two thinkers, he argues, those differences should not be conceived as insurmountable. He thereby echoes some of Rudolf Boehm's claims in his "Husserl and Nietzsche." I agree with Ansell-Pearson when he says, "I think we can most productively relate Nietzsche's thinking to phenomenology through exploring two core and related issues: consciousness and individuation."[8] I also wish to go further than Peter Poellner, who claims, "It is in Nietzsche that we find the philosophical underpinnings of the phenomenological turn in philosophy."[9] Unlike Poellner, I see this phenomenological turn as being in full swing in the first chapter of *Human, All Too Human* and consolidating itself in the works that follow.

A Kantian Nietzsche?

Nietzsche's relation to Kant is very complex. R. Kevin Hill has shown that Nietzsche is a very attentive reader of Kant.[10] It was thought for a long time that Nietzsche's knowledge and understanding of Kant relied on Schopenhauer's treatment of him as well as other secondary sources on Kant. Hill shows that Nietzsche read Kant directly and that he read the *Critique of Judgment* first, before the *Critique of Pure Reason.* He was particularly interested in critical philosophy. Hill explains that, in Nietzsche's mid-career works, from 1878 to 1882, "references to Kant's metaphysics and epistemology stress the skeptical motif at the expense of any positive claims about the thing-in-itself."[11] After *The Birth of Tragedy*, Nietzsche elaborated a method that would bring him to make proposals for a positive philosophy. This method is the *historische Philosophie,* or historical philosophizing (which will later become genealogical thinking). It is this method that will allow him to wrestle with "the first and last things," namely with the illusory concepts of metaphysics. The question for Nietzsche is the following: On what ground are our truths erected? Kant's philosophy also aims at the foundation of knowledge. The critique seeks to explain how reason elaborates the object of its knowledge.

According to Kant, the epistemic process is as follows.[12] A rational consciousness perceives an object. Perception occurs thanks to it but is limited and conditioned by the categories of understanding. These categories allow for perception to happen but also shape the perception itself. The thing in-itself is limiting and allows for the epistemic relation between subject and object to take place. According to some interpretations—which Nietzsche appears to follow at times—Kant's proposal is that the object of perception is causally supported by the thing in-itself. The object is a phenomenon for the subject, and, as such, it is not the genuine object. In some way, the object in-itself would ground the object as phenomenon for the subject. For Nietzsche, it is tempting to posit a noumenal world to explain the phenomenal world, which is the only world to which we can ever have access. Hill goes so far as to say that the aesthetical metaphysics found in *The Birth of Tragedy* is the outcome of this temptation: Nietzsche would have given in to it and explored its possibility in this early work. However, with *Human, All Too Human*, Nietzsche takes a new path.

For Nietzsche, it is clear that the noumenal realm, if it exists, is without any significance. Aphorism 9 of *Human, All Too Human I* is very clear:

> It is true, there could be a metaphysical world; the absolute possibility of it is hardly to be disputed. We behold all things through the human head and cannot cut off this head; while the question nonetheless remains what of the world would still be there if one had cut it off. This is a purely scientific problem and one not very well calculated to bother people overmuch. . . . For one could assert nothing at all of the metaphysical world except that it was a being-other, an inaccessible, incomprehensible being-other; it would be a thing with negative qualities.—Even if the existence of such a world were never so well demonstrated, it is certain that knowledge of it would be the most useless of all knowledge: more useless even than knowledge of the chemical composition of water must be to the sailor in danger of shipwreck. (HTH I §9)

This is a key passage for the interpretation that I wish to present here. Nietzsche is not rejecting the possibility of a noumenal world; he merely declares it to be without any effect. What really matters to the human being is the phenomenal world, and this world depends entirely on our human head. It is therefore thanks to the existence of our consciousness that the phenomenal world is born, the only world that matters to us. It is the human being that makes its world, this world that is "so marvelously variegated, frightful, meaningful, soulful, it has acquired colour—but we have been the colourists: it is the human intellect that has made appearance appear and transported its erroneous basic conceptions into things" (HTH I §16). One may want to consider this passage under the following light: Nietzsche is providing an explanation here of the way in which the human being has created truths for himself. This would thus be an explanation of how truths are really errors, untruths (in the sense of truth given by a correspondence theory of truth). I do not reject this. I think that Nietzsche is very clear about this in the passage. However, I believe that the passage is also very clear on the nature of consciousness as intentional. Nietzsche says, "It is the human intellect that has made appearance appear." Thus it is our human head that makes the phenomenon be as it encounters the world. It encounters something, an *etwas*, and the human head colors it, interprets it, constitutes it as a phenomenon, in a way very similar to—although different from—the Kantian rational subject who imposes the categories of his understanding on his perception. I find it to be akin to the work of the Husserlian subject, which is constituted by the world it encounters and shapes it as it encounters it. The constitutive process is a two-way process in Husserl, which is why Nietzsche stands closer to him than to Kant after all. In the passage quoted above, Nietzsche explains that the human intellect colors the world, and the self emerges from this dual act of perception/creation of the phenomenon.

The general problem of the distinction between phenomenal reality and noumenal reality, or that of the distinction between phenomenon and thing in-itself, is one that generates many interesting questions and problems. One can try to work out an explanation of how the phenomenon's existence rests upon that of the thing in-itself. That is Kant's goal. Nietzsche leaves that problem aside since the thing in-itself, according to him, does not matter to the life of consciousness. He says, "The thing in itself is worthy of Homeric laughter: that it appeared to be so much, indeed everything, and is actually empty, that is to say empty of significance" (HTH I §16). If Nietzsche drops the problem of the determination of the thing in-itself and of its link to the phenomenal world, there remains the very interesting problems of the generation of phenomena and of the self in the relation between consciousness and the world—a world whose very constitution consciousness is responsible for. There are two interrelated aspects to this problem for Nietzsche. First, one needs to explain how the human world has become what it is through the erection of truths and lies by the human being. Historical philosophizing, or genealogy, is the best tool for this. It allows for bracketing off all the false judgments that have built the world, that have veiled the raw experience of the world, thereby creating an illusory world.[13] That exercise leads to the fundamental relation between consciousness and the world. One must return to the fundamental phenomenon, which is that of consciousness as "weaved with the world."[14]

One may want to object at this point that, for Nietzsche, consciousness is merely an epiphenomenon. There is a strand of interpretation of Nietzsche's philosophy that puts all of its emphasis on the primacy of the body and of the physiological processes. This approach posits that consciousness is merely a phenomenon at the margins of all physiological processes, an epiphenomenon. What matters—what is primary and worthy of investigation—is the body, instincts and drives, forces at work within and through the body. Something like a consciousness emerges out of this physiological activity and, following the emergence of a conscious-like epiphenomenon, a self also emerges. But this self or phenomenon of consciousness is far from primary. To these interpreters of Nietzsche, there is no individual having these experiences. The experiences of this body trigger conscious individuation. I do not want to deny this; it is a plausible explanation of the origin of consciousness. However, as soon as consciousness exists, it becomes necessary to explain its relation to the world, no matter what the origins of consciousness might be. The physiological explanation delineated above does not tackle this problem, and yet it is the problem that Nietzsche constantly wrestles with. Poellner has suggested that the physiological reading and the phenomenological reading of Nietzsche's philosophy are not mutually exclusive. I agree with him. It is undeniable that Nietzsche grants an unprecedented place to the body. Consciousness is necessarily an embodied consciousness. Is it generated by the very activity of this body? Maybe. But once it is there, its perception of the world and its action on the world are real and explainable phenomena. Poellner says, "The correct description of the cognitive interests that motivate even non-phenomenological explanations therefore essentially requires reference to phenomenological facts—to consciousness and its content."[15]

Consciousness and World in Husserl

I have chosen to focus on the Husserl of the *Cartesian Meditations* for my analysis. This may seem like an odd choice to many who would expect other Husserlian writings to be brought to bear on Nietzsche. However, there is a good rationale for my approach. There are definitely methodological parallels to be drawn between Nietzsche and Husserl when one considers and compares their respective approaches.[16] Already, in *Human, All Too Human*, Nietzsche is putting historical philosophizing to work. The point is to go back to the fundamental experience of being a consciousness in the world and to dismiss the false judgments that pervert and mask it. Reading the following passage, one might think it was written by Nietzsche:

> I realized that it was necessary, once in the course of my life, to demolish everything completely and start again right from the foundations if I wanted to establish anything at all in the sciences that was stable and likely to last. . . . I will devote myself sincerely and without reservation to the general demolition of my opinions. . . . For the purpose of rejecting all my opinions, it will be enough if I find in each of them at least some reason for doubt.[17]

Although this could have been written by Nietzsche, it is actually from Descartes, in the first of his *Meditations on First Philosophy*. These meditations, as we know, prompted Husserl's *Cartesian Meditations*, as Husserl clearly indicates in the introduction to his work. Thus he suggests that one may refer to phenomenology and transcendental philosophy as a neo-Cartesianism:[18] "We do not as yet accept any normative ideal of science; and only so far as we produce one newly for ourselves can we ever have such an ideal. But this does not imply that we renounce the general aim of grounding science absolutely" (CM §3, 8). While Nietzsche does not aim to establish an absolute ground for science, he does want to ground it on new bases. At the time of writing *Human, All Too Human*, he is driven by the same search for truth and knowledge that Descartes and Husserl share. He quotes Descartes in lieu of a preface to the first edition of *Human, All Too Human*, and the passage he is quoting sees Descartes opting to "devote [his] whole life to cultivating [his] reason and advancing as far as [he] could in the knowledge of the truth."[19] This is the goal Nietzsche has set for himself as early as his first essays, such as "Truth and Lies in a Nonmoral Sense."

This critical approach is that of Descartes, Kant, Nietzsche, and Husserl. However, what are we to make of the judgments that are erected upon this critique? Indeed the task is not merely to demonstrate how certain judgments we hold are in fact erroneous and of our own making. Rather, the task is to describe what remains after the elimination of these erroneous judgments. In Descartes, what remains is the experience of the *cogito ergo sum*. In Kant, we are also left with this rational subjectivity—the understanding and its categories—that organizes and conceptualizes the world. In a Cartesian fashion, Kant proclaims that "it must be possible for the 'I think' to accompany all my representations."[20] With Husserl, bracketing is the method by which we will uncover the irreducible core that grounds conscious life. It is "the radical and universal method by which I apprehend myself purely: as Ego, and with my own pure conscious life, in and by which the entire Objective world exists for me and is precisely as it is for me" (CM §8, 21). Husserl thinks that beyond the intentional conscious life there is such a thing as a pure ego that grounds and allows for the conscious life to be. He explains:

> If I put myself above all this life and refrain from doing any believing that takes "the" world straightforwardly as existing—if I direct my regard exclusively to this life itself, as consciousness *of* "the" world—I thereby acquire myself as the pure ego, with the pure stream of my *cogitationes*.
>
> Thus the being of the pure ego and his *cogitationes*, as a being that is prior in itself, is antecedent to the natural being of the world—the world of which I always speak, the one of which I *can* speak. Natural being is a realm whose existential status [*Seinsgeltung*] is secondary; it continually presupposes the realm of transcendental being. (CM §8, 21)

There is in Husserl, therefore, a pure ego which has a transcendental nature and which allows for intentional consciousness to exist as such. The pure ego is what orientates and directs intentionality. What, then, would this pure ego and its *cogitationes* be without the world? If consciousness is essentially intentionality—this movement out of oneself that brings back its experiences of the world into the self, its experiences as a consciousness-in-the-world—what can the pure ego be? Would the pure ego be something like a potentiality?[21] Husserl insists, however, that the pure ego is not merely a simple structure that renders consciousness possible (although it is that too). The pure ego possesses, or is the author of, a pure flow of *cogitationes*. The pure ego is something substantial. What is it, then?

Husserl distinguishes between a transcendental and a psychological ego in the last section of the first meditation in order to reject the psychological ego. This is what the phenomenological *epochē* allows for: it reduces the natural human ego, the psychological ego, to the transcendental ego. The reduction also allows him to explain how, "just as the reduced Ego is not a piece of the world, so, conversely, neither the world nor any worldly Object is a piece of my ego" (CM §11, 26). The transcendental ego is a necessary premise[22] for the world. In the natural attitude, I do not realize that I am at every moment also a transcendental ego.

The problem of the existence of the world in itself is not a problem for Husserl. In fact he stipulates at the beginning of the *Meditations* that there is no apodictic evidence of the world. The world is a phenomenon for consciousness, as Husserl explains in his definition of intentionality: "Every conscious process is, in itself, consciousness *of* such and such, regardless of what the rightful actuality-status of this objective such-and-such may be, and regardless of the circumstance that I, as standing in the transcendental attitude, abstain from acceptance of this object as well as from all my other natural acceptances" (CM §14, 33).

It is important to distinguish between the world as phenomenon, constituted by intentional consciousness, and the world in itself. It is only in so doing that we may understand some claims made by Husserl, such as the following:

> That the being of the world "transcends" consciousness in this fashion (even with respect to the evidence in which the world presents itself), and that it necessarily remains transcendent, in no way alters the fact that it is conscious life alone, wherein everything transcendent becomes constituted, as something inseparable from consciousness, and which specifically, as world-consciousness, bears within itself inseparably the sense: world—and indeed: "this actually existing" world. (CM §28, 62, translation altered)

There is thus a world that transcends consciousness and about whose being one cannot inquire. Passages such as these indicate that this world is out of our reach, inaccessible. However, there is this other world, the one that matters to the human being, namely, the world as phenomenon. This is the world that we constitute through the activity of our intentional consciousness. Further, this constituting activity is also constitutive of our being. The transcendental ego constitutes the world as phenomenon, but this constitution is its very being. The being of the transcendental ego is intentionality. It is therefore difficult, even impossible, to conceive of a pure ego that would be empty of the world.

This is the criticism that both Sartre and Merleau-Ponty make of Husserl's philosophy in the *Cartesian Meditations*. As Eric Matthews puts it, Merleau-Ponty rejects the idea of a pure subjectivity or a pure consciousness because "a *cogito*, an 'I' or 'self' can exist only in relation to a situation, involving both a world of things and other people."[23] Likewise Sartre, in *The Transcendence of the Ego*, rejects this Husserlian concept since, according to him, "phenomenology does not need to appeal to any such unifying and individualizing *I*."[24] Indeed, for Sartre, the transcendental ego does not resist the phenomenological reduction. He explains: "The *Cogito* affirms too much. The certain content of the pseudo-'Cogito' is not '*I have* consciousness of this chair,' but 'There is consciousness of this chair.'"[25] In the conclusion to his essay, and after having demonstrated that the I is an object of the world (thence the title of the essay), Sartre declares, "This absolute consciousness, when it is purified of the *I*, no longer has anything of the *subject*. It is no longer a collection of representations. It is quite simply a first condition and an absolute source of existence."[26] However, as such, it is pure potentiality, a void, a nothingness, as he will describe it in his later *Being and Nothingness*. At this point we must go back to Nietzsche in order to see if we can shed some light on the problem that is emerging here in Husserl.

Consciousness, Intentionality, and World in Nietzsche

In her essay on Nietzsche and biology, Barbara Stiegler suggests that the Nietzschean subject is nothing else but a biologized Kantian subject. According to her, the Nietzschean subject keeps its double Kantian sense of being both an empirical subject and a transcendental subject. It is both and at all times in flux and a unificatory act.²⁷ She also suggests that "the biologization of the Kantian subject, rather than emptying the subject of its corporeity, reminds us, on the contrary, that *every living subject is first an affected subject who suffers from these affects*."²⁸ Stiegler's claim seems to me to be going too far. That said, the Nietzschean innovation—the phenomenological turn in his thought—lies in this biologization of the subject which is definitely at work in his philosophy. The anchoring of consciousness in the body is the foundation stone of the phenomenological understanding of the human being and his relation to the world. Indeed, as Hill puts it, we find in Nietzsche a "Kantian constructivist account of how the mind produces phenomena."²⁹ But this production of phenomena—this construction of the world—is done by an embodied consciousness and not by a solely rational subject: a Kantian pure reason that operates with its categories of understanding.

Some of the quotations that I cited earlier to show Nietzsche's dealings with the Kantian noumenal/phenomenal distinction can be revisited here. This will be useful as they give us important clues to Nietzsche's conception of the individual as an embodied consciousness. The following are particularly interesting. Nietzsche says, "We behold all things through the human head and cannot cut off this head" (HTH I §9). And then, in another aphorism of "Of First and Last Things" he says, "We have been the colourists [of the world]: it is the human intellect that has made appearance appear and transported its erroneous basic conceptions into things" (HTH I §16). What Nietzsche is saying here is that consciousness perceives and shapes the world as soon as it encounters it. The world is a phenomenon for consciousness. That is the real world for consciousness, and whatever world in itself there might be is without effect on it. This point of view is to be found in the writings that follow *Human, All Too Human*. An example is this passage from *The Gay Science* (hereafter GS):

> How should explanations be at all possible when we first turn everything into an *image*, our image!
> It will do to consider science as an attempt to humanize things as faithfully as possible; as we describe things and their one-after-another, we learn how to describe ourselves more and more precisely. (GS §112)

In this aphorism of book 5 of the *Gay Science*, written and published after the publications of *Thus Spoke Zarathustra* and *Beyond Good and Evil*, Nietzsche dismisses scientific explanations, namely those that aim at providing an explanation and description of the world as it is in itself: "A 'scientific' interpretation of the world, as you understand it, might therefore still be one of the *most stupid* of all possible interpretations of the world, meaning that it would be one of the poorest in meaning" (GS §373). One may also consider the following quote from *Beyond Good and Evil* (hereafter BGE): "It always creates the world in its own image; it cannot do otherwise. Philosophy is this tyrannical drive itself, the most spiritual will to power, to the 'creation of the world,' to the *causa prima*" (BGE §9). While this quote is about philosophy, Nietzsche is also talking about thought processes and consciousness since, as we will see later, the will to power he is referring to here is the grand reason of the body, namely embodied consciousness.

It seems therefore that Nietzsche shares Husserl's point of view and that his biologized Kantian subject—"embodied" would be more appropriate—is this consciousness that creates the world as phenomenon. In *Daybreak* (hereafter D), Nietzsche says, "Only when he has attained a final knowledge of all things will man have come to know himself. For things are only the boundaries of man" (D §48). Here Nietzsche is dealing with the understanding of things as things in themselves and as phenomena. Things in themselves are indeed the limits of human consciousness: when consciousness encounters the thing in-itself, the phenomenon arises as consciousness constitutes it as a thing for itself, as an object for consciousness. Consciousness is also constituted through this process: its constituting of the phenomenon constitutes itself as it perceives and shapes the object and the world. Being a consciousness of and in the world, it is modified and constituted by what it constitutes. Consciousness is constituted by this movement out of itself that it is as intentionality. Poetically put: "There is absolutely no escape, no backway or bypath into the *real world*! We sit within our net, we spiders, and whatever we may catch in it, we can catch nothing at all except that which allows itself to be caught in precisely *our* net" (D §117).

It is important to look very closely at what Nietzsche says of the self, or the ego, in *Daybreak* and *Beyond Good and Evil* because these are the concepts over which the connection with Husserl undoes itself. Indeed the pure ego proposed by Husserl finds no equivalent notion in Nietzsche, for whom the notion of an ego is really problematic. According to him, one of the most common human errors is to have faith in language. Thus we come up with an erroneous concept of ourselves partly because of the limited vocabulary at our disposal to give an account of our "inner life," which, in fact, cannot be articulated linguistically. Thus Nietzsche says that "we misread ourselves in this apparently most intelligible of handwriting on the nature of our self" (D §115). The subject is a fiction that we have posited as a substratum for our thoughts and our deeds. Taking aim at the cogito, Nietzsche speaks of a "superstition of logicians" and suggests that

> it is a falsification of the facts of the case to say that the subject "I" is the condition of the predicate "think." *It* thinks; but that this "it" is precisely the famous old "ego" is, to put it mildly, only a supposition, an assertion, and assuredly not an "immediate certainty." After all, one has even gone too far with this "it thinks"—even the "it" contains an interpretation of the process, and does not belong to the process itself. (BGE §17)

What is it, then, that thinks? Are we dealing with an "it thinks," a "there is consciousness" which would individualize itself through its own process of interacting and constituting the world and itself?

In fact, for Nietzsche, the point is not to completely eliminate the process of individuation that eventually consolidates into an ego. The point is, through historical philosophizing, to demonstrate its origins and to put it in its right place. This place is no longer that of the substratum of conscious existence. To posit a pure ego, as Husserl does, or a transcendental subject, as Kant does, or a thinking substance, as Descartes does, upon which we can erect our knowledge of the world is erroneous. Rather—and closer to Sartre's and Merleau-Ponty's approaches—Nietzsche wishes to talk about a consciousness that is not already individuated, an impersonal consciousness that is the substratum for conscious existence. This consciousness is an embodied consciousness, and, as such, it is "a social structure composed of many souls" (BGE §19). Nietzsche explains, "For the longest time, conscious thought was considered thought itself. Only now does the truth dawn on us that by far the greatest part of our spirit's activity remains unconscious and unfelt" (GS §333).

Thinking emerges as a result of bodily activity, of the sensations and emotions that the body experiences.[30] In the section "Of the Despisers of the Body" in *Thus Spoke Zarathustra*, Nietzsche clearly explains how he conceives of this "social structure composed of many souls." There he speaks of the soul as "only a word for something in the body" and the "I" of which we are so proud, our "ego," is in fact the product of the activity of the body in the world, something like a Sartrean transcendent ego. Nietzsche further explains, "Your body and its great intelligence . . . does not say 'I' but performs 'I.'" However, the body is not a sum of unconscious physiological processes, since Nietzsche also talks about a Self (*Selbst*), a grand reason (*große Vernunft*) that the body is: "Behind your thoughts and feelings, my brother, stands a mighty commander, an unknown sage—he is called Self. He lives in your body, he is your body. There is more reason in your body than in your best wisdom." This is intentional consciousness which individuates itself in a transcendent ego once engaged in the world through its activity. Thus, as in Sartre (and possibly Merleau-Ponty), the ego is relegated to a secondary role.

What are we to make of this mighty commander, this self that the body is (though not to be equated with the "I," the Ego which is a worldly object)? Is the embodied intentional consciousness the will to power? Examining closely what Nietzsche has to say in aphorism 36 of *Beyond Good and Evil* might help shed some light on this question:

> Suppose nothing else were "given" as real except our world of desires and passions, and we could not get down, or up, to any other "reality" besides the reality of our drives—for thinking is merely a relation of these drives to each other: is it not permitted to make the experiment and to ask the question whether this "given" would not be sufficient for also understanding on the basis of this kind of thing the so-called mechanistic (or "material") world?

What is it that "causes" thinking?[31] The mutual relation of instinctual activity—of the body's activity. This is the *Selbst* at work, the grand reason of the body. The consciousness of this body in the world constitutes itself through its encounter with the world and constitutes the world at the same time. This is the bidirectional process of intentionality. This is what allows Nietzsche to conclude:

Suppose, finally, we succeeded in explaining our entire instinctive life as the development and ramification of *one* basic form of the will—namely, of the will to power, as *my* proposition has it; suppose all organic functions could be traced back to this will to power and one could also find in it the solution of the problem of procreation and nourishment—it is *one* problem—then one would have gained the right to determine all efficient force univocally as—*will to power*. The world viewed from inside, the world defined and determined according to its "intelligible character"—it would be "will to power" and nothing else. (BGE §36)

The will to power—this grand reason that the body is—shapes the world as will to power since this intentional consciousness constitutes and creates the world for itself as phenomenon. The world as phenomenon is nothing else but will to power.

An interesting question arises here: Is it permissible to bring together this will to power and the pure ego as proposed by Husserl? Does this "it thinks," which is not a thing but rather a fluctuating bundle of relations, correspond to Husserl's pure ego? The will to power is the intelligible character of the world as phenomenon. It is therefore that thanks to which individuation can occur. This movement of intentional consciousness or will to power allows for the world and the ego to emerge. However, a will to power empty of the world would be as incomprehensible as a Husserlian pure ego empty of the world. If Husserl hangs on to the concept and refuses that this pure ego be something like the will to power—namely a principle and character of intelligibility for the world—then it is impossible to equate the pure ego and the will to power.[32]

Conclusion

Understanding Nietzsche as engaged in a dialogue with Kant (and Descartes) and bringing him closer to Husserl by drawing some parallels between his proposals and those of the *Cartesian Meditations* allows for an innovative reading of Nietzsche's philosophy. The Nietzsche that emerges out of my reading is one that is not so obsessed by physiology and the destruction of the subject. In the end, we are dealing here with a Nietzsche who remains preoccupied by the question of truth but who approaches it from the phenomenological point of view according to which consciousness constitutes its world and, accordingly, its truths and its own being. Nietzsche rhetorically questions whether "all our so-called consciousness is a more or less fantastic commentary on an unknown, perhaps unknowable, but felt text" (D §119). The in-itself, the noumenal, is this unknown text that we can feel but from which we are always separated by the constitutive act of consciousness which posits the phenomenal world. Indeed the language in Nietzsche is not so clear. He is not using any of the vocabulary that Husserl introduces and uses. And even if there are overlaps and parallels from one to the other, the thorny question of the pure ego and its status remains. That said, the analysis provided here clearly demonstrates that Nietzsche's understanding of consciousness as intentional as well as the way in which he conceives its relations with the world make him a phenomenologist avant la lettre.

I quite like the formula used by Vincent de Coorebyter to refer to Sartre's thought before he started reading Husserl. De Coorebyter explains that, until then, Sartre "had practiced a wild phenomenology which was not conscious of itself."[33] I think that this formula applies equally well to Nietzsche. Had he encountered Husserl's philosophy, would he have had the same criticisms as Sartre? Would he have made the same appropriations? One can only speculate. But the pursuit of truth, the method used, and the concepts presented are very close. Thus responding to Ansell-Pearson's call and exploring the points at which Nietzsche's and Husserl's paths cross is extremely fruitful and allows us to see Nietzsche in a different light. I believe that reading him as a phenomenologist will necessarily entail having to reread his ethical and political views. This task, however, will have to be left aside for the moment.

Notes

1. *Human, All Too Human* is one of the most neglected of Nietzsche's writings. It is often considered to be a positivistic interlude, one that would not articulate Nietzsche's philosophy as found in subsequent texts. I consider this point of view to be erroneous. Indeed once one reads the work very closely, one discovers a new Nietzsche. I would go so far as to say that the Nietzsche of *Human, All Too Human* is even more interesting than the one we are more familiar with. It is a Nietzsche who is engaged in an important dialogue with the philosophical tradition that he is trying to reevaluate. Despite Nietzsche's own description of the book as a monological book (*monologische Buch*) in the epigraph, it is a genuine dialogue. The English edition omits the inclusion of this very interesting epigraph as well as the quotation from Descartes that Nietzsche uses as a preface for the first edition in 1878.

2. My translation of "einem der grössten Befreier des Geistes" (Nietzsche, *Menschliches, Allzumenschliches*, 10). The text of the whole epigraph is as follows: "This book, a monologue, emerged during a winter sojourn in Sorrento (1876–1877). I would not have presented it to the public now, had the approaching date of 30th of May 1878 not awoken such a vibrant desire to present a personal homage to one of the greatest liberators of the spirit." (My translation of "Dieses monologische Buch, welches in Sorrent während eines Winteraufenthaltes [1876 auf 1877] entstand, würde jetzt der Oeffentlichkeit nicht übergeben werden, wenn nicht die Nähe des 30. Mai 1878 den Wunsch allzu lebhaft erregt hätte, einem der grössten Befreier des Geistes zur rechten Stunde eine persönliche Huldigung darzubringen.")

3. As mentioned earlier, Nietzsche offers a quote from Descartes's *Discourse on Method* in lieu of a preface for the first edition of 1878 of *Human, All Too Human*:

> Finally, to conclude this moral code, I decided to review the various occupations which men have in this life, in order to try to choose the best. Without wishing to say anything about the occupations of others, I thought I could do no better than to continue with the very one I was engaged in, and devote my whole life to cultivating my reason and advancing as far as I could in the knowledge of the truth, following the method that I had prescribed by myself. Since beginning to use this method I had felt such great satisfaction that I thought one could not have any sweeter or purer enjoyment in this life. Every day I discovered by its means truths which, it seemed to me, were quite important and were generally unknown by other men; and the satisfaction they gave me so filled my mind that nothing else mattered to me. (*Discourse on Method*, III, 33)

In his 1886 Preface, Nietzsche elaborates in his own words. He indicates that his writings "have been called a schooling in suspicion, even more in contempt, but fortunately also in courage, indeed in audacity. And in fact I myself do not believe that anyone has ever before looked into the world with an equally profound degree of suspicion" (*Human, All Too Human*, I Preface §1 [hereafter HTH]). He is indicating here that his skepticism is magnified in comparison to that of Descartes and Kant. It is still, however, and for all of its profundity, informed by Descartes's and Kant's. For more on Nietzsche's skepticism, see Berry, *Nietzsche and the Ancient Skeptical Tradition*; Welshon, "Skepticism, Antirealism, and Perspectivism in Nietzsche's Epistemology"; Rayman, "Nietzsche, Truth and Reference."

4. Nietzsche, "Truth and Lies in a Nonmoral Sense" (hereafter TL). I am using Daniel Brazeale's translation as it appears in *The Nietzsche Reader*.

5. I take phenomenology to be a philosophical approach that examines the being-in-the-world of the human while going beyond interpretations and theoretical frameworks in order to go "back to the things themselves." Its object of inquiry is consciousness as embodied and woven into a pregiven world. The encounter between intentional consciousness and the world is creative to a degree, since consciousness constitutes the world in which it is already involved. Through phenomenological "reduction," the philosopher can explain how experience is constituted by a consciousness that is in-the-world. Thus the object of perception is shown to be truly the fruit of the constitutive subject's encounter with the world. Existential phenomenology focuses on how the human lives its being-in-the-world as intentional consciousness. I believe that this is what Nietzsche's philosophy does.

6. We will see later in this essay that Nietzsche's view of consciousness is complex. He distinguishes between the self and the ego, the self being our embodied consciousness and the ego being an outcome of our activity in the world.

7. There is indeed a lot to be said about the Husserl-Nietzsche connection. Rudolf Boehm, as early as 1962, was already pointing to some pathways (see chapter 1 in this volume). My essay, as well as a few others in this volume, uncover the many concepts that Nietzsche and Husserl share.

8. Ansell-Pearson, "Incorporation and Individuation," 62.

9. Poellner, "Nietzsche and Phenomenology," 13.

10. See Hill, *Nietzsche's Critiques*. Hill's study is an excellent analysis of the relation between the two philosophers and of Nietzsche's reception of Kant. For another, less exhaustive, study, see Reboul, *Nietzsche Critique de Kant*.

11. Hill, *Nietzsche's Critiques*, 21.

12. I acknowledge that this account will be all too brief, but it serves the purposes of my essay. Despite its brevity, I think it will still be fair to the gist of Kant's proposals.

13. In *Twilight of the Idols*, we find the very famous passage titled "How the 'Real World' at Last Became a Myth: History of an Error." In this rather short section, Nietzsche encompasses the whole history of the real world, the realm of the thing in-itself, and how it gained the prominence and value it did for human beings. He concludes by saying, "We have abolished the real world: what world is left? the apparent world perhaps? . . . But no, with the real world we have also abolished the apparent world!" What he is rejecting here is not the phenomenal world of experiences. With the construct "real world" came the construct "apparent world," the needed opposite to the real world, and both together were veiling the phenomenal reality of human experience in the world. This phenomenal reality is the raw experience of the world. It is impossible to experience if one has not shown the illusions of the "real world" and the "apparent world" to be what they are through historical philosophizing.

14. Here I am using an expression that Lyotard uses when speaking of the phenomenological concept of consciousness. In French, consciousness is "tissée avec le monde." See his *La Phénoménologie*, 6. See also note 4 above and how I have used it in my definition of phenomenology.

15. Poellner, "Nietzsche and Phenomenology," 26.

16. Although, as will become clear throughout the essay, parallels are not only to be drawn with regard to methodology but also to certain conceptual content of their philosophies.

17. Descartes, *Meditations on First Philosophy*, 76

18. Furthermore, he explains:

The longing for a fully alive philosophy has led to many a renaissance. Must not the only fruitful renaissance be the one that reawakens the impulse of the *Cartesian Meditations*: not to adopt their content but, in *not* doing so, to renew with greater intensity the radicalness of their spirit, the radicalness of self-responsibility, to make that radicalness true for the first time by enhancing it to the last degree, to uncover thereby for the first time the genuine sense of the necessary regress of the ego, and consequently to overcome the hidden but already felt naïveté of earlier philosophizing? In any case, the question indicates one of the ways that has led to transcendental phenomenology. (Husserl, *Cartesian Meditations*, 6; hereafter CM)

The latter part of the quote is already indicating the point at which Nietzsche and Husserl will have to part ways, namely Husserl's acceptance of eternal values as well as the embrace of the notion of a pure ego.

19. Descartes, *Discourse on Method*, III, 33. See note 3 above.

20. Kant, *Critique of Pure Reason*, second edition, §16, 152.

21. In the Aristotelian sense of *potentia*?

22. Husserl refers to it as an "apodiktisch evidente Prämisse" (*Cartesianishe Meditationen*, 66).

23. Matthews, *The Phenomenology of Merleau-Ponty*, 33.

24. Sartre, *The Transcendence of the Ego*, 38.

25. Ibid., 53.

26. Ibid., 106.

27. Stiegler, *Nietzsche et la biologie*, 20–21.

28. My translation of "La biologisation du sujet kantien, plutôt que de vider le sujet de sa corporéité, rappelle donc, au contraire, que *tout sujet vivant est d'abord un sujet affecté, et qui souffre de ses affections*" (ibid., 35).

29. Hill, *Nietzsche's Critiques*, 103.

30. What follows is a brief account of a more detailed analysis that I have presented in the article "Nietzsche's Notion of Embodied Self."

31. I am using this verb with extreme caution because Nietzsche is far from adopting a causalist view.

32. For another approach that takes into consideration the later Husserl in contrast to Nietzsche, see the essay by Bettina Bergo in this volume.

33. My translation of "avait pratiqué une phénoménologie sauvage et inconsciente de soi" (de Coorebyter, "Introduction," 21).

Bibliography

Ansell-Pearson, Keith. "Incorporation and Individuation: On Nietzsche's Use of Phenomenology for Life." *Journal of the British Society for Phenomenology* 38, no. 1 (2007): 61–89.

Berry, Jessica. *Nietzsche and the Ancient Skeptical Tradition*. Oxford: Oxford University Press, 2011.

de Coorebyter, Vincent. Introduction to *La Transcendance de l'Ego et autres textes phénoménologiques*, by Jean-Paul Sartre. Paris: Vrin, 2003.

Daigle, Christine. "Nietzsche's Notion of Embodied Self: Proto-Phenomenology at Work?" *Nietzsche-Studien* 40 (2011): 226–43.

Descartes, René. *Discourse on Method*. In *Descartes: Selected Philosophical Writings*. Translated by John Cottingham, Robert Stoothoff, and Dugald Murdoch. Cambridge: Cambridge University Press, 1998.

———. *Meditations on First Philosophy*. In *Descartes: Selected Philosophical Writings*. Translated by John Cottingham, Robert Stoothoff, and Dugald Murdoch. Cambridge: Cambridge University Press, 1998.

Hill, R. Kevin, *Nietzsche's Critiques: The Kantian Foundations of his Thought*. Oxford: Clarendon Press, 2003.

Husserl, Edmund. *Cartesian Meditations: An Introduction to Phenomenology*. Translated by Dorion Cairns. Norwell, MA: Kluwer Academic, 1999.

———. *Cartesianische Meditationen und Pariser Vorträge*. Edited by S. Strasser. The Hague: Martinus Nijhoff, 1973.

Kant Immanuel. *Critique of Pure Reason*. Translated by Norman Kemp Smith. New York: Palgrave Macmillan, 2003.

Lyotard, Jean-François. *La Phénoménologie*. Paris: PUF, Que sais-je?, 2004.

Matthews, Eric. *The Phenomenology of Merleau-Ponty*. Montreal: McGill/Queen's University Press, 2002.

Nietzsche, Friedrich. *Beyond Good and Evil*. Translated by W. Kaufmann. New York: Vintage Books, 1989.

———. *Daybreak: Thoughts on the Prejudices of Morality*. Edited and translated by R. J. Hollingdale, M. Clark, and B. Leiter. Cambridge: Cambridge University Press, 1997.

———. *The Gay Science*. Translated by W. Kaufmann. New York: Vintage Books, 1974.

———. *Human, All Too Human: A Book for Free Spirits*. Translated by R. J. Hollingdale. Introduction by R. Schacht. Cambridge: Cambridge University Press, 1996.

———. "Truth and Lies in a Nonmoral Sense." Translated by D. Brazeale. In *The Nietzsche Reader*. Edited by Keith Ansell-Pearson and Duncan Large. Oxford: Blackwell, 2006.

———. *Twilight of the Idols/The Anti-Christ*. Translated by R. J. Hollingdale. London: Penguin Books, 1990.

Poellner, Peter. "Nietzsche and Phenomenology, Or: How to Get the Relation between Phenomenology, Science, and Metaphysics Right." In *A Companion to Nietzsche*, edited by Keith Ansell-Pearson. Oxford: Blackwell, 2006.

Rayman, Joshua. "Nietzsche, Truth and Reference." *Nietzsche-Studien* 36 (2007): 155–68.

Reboul, Olivier. *Nietzsche Critique de Kant*. Paris: PUF, 1974.

Sartre, Jean-Paul. *The Transcendence of the Ego: An Existentialist Theory of Consciousness*. Translated by Forrest Williams and Robert Kirkpatrick. New York: Hill and Wang, 1991.

Stiegler, Barbara. *Nietzsche et la biologie*. Paris: PUF, 2001.

Welshon, Rex. "Skepticism, Antirealism, and Perspectivism in Nietzsche's Epistemology." *Journal of Nietzsche Studies* 37 (Spring 2009): 23–43.

3 On Nietzsche's Genealogy and Husserl's Genetic Phenomenology

The Case of Suffering

Saulius Geniusas

THE QUESTION OF suffering played a prominent part in philosophical reflections until the end of the nineteenth century. In contemporary philosophy, this question is almost entirely forgotten. Of course, one could object to such a claim and suggest that nowadays philosophers address suffering *indirectly* when they turn to the question of pain—an issue by no means uncommon in contemporary philosophical discussions. And yet in these analyses pain is addressed as a phenomenon that falls into the larger class of sensations known as bodily sensations, such as itches, tingles, and tickles.[1] It is highly doubtful whether such a framework can do full justice to our experience of pain.[2] In the present context, suffice it to stress that the reduction of the problematic of pain to the level of bodily sensations cannot tell us what suffering is, if only because, in the words of Gary Madison, suffering is not a neurological but an existential phenomenon.[3] Or as Eric Cassell has put it, "Bodies do not suffer, persons suffer."[4]

Taking the neglect of the question of suffering into account, let me preface this essay with two observations. First, suffering is a subjective experience, and in two distinct senses. This experience is subjective in that it can be directly given only from the first-person perspective; it is also subjective in that no one else can access my own suffering. *Suffering is thus a paradoxical phenomenon, both indubitable and unverifiable.* Such a state of affairs allows one to pinpoint the peculiar evidence characteristic of our experience of suffering. Taking into account the broadening of the notion of evidence in phenomenology (where evidence is understood as an agreement of what is meant and what is intuited) and the conceptual distinctions between the different forms of evidence phenomenology has introduced, one could say that *our experience of suffering is assertoric and apodictic, yet by no means adequate.* On the one hand, this evidence is assertoric and apodictic insofar as the experience of suffering carries the certainty that the nonbeing of this very experience is unimaginable and inconceivable. On the other hand, this experience is inadequate insofar as it principally lacks intersubjective verification.

Second, despite being a subjective experience, suffering is always already dressed up in particular interpretations, many of which are not of our own making. Since I, as a human being, am not just a natural but also an intersubjective, historical, and cultural being, my most private suffering is shot through with the interpretations of suffering that are inherited and appropriated from others.

Thus sensitivity to experience and caution about the possibility of drawing a clear distinction between experience and interpretations of experience are called for especially when it comes to the philosophical analysis of suffering. Few other thinkers have shown such sensitivity and such caution as vigorously as Nietzsche and Husserl. It is, however, of great philosophical interest that their analyses of suffering took them in almost opposite directions. On the one hand, it is *suffering as an experience* that attracts the attention of Husserl, whose phenomenological inquiry aims to liberate suffering from the inadequate interpretations that have been imposed on it. On the other hand, Nietzsche's primary interest lies in the *interpretations of suffering* and both the blinding and the liberating function performed by different interpretations.[5]

The significance of Nietzsche's and Husserl's reflections on suffering can be best seen in light of the nowadays dominant perspective on suffering, to whose brief description I now turn.

Three Visions of Suffering

According to one of the central hermeneutical principles, we understand a thesis only when we reconstruct the question to which it aims to provide an answer. The nowadays dominant view on suffering springs from the attempt to answer the following question: What must I do in order to eliminate suffering? Let me turn to a few illustrations, which will confirm the central significance of this question for the nowadays dominant view on suffering.

In the context of *religious* life, suffering is conceived as a curse that was cast on human existence, a curse that religious practices can help us escape.[6] In a *technological* context, we encounter the same mind-set, but this time dressed in secular garb. We hear that for suffering to be eradicated, there is no need to wait for a better world to come. Supposedly the unprecedented technological discoveries will enable us to abolish suffering *hic et nunc.* On the *political* level, all the talk of changing things, improving them, of making progress is for the most part conceived in terms of diminishing suffering. And when it comes to *medical culture,* alongside the religious, technical, and political *machinery of salvation* we have found an equivalent *machinery of concealment*: so as not to upset fellow human beings, we hide suffering behind closed doors, be it in hospitals, hospices, or elsewhere.

One could object that such a portrayal of the nowadays dominant view does not take into account the mounting representation of suffering in popular culture. Yet one need not overlook that here we face something quite paradoxical: *pain that does not hurt* and *suffering from which one does not suffer*. The representation of suffering in films, television, comics, and computer games gives rise to an experience of *suffering at a distance*, that is, to the suffering of actual or virtual *others* who are *far away* and whose lives are unconnected to our own.[7] The pleasure associated with our capacity to stomach the pain of others represented within a virtual medium is associated with our alleged freedom from suffering, that is, the comfort and reassurance that, supposedly, our attempt to eliminate suffering has, at least to some degree, been successful. The transformation of suffering into entertainment, which distracts one from actual concerns and helps one overcome boredom, only strengthens the tacit assumption that life without suffering is possible.

In short, according to the first vision, suffering is a wholly *unnecessary* and perfectly *dispensable* dimension of human existence.[8] By contrast, the second vision sees suffering as a *revealing* phenomenon. The second vision arises out of the question, What does suffering tell me about the human condition? The approach that this second vision takes toward the first one is both ironic and critical: ironic, because it knows that the alleged elimination of suffering would equal the elimination of the human condition; critical, because the attempt to eradicate suffering arises out of the refusal to admit the constitutive role that suffering plays in human existence. For the second vision, the first approach to suffering, that is, *our* approach, misses its target. It is not that *we* misunderstand suffering; in fact we understand it quite well, yet we find compelling ways to cover up and alter this understanding. As we will soon see, Husserl's genetic phenomenology represents this second vision most forcefully.

In contrast to the first and the second visions, the third addresses suffering as a *concealing* phenomenon. This vision is primarily concerned with the following question: How exactly does a particular perspective on suffering relate to the life of the one suffering? Does the perspective in question affirm life, or is it rather a rebellion against it? I will suggest that Nietzsche's *Genealogy of Morals* provides us with the most robust resources that underlie this perspective.

The dominance of the first vision in our culture is so overpowering that it is often assumed to be the only available perspective. With this in mind, I would now like to turn to a more detailed analysis of the second and third visions with a focus on their critical functions. I leave the question regarding the relation between the second and the third visions for the final section.

Suffering as a Revealing Phenomenon

My earlier remark, that the second vision of suffering has its resources in Husserl's phenomenology, might sound highly counterintuitive. After all, Husserl's phenomenology has often been attacked for being too epistemological, solipsistic, and idealistic and thus incapable of addressing such existentially charged themes as suffering. While the problematic of suffering is bound to the problematic of finitude, all too often one hears that in the face of finitude, Husserl's phenomenology was to encounter its own limit. As Gadamer suggests, the drawback of Husserl's exclusive preoccupation with essences led him to overlook the "actuality of what is actual," the "factuality of what is factual," that is, our own facticity.[9]

Allegedly Husserl's fixation on the problematic of self-evidence constitutes another reason that makes his phenomenology so poorly suited to address the problematic of suffering. "Why are you so furiously set against Husserl?" Max Scheler had asked Lev Shestov during their last meeting. In an article that he completed only a few weeks before his death,[10] Shestov answers Scheler's question by juxtaposing self-evidence with suffering: "European thought, bewitched by self-evidence, considers itself to have 'risen above' a 'revealed' truth for which human tears are more powerful than the necessities disclosed by self-evidence. . . . One must either absolutize truth and relativize life or else refuse to obey the compulsion of truth in order to save human life."[11] Shestov's critique of Husserl, presented with great admiration, stems from what Shestov sees as the incompatibility of two conceptions of philosophical praxis. Philosophy can be conceived either as reflection (Husserl) or as a struggle (Shestov). For Shestov, only the latter model, conceived precisely as a struggle against self-evidence, can do justice to human suffering.

Admittedly the problematic of suffering does not constitute a central problem in Husserl's phenomenology. Yet arguably these standard critiques dismiss the richness of Husserl's phenomenology too quickly, and thus they overlook how his phenomenology could enrich our understanding of suffering. In this regard, the recent publication of Husserl's *C-Manuscripts*[12] is of central significance. In these manuscripts, we encounter Husserl's intriguing analyses of birth, death, and sleep. All in all, Husserl has left us with more than two hundred pages of manuscripts dedicated precisely to this problematic.[13]

To clarify the transcendental context, within which the Husserlian perspective on suffering takes root, let me start with a rather basic observation: Neither I, nor you, nor anyone else has a single memory of his or her birth; neither I, nor you, nor anyone else will ever experience his or her death. Experience does not corroborate my finitude. On the contrary, about each experience I can always say that there are other experiences that precede it, just as there are other experiences that follow it. Thus on the one hand, my own experience motivates me to speak of an infinite extension of experience; yet on the other hand, I am also certain that my existence has a beginning and that it will come to an end. Where does this certainty come from?[14]

It is almost a matter of philosophical platitude to escape this embarrassment by stating that my awareness of my own finitude relies exclusively on my experience of others and their finitude. To be sure, I cannot experience *my own* birth, death, or sleep; yet just as surely, I can "experience" the birth, death, and sleep of *others*. I see others come into this world and leave it, and I know that in this regard, my nature is the same as theirs. The beginning and the end of the existence of my fellow human beings *seems* to be the source of evidence on which the recognition of my own finitude rests. Voltaire represents this view most elegantly when he writes, "The human race is the only one that knows it must die, and it knows this only through its experience. A child brought up alone and transported to a desert island would have no more idea of death than a cat or a plant." Yet according to Husserl, *human subjectivity, even when taken in transcendental isolation from all others, is already aware of its own finitude.* In contrast to Voltaire, Husserl's analyses bring to light that a human being, transported to the "transcendental island" of his or her own inwardness, is already aware of birth and death as limit-phenomena.

Let us begin with the problematic of birth. If my consciousness of birth does not derive from my experience of others, where exactly does it take root? We find Husserl struggling with this question in a short text, "The Finitude of the Primordial Ego,"[15] a text that he qualified as "possibly the best presentation of limit-phenomena."[16] We know that each experience subjectivity undergoes has its own horizons of sense. We also know that, for instance, in childhood, these horizons did not yet entail numerous dimensions of sense that subsequent experience suffused them with. This means that the horizons of sense, from which my experience is inseparable, admit of accretion and remodeling of sense.

On the basis of this rudimentary awareness, I can always ask myself: What would the world look like if it were stripped of all horizons of sense? By addressing this question, subjectivity can come to terms with birth as a limit-phenomenon. Such a disclosure of the sanctuary of pure phenomenality within the primordial world can be considered subjectivity's dim awareness of the dawning world-experience.

In this short text (as well as elsewhere) Husserl likens such a consciousness of birth to *awakening.* This is, however, a dangerous analogy. For let us ask: What does the consciousness of awakening entail? To be conscious of awakening is to be already aware that the I that awakens is the same I as the one that had earlier fallen asleep. Not being conscious of the unity of my life, I would either conceive of my former self as another ego, or I would not be conscious of my former self at all. In either case, not being conscious of a unified self, I would not be conscious of sleep. Yet the I that awakens into this world is not conscious of the unity that spans its life. The sleep from which this I awakens is essentially different from ordinary sleep. So as not to lose sight of this inimitable phenomenality of birth, Husserl qualifies it as awakening from *primordial sleep (Urschlaf).*

Just as consciousness of my birth, so also consciousness of my death need not be derived from my experience of others. Consciousness of sleep procures the givenness of birth and of death as limit-phenomena. As we just saw, the phenomenality of birth is interceded by my direct consciousness of awakening. When it comes to the problematic of death, Husserl argues that my awareness of death is corroborated by my direct consciousness of falling asleep. This means that my consciousness of *my own* death is transcendentally more rudimentary than my awareness of the death of *others*: the phenomenon of death is already given to me as a dim awareness of a *dreamless sleep from which I will never wake up.*

Yet the hindrance encountered in the discussion of birth reemerges in Husserl's analysis of death. Just as the common sense of awakening is coupled with the sense of a foregoing falling asleep, so the common experience of falling asleep motivates one to assert that there is no final sleep over which life does not triumph.[17] This means that, to obtain the sense of death as a limit-phenomenon, I must couple the experience of falling asleep with some other experiences I undergo still within the primordial world.

It is these other experiences that finally bring us to the problematic of suffering. These other experiences are those of the diminution of powers (*Kräfteeinschränkung*) and of taking sick (*Erkrankung*). These experiences bring about the dilapidation of my body (*Leib*), which in its own turn gives rise to the constriction of the experienced world. When I couple such experiences with that of falling asleep, I obtain an awareness of my death as a limit-phenomenon.

Thus already within the "transcendental island of inwardness," that is, within the primordial reduction, I am aware of my own finitude. My own life is given to me as finite because I am aware of my own birth and death as limit-phenomena. I am conscious of my birth as the first awakening from the primordial sleep; I am aware of my own death as the sinking of my life into primordial sleep. What makes birth, as a limit-phenomenon, possible is the conception of pure phenomenality in the absence of any horizonal sense. What makes death as a limit-phenomenon possible is the experience of suffering and pain.

Why is this phenomenology of pain and suffering significant? This phenomenology brings to light that in the absence of pain and suffering, human subjectivity would not be aware of death as a limit-phenomenon. One is thus fully justified in speaking of suffering as a *revealing* phenomenon. As I mentioned earlier, the second vision of suffering arises out of the question "What does suffering tell me about the human condition?" Now we have an answer to this question: suffering reveals the finitude of human existence.

Yet this answer remains imprecise. It invites one to ask: Are we then to draw an analogy between Husserl and Heidegger and say that just as for Heidegger *Angst* reveals the certainty of death, so for Husserl too suffering is inseparable from an identical *certainty*, conceived as adequate evidence? I would suggest that such an approach would be inappropriate. Just as Heidegger draws a distinction between an authentic and an inauthentic being-toward-death, so a similar distinction could be drawn in Husserl's case. And yet the meaning of these terms (i.e., *authentic* and *inauthentic*) would be essentially different in Husserl and Heidegger. For Heidegger, the difference between authentic and inauthentic notions of death has to do with the phenomenological origins from which the phenomenon of death is derived. Insofar as the conception of death derives from others (i.e., from *das Man*), the conception of death is inauthentic.

Insofar as the conception of death derives from my own being-toward-death, I face an authentic notion of finitude. In Husserl, the situation is quite different.

What could these terms, *authentic* and *inauthentic*, mean in the context of Husserlian phenomenology? I would suggest the following: *If I have any certainty about death or its absence, I can rest assured that I face an inauthentic notion of death.* As seen from the Husserlian standpoint, the authentic notion of death consists in its *paradoxical* phenomenality.

The phenomenality of death is paradoxical because it stands in conflict with the temporal structure of experience. Cessation, just as inception, is conceivable only as a cessation of something or someone given to consciousness that conceives it. That is, cessation presupposes noncessation—consciousness to which the cessation is given.[18] Both beginning and end (as far as they are phenomena) are possible only in process and not as the beginning or the end of the process. Thus the problematic of birth and death point to a more rudimentary immanent time that renders them phenomenal. This conflict between the givenness of immanent time and the inescapability of death inflicts upon death its paradoxical phenomenality: "But is it not paradoxical that living in the streaming present, I must continuously believe that I will continue to live, when I nonetheless know, that my death is imminent?" (Hua Mat VIII, 96).[19]

Suffering is a revealing phenomenon. Yet what does it reveal? I earlier remarked that suffering reveals my own finitude. Yet suffering also reveals something else: it reveals that finitude *can never be given with certainty.* Suffering first and foremost reveals the *paradoxical* phenomenality of finitude, that is, the irresolvable tension that qualifies human existence, a paradoxical tension that human beings can cover up but cannot escape. Suffering reveals the limits of certainty; it reveals the *enigma of finitude.*

Once the nowadays common approach to suffering is viewed from this perspective, one has to say that the dominant tendency in our culture is precisely that of covering up the paradoxical phenomenality of finitude. As I suggested above, we find this concealment at work in the *political* and *technical* cultures, which make repeated promises to eliminate suffering; we find it also in the *medical* culture, in its fixed tendency to find for suffering efficient hiding places. And let us ask: What is the approach that we take to these political, technical, and medical promises? On the one hand, we are secretly aware that these promises cannot be fulfilled. On the other hand, we do not discard them; in a clumsy way, we continue to believe in them, while realizing their absurdity and unattainability.

This tendency to cover up the paradoxical phenomenality of suffering is strongly inscribed in the religious consciousness, if by this one means a kind of *certainty* that, sooner or later, suffering will be eradicated and life will triumph over death. This tendency is just as strongly inscribed in secular consciousness if it is filled with *certainty* regarding the inescapability of death.[20] As seen from the Husserlian perspective, both alternatives are built on the same false assumption that *certainty* regarding finitude is possible. Yet this certainty, whether it expresses itself as a thesis or an antithesis, is a mark of the inauthentic phenomenality of finitude. If suffering reveals the limits of certainty, then both perspectives cover up the enigma of suffering. As seen from the Husserlian point of view, the nowadays dominant perspective on suffering misses its target in that it is built upon the refusal to admit the paradoxical phenomenality of suffering.

Suffering as a Concealing Phenomenon

The standard critiques of Husserl's phenomenology have given rise to the impression that the problematic of suffering lies beyond the boundaries of Husserl's phenomenology. Yet even though the problematic of suffering emerges at the margins of Husserl's phenomenology, it is by no means just of marginal significance either for our understanding of his phenomenology or for our understanding of suffering. As we turn to the third perspective on suffering, which has its sources in Nietzsche's writings, we find ourselves in an entirely different situation. To begin with, suffering is by no means tangential in the context of problems that Nietzsche himself has addressed. Furthermore, few other inquiries into suffering have been as influential as Nietzsche's. In the first half of the twentieth-century, some of the most fascinating analyses of pain and suffering were Nietzschean at their core.[21] More recently we have witnessed a growing interest in Nietzsche's reflections on suffering not only in philosophy but also in other disciplines, such as literature, nursing, and political science. Given this plethora of interpretations, I will address Nietzsche's reflections on suffering not by repeating its well-known aspects but rather by juxtaposing his position to Husserl's.

Nietzsche's reflections on suffering are designed to answer two significantly different concerns. On the one hand, Nietzsche addresses suffering as a basic and irreducible dimension of human existence. In this regard, he draws a distinction between meaningful and meaningless suffering and argues that any thematization of suffering transforms meaningless suffering into a concealing phenomenon. On the other hand, Nietzsche also addresses suffering as the most severe trial that existence can face. Within this trial, he approaches our reactions to suffering as symptoms of a hidden evaluation of existence. This "symptomatic" analysis is geared toward the discovery of a meaningful response to suffering that would enhance the significance of existence.[22]

Let us turn to a claim we encounter repeatedly in Nietzsche's writings. In the second book of his *Genealogy of Morals*, Nietzsche writes, "What really arouses indignation against suffering is not suffering as such but the senselessness of suffering" (GM 68). In the final section of the third book of the *Genealogy*, we encounter a reiteration of this claim: "The meaninglessness of suffering, not suffering itself, was the curse that lay over mankind so far" (GM 162). What sense are we to make of the meaninglessness of suffering? George F. Sefler offers a possible answer:

Of itself, suffering is irrational; it has no meaning or purpose. Meaning is given to suffering—as to all the other aspects of life—by man himself. Thus, the *human* problem of suffering is not to prove that it exists (that is a fact), but to determine the *meaning* of its existence. If suffering, then, is to have a sense, or meaning, this is to be supplied by the individual person.[23]

When Nietzsche is read alongside Husserl, it becomes clear that this answer does not solve the problem we face. In light of the central phenomenological thesis regarding the intentionality of lived experience, *it suffices to cut off any phenomenon from experience to render it meaningless.* Thus of course, "meaning is given to suffering," but to this one also needs to add: just as meaning is given to everything else. Yet as soon as this addition is made, it becomes incomprehensible why Nietzsche would claim that the meaninglessness of suffering is "a curse that lay over mankind so far."

It is of central importance not to overlook the latter claim. *The meaninglessness of suffering can be seen as a curse only insofar as it can be experienced.* After all, if the meaninglessness in question lay beyond the bounds of experience, it would not affect us, and therefore we could only remain indifferent to it. It is not that suffering is irrational, meaningless, and purposeless "of itself." Strictly speaking, suffering has no "of itself"; it exists only insofar as it is experienced. *The distinction between meaningless and meaningful suffering,* if it is to be intelligible, *must fall within the boundaries of experience.*[24]

In the two passages from the *Genealogy of Morals* that I quoted earlier, Nietzsche's claim is twofold: first, he asserts that suffering itself is *meaningless*; second, he also asserts that for mankind, the meaninglessness of suffering is *unbearable.* What consequences follow from these theses? If suffering is meaningless and if this meaninglessness is unbearable, then the only thing left is to transform suffering into something it is not, to dress it up in a variety of (mis)interpretations that will help us hide from the unbearable meaninglessness of suffering. Thus the third vision announces that the human confrontation with suffering has always been that of forcing meaning onto something that is meaningless. Why? Because some sense—even if it is inappropriate—is better than no sense (GM 162), better because it helps humanity overcome what Nietzsche calls "suicidal nihilism" (GM 162).

Thus, much like the second vision, the third perspective proclaims the same diagnosis: the nowadays dominant view is a misinterpretation of suffering. Yet in contrast to the second vision, which contrasted this misinterpretation with what it identified as the truth of suffering, the Nietzschean perspective announces that, in a good sense, one cannot help but misunderstand suffering. The nowadays common misinterpretation of suffering in this regard is no exception.

Yet are we then to conclude that the phenomenon of suffering lies beyond understanding? Not necessarily. We can always obtain a better sense of suffering by tracing the genealogy of particular narratives within which suffering has been dressed up. In their readings of Nietzsche, commentators sometimes ignore that his own account of such a genealogy is ambiguous and self-contradictory. In the final section of the *Genealogy of Morals*, he famously claims that the interpretation of suffering through the ascetic ideals has been the only available interpretation. The meaning offered through the ascetic ideals "was the only meaning offered so far; any meaning is better than none at all. . . . In it, suffering was interpreted; the tremendous void seemed to have been filled; the door was closed to any kind of suicidal nihilism" (GM 162). And even though this *only interpretation* brought with it new suffering that arose through the emphasis on internalization and guilt, nonetheless a human being was saved. A human being "now possessed a meaning, he was henceforth no longer like a leaf in the wind, a plaything of nonsense. . . . *The will itself was saved*" (GM 162).

Such is the view presented in the third part of the *Genealogy*. In the second part, we find a somewhat different position. Here Nietzsche identifies the interpretation of suffering on the basis of the ascetic ideals as *one possible interpretation*. Alongside this interpretation, he also speaks "of the naive man of more ancient times, who understood all suffering in relation to the spectator of it or the causer of it" (GM 68). Here Nietzsche does not present these two perspectives as the only ones available. His point rather is that "neither for the Christian, who has interpreted a whole mysterious machinery of salvation into suffering," nor for the more ancient perspective of which I just spoke, "was there any such thing as *senseless* suffering" (GM 68). Keeping in mind the distinction between meaningful and meaningless suffering, one can say that the saving power of these interpretations comes along with their concealing powers. Like Proteus, as soon as it is seen, suffering becomes something it is not; as soon as it is objectified, suffering is already domesticated, rendered livable, transformed into what it is not.

I would now like to turn to what I earlier identified as the second central concern that guides Nietzsche's reflections on suffering: Could it not be that suffering has the function of evaluation? Even more, could suffering not be a symptom of our most fundamental evaluations of existence? Let me turn to this principal issue by raising an operational question: How does the genealogy of different narratives on suffering help us understand the phenomenon of suffering? Clearly, the goal of genealogy cannot be simply that of cataloguing all the available positions on suffering. Rather, as Deleuze has emphasized so compellingly, the point of genealogy is to unmask those forces that underlie and determine particular perspectives on values.[25] As is well known, for Nietzsche, there are two such forces: active and reactive. While the active forces manifest themselves in terms of the affirmation of life, the reactive forces give rise to the rejection of life. Herein lies the criterion according to which the third vision discriminates between different perspectives on suffering. Moreover herein lies the reason why the third vision is critically disposed toward our vision of suffering: our vision derives from reactive forces; it does not affirm life but rather is a reaction against it.

One can further support such a critical diagnosis by highlighting two of Nietzsche's claims. First, according to Nietzsche, a life lived in avoidance of suffering results in the incapacity to experience any joy.[26] Second, and more important, a life lived in avoidance of pain and suffering can never be profound.[27] These claims make it clear that the critical function of Nietzschean genealogy is not meant to be only diagnostic. Rather the Nietzschean "reevaluation of all values" strives to show how suffering may be freed from reactive forces and absorbed by the active ones. Put otherwise, it is meant to show how suffering, conceived as "a principal argument against existence," may be freed from its reactive interpretations and be conceived as a necessary dimension of a more meaningful existence.

When life is conceived in terms of self-preservation, what is good might very well be conceived as the absence from and prevention of suffering. Yet Nietzsche invites us to think of life not in terms of conservation but in terms of intensification and deepening. Once life is conceived not in terms of self-preservation but in terms of self-surpassing, suffering turns out to be a necessary dimension of meaningful existence.

Nietzsche is rightly credited by the classicists for his insights into the function of contest, *agon*, in antiquity. Yet, as one commentator has remarked, Nietzsche's "truly creative stroke . . . was to then take this concept [of *agon*] and turn it inward, to apply it to the theater of the mind and heart, to convert it into a universal principle of individual creativity."[28] This "turning inward" of the Greek *agon* is exactly what transforms suffering into a new kind of a phenomenon; it transforms suffering from "the worst question mark" into the promise of a more meaningful existence. Indeed once *agon* becomes a universal principle of creativity, one can no longer identify the good life with the absence of and prevention from suffering. In the words of Meister Eckhart, which in *Schopenhauer as Educator* Nietzsche cites with approval, "The beast that bears you fastest to perfection is suffering."[29] The "turning inward" of *agon* transforms negation into affirmation, suffering into vitality, evil into growth;[30] it brings to light the constitutive role that suffering plays in a life conceived on the basis of intensification and deepening, self-cultivation and self-surpassing.

To reiterate: the nowadays dominant view conceives of suffering as something that needs to be lessened, disposed of, and eliminated. The third vision of suffering mounts an attack against such a view, yet not because it is false but because it denies the essential condition that can make existence joyful, profound, and meaningful.

Concluding Observations

Let us return to the three visions of suffering. In my analysis, I have shown the one thing that the second and the third visions share: both are critically disposed to the nowadays dominant view. Still, in the aftermath of the foregoing analysis, it remains unclear how the second and the third visions of suffering relate to each other. In this concluding section, I would like to suggest that the second and third views are just as sharply opposed to each other as they are opposed to the nowadays dominant view.

Let us look at this matter a little more closely. The phenomenological perspective on suffering faces resistance from the genealogical perspective, and, I would suggest, it cannot find the means to respond to this resistance in a way that a genealogist would find convincing. In its aim to overcome the prevalent misinterpretations of suffering, in its claim to have reached the *truth* of suffering, what the phenomenological position offers is in fact yet another narrative on suffering. It is precisely this: *a narrative*. But once so much is said, it becomes clear that *the phenomenological perspective becomes a genealogical theme*, and thus, for a genealogist, it is yet another *misinterpretation* of suffering, yet another attempt to *escape* the meaninglessness of suffering.

And how does the relation between these two perspectives appear when one begins with the genealogical point of view? Analogically, we are led to the realization that the genealogical perspective is limited by the phenomenological one. The genealogical claim that all perspectives on suffering are misinterpretations that derive from the attempt to cover up its meaninglessness calls for a *philosophical* justification. But this view—so the phenomenological critique would propose—can be justified only if one obtains *direct access* to the meaninglessness of suffering itself. Otherwise the essential building block of the genealogical analysis would be a philosophically unjustified conjecture. But how could genealogy justify its starting point when it explicitly declares that the phenomenon of suffering is unbearable, and thus is always already covered up, transformed into what it is not?

Thus the second vision emerges by suppressing the third, just as the third vision is possible only by dismissing the second. If these positions on suffering can be taken as representative of genetic phenomenology and genealogy in general, then the foregoing analysis leads to the realization that *genealogy is the bad conscience of genetic phenomenology, and vice versa.* That is, genealogy and genetic phenomenology share the same thematic field, yet they draw us in opposite directions by covering up the alternatives they dismiss—and covering them up always too quickly and illegitimately.

Arguably the conflict between these two visions of suffering derives from a more radical dispute about the nature of *reflection* and *self-consciousness*. After all, suffering (in contrast to illness) is a phenomenon of lived experience. What Elaine Scarry says about pain can also be said about suffering: "One aspect of great pain . . . is that it is to the individual experiencing it overwhelmingly present . . . and yet is almost invisible to anyone else, unfelt, and unknown."[31] Indeed, as Scarry shows, for the one who suffers, suffering cannot be denied; for all others, it cannot be confirmed. This means that the turning back upon oneself that self-consciousness and reflection give rise to provides us with the only reliable access to such phenomena as suffering. And yet it is one thing to speak of the accessibility of the *phenomenon* of suffering through reflection; it is an entirely different matter to articulate the *meaning* of this phenomenon. Although it makes little sense to doubt the experience of suffering while one undergoes it, it makes perfectly good sense to question whether or not one understands the meaning of this experience. Does the meaning of suffering lend itself to accurate articulation through self-consciousness and reflection? With this question, we find ourselves at the point at which Nietzsche and Husserl part ways. Let us briefly turn to this issue.

On the one hand, Husserl's reflections on the meaning of suffering are to a large extent based on the trust in self-consciousness and reflection. Suffice it to say that in his phenomenology, the whole problematic of the reduction is meant to ground the philosophical legitimacy of reflection. On the other hand, Nietzsche's inquiry into the meaning of suffering is grounded in the mistrust of the principle of self-consciousness. In direct contrast to Husserl, Nietzsche calls for (to use Gadamer's expression) a "dedogmatizing of self-consciousness": he insists that self-consciousness is precisely what philosophy must doubt more fundamentally than it doubts anything else.[32] In direct contrast to Husserl, for Nietzsche skepticism about the claims of self-consciousness and reflection is unavoidable.

Given the radical differences in Nietzsche's and Husserl's approaches to self-consciousness and reflection, I would suggest that the conflict between the second and third visions of suffering is *irreconcilable*. Without hermeneutical violence to Nietzsche, Husserl, or both, no harmony between these perspectives can be established. What implications does this realization have for the dialogue between Nietzsche and phenomenology?

I would suggest that a meaningful dialogue could be pursued in at least two different ways. The first way would stem from the realization that the recognition of irreconcilable differences is irreplaceable if one is to gain understanding of genealogy or phenomenology. It is surprising that, so far, such a way of opening up a dialogue between Nietzsche and Husserl has not been pursued, especially because the recognition of the significance of this insight has been operative in both phenomenological and genealogical literature. Recall, for instance, Deleuze's famous analysis of the irreconcilable differences between genealogy and dialectic.[33] Could a similar approach not also assist us in understanding the relation between genealogy and phenomenology? Or consider Shestov's account of one of his last meetings with Husserl. During this meeting, Husserl demanded with extraordinary insistence that Shestov read Kierkegaard precisely because Kierkegaard's position was the one that Husserl was unyieldingly opposed to, starting with his earliest and ending with his latest works. As Shestov remarks in passing, "He [Husserl] might just as well have insisted that I study Nietzsche."[34]

Another way to open a dialogue between Nietzsche and Husserl would lead one to pursue the numerous ways in which Nietzsche's concrete analyses call for a phenomenological grounding, and vice versa. While recognizing the irreducible differences between Nietzsche and Husserl, one would nonetheless decontextualize particular analyses, and one would bracket these differences with the aim of enriching our understanding of phenomena under scrutiny. The problematic of suffering is a good case in point. Recall the distinction Nietzsche draws between meaningful and meaningless suffering. One might wonder, how exactly is meaningless suffering *experienced*? Nietzsche's answer to this question is far from clear or detailed. I would suggest that phenomenology— a philosophy that considers lived experience the highest court of appeal—could provide the needed resources to answer this question. By bringing to light how suffering is experienced as pure negativity, how it obliterates the other contents of consciousness, how it resists expression and any other means of objectification, phenomenology could fill this gap in Nietzsche's genealogy of suffering. On the other hand, this distinction between meaningless and meaningful suffering also has great merit for phenomenology. By appropriating this Nietzschean insight, phenomenology would be able to identify suffering as a phenomenon that lies at the boundary of meaninglessness and meaning, that is, as a theme that resists thinking and in its resistance gives rise to thought.

This resistance of suffering to objectification and reflection sheds more light on what I have identified as the first vision of suffering. As I argued earlier, the first vision proclaims that suffering is a superfluous dimension of human existence, yet this proclamation is made in bad faith, since it is accompanied by the simultaneous recognition of the existential irreducibility of suffering. The dialogue opened between Nietzsche and Husserl could lead to the recognition of some of the central reasons that underlie the first vision of suffering. If suffering indeed resists thinking, and in this resistance gives rise to thought, it should no longer be surprising that the first vision would in one and the same breath affirm and deny the irreducibility of suffering. The first vision of suffering could be said to be a natural means to cover up such a paradoxical phenomenality of suffering.

Such, then, is the curious relation between the second and third visions of suffering. On the one hand, they are radically and irreconcilably opposed to each other. On the other hand, the philosophical development of both positions largely depends on their capacity and willingness to incorporate each other's insights. Needless to say, such appropriation does not indicate an abolishment of fundamental differences, which reach back to the problem of self-consciousness. It remains to be seen if this fundamental problem ever will receive a straightforward solution. Until then, we will continue to evaluate such philosophical traditions as phenomenology and genealogy on the basis of their ability to thematize concrete phenomena such as suffering.

Notes

1. The so-called sense-datum theories, perceptual theories, representational theories, evaluative theories, and motivational theories of pain are built upon this assumption.

2. To be sure, the stimuli that cause physical pain have remained constant over history. And yet the human experience of these stimuli has varied greatly. Nietzsche emphasizes this variability especially forcefully when he writes, "The combined suffering of all the animals ever subjected to the knife for scientific ends is utterly negligible compared with *one* painful night of a single hysterical bluestocking" (*On the Genealogy of Morals*, 68; hereafter GM).

3. See Madison, *On Suffering*, 7. Madison's analysis constitutes a remarkable exception to the otherwise almost complete philosophical silence when it comes to the question of suffering.

4. Cassell, "The Nature of Suffering and the Goals of Medicine," 693–745.

5. The subsequent inquiry into these crucial differences should not overshadow a common concern that underlies both Nietzsche's and Husserl's reflections on suffering: what matters to both are the effects of suffering on the *person* and not just on the *physical body*. Since this distinction between persons and bodies will be operative in what follows, a few qualifications are in place. Here the notion of the body is to be understood in terms of what Husserl has called *Körper* rather than *Leib*, namely as a physical body, which lends itself to neurobiological analysis. By drawing a distinction between *body* and *person*, I suggest that we perform a category mistake when we follow the common tendency and view a human being as a neurobiological and homeostatic machine. As Gary B. Madison has put it, "This technoscientfic view of the human being is one that has come in large part to dominate

both modern medical science and the practice of healthcare . . . as is evidenced in the widespread and uncritical reliance on pharmaceuticals and neurobiological 'enhancement technologies' on the part of the medical profession as a means for dealing with human suffering and the imperfections of human nature" (*On Suffering*, 2).

6. Since a detailed inquiry into this theme would take me too far afield, in the present context a few general remarks will have to suffice. One can conceive of the Christian doctrine of suffering as a middle path between passive endurance of suffering and active resistance: the "royal way of the cross" is an invitation to achieve *redemption from suffering through suffering* by the love of God. What we face here is a strange *coincidence of active and passive heroism*: this path invites one both to resist misery and malice and to privilege passive endurance of suffering *over* active resistance. By contrast, the teachings of Buddha as well as of the Brahman Upanishads represent a different confrontation with suffering: what we find in both is what Max Scheler has called *the Eastern ideal of passive heroism*, that is, an *ethic of nonresistance* and passive acceptance of suffering. In these contexts, the religious doctrine is meant to terminate the restless wandering by separating the superindividual self from every drive for individuality. Yet despite the highly significant differences between these religious frameworks and despite the crucial implications that stem from them, one should not overlook the common element that all these frameworks share, namely the *conjecture that life without suffering is possible*. In the present context, I will limit myself to highlighting this common conjecture.

7. As Susan Sontag has compellingly argued in *Regarding the Pain of Others*, "The more remote or exotic the place, the more likely we are to have full frontal views of the dead and dying" (70). It is certainly telling that when exceptions occur, we liken them to the irreal representation of suffering: "It's like in the movies."

8. As we are soon to find out, to commit to this vision means to tacitly admit the existential irreducibility of suffering, while patently covering it up and explicitly denying its necessity.

9. See Gadamer, "Die Phänomenologische Bewegung," 109; "The Phenomenological Movement," 135.

10. Shestov, "Pamyati velikogo filosofa (Edmund Husserl)," 126; "In Memory of a Great Philosopher: Edmund Husserl."

11. "In Memory of a Great Philosopher: Edmund Husserl," 469.

12. Husserl, *Späte Texte über Zeitkonstitution (1929–1934): Die C-Manuskripte*, vol. VIII (hereafter Hua Mat VIII).

13. The remaining portion of this section addresses themes that I have also treated elsewhere. See Geniusas, "On Birth, Death, and Sleep in Husserl's Late Manuscripts on Time."

14. The notion of certainty in this context stands for what I earlier identified as apodictic and assertoric, yet not adequate, evidence.

15. See "Die Endlichkeit des primordialen Ego" (Hua Mat VIII, 154–67).

16. See Hua Mat VIII, 159.

17. See Hua Mat VIII, 445.

18. See Husserl, *Analysen zur passiven Synthesis*, 378.

19. Here we reach the fundamental difference between Husserl's and Heidegger's analyses of death. While Heidegger invites us to think time on the basis of death, Husserl invites us to think death on the basis of time. For this reason, while for Heidegger authentic temporality amounts to the "possibility of impossibility," conceived as pure destruction, for Husserl authentic temporality is the ultimate condition of all phenomenality, including that of destruction. *As far as death is phenomenal, it is coupled with the impossibility of nothingness.*

20. In his recent study *On Suffering*, Gary B. Madison has also emphasized the common roots of both the mythical and the secular approaches to suffering: "In biblical times those who suffer were thought to be inhabited by demons or evil spirits and to be 'unclean.' In our own times medical science, under the influence of mechanistic-materialism, is inclined to view the distress people may

experience in life as something which is similarly beyond their control and which, if not directly attributable to their genetic make-up, is, in any event, a matter of 'brain chemistry' pure and simple, a case of 'neurochemical malfunction'—as a 'disease' of which people need to be cleansed by medicinal means" (276).

21. In the present context, a brief reference to Max Scheler's and Ernst Jünger's studies will have to suffice. See Scheler, "Vom Sinn des Leides," 36–72; "The Meaning of Suffering," 82–116. See also Jünger, "Über den Schmerz," 149–98; *On Pain*.

22. Paul J. M. van Tongeren has drawn a similar distinction in Nietzsche's reflections on suffering in "A Splendid Failure," 23–34.

23. Sefler, "Nietzsche and Dostoevsky on the Meaning of Suffering," 145.

24. This distinction between meaningful and meaningless suffering places a significant limit upon the phenomenological accounts of suffering. For instance, Max Scheler's claim that all suffering can be subsumed under the general concept of sacrifice does justice only to meaningful suffering. Thus, on the one hand, this distinction calls phenomenology to deepen its account of suffering. On the other hand, since in Nietzsche's writings it remains unclear how this meaninglessness is experienced, phenomenology can in significant ways enrich a Nietzschean account of suffering. I will return to this issue in the concluding section.

25. See Deleuze, *Nietzsche and Philosophy*, 2.

26. As Nietzsche puts it in *Gay Science*, "Either as *little displeasure as possible*, painlessness in brief . . . or as much *displeasure as possible* as the price for the growth of an abundance of subtle pleasure and joys that have rarely been relished yet. If you decide for the former and desire to diminish and lower the level of human pain, you also have to diminish and lower the level of their capacity for joy" (86; hereafter: GS). In the words of Nietzsche's Zarathustra, "Did you ever say yes to a single joy? Oh, my friends, then you said Yes too to all woe. All things are chained together, entwined, in love" (*Thus Spoke Zarathustra*, 283).

27. "I have often asked myself whether I am not much more deeply indebted to the hardest years of my life than to any others. . . . And as to my prolonged illness, do I not owe much more to it than I owe to my health? To it I owe a *higher* kind of health, a sort of health which grows stronger under everything that does not actually kill it!—*To it, I owe even my philosophy*. . . . Only great suffering is the ultimate emancipator of spirit . . . the suffering that takes its time—forces us philosophers to descend into our nethermost depths" (Nietzsche, *Nietzsche Contra Wagner*, "Epilogue").

28. Hillesheim, "Suffering and Self-Cultivation," 173.

29. See Nietzsche, *Schopenhauer as Educator*, 153. Why would Nietzsche approve of this claim? Consider the following: "Ask yourselves whether a tree that is supposed to grow to a proud height can dispense with bad weather and storms; whether misfortune and external resistance . . . do not belong among the *favorable* conditions without which any great growth even of virtue is scarcely possible. The poison of which weaker natures perish strengthens the strong—nor do they call it poison" (GS, 91–92).

30. See Hillesheim, "Suffering and Self-Cultivation," 177.

31. Scarry, *The Body in Pain*, 51.

32. See in this regard Gadamer, "The Problem of Intelligence," 45–60.

33. As Deleuze has it, "[Dialectical] opposition can be the law of the relation between abstract products, but difference is the only principle of genesis or production. It is this irreconcilable difference between Nietzsche and Hegel that allows us to better understand both" (*Nietzsche and Philosophy*, 157).

34. Shestov, "In Memory of a Great Philosopher: Edmund Husserl," 462.

Bibliography

Cassell, Eric. "The Nature of Suffering and the Goals of Medicine." *New England Journal of Medicine*, no. 306 (1982): 693–745.

Deleuze, Gilles. *Nietzsche and Philosophy*. Translated by Michael Hardt. New York: Columbia University Press, 2006.

Gadamer, Hans-Georg. "Die Phänomenologische Bewegung." In *Kleine Schriften*, vol. 3. Tübingen: Mohr, 1972.

———. "The Phenomenological Movement." In *Philosophical Hermeneutics*. Translated by D. E. Linge. Berkeley: University of California Press, 1976.

———. "The Problem of Intelligence." In *The Enigma of Health*. Translated by J. Gaiger and N. Walker. Stanford: Stanford University Press, 1996.

Geniusas, Saulius. "On Birth, Death, and Sleep in Husserl's Late Manuscripts on Time." In *New Contributions to Husserl's Theory of Time-Constitution*, edited by D. Lohmar and I. Yamaguchi. Dordrecht: Springer, 2009.

Hillesheim, James. "Suffering and Self-Cultivation: The Case of Nietzsche." *Educational Theory* 36, no. 2 (1986): 171–78.

Husserl, Edmund. *Analysen zur passiven Synthesis: Aus Vorlesungs- und Forschungsmanuskripten, 1918–1926. Husserliana XI*. Edited by Margot Fleischer. The Hague: Martinus Nijhoff, 1966.

———. *Späte Texte über Zeitkonstitution (1929–1934): Die C-Manuskripte. Husserliana Materialien VIII*. Edited by Dieter Lohmar. Dordrecht: Springer, 2006.

Jünger, Ernst. *On Pain*. Translated by David C. Durst. New York: Telos Press, 2008.

———. "Über den Schmerz." In *Essays I: Betrachtungen zur Zeit*. Stuttgart: Ernst Klett Verlag, 1960.

Madison, Gary B. *On Suffering: Philosophical Reflections on What It Means to Be Human*. Hamilton, Ontario: Les Érables, 2009.

Nietzsche, Friedrich. "The Case of Wagner." In *Nietzsche Contra Wagner and Selected Aphorisms*. Translated by Anthony M. Ludovici. Edinburgh: Dodo Press, 2008.

———. *Gay Science*. Translated by Walter Kaufmann. New York: Vintage Books, 1974.

———. *On the Genealogy of Morals and Ecce Homo*. Translated by Walter Kaufmann. New York: Vintage Books, 1967.

———. *Schopenhauer as Educator*. In *Untimely Meditations*. Translated by R. J. Hollingdale. Cambridge: Cambridge University Press, 1997.

———. *Thus Spoke Zarathustra*. Translated by Graham Parkes. Oxford: Oxford University Press, 2005.

Scarry, Elaine. *The Body in Pain*. Oxford: Oxford University Press, 1985.

Scheler, Max. "The Meaning of Suffering." In *On Feeling, Knowing, and Valuing*, edited by Harold Bershady. Chicago: University of Chicago Press, 1992.

———. "Vom Sinn des Leides." In *Schriften zur Soziologie und Weltanschauungslehre*, edited by Maria Scheler. Bern: Francke Verlag, 1963.

Sefler, George F. "Nietzsche and Dostoevsky on the Meaning of Suffering." *Religious Humanism* 4, no. 1 (1970): 145–50.

Shestov, Lev. "In Memory of a Great Philosopher: Edmund Husserl." *Philosophy and Phenomenological Research* 22, no. 4 (1962).: 449–71.

———. "Pamyati velikogo filosofa (Edmund Husserl)." *Russkiye zapiski,* no. 12 (1938): n.p.

Sontag, Susan. *Regarding the Pain of Others*. New York: Farrar, Straus and Giroux, 2003.

van Tongeren, Paul J. M. "'A Splendid Failure: Nietzsche's Understanding of the Tragic." *Journal of Nietzsche Studies* 11 (1996): 23–34.

4 Live Free or Battle

Subjectivity for Nietzsche and Husserl

Kristen Brown Golden

IT IS WELL known that Husserl identified the approach and themes of existentialists like Nietzsche with irrationalism. He perceived them as a threat to universal science. Their supposed excesses, seeming dilettantism, and cult-like popularity were a provocation for Husserl's final version of phenomenology. But as David Carr notes in his introduction to that work, *The Crisis of European Sciences and Transcendental Phenomenology*, in the years leading up to World War II, Husserl could not deny that existentialist approaches with which his project of universal science had long been at odds had brought to people's attention "something real: a deeply felt lack of direction for man's existence as a whole, a sense of the emptiness of Europe's cultural values, a feeling of crisis and breakdown, the demand that philosophy be relevant to life."[1]

If the *Crisis* is Husserl's attempt to fortify his project of rational ideas against a tide of "irrationality" and malaise sweeping Europe in the 1930s, it is also a seepage of intriguing concessions to existentialists. The *Crisis* is Husserl's most genealogical work dealing with Cartesianism, empiricism, Kantianism, and psychology. I shall focus on it through a comparison with Nietzsche's *On the Genealogy of Morals*. Specifically, I shall look at part III (B), "The Way into Phenomenological Transcendental Philosophy from Psychology," in the *Crisis* and essays 1 and 3 in the *Genealogy*. The *Crisis* selection is an area in the text where Husserl describes the lived world for the perceiver using an approach that, compared to Nietzsche's, is staid and relatively lacking in experiential specificity. But its general sense has similarities with Nietzsche's concept of perspectivism.

I shall show that both Nietzsche's and Husserl's projects place renewed emphasis on the importance of reckoning with the implications of the full force of a subjective viewpoint, but for projects whose orientations remain vastly different. Husserl is inspired to affirm what could seem an extreme faith in rational ideals. Nietzsche is inspired to dig up these ideals and interrogate the plays of power and idea that ground them. Husserl is more forward-looking, concentrating on the naïve objectivist standpoint of present existence, but only in order to bring about a future transcendental subjectivist outlook for that existence. The Nietzsche of the *Genealogy* is more backward-looking—interested in identifying the species of chains holding our subjectivity in predictable psychic cycles. Whether and to what extent each of their genealogies evokes aspects of modern subjectivity in a manner that meets the perceived demand that "philosophy be relevant to life" (TI xxv–xxvi) shall form the framing question of my chapter. To begin I shall examine Husserl's genealogical approach to subjectivity.

Husserl's Genealogy: The Problem and the Goal

Husserl's genealogy of subjectivity locates the science of psychology at the core of the grounding of the modern science he criticizes. To understand his meaning of *psychology* and to appreciate the task he believes modern psychology poses for attaining a properly oriented psychology, I shall first explain his concept of genealogy. The Husserl of the *Crisis* has decided that a more effective way than via mathematical objects for showing the constituted nature of human experience is through social and cultural objects. His interest in the life-world[2] focuses on one aspect of everyday awareness: the way scientific consciousness emerges from ordinary, nontheoretical intuition. By the 1930s Husserl has come to see the everyday objects of the natural and scientific attitudes to be conditioned by historically constituted meanings. The *Crisis* focuses on the way scientific attitudes move from quotidian awareness of the ordinary to a pervasive set of assumptions. It concentrates on how new theoretical ideas can sediment into decisive cultural meanings to form the hidden structures that make possible everyday awareness. Subjective states, it would seem, are not bound to a universal framework that remain constant despite changes through history. Understanding our existence to be historical in essence,[3] Husserl saw the need to investigate our current attitudes genealogically. He wanted to show the way the unfolding of a potentially unified science since the Greeks becomes a deformed rationalism. He wanted to inspire others with the idea that "faith in the possibility of philosophy as a task, that is, in the possibility of universal knowledge, is something we cannot let go" (C 16).

Husserl construes the brandishing of naïve objectivist attitudes about science and the parceling up of the sciences to be the crucial misstep, furthering a societal breakdown that would culminate in National Socialism. The object of his grinding axe is that modern scientists choose to exclude consciousness from the philosophical framework of modern science. He believes a science grounded in "physicalism," that is, in naturalism and the psychophysical dualism and naïve objectivism implied therein, to be a conception of the world that is "absurd for it to [an] insurpassable degree" (C 265), absurd because it fails to "notice the very subjectivity which made genuine rational objectivity possible."[4] Only through intentional phenomenology can humankind apprehend the deformity of Enlightenment rationalism and redirect a scientific consciousness. Only through a full transition out of a naturalistic objectivist orientation into the nascent ideals of universal science can "true liberation from the traditional temptations" happen (C 263).

Psychology: The Decisive Discipline

If both Nietzsche and Husserl employ genealogy to reveal an inner world of subjectivity and a process of ideation conditioning experiential forms through centuries, Nietzsche emphasizes a subject of conflict and bondage while Husserl emphasizes a subject capable of self-giving freedom.[5] Husserl's view that hidden in the development of the European sciences is a path to universal transcendental philosophy leads him to modern psychology (C 202–3). Psychology has moved to the focal point of the last part (part III B) of the genealogy in the *Crisis*. It is the discipline whose subject matter of universal subjectivity, Husserl believes, can reveal the mistake of the objectivist basis of the modern sciences. "Psychology is the *truly decisive field*," he writes (C 208). "It is this precisely because, though it has a different attitude"—by which presumably he means it assumes a natural attitude, and thus it has a different orientation than the transcendental philosophical point of view—"and [though it] is under the guidance of a different task," that is, struggling across a continuum of naïve objectivist positions that span camps of psychophysical dualism on the one side and idealism on the other, "its subject matter is universal subjectivity, which in its actualities and possibilities is *one*" (C 208). The *"one"* here intimates the universal transcendental ego.[6]

A transcendental psychology is a transcendental philosophy, writes Husserl (C 257). It provides the comprehensive philosophical transformation needed for the sciences by changing the scientific outlook from a pervasively objectivist grounding to a primarily subjectivist grounding. The emergence of a transcendental psychology would provide for the sciences the transcendental outlook required: conscious recognition that consciousness is the beginning of all knowledge and value.

Specifying the Problem of Psychology for Husserl

Both Nietzsche and Husserl emphasize lived awareness as a starting point for the formation of human objects. The general problem of traditional psychology for Husserl is its structuration by the assumptions of philosophical objectivism. Philosophical objectivism is the "transcendental naiveté" that will "not die out" (C 193). What he views as its consequence, "the fashionable degenerations of philosophy into irrationalistic busy-work substituted for the inextinguishable idea of philosophy as the ultimately grounding and universal science," Husserl judges to be irresponsible (C 197). His criticism of psychology after Kant emphasizes its unexamined acceptance of theoretical naturalism: "The task set for modern psychology, and taken over by it, was to be a science of psychophysical realities. . . . Here all theoretical thinking moves on the ground of the taken-for-granted, pregiven world of experience, the world of natural life." The problem with the philosophical objectivism of the sciences is their viewing their objects as possessing "true-being-in-themselves" (C 204). What is warranted, says Husserl, is a transcendental psychology. A transcendentally oriented psychologist would "understand that in fact an indissoluble inner alliance obtains between psychological and transcendental philosophy" (C 206).

Husserl would perceive the approaches to psychology of most of his peers to operate under naïve views of naturalism. I shall briefly indicate the scene of psychology with which he is interacting. Important to remember is that by the 1930s, when Husserl conceived the *Crisis*, the disciplines of psychology and philosophy were becoming decisively separate. The formalization in England and the United States of what was called "psychology" and "science" on the one hand, and "philosophy" as a humanities discipline, on the other, reflects the inability of two opposing forces in nineteenth-century psychology that were unable to reconcile. To put it somewhat reductively, on the one side were empiricist and experiment-based approaches to psychology (J. S. Mill [1806–73], Alexander Bain [1818–1903], Franz Joseph Gall [1758–1828], Herbert Spencer [1820–1903], and Wilhelm Wundt [1832–1920]) adopting methods of the natural sciences as a model. On the other side were romanticists and/or systematizers (Friedrich Nietzsche [1844–1900],[7] Benedetto Croce [1866–1952], Edward Caird [1835–1908], Franz Brentano [1838–1917], and Edmund Husserl [1859–1938]) applying critical analysis to the sources of cognition. The former anointed their methods with the monikers of "psychology" and "science." The latter, by contrast would become formally known as "philosophers," despite their claims to contributions to psychology and science. Daniel Robinson summarizes matters thus:

> Even the phenomenology of Brentano and Husserl, so radically different from what Hegel had in mind, would be forged into a "descriptive psychology," more philosophy than psychology and never an "empirical" science. Thus, in Europe, where the idealist tradition was deepest, the psychologist could either become a Wundtian, a neo-Hegelian, or a physiologist in psychologist's clothing. In England and America the alternatives were further reduced. One was either a philosopher or an experimentalist.[8]

The significance of this history for my purposes is that it helps to distinguish Husserl from other psychologists like Wundt and Dilthey along a psychology spectrum determined by materialists on one end and idealists on the other.

Wundt espouses an inductive strategy embedded in a lineage that Mill did much to initiate and promote. Mill thought psychology should model its methods after those of the natural sciences. He believed it needed to distinguish itself from the discipline of philosophy, whose techniques he believed too speculative for psychological science (IHP 276). Psychologists who held views similar to Mill about the importance of separating psychology from philosophy include Bain, Gall, Spencer, and Wundt. Though these investigators varied in the extent to which they based their theories in materiality, they shared a general framework of psychophysical parallelism that reflected the empiricist naturalism framing the natural sciences that operated as their model. Robinson writes that "Bain and Spencer did all but found experimental psychology" (IHP 278). The criteria for such a distinction, Robinson explains, are that they "cemented the new science to the new biology" (IHP 278); they presented the empiricist laws of association in effective new ways; and "they fought successfully for the independent status of the science" (IHP 278). It would be Wilhelm Wundt, the slightly younger colleague of Bain and Spencer, who would go on record as experimental psychology's founder. He was able to carry out two additional tasks deemed central to the discipline: he established a workplace and equipment for conducting psychological research and put the facilities to use conducting psychological research. The first of such psychology laboratories Wundt launched at the University of Leipzig in 1879 (IHP 278).

Husserl's and Nietzsche's genealogical works place an emphasis on showing subjective experience internally. Nietzsche does this through the flow of credal, emotive, and evaluative experiences arising for the genealogist, which I shall discuss shortly. For the Husserl of the *Crisis*, the *"enigma of subjectivity"* presupposes its conditioning within the mentioned lineage of modern psychology (C 5). From within this tradition subjects habituate themselves to a naïve naturalism fracturing "the history of philosophy seen from within" from a relentless "skepticism [that] insists on the validity of the factually experienced" (C 13). Subjectivity has become splintered on the basis of questionable concepts of "inner" versus "outer" (C 219). Husserl examines the problem of the concepts of inner versus outer, in order to clarify anew "what is actually experienced." According to modern conceptual habits, beliefs about subjective experience conform to the modern theoretical conception that physical nature is "supposed to be based on outer" experience while psychological nature is supposed to be based on inner experience (C 219). The unnoticed tendency to separate objects of the supposed inner versus outer domains, suggests Husserl, draws a curtain between our thoughts about our experience and our experience as it actually appears. "To put it more precisely: what is actually experienced is the world as simply existing, prior to all philosophy and theory—existing things, stones, animals, men. In natural, direct life, this is experienced as simply, perceptually 'there' (as simply existing, ontically certain presence) or, just as simply, in terms of memory, as 'having been there,' etc." (C 219). And to this natural life, Husserl adds, "necessary straightforward reflection belongs." He removes a distinction between life-world and theoretical world, or more precisely, he indicates that a nontheoretical-theoretical distinction does not have to present a barrier to actual experience, nor to a science of actual experience. When what is experienced as "there" perceptually is reflected upon as what is "there" perceptually, and when what is experienced as "there" is not reordered and hidden behind naturalist concepts that obscure intended life, a nontheoretical-theoretical distinction and, what's similar, a descriptive-explanatory distinction can find a usefulness in psychology (C 222–23).

Remedy for Psychology through Correction to Dilthey

In order to appreciate what I call Husserl's future-oriented presentation of subjectivity and its contrast with Nietzsche's more past-oriented presentation of subjectivity, an understanding of the place of Dilthey's descriptive psychology in transcendental psychology shall be useful. Husserl employs ideas from Dilthey's *Ideas for a Descriptive and Analytic Psychology* (1894) to operate like a pivot upon which to move traditional psychology to transcendental psychology. Dilthey argues against the tide of experimental psychologists for indiscriminately adapting natural science methods to psychological science. Basing his criticism on a distinction between "explanative" and "descriptive" argumentation, he takes issue with what he construed as experimental psychologists' unjustifiable application of assumptions (which he calls "hypotheses") at the beginning of investigations, and thus proceeding with an empiricist deduction. If Dilthey saw the borrowed methods of the new psychologists as appropriate for those they borrowed them from, natural scientists—an obvious difference from Husserl—he did not think them appropriate for psychological scientists. The deductive argument of explanation whose premises are verifiable empirically through repeatable experiments produce results that are "no longer subject to doubt."[9] Dilthey subscribed to a theory of "outer phenomena" that replicates a blend of Humean and Kantian ideas about the "coexistence and succession" of perceptions. He accepted the idea that "a causal nexus can only arise in our conception of nature through inference" and that "the hypothesis is therefore the necessary tool for progress in cognizing nature" (IDAP 116). He presumed that the natural sciences could use a more precise method (explanation) and yield more stable knowledge than psychological science.

In assuming the more exactness of the natural sciences, Dilthey would be guilty of what Husserl saw Kant guilty of: seeing nature as real in-itself and not recognizing the historical nature of the mathematical and physical concepts holding naturalism in place. "It is the strength of the natural sciences," Dilthey writes, "that mathematics and experimentation provide them the tools for testing hypotheses with the highest degree of exactness and certainty" (IDAP 116). Achievements in modern science—Galilean, Cartesian, Newtonian—that Husserl sees based in ideas that are historical in their possibility for consciousness, Dilthey seems to see as decidedly justified. If in some way Dilthey's thought is able to account for the temporal nature of human ideas (IDAP 166), he does not work out clearly how human historicality would affect scientific ideas.[10] With this in mind, the following example from *Ideas for a Descriptive and Analytic Psychology* indicates Dilthey's absorption in the naturalist objectivism so pervasive then—and now.

> The Copernican hypothesis, according to which the earth rotates on its own axis every twenty-four hours (minus four minutes) and simultaneously revolves around the sun every 365 ¼ days, is the best and most instructive example of how a hypothesis is transformed into an assured scientific result. Progressively developed and

grounded by Kepler, Galileo, Newton, Foucault, and others, it has become a theory no longer subject to doubt. (IDAP 116)

Dilthey appears to limit the influence of psychic givenness by reifying outer objects of natural science. He explicitly separates them from the objects of the human sciences, which he locates in a pregiven psychic nexus relating to one another dynamically as a "living continuum" (IDAP 119). How different is Husserl's emphasis—or "calling." It focuses on clarifying that all ideas, whether of "inner" objects or "outer" objects, begin with the subject. A consequence of realizing the self-giving intuition of the transcendental ego is that everything subjective, every so-called thing "is part of an indivisible totality" (C 220). If the subject is essentially historical, all of its ideas, whether inner or outer, are given to subjective intuition historically too—that is to say, according to our essentially temporal nature. In this sense, we see that the temporal essence that subjectivity is determines the constraints that subjectivity undergoes. Subjectivity is the master and the slave of its own dynamic formation.

Dilthey's psychology is important because of the role Husserl has it play in the movement to transcendental psychology. From descriptive psychology Husserl launches his transition from an objectivism-laden modern psychology to a phenomenological-psychological reduction. Reworking Dilthey's descriptive-explanative distinction, he contends that there is a place for not only description but also explanation in psychological science. Required, however, is recognizing the proper place of the psychic as the original site of the formation of ideas (C 223). "This results, as it does everywhere, in an applicable and indispensable sense of description and of descriptive science and also, at a higher level, of 'explanation' and explanatory science." Explanation in psychology "occurs on the basis of 'descriptive' knowledge" (C 223). Husserl calls explanation a "scientific method" that "ultimately verifies itself by means of the descriptive data" (C 223). And for him, this pattern of description as a basis and explanation as an "elevated level" culled from analysis extends to "*all* sciences" (C 223). Thus Husserl sees himself correcting Dilthey's position by showing the proper application of both description and explanation to psychology, the condition being that the scientist—in this case the psychologist—implement the right stance, that he or she perform the proper *epoché*.

In the case of the psychologist, the new reduction applies "to all souls, and thus to the psychologist's own. For a "truly descriptive psychology," the psychologist must perform a "universal epoché" (C 239). "'With one blow' he must put out of effect the totality of his participation in the validities explicitly or implicitly effected by the persons who are his subjects and this means all persons" (C 239). This criterion would seem to require almost superhuman abilities. To his credit, or crazed wishfulness, Husserl remained dogged in his faith that a fully disinterested subjectivity is humanly possible.

The Universal Problem of Intentionality and Its Relation to Nietzsche

If one attains a properly detached attitude to one's validities, what is experienced as perceptually not "there," according to Husserl, is the object supposed by the legacy of objectivism, that is to say, the tradition of assuming an object that is in itself real. But it is precisely to renew our vision against the modern orientation that assumes realness of the "entity itself" that Husserl would have us turn our attention from the presuppositions of psychophysical dualism and naïve objectivism to the particularity of a present "flowing life-world" (C 220). He directs us to misleading ideas about "outer experience" of bodily things so that he might then redirect us to the lived experience of intended bodily appearances.

> Here, in immediate givenness, one finds anything but color data, tone data, other "sense" data or data of feeling, will, etc.; that is, one finds none of those things which appear in traditional psychology, taken for granted to be immediately given from the start. Instead, one finds, as even Descartes did (naturally we ignore his other purposes), the cogito, *intentionality* in those familiar forms which, like everything actual in the surrounding world, find their expression in language: "I see a tree which is green; I hear the rustling of its leaves, I smell its blossoms." (C 233)

Husserl's attunement to the world as immediate intended appearance reminds one of the familiar complaint made by Nietzsche.

Philosophers mistake "the last for the first."[11] They place the "emptiest concepts," the so-called highest concepts, "at the beginning *as* the beginning" (TWI 47). An exasperated Husserl asks, "Why does the whole flowing life-world not figure at the very beginning of a psychology as something 'psychic,' indeed as the psychic realm which is primarily accessible, the first field in which immediately given psychic phenomena can be explicated according to types?" (C 220). "Why," he protests, "is the experience which actually, as experience, brings this life-world to givenness and, within it, especially in the primal mode of perception, presents mere bodily things—why is this experience not called psychological experience rather than 'outer experience,' supposedly by contrast to 'psychological experience?'" (C 220). Husserl draws attention to—yet again—a tenet of the modern subject that appears both obvious and obscure.

It would seem patent that all seeing is a perspectival seeing (Nietzsche), or that all appearances are a subjective givenness (Husserl). But these are deceptively simple themes and, for this reason, oft-traversed by Husserl and Nietzsche and in their literatures. Husserl emphasizes the tendency of modern humans to take for granted the significance of "the fact that everything about the life-world is obviously subjective" (C 220). The modern inability to credit subjective experience acts as a barrier to revealing from its own self-evidence the ground of transcendental philosophy. For Husserl, modern subjects are liable to keep hidden from themselves the significance of the universality of our psychological lives for a project of a universal science. The *Crisis* is in part a response to the predicament Husserl delineates as experience. Existence as subjectively directed needs to be brought "to mind here with renewed, lively, clarity" (C 220). And Nietzsche makes contributions on this front. Husserl beseeches us to meditate on the sleight of mind by which subjective experience, the source, becomes "merely subjective appearance," the last. Like a Zen teacher striking a slouching monk to awake, Husserl implores modern subjects to look at the positioning of their subjectivity. For Husserl, it begins with the givenness of the world. Admitting the differences in experiencing a mountain, bird, or tree as opposed to a musical lyric, childhood memory, or geometrical concept, and the difficult problems they may raise for a universal science of psychology, an incredulous Husserl demands, "Does this change the fact that everything about the life-world is obviously 'subjective'? Can psychology, as a universal science, have any other theme than the totality of the subjective?" (C 220).

Nietzsche's Psychology: Perspectivism and the Chains of Subjectivity

That Nietzsche's writings also emphasize psychology, and in particular, the singularity of human perception in his concept of perspectivism, has been extensively commented upon in the Nietzsche literature.[12] I shall spotlight a few examples of his narrative point of view in *On the Genealogy of Morals* to display the limits of subjectivity he suggests. The examples adumbrate subjective experience as bound despite its generativity. I shall show how Nietzsche's genealogist viewpoint inflects Husserl's emphasis in the *Crisis* on life-world, or rather, one sense of his idea of life-world: absorption in the flow of the quotidian. But whereas Husserl's focus reveals the subjective sources of everyday experience in order to free subjectivity from irrational aspects of the modern everyday, Nietzsche's emphasis reveals contradictions in celebrated ideals that limit subjectivity in surprising ways to the everyday.

Before I address Nietzsche's display of the world of subjectivity as perspectivism, a few words about his position in the discourse of nineteenth-century psychology will be useful. As Robert Holub notes, Nietzsche's use of the term *psychology* develops at least two dominant regions of meaning: "The first is an older, commonsense designation of psychology as the art of knowing other people, of understanding what motivates and moves people to behave in the way they do."[13] The other field of meaning for psychology, I agree with Holub, is ethics: "In this context the word 'psychology' assumes multiple meanings. It refers at times to the mentality of those people who adhere to a system of moral values informed by a Christian ethical system, and at other moments to the mental mechanisms of individuals identified with that system, or to certain abstract principles, such as in the phrases the 'psychology of belief,' or 'the psychology of conviction'" (BP 155). Nietzsche's study of psychology is speculative in approach and rooted in books of the humanities. He appears to have paid little attention to the developments in nineteenth-century psychology favoring experiments. When he employs the term *psychology* he generally pulls from a philosophical tradition which he relates to morality (BP 162). In contemporary terms, "most of Nietzsche's psychology would be most properly termed 'moral psychology'" (BP 162). The purpose to which I shall now turn is the manner of Nietzsche's genealogy that can be viewed as a relative of Husserlian phenomenology. Nietzsche employs a style of narrative viewpoint that emphasizes a broad theme of philosophical psychology: subjective confinement to the everyday.

A parallel exists between Husserl's idea of the natural point of view of the subject in which one validates the flow of phenomena arising for subjectivity (having-in-validity; C 237) and Nietzsche's idea of perspectivism according to which the genealogist validates a stream of experience emerging for the narrator. A comparison can also be drawn between Husserl's correlative idea of putting out of play an emotion or feeling or judgment and Nietzsche's suspending judgment about the world beyond what we can know through human perceptual limits.[14] The possibility of the respective subjective identifications and the explicit distinction of identification with the quotidian from an ultimate identification with true being remain nodes of intersection for Nietzsche and Husserl. Their subjectivity distinguishes everyday absorption of subjectivity from universally objective agreement about the reality in-itself of the objects a subject validates.

Husserl and Absorption in the Everyday

Husserl's idea of absorption in the everyday not only discloses strictures under which humans must exist; it refers to the "realness" status that particular undergoings of modes of existence (emotive, evaluative, pragmatic) have for a person. Husserl states emphatically that the psychologist's viewpoint with respect to the perceiving person to whom he or she listens does not change the fact that the other's perceptions have validity for that person. I shall draw attention to both the idea of the modes of certainty presented for the person being observed and the idea of putting certainty out of play as the role assigned the psychologist witnessing the person's account of his or her experience. As to the first, the modes of certainty for the absorbed subject being observed, Husserl writes:

> What is essentially proper to the soul includes all intentionalities, the experiences of the type called "perception," for example, considered precisely as those performed by the person serving as an example and exactly in the way he accomplishes them; . . . one thing is clear: whether the perceived [object] exists or not, whether the perceiving person is mistaken about this or not, and also whether I, the psychologist, who in my empathetic understanding of the person unhesitatingly concur in the belief in the perceived [object], am mistaken about it nor not—this must remain irrelevant for me as a psychologist. None of this may enter into the psychological description of the perception. (C 236–37)

Descriptive statements about the experience of the person witnessed are not identical to the originals perceived; they "necessarily go beyond what is purely essentially proper to these subjects" (C 237). Husserl's following point is that the psychologist cannot remove from his or her perspective the extent to which he may credit or discredit some of the person's beliefs—and likewise, that the person the psychologist witnesses cannot either: "One cannot transform certainty into doubt or negation, or pleasure into displeasure, love into hate, desire into abhorrence" (C 237). But that one cannot change a present belief or mood or taste at will does not preclude one from "putting its performance out of play for certain particular purposes" (C 237). In other words, the person the psychologist witnesses and the psychologist alike can put the performance of their own or others' beliefs "out of play for particular purposes" (C 237). Husserl's point is that descriptive analysis of one's validities helps move subjectivity to a transcendental philosophical outlook. The psychologist recognizes the conditioned nature of her and another's beliefs and accomplishments.

Nietzsche and Absorption in the Everyday

If I focus on the genealogist's perspective in *On the Genealogy of Morals*, as though she represents Husserl's perceiving person sitting opposite the transcendentally transformed psychologist, I am not going to be very convincing if I try to argue that she is not undergoing this belief, or that she is not intending that disavowal, or that she is not feeling that flash of joy. The reader of *On the Genealogy of Morals* is afforded a window into an unfolding series of points of view by the representation of a single subject. For the sake of argument I will assume the genealogist's sincerity respecting descriptions of her emotive, evaluative, and cognitive experience. I can look at her experience of the concept of guilt and bad conscience. When she writes that "'guilt,' conscience,' [and] 'duty,' . . . had its origin . . . soaked in blood thoroughly and for a long time" (GM II §6) and proceeds to list a variety of torture techniques, I may disagree with the historical validity of her idea but not with the fact that the idea held validity for her. When she associates a poorly working faculty of forgetting with indigestion (GM II §1), I may disagree that "forgetting represents a force, a form of *robust* health" (GM II §1) but not that the idea that certain forms of memory are signs of decline made sense to her. When she describes the modern subject's enormity of guilt and its treatment through a kind of herd-organization "*orgy of feeling*" (GM III §19), I may doubt the factual truth of her claim but not that the claim is associated with intense feelings of disgust in her.

I care about the fact of the genealogist's absorption in instances of emotive, credal, and imaginative validities not because, on Nietzsche's terms, these make up the stuff of her life—which they do—but because it discloses a kind of chain binding her life. Husserl's text makes this point less dramatically than Nietzsche's, but it does nonetheless.

The signature expressiveness of Nietzsche and his genealogist shown piecemeal in the absorption examples above is well-known. I assume these genealogist points of view to be examples of modes of Nietzsche's concept of perspectivism, the idea that point of view conditions all knowing and all valuing.[15] I also assume that Husserl's idea of everyday validities explicitly formalizes the point I made earlier, namely that the force of lived perspectivism as Nietzsche indicates it, or rather, the primacy of the subjective as Husserl indicates it, needs to be reckoned with, although for projects whose orientations remain in significant ways opposed. Husserl's attraction to an analysis of subjectivity is motivated by a desire for a theory that would unify a science of all psyches. Nietzsche's attraction to a reconstruction of formative roots of subjectivity is motivated by the genealogist's alternate anguish from, and joy within, present existence. Husserl's orientation is to attend to naïve or natural existing but in order to affect a certain future for that existing that would reveal a hidden theoretical framework that could become part of a future life-world. Nietzsche's genealogist seems aware of the future, but mostly incidentally.

Nietzsche: Subjectivity and Conflict

In the *Genealogy*, Nietzsche does not try to perform a Husserlian *epochē*. He does not make phenomenological reductions a strategy and theme in his work. But he emphasizes a relationship analogous to that between Husserl's psychologist and the person whose perceptions the psychologist witnesses. The parallel relationship in Nietzsche's text rests between the broad structure of the essays and the serial appearances they unreel through the perspective of the genealogist. Though the momentary contexts evince specific value judgments about this particular slavish behavior or that particular guilt-formation, the text's framing suggests that any absolute scientific judgment about the nature of being per se or the nature of good and evil per se or the nature of any appearance per se is best held in abeyance.

In Nietzsche's emphasis on subjectivity through the flow of appearances of the genealogist, the idea of conflict remains not only a central theme but also a basic structure. The narrator's absorption in a stream of battling assessments divulges the difficulty of existing that is singular subjective experience for Nietzsche. In one not much discussed area of the "First Essay," the genealogist's viewpoint fastens on what I will call "Hesiod's obstacle": how to represent the viewpoints of two diametrically opposing worlds of a single epoch. Hesiod's answer, according to Nietzsche: split them up, and not just existentially but chronologically (GM I §11). The first world will display the perspective "of the heroes and demigods of Troy and Thebes, the form in which that world had survived in the memory of the noble races who were those heroes' true descendants" (GM I §11). The genealogist beholds Homer's world presenting to Hesiod a "dilemma" and a "contradiction" (GM I §11). It is "magnificent but at the same time so shockingly violent." Like Hesiod, the genealogist is struck, at first, by the majesty of Homer's world and, second, but no less deeply, by its horror. Her tendency to diatribe against the weak is halted as she turns her gaze and empathy from the first world of Achilles and the Achaeans to the second world of Andromache and the Trojans. She imagines how "that same world [of Achilles] appeared to the descendants of the downtrodden, pillaged, mistreated, abducted, enslaved: an epoch of bronze . . . hard, cold, cruel, devoid of feeling or conscience, destructive and bloody" (GM I §11). Jolted from one directional state to its opposite, the narrator "has" each world, which is to say, she validates each and identifies with each but not at once. The apparent agility of her perspective, its ability to imagine Achilles' pride, relative stability, and war-spoil comforts, on the one side, and its alternate concern for Andromache's misery, total destabilization, and wrecked domesticity, on the other, suggests having lived through some things—loss, perhaps the destabilizing effects of terror, but also personal triumph. Through the narrator's perspective, Nietzsche conveys something like intuitive self-evidence of experience (Husserl's point) and the radical dissonance of modern subjective existence (Nietzsche's point).

Not only does Nietzsche write about the battling viewpoints, making conflict a theme, but he discloses states of conflict to be formations a subject undergoes constitutively and in relation with others. Nietzsche's genealogist exists in this conflict. The series of emotional states and mental attitudes the genealogist expresses toward ascetic ideals in the "Third Essay" exhibits Nietzsche's modern subject existing across stressed forces. The latter is significant as antecedent to Husserl's writing of the *Crisis* because of the importance the critique of ascetic ideals places on the problem of the meaningfulness of existence for individuals. Husserl's *Crisis* acknowledges in ways his earlier works do not "the profound malaise among the educated to which the existentialists were directly speaking" and to which Nietzsche's discourse of ascetic ideals also speaks (TI xxv).

Nietzsche's Ascetic Ideals and Affectional Expressions: Subjectivity as Structural Conflict

Ascetic ideals indicate that human existence is a meaningless breach.[16] Nietzsche characterizes this as a gap separating "animal and angel." Like punishment for Nietzsche, ascetic ideals have meant many things in Europeans' lineage. But a compendium of different meanings of ascetic ideals poorly conveys the spirit of the essay's narrative voice, whose tone represents subjectivity's absorption by expansive emotive and evaluative registries. The genealogist's disgust at the *Parsifal*-Wagner turns into a rant: "Must one really see in [*Parsifal*] (as someone once put to me) 'the product of an insane hatred of knowledge, spirit and sensuality'? A curse on the senses and the spirit in a *single* breath of hatred? An apostacy and return to morbid Christian and obscurantist ideals?" (GM III §3). The genealogist's submitting Schopenhauer's "disinterested" aesthete to a second round of disinterest testing (to show Schopenhauer's subject of sublimity to be anything but disinterested) turns into mean levity:

> Above all, we should not underestimate the fact that Schopenhauer, who treated sexuality as a personal enemy . . . *needed* enemies in order to keep in good spirits; that he loved bilious, black-green words, that he scolded for the sake of scolding, out of passion; that he would have become ill, become a *pessimist* (for he was not one, however much he desired it), if deprived of his enemies. (GM III §7)

The genealogist's variegating assessments of how philosopher-types generally manipulate the ascetic ideal turns into stern irony:

> [For] their *fairest* fruitfulness . . . it is quite possible that [philosophers'] dominating spirituality had first to bridle their unruly and tetchy pride or their wanton sensuality, or that they had to struggle hand and soul to maintain their will to the "desert" against love of luxury and refinement. (GM III §8)[17]

In communicating the different ends toward which Wagner, Schopenhauer, and philosophers put ascetic ideals, Nietzsche deploys the narrator's evaluative and emotional swings without apology or explanation. The genealogist's tone opposes a philosophical tradition of cool neutrality, next to which Nietzsche's style appears excessive. For the German academic tradition epitomized by Kant, philosophical writing should obscure the individual personality, building narrative tone that conveys objectivity and a language that avoids the tinge of mood, emotion, or personal taste. Nietzsche's affectional style exaggerates subjectivity's immersion in emotive, credal, and evaluative states. It mimics specific aspects of lived experience (C 220)[18]—its emotive, torn, sometimes in-crisis mode—forms of expression that Husserl's writing tends to exclude.[19]

Nietzsche's demonstrative genealogy conveys the sense that existence, if intersubjective in some ways, is nevertheless radically singular in others. If all emoting and valuing is *"only* a perspective seeing, *only* a perspective 'knowing'"* (GM III §12), if experience is always a singular becoming, as the world of Nietzsche's genealogist suggests, then subjectivity for Nietzsche is largely unknowing about where, in a vast metaphysical sense, it has been or whither, in an ultimate evaluative sense, it should go. It indicates that experience presupposes something akin to Husserl's and Merleau-Ponty's descriptions of consciousness as an emergent directedness toward an as yet indefinite but possible object. Nietzsche's genealogical subjectivity displays consciousness driven by buried drives toward objects it cannot entirely fathom.

His narrative style and genealogical subject suggest that we are not bodies subtended from ideaphoric minds nor angels separable from predatory animals.[20] We exist in the crossings of our bodily affect, of our passing ideas, of our deeply incised fears, of our cycling aspirations. Moreover the interstices of the metaphoric fabric that subjects live for Nietzsche would not so meet in us were they not also stretched across others. Others surround us now, breathing and alive in our midst or generationally transmitted through our embodied practices and our phonetic writing. The embeddings Nietzsche assembles have inchoate likeness to the concept of flesh that Merleau-Ponty would develop decades later.

Merleau-Ponty's co-enveloping subjectivity, reminiscent of Husserl's "transcendental intersubjectivity" (C 262), is for Nietzsche constricture: laced with violence. On Nietzsche's terms, guilt, ascetic ideals, and the violence formative to them circumscribe just about everyone in the Western tradition, as shown in the genealogist's experience of the opposed worlds of Achilles and Andromache. Nietzsche specifies contorting existences strewn across the lives of philosophers, artists, and the religiously devout. Across even millennia. His discourse intimates a striving that tears across centuries and their subjects, including ours. I like the way Charles Scott describes the pressure that ascetic ideals place on contemporary subjectivity. Conveying a cheeky irony about our predicament, he writes:

> We are naturally inclined by our discourses to find the highest forms of worship, the best forms of criticism, the most subtle wines, the loftiest music, the purest foods, the most salubrious methods of health care, the best cause for social action, the most

sterling morality, the formulae for realizing our true and best nature, the best and truest thoughts. We are driven by our discourse to find the truth of ourselves by disciplines of self-realization and self-denial, like the athlete who trains for movement and endurance by austere denial of most satisfactions and by elevating a few severe activities. (QE 36)

It is difficult to deny that modern subjects strain under a vast array of bizarre ideals. In our attempts to measure up to expectations whose origins far exceed modernity and whose shape often meanly forms its subjects, it would seem that Nietzsche-like responses—a burst of laughter, a music mocking the modern chains that make it—are certainly in order. To be a modern subject, for Nietzsche, is to undergo antipodes— often ancient—that contort our psyches, that violate our being, and that make possible a stunning range of configurations with others.

Concluding Remarks: Subjectivity as Bondage or Freedom

In comparing the narrator's perspective in Nietzsche's *Genealogy* with Husserl's approach to a phenomenological-psychological reduction in the *Crisis*, I have underscored the importance of subjective experience for Nietzsche's and Husserl's projects. If one can refrain from fully identifying with the absorptions of everyday experience, and Husserl and Nietzsche, in their own ways, suggest that one can, the extent of this freedom and its circumstances remain murky (C 237). Their genealogies indicate that we have singular attachments to perceptual modes (emotive, evaluative, pragmatic) from which we cannot divest ourselves as though we were changing a garment.[21]

Husserl anticipates conceptual structures enforcing a more rational world. Nietzsche anticipates subjectivity characterized by more life affirmation and more acceptance and awareness of the apparent disunity grounding modern reason. Husserl's project magnifies absorption in the day-to-day in order to put it out of play and make way for "absolute freedom from prejudice" and for "true liberation" (C 263). Nietzsche's genealogy of structures, if attaining a measure of distance from the frameworks he shows us caught by, would seem more a resignation to them, in the sense that it calls for affirming life, chains and all. Husserl's vision requires a different kind of resignation, that of a master renunciant, not unlike those of Buddhism.

Nietzsche's genealogy articulates an implicit ontology of subjectivity whose being is for him mere probability and historical contingency. The prevalence of ascetic ideals structuring this being cannot be overstated on his terms: their trace of the master-moral, slave-moral systems etymologically; their trace of mnemonic habits of guilt rooted in forms of torture; their connecting hypotheses rooted in ancient practices to embodied stresses we live now. And yet ascetic ideals have little to do with assumptions or judgments about ontology; to the extent that Nietzsche makes ontological judgments about the being of ascetic ideals, he qualifies them through historical and cultural observations. In this we see Husserl's late work become akin to his genealogical predecessor. That both reveal ways human idealizations are conditioned by subjectivity's experience qua temporal and historical being, that both show ways we are grabbed by a supposed immediacy to experience, that both point to frameworks and reflective processes that can gain distance on or can restrain identification with our naïve attitudes indicates sources in Nietzsche for Husserl's phenomenology. But whereas Nietzsche's subjectivity highlights the formation of our experience that binds, Husserl emphasizes a subjectivity that can be free.

To the extent that we are embattled subjects, finding it all but impossible not to identify with the strictures we live by, it would seem Husserl's cool neutral methodology does not reflect life as well as Nietzsche's passionately invested approach. To the extent that people's experience registers deeply ingrained discordances forming it, to the extent that people consider specific angles on past predations or attune themselves to disturbing transgenerational habits that enliven us at the same time they cut into us, it would seem that Nietzsche's genealogy captures life capturing us more resonantly than Husserl's does. To the extent that one's experience carries an incorrigible commitment to a future that is less embattled, to the extent that one's experience maps rationality and irrationality as opposites and has faith in humanity's ability to disclose unity in a science inspired by the Greeks, or to the extent that one's present is driven by confidence in the possibility of a free subjectivity detached from the hold of everyday validities (C 239), Husserl's passionate commitment to transcendental subjectivity reflects life attempting a salve for real ailments, including ascetic ideal pathologies. It reflects a more Apollonian, more resolute manner than Nietzsche's, and on its terms is a philosophy that meets the demand that "philosophy be relevant to life" (TI xxv–xxvi).

On Nietzsche's terms, hoping for a future without brutality is an enactment within the cycling of ascetic ideals. But Husserl suggests that one can overstate the prevalence of the ascetic ideal in our lives and intimates that Nietzsche is guilty of doing so. Though to Nietzsche, Husserl's hope would seem a mad faith, yet another manifestation of being caught within the cycles of ascetic ideals, to Husserl and like-minded idealists only an "unsurpassable radicalism of the full transcendental epochē" can release us from the irrational predicaments of the twenty-first-century heirs of modernity. A complete reduction of subjectivity would seem "the only [portal] to absolute freedom from prejudice" (C 263), making "possible a true liberation from the traditional temptations" (C 263).

Nietzsche does not give up on humanity's will to freedom, its will to create, or its will to change. But in the *Genealogy* he is willing to assume a position of detached acquiescence with respect to the bondage of modern subjectivity.[22] Husserl fights for a different kind of detachment, one that can be realized only by a refusal to settle with predicaments of reason and that can be attained only by an extraordinary optimism about humanity's capacity for restraint in the face of everyday subjective absorption.

Notes

I would like to thank Steve Smith for his comments on early versions of this chapter, and Nick Brown, Patrick Hopkins, Élodie Boublil, and Christine Daigle for their suggestions. Of course, I take responsibility for any shortcomings in the final version and recognize them as entirely my own.

1. Carr, "Translator's Introduction," xxv–xxvi (hereafter TI).

2. Problematic for the variegated senses of *life-world* is whether they can work together, a point David Carr makes (TI xl–xli). In its most basic sense the term *life-world* means ordinary every-day experience. Sometimes the sense communicates immediacy that is prepredicative, sometimes a meaning that is pretheoretical. (But the pretheoretical it would seem, cannot be prepredicative.) Likewise the genealogy of philosophical concepts indicates that certain generationally passed-down world frames—planes versus depth, psychophysical dualism versus lived intentionality for which embodied objects are of the "psychic" realm—mediate the supposed "immediate."

3. Husserl, *The Crisis of European Sciences*, 15 (hereafter C).

4. Moran, *Introduction to Phenomenology*, 180.

5. Were one interested in focusing on other texts by Nietzsche and Husserl, and other aspects of those texts than I'm interested in here, a contrary point could be argued. Nietzsche's concept of the *Übermensch* could be seen to be capable of a self-giving freedom, and Husserl's subject of the natural attitude could be seen to be bound to a misrepresentation of the world.

6. This interpretation works given the sequence of ideas that follow. In §59 a psychology after a transcendental reduction discloses that "the previously naïve ego was none other than the transcendental ego in the mode of naïve hiddenness" (C 210).

7. For my purposes here Nietzsche is a "romanticist" and Husserl a "systematizer." What holds this otherwise odd pairing together is a commonality in their approaches: they eschewed experimental method.

8. Robinson, *An Intellectual History of Psychology*, 337 (hereafter IHP).

9. Dilthey, "Ideas for Descriptive and Analytic Psychology," 116 (hereafter IDAP).

10. Rudolf Makkreel suggests that Dilthey's project may be more sensitive to the conditioned nature of scientific knowledge than my argument concedes: "What is most significant here is that the categorial structures that engage us with the world are not artificially imposed or deduced but educed from the givenness of life. These structures are basically reciprocal in nature and capable of making sense of historical development" ("Introduction to Volume II," IDAP, xxviii).

11. Nietzsche, *Twilight of the Idols*, 47 (hereafter TWI).

12. For a useful examination of Nietzsche's thought as it relates to psychology see Golomb, Lehrer, and Santaniello, *Nietzsche and Depth Psychology* (hereafter NDP).

13. Holub, "The Birth of Psychoanalysis from the Spirit of Enmity," 154 (hereafter BP).

14. The idea that all human knowing and valuing is conditioned by one's point of view, which Nietzsche calls "perspectivism," is thematized in many of his writings. He writes, "There is *only* a perspective seeing, *only* a perspective 'knowing'; and the *more* affects we allow to speak about one thing, the *more* yeses, different eyes, we can use to observe one thing, the more complete will our 'concept' of this thing, our 'objectivity,' be" (*On the Genealogy of Morals*, III, §12; hereafter GM; the first number refers to the chapter, the second refers to the section). A concept of perspectivism arises as early as 1872 in *On Truth and Lying in a Non-Moral Sense*: "Only because man forgets himself as subject, and indeed as *an artistically creative* subject, does he live with some degree of peace, security, and consistency; if he could escape for just a moment from the prison walls of this faith, it would mean the end of his 'consciousness of self.' He even has to make an effort to admit to himself that insects or birds perceive a quite different world from that of human beings, and that the question as to which of these two perceptions of the world is the more correct is quite meaningless, since this would require them to be measured by the criterion of the *correct perception*" (TL 148).

15. "There is *only* a perspective seeing, *only* a perspective 'knowing'" (GM III, §12).

16. Scott, *The Question of Ethics*, 35 (hereafter QE).

17. I have modified the Kaufmann translation to combine aspects of the translation by Carol Diethe in Nietzsche, *On the Genealogy of Morality*.

18. "This normal, straightforward living, toward whatever objects are given indicates that all our interests have their goals in objects. The pregiven world is the horizon which includes all our goals, all our ends, whether fleeting or lasting, in a flowing but constant manner. . . . World is the universal field into which all our acts whether of experiencing, of knowing, or of outward action, are directed. From this field, or from objects in each case already given, come all affections, transforming themselves in each case into actions" (C 144).

19. Husserl expresses disdain for modern proliferations of philosophies that can be distinguished merely by their "aesthetic styles." Philosophy's fate cannot simply be to dissolve into the "many literary products of the day" (C 196–97).

20. I assume the reader is more familiar with Nietzsche's works than with the comparatively vast phenomenological tradition that includes Husserl's *Crisis*. Thus I occupy comparatively less space detailing the Nietzschean concepts I use for this argument than I do for the Husserlian concepts I develop.

21. C 237; Nietzsche, *Philosophy in the Tragic Age of the Greeks*, 63.

22. Alongside a seeming impatience with, and distaste for, the European subject's besetment with ascetic ideals, its "will to nothingness," its "rebellion against the most fundamental presuppositions of life" (GM III §28), Nietzsche's genealogist concludes the *Genealogy* with an attitude suggesting the narrator's resignation to subjectivity's bondage: "But it is and remains a will!" (GM III § 28). Despite our entrapped existence, he declares, we still have aspiration; we still have passion; we still have life!

Bibliography

Carr, David. "Translator's Introduction." In *The Crisis of European Sciences and Transcendental Phenomenology*, by Edmund Husserl. Evanston, IL: Northwestern University Press, 1970.

Dilthey, Wilhelm. "Ideas for Descriptive and Analytic Psychology." In *Wilhelm Dilthey: Selected Works*, vol. 2: *Understanding the Human World*. Edited by R. Makkreel and F. Rodi. Princeton: Princeton University Press, 2010.

Golomb, Jacob, Weaver Santaniello, and Ronald Lehrer, eds. *Nietzsche and Depth Psychology*. Albany: State University of New York Press, 1999.

Holub, Robert C. "The Birth of Psychoanalysis from the Spirit of Enmity: Nietzsche, Rée, and Psychology in the Nineteenth Century." In *Nietzsche and Depth Psychology*, edited by Jacob Golomb, Weaver Santaniello, and Ronald Lehrer. Albany: State University of New York Press, 1999.

Husserl, Edmund. *The Crisis of European Sciences and Transcendental Phenomenology*. Translated by David Carr. Evanston, IL: Northwestern University Press, 1970.

Moran, Dermot. *Introduction to Phenomenology*. London: Routledge, 2000.

Nietzsche, Friedrich. *On the Genealogy of Morality*. Edited by Keith Ansell-Pearson. Translated by Carol Diethe. Cambridge: Cambridge University Press, 1994.

———. *On the Genealogy of Morals*. Translated by Walter Kaufmann. New York: Random House, 1967.

———. "On Truth and Lying in a Non-Moral Sense." In *The Birth of Tragedy and Other Writings*. Translated by Ronald Speirs. Cambridge: Cambridge University Press, 1999.

——. *Philosophy in the Tragic Age of the Greeks*. Translated by Marianne Cowan. Chicago: Gateway 1996.

——. *Twilight of the Idols/The Anti-Christ*. Translated by R. J. Hollingdale. London: Penguin Books, 1990.

Robinson, Daniel. *An Intellectual History of Psychology*. 3rd ed. Madison: University of Wisconsin Press, 1995.

Scott, Charles. *The Question of Ethics: Nietzsche, Foucault, Heidegger*. Bloomington: Indiana University Press, 1990.

5 Giants Battle Anew

Nihilism's Self-Overcoming in Europe and Asia (Nietzsche, Heidegger, Nishitani)

Françoise Bonardel

At the still point of the turning world. Neither flesh nor fleshness;
Neither from nor towards; at the still point, there the dance is.

—T. S. Eliot, *Burnt Norton*

TRANSPLANTED INTO THE "ground" of Being, words take on new meaning.[1] Thus some clarification is in order when Heidegger announces that presentation and interpretation will necessarily interpenetrate each other in his "argument" (*Auseinandersetzung*) with Nietzsche. This argument is in no sense demonstrative, as the term is commonly understood, and there is nothing representational about the presentation, which opens the way to the essence of what Nietzsche would have only incompletely thought: nihilism, as the "covert basic law of Western history."[2] What, then, does it mean to interpret? It is anything but an intrusion of subjectivity into what is meant to freely unfold; rather, it is a way of *consenting* "so essentially to what is in question that Nietzsche's words are allowed to remain intact and to resonate purely from that which is in question."[3] Simply an *accompaniment*, then, paired with a consent to being led not by the thinker but by the question the thinker himself has accepted being led by, an attention so scrupulously careful, in short, that Heidegger calls it "compassionate" (*mitleidig*) and talks about a "meditative thinking" that underscores the singular "piety" (*Frömmigkeit*) of thought. When Heidegger adds that one only accedes to the Unthought in the thought of a great thinker if one enlarges yet more on "what is great in him,"[4] we may ask ourselves if he has actually reached his goal, or if he has only highlighted "all of Nietzsche's twilight grandeur, on whom the Platonic sun, on the verge of expiring, was casting its last rays."[5]

Assuming one has understood the essential tone in Heidegger's question of 1953—"Who is Nietzsche's Zarathustra?"—one may rightfully ask, *Who is* Heidegger's Nietzsche? The answer, at first glance, appears simple and may be given in few words:

"the last metaphysician of the West" and, as such, "the henchman to Western fatality," he who, taking upon himself all the consequences of the "death of God," first brought to light the heretofore occult connection between metaphysics and nihilism. If his thought is in this sense a passage allowing us to see in him "the name of an age of the world," Nietzsche would have nonetheless failed to conceive the essence of nihilism— its originary ontological unfolding (*Wesen*)—for he remained a metaphysician, despite (or because of) his desire to reverse values and invert Platonism. Also, it would appear that he failed to complete the project announced in a note (dated 1887) included in *The Will to Power*: "*Nihilism overcoming itself*, an attempt to say yes to all that had been denied up to now."[6] Speaking of *self*-overcoming (*Selbstüberwindung*), then, Nietzsche was aware that the triumph for which he would have laid the groundwork would not be his own; the important thing, Heidegger pointed out, was to know if he had crafted a mere going-beyond, the mere perfection of metaphysics, or had taken on a true overcoming, bringing about "the historical moment in which the *essential possibilities* of metaphysics are exhausted"[7] and nihilism thus definitely overcome.

Be that as it may, Heidegger was convinced that he was initiating "a dialogue" with Nietzsche, whose "own way is preparing a transition"[8] toward the other shore, if not to the promised land of nihilism's self-overcoming. Taking on the aura of an explorer, whose "Asiatic and supra-Asiatic eye" delved into "the most world-negating of all possible ways of thinking,"[9] had Nietzsche merely been rapt in dreadful awe while remaining incapable of the revelation with which Heidegger, assuming the role of ultimate ferryman, intended to proceed? It is in relation to this decisive "passage," and to the prior appropriation (*Verwindung*) of the essence of metaphysics it implies, that Heidegger refers to East Asian discourse and its possible engagement with European discourse, neither of which he deemed "able on its own to open or to found this realm."[10]

Reading Nietzsche in light of the "question of Being" (*Seinsfrage*) over the course of twenty years[11] and then broadening the horizon of his thought to encompass Taoism and Buddhism, Heidegger seems to have failed to consider the equally historical import of an interrogation originating in Japan at about the same time, one that was turning toward Western philosophy, of which he was then the most eminent representative. Japan, divested of its own philosophical and religious traditions by its rapid Westernization, was all the more concerned with the crisis of European nihilism. Yet it is by way of a "remembrance" (*Andenken*) akin to Heidegger's meditations on the Pre-Socratics that the philosopher Nishitani Keiji (1900–1990)—who attended Heidegger's class on Nietzsche in Freiburg (1936–38)—drew on the Buddhist notion of emptiness (*śūnyatā*) while elaborating the conditions of this self-overcoming. Nishitani considered this overcoming to have been fully accomplished in Nietzsche, whose more ambitious intuitions regarding the possibility of a future religion Heidegger had mostly ignored. If an authentic encounter with a thinker enables one to bring to light the *Unthought* in his or her thought, Heidegger is no exception to the hermeneutic rule, and his "crucial encounter" with Nietzsche could well have taken place "on the central, though unacknowledged theme of Heidegger's philosophy: the religious problem."[12] This theme may well shed new light on Asian echoes from the encounter between these two giants of Western thought.

A Problematic "Overcoming"

If it is true that in ending the hegemony of the suprasensible, nihilism does away with the opposition between the "real world" and appearances—a fateful opposition underlying all Western metaphysics—can the philosopher carefully thinking the act of appearing without reducing it to pure appearance be anything but somewhat of a phenomenologist?[13] As Ricoeur reminds us, "Phenomenology, in temporarily or definitively bracketing the question of Being, is born as soon as one treats the way in which things appear as an autonomous problem."[14] Yet it is precisely such bracketing that Heidegger refused to exercise throughout his lengthy and intense "argument" with Nietzsche; the latter, insensible to the "question of Being," had not measured up to "the demands of what must be thought"[15] regarding nihilism: "If to be present itself is thought of as appearance, then there prevails in being present the emergence into the openness in the sense of unconcealedness. This unconcealedness comes about in the unconcealment as a clearing: but this clearing itself, as occurrence, remains unthought in every respect," as Heidegger states in his *Dialogue on Language: Between a Japanese and an Inquirer*.[16] Reformulating phenomenology's vocation in this way, how could he not minimize all that Nietzsche's "phenomenalism" had contributed to the self-overcoming of nihilism? Heidegger seems to be constantly tightening the vise, which, while circumscribing the field of metaphysics so as to better liberate the "truth of Being" from its fateful hold, has partly determined his vision of Nietzsche and clipped his Dionysian wings in advance.

An analytic listing of Heidegger's many definitions and redefinitions of metaphysics would be instructive in this regard, though they may be reduced, more or less, to a single formulation: "Metaphysics speaks of beings as such and as a whole, thus of the *Being* of beings."[17] Considered as such and playing the role of cause or foundation, the Being of beings only says of Being what it contains in the most general and abstract sense, while there remains, unthought, the *florescence* that enabled the advent of being, bearing the mystery of Being without ever fully revealing it. Heidegger had therefore not been content, as Kant had before him, to bring back to beings the dove that had gone astray in the suprasensible. It is on *another ground* that he invites the thinker to follow in the dove's careful steps, a ground whose stability one restores only after becoming familiar with Nothingness, and in much more radical a manner than Nietzsche was supposed to have done: his metaphysics—that of the Will to Power—would have remained nihilistic in spite of his wish to overturn the values which, favoring the suprasensible, had ushered the great nihilist deflation. Thinking the essence of nihilism more essentially—more authentically—therefore required that one does not think the *nihil* in a nihilistic way, while also refraining from turning it into a "being." Yet was that not precisely what Nietzsche had done, in his way?

We must certainly be grateful to Heidegger for having shed light on the nearly methodical consistency of "Nietzsche's metaphysics," though it was at the expense of some of its components (and not the least significant). Often meditating on the five "fundamental terms" defining this metaphysics—will to power, nihilism, eternal return of the same, the overhuman, justice—Heidegger pointed out their *interdependence*, even inscribing them in an implicit circularity; the *order*, however, in which he broaches these terms clearly points to the linchpin and driving force of the circular movement: the Will to Power—undeniably in full agreement with Nietzsche, for whom it is "the force that metamorphoses and remains the same."[18] Yet, it is at the cost of an interpretative slippage that Heidegger went from the will to power in art, where it still figures as a creative antidote to nihilism (lecture of 1936), to the "will to will," which, legitimizing the necessity of the Return—for other reasons, it is true, than those put forth by Nietzsche (lecture of 1939)—confirms the transition to *modern* metaphysics as a domination of the totality of beings by way of enframing (*Gestell*). Heidegger comes to superpose the two circles, as if the critical recurrence of the "will to will" found its culmination in Nietzsche's "abyssal thought" (*abgründlicher Gedanke*) regarding the Eternal Return: "Everything goes, everything comes back; eternally rolls the wheel of being. Everything dies, everything blossoms again; eternally runs the year of being."[19]

Under Nietzsche's decisive influence, metaphysics would thus have given birth to the modern epoch's characteristic "greatest passion for beings,"[20] a forgetfulness of Being all the more resolute in extending its domination (*Herrschaft*) over the totality of beings. Having brought *modern* metaphysics to its conclusion and identified the nihilist poison corrupting it from the root, Nietzsche would have fully taken up the "inclusive" inquiry, but in no case had he overcome the nihilism that made its hidden essence manifest: "The will to will can will nothing other than empty nothingness, in the face of which it asserts itself without being able to know its own completed nullity."[21] By canceling out the combined effects of these two nullities—the wish to self-annihilation and the inanity of this wish—nihilism overcomes itself. And to better mark the limits of Nietzsche's thought, Heidegger replaces the Nietzschean *Umwertung aller Werte* with an apparently more radical term designating a reversal (Turn) of metaphysics on which, to his mind, nihilism's self-overcoming depends, *Umkehrung,* which suggests a wrenching of oneself from oneself that takes a novel form, an internal transformation that becomes operative *within* nihilism itself—Heidegger here is in agreement with Nietzsche—and not a frontal assault or heroic recapture.

Nonetheless Heidegger uses the same term as Nietzsche to denote the process, *Überwindung,* while disputing that a mere going-beyond resulting from the completion (*Vollendung*) of metaphysics constitutes a true overcoming; this semantic difficulty sometimes prompted him to introduce another term, *Übergang,* to take into account what he thought differentiated him from Nietzsche: "Der Übergang ist jedoch nicht die Überwindung, sondern nur die Eingang ein sie als Geschichte."[22] For over-coming, in the historical sense intended by Heidegger, paradoxically involves aban-doning any notion of going-beyond so as to be attuned to Being, the interrogation of which only becomes audible if one first consents to emptying one's chalice (the heavily connoted image crops up in Jünger)[23] to attain, in the end, *a point of reversal* as myste-rious as it is immeasurable since it is no longer a matter of an inversion perpetuating a prior state in contrary form. Heidegger is thus battling on two fronts: that of values, to which he deems Nietzsche to have been too beholden to imagine that he had himself effectuated a *trans*valuation; and that of an exit from nihilism, requiring of the thinker a strategy adapted to its nature: one only overcomes nihilism, "the most worrying of all hosts," by feeling the intimate interconnection of Being and Nothingness in the inmost depths of one's being. To this ultimately initiatory trial, Nietzsche subjected himself with the enthusiasm of a prophet envisaging a new Dawn, and Heidegger with the steadfastness of a battle-weary veteran going into a night in which the world might well come undone.

Highlighting the close connection between will and power, each calling upon the other indefinitely, and insisting on the creative impotence and deepening nihilism inherent in indefinitely willing one's own will, Heidegger remained silent about that which, in the exercise of power, was in Nietzsche's view an *ecstatic nonvolition* renounc-ing all domination. But how can the Overhuman advocate an unconditional "yes" to the thought of the Eternal Return—one might say, to the end of resentment regarding time—while also embodying a future "type" comprising the qualities required of man's mechanized domination of the Earth? That which is dynamic tension in Nietzsche, working toward nihilism's self-overcoming in the superior man, "conqueror of both God and of nothingness,"[24] tends to become a cleavage in Heidegger, who, conceiving domination in close relation to enframing, obliterates the "sovereign" aspect it has in Nietzsche, while eschewing the nearly eremitic dimension and profound sense of ecstatic nihilism in the creative vocation of the Nietzschean *Übermensch*. Criticizing religions as vectors of nihilism, did Nietzsche not also consider them the only labora-tories capable of fashioning such superior types as the hermit and the saint? Georges Bataille's crucial distinction between *mastery* and *sovereignty*[25]—which does full jus-tice to Nietzsche's sovereign vision—highlights a frequent ambiguity in Heidegger, who conflates the two terms when he speaks of the Nietzschean Overhuman, "master of such domination"[26] (*Herr dieser Herrschaft*), but dissociates them when he wishes to show that *sovereignty* belongs to Being while supremacy (*die Vormacht*) is the preroga-tive of beings.

Similarly we may appreciate the significance of Heidegger's judgment on the nihil-ist character of Nietzsche's valuation process only if we examine the precise mean-ing of the famous expression *Umwertung aller Werte*, by turns translated as *inversion, reversal, overturning, transmutation, transvaluation, revaluation*. The difficulty is that Nietzsche's texts justify nearly all these variant translations. Two semantic orientations nevertheless emerge, one favoring the figures of reversal, or inversion, while the other refers to a more mysterious operation, of an "alchemical" order, righting the harm done by "nihilist counterfeiting," to which Nietzsche attributes a first reversal that had subjugated the Will to Power of the strong to that of the weak.[27] The choice between the two is not a trivial one, to the extent that the first tends to justify Heidegger's judgment, by which "the reversal of a metaphysical statement remains a metaphysical statement,"[28] while the other credits Nietzsche's thought with a horizon at once more uncertain and more distant, lending credibility to the transformation of poison into medicine taught by Zarathustra.

Did Nietzsche himself hesitate between these two seemingly opposite possibilities, or had he only uttered the one—"We, men of reversal" (*Wir Umgekehrten*)[29]—to initiate a movement leading to the other? Similarly one may consider the *transmutation* of values (to which Nietzsche explicitly refers, paying an emphatic homage to the makers of gold)[30] as the prerequisite for an extensive *transvaluation*, not the adoption of one value as superior to all others—a supreme being among all beings, Heidegger would say—but as *one beyond all values*, helping to truly overcome nihilism and *transfigure* the world. Claiming to see in the Nietzschean *amor fati* "the will as transfiguration . . . [that] erects and exposes what it will in its essence to the supreme possibilities of its Being,"[31] Heidegger readily admits the jubilant nature of Dionysian intoxication, but not for a moment does he credit it with the ability to emerge from the circle of beings. Giving philosophical and religious credence to the "philosopher Dionysus" and his *transfiguration* of life and the world, Nietzsche was setting the first stone for the only "religion" he thought capable of meeting the expectations of the man of the future—evidently quite different from Heidegger's highly cautious rediscovery of the sacred, more attuned to the "presence of failure"[32] than to the glorious epiphany of a stricken God.

It is commonly accepted—and Heidegger hardly disputes it—that the God whose death Nietzsche announced is of a piece with the suprasensible sphere whose devaluation brought about the ineluctable progress of European nihilism (its *decomposition* [*Verwesung*], says Heidegger, set on breaking away from all valuation). Pointing out that it was the *moral* God who fell to the murderers' blows, Nietzsche felt that a renewal of the divine could very well emerge from this deicide: "You say 'destruction of God by his own hands' when it is in fact a question of his molting: he is sloughing off his moral skin! And besides, you'll see him soon enough, beyond good and evil."[33] Will the suprasensible ideals also *molt*, like the God whose death the Madman announces in §125 of the *Gay Science*? Either way, if it is a matter of *devaluation*, why speak of "death" in connection with God? One may be surprised by this sudden dramatization when Nietzsche's prior statements suggested a rather more decadent vision of the twilight of the gods: "I believe in the ancient German saying: All gods must die."[34] Associating God's death and the devaluation of supreme values in a single nihilating movement, thus speaking of "God's default" (*Entgötterung*) in a world in which God is neither efficient nor present, Heidegger is in fact reformulating Nietzsche's thought:

For meditative thinking, this means: God thought in terms of value, be it a supreme value, is not God: God is therefore not dead. For his divinity lives. It is nearer thought, even, than it is to faith, if it is true that divinity originates from the truth of Being and if Being as appropriating commencement [*ereignender anfang*] "is" other than the foundation and cause of beings.[35]

One wonders still if Heidegger, basing his conception of both the death of God and the decomposition of suprasensible ideals on the essence of metaphysics, hasn't obliterated that which helped differentiate them in Nietzsche. Advocating the shock treatment of relearning tragic suffering, Nietzsche could not have been entirely unaware of the difference between the two evils of Christianity and Platonism, more distinct in his discourse than in Heidegger's. Emphasizing the vicious circle lodged around the will to will, Heidegger could only contemplate its weakening and a loss of power contrary to its essence. Is it because Nietzsche had discussed these central questions from a "fundamental metaphysical position" very different from his own that Heidegger preferred to ignore the many texts pertaining to a future God? Is this not *the* question likely to show whether Nietzsche, prophet of the "death of God" and herald of nihilism, had sufficiently *accompanied* the ambiguous process to have at least adumbrated its self-overcoming?

What God for What Future?

Nietzsche could not have seriously considered a nihilism that taught him to mistrust any potentially nihilizing "being" (substance, idea, subject) while also attempting to reify its negative, nothingness: the one could not be deflated without deflating the other. Also, the "death of God" actually presides over an unprecedented *voidance* since what we had thought full turns out to be empty: "To sacrifice God for nothingness—that paradoxical mystery of the final cruelty has been reserved for the race that is now approaching: by now we all know something about this."[36] Nietzsche therefore did not merely speak of the "murder of murders" in the tones of high tragedy: "How may such a murderer be consoled? How purified?"[37] More important, he reported that nihilism, to be well understood, requires that one think of its action by way of a *withdrawal*: something was that is no longer, having withdrawn without our knowing whether it is a temporary eclipse—perhaps a form of "work of the negative"—or a definitive annihilation. The difficulty, then, lies in not forgetting that it is a matter of an emptying, a *vacuum*, inducing a devaluation of strengths and forms and proscribing any reification of this *nihil*, the translation of which remains problematic, like that of the German *das Nichts*: Is it a question of nothingness here, or of nothing, of an emptiness? A minuscule point of reference in any case (*ne hilum*), on which thought labors only to arrive at a final subtraction: of what was there remains "nothing," nothing but the trace of that withdrawal and the nostalgia it can induce in individuals as exhausted as the Europeans before a nonbeing (*ne ens*) verging on nothingness.

Nietzsche was then fully aware that he could grasp the essence of nihilism only if he accompanied it through its characteristic withdrawal while resisting its pull toward an irreversible and complacent decadence; the art of "civilization's physician" consisted of discovering the formula for a redemptive letting-go that would enable the transformation of one's poisons into medicine, whereas the weak, having no healing instinct, "seek as remedy that which speeds their ruin."[38] Did Heidegger not learn this strategy from Nietzsche before making it his own? Nietzsche's insightful description of "the spreading violence of actual nihilism"[39] and his active participation in the destruction of former values cannot take away from the boldness and inventiveness of his approach to religion. Suggesting that the essence of nihilism may well reside "in the fact that the essence of nihilism consists in *not* taking the question of the nothing seriously,"[40] Heidegger could deal with Nietzsche only through a reductive understanding of his process of annihilation, which goes beyond metaphysics precisely in that it is not reducible to a mere "insurrection against nothingness."[41]

Heidegger had nonetheless given more demanding thought than Nietzsche to the conditions for an ontological-existential mutation of nihilism. Conceiving the essence of nihilism without reducing it to the devaluation it brings about required that one not confuse its most radical manifestation—the drifting of all being into Nothingness—with a "complete dissolution into vacuous nothingness" (*in das nichtige Nichts*),[42] a nothingness that Heidegger deems "vulgar" in that it is still only the inverse of the being it remains bound to: "The nothing of being follows the Being of being as night follows day."[43] Extending this nothingness-making's sphere of influence to the totality of beings—the modern temptation par excellence—will not help one understand Nothingness in relation to Being, only to the Being of beings: "In contrast, to go expressly up to the limit of Nothing in the *question* about Being, and to take Nothing into the question of Being—this is the first and only fruitful step toward the true overcoming of nihilism."[44] Amazed that there *are* beings rather than nothing, metaphysics turned in dread (*horror vacui*) from what it took for Nothingness, though it is no more nothingness than Being may be reduced to the totality of beings. The difficulty lies in reaching this authentic Nothingness, anterior to the "no" of negation and both inherent in and concealed in Being.

If the true import of Nothingness is revealed through the existential tone of anxiety, one must admit that Nietzsche remained immune to it. May we then conclude that he could in no way convert nihilist negation into another form of annihilation, revelatory of a mode of being on which Nothingness has no hold? Expelling the existent from the reassuring domain of beings by offering to meet its totality in the mode of withdrawal, anxiety allows it to experience that rare moment of its emergence from Nothingness, by which it then feels mysteriously "held back." Still, *Dasein*, sensing the totality of beings pulled out from under it, must offer no resistance to this apparent annihilation until it finally touches the bottom of a "place," nearer emptiness than Nothingness, where it will experience "the pervasive expanse of that which gives every being the warrant to be."[45] Thus supporting the existent in its fall, Being, in Heidegger's discourse, plays a role comparable to that of the Deity (*Gottheit*) that Meister Eckhart said was "nothingness" (nonbeing) gathering within it the soul that, in its abandonment, risks obliteration. What does Heidegger undertake in these analyses unmatched in Nietzsche's works? He introduces into meditative thought an *apophatic* dimension arduously appropriated from theology. Yet when Heidegger claims to see in the Nietzschean determination of the entire universe "a negative theology without the Christian God,"[46] it is still *theology* for him, which is as much as to say metaphysics.

Nietzsche, though, has associated Christianity too closely with nihilism for us not to take him seriously when he says, "In me, it is Christianity that triumphs over itself through self-overcoming,"[47] which recalls the admonishment, "If we fail to make the *death of God* a grand *renunciation* and a perpetual *victory over ourselves*, we will have to *suffer the loss*."[48] What renunciation will alleviate the sense of an irreparable loss? Coupled in his thought, renunciation and loss compound their nihilating effects if the one does not counterbalance the negative effects of the other: one does not lose what one has renounced. A stunning transformation of ascetic ideals, first rejected for having encouraged a will to nihilist annihilation, reappearing transformed by a redemptive Will to Power! Breaking the substantiality of beings and thus the representation of their totalizing wholeness, this deconstruction certainly helps snatch the Will to Power's world from the maw of Nothingness and justify the striking transformation of apparently nihilist religions (Christianity, Buddhism) in the later Nietzsche.

Is there, then, a connection between the Nietzschean conception of justice, "the truth of what is—which now is in the mode of the Will to Power,"[49] and the fact that the void left by God's death may, according to Heidegger, remain *empty* a long time, or even forever? The question is all the more important given that in "Overcoming Metaphysics" (1936–46) Heidegger wrote that "*Iustificatio*, in the sense of the Reformation and Nietzsche's concept of justice as truth, are the same thing."[50] The conflation is surprising: Might Luther have unwittingly heralded the Will to Power? If his vision of justice had been confirmed by Luther's, would Nietzsche have accused the "great solemn yet oppressive Reformation"[51] of having accelerated Europe's decadence? Indeed Nietzsche called Luther a "benefactor" for the sole reason that he had devalued ascetic ideals, opening the way for a "non-Christian *vita contemplativa*," which one imagines as Dionysian even if Nietzsche does not mention it, though he expresses approval for works discredited as much by Socrates and Plato as by Luther: "Works, first and foremost! That is to say, doing, doing, doing! The 'faith' that goes with it will soon put in an appearance—you can be sure of that!"[52] At the very least, Nietzsche's critical stance regarding Luther and the Reformation affords us an opposing idea of what a religion of the future might be in his view—something Heidegger, in his reading of Nietzsche, speaks so little of.

The issue is significant, however, because if religion, whatever its form, is reborn not only after but *from* the great nihilist deflation, it means Christianity and Buddhism have not exhausted the essence of the religious nor definitely corrupted the potential for an authentic relation to the divine: "Only after the death of religion may invention proliferate again in the field of the divine,"[53] says Nietzsche, more than ever speaking as a creator, as a philosopher-artist. Perhaps it is because Heidegger found the poetic expression of this more authentic relation in Hölderlin that he has so little to say about Nietzsche's propositions regarding this "sacred pathos." He also suggests that the vacancy left by God's death would long remain empty: vacant but available, definitively void of the suprasensible, or so empty—of an emptiness one must refrain from redefining so as not to render it as value—that whatever divine figure is reestablished therein would have little to do with the God that deserted it. On this point, as on so many others, Heidegger's historical tempo is not Nietzsche's. Evoking multiple possibilities—radical atheism, "Buddha-like atheist religion," the advent of an unknown God—Nietzsche finally concludes, "And how many new gods are still possible! As for myself, in whom the religious, that is to say god-forming, instinct occasionally becomes active at impossible times—how differently, how variously the divine has revealed itself to me each time!"[54] For his part, considering that the true murder and least pardonable blasphemy was to think God as a value, Heidegger held to the strictest *reserve* while implicitly positioning himself as the guardian of a place whose emptiness, as disorienting as it may be, was preferable to a new usurpation of the divine by some "value" or other. And it is not a concern for decoupling theology and philosophy that keeps him from speaking on the identity of the God-to-come, aside from the *Beiträge* (1932–35), where he furtively takes on the figure of Proteus.[55]

Making the "question of God" contingent on that of Being, Heidegger could not help but be untrue to Nietzsche, the paradox being that the very magnitude of his "argument" with him contributes to obscure and restrict his ultimate position with respect to religious innovation since, with God stripped of a moral dimension, nihilism also turns out to be "a divine way of thinking," reaching its apogee in the unconditional acceptance of the Return as the "religion of religions."[56] It hardly matters *who* Nietzsche's intimated God will be—Dionysus, or some as yet unknown god—when his impassioned evocation contradicts Heidegger's assertion that he had only conceived God as a supreme value, while he had indeed begun a process of overcoming all valuations: "'God' as a culminating moment: existence, an eternal divinization and de-divinization. *But AS SUCH not a culminating point of value*, only culminating points of power."[57] In short, the logical consequence of a vision of the Will to Power which, encompassing the totality of being in the Return, sanctifies becoming within each moment, thus eschewing that source of resentment, time: "Becoming must appear justified at every moment," says Nietzsche, adding that "justified" becoming is *unvaluable*.[58] Eternalized, in short, made divine, like the scintillating sea at Noon on which Nietzsche's admiring gaze paused so often, convinced that tomorrow's religiosity would have nothing to do with metaphysics, nor with faith—"The man of belief is the opposite of the religious man"[59]—and that a profound transformation would change the very notion of "religion" through and through.

Of Christianity, excoriated in *The Antichrist* as a moral religion, Nietzsche grasped that it was above all a "state of heart," and of Buddhism, heretofore accused of weakening an already decadent Europe, that it was also a healthy way of life, founded on inexhaustible gratitude toward life: "It stands, as I put it, beyond good and evil."[60] Most peculiar, then, that Nietzsche, who saw only the nihilist component in Buddhist emptiness (*śūnyatā*), had nonetheless sensed that as a *practice*, foreign to Western metaphysics, Buddhism could relate to his own effort in overcoming nihilism; Heidegger saw in this burgeoning dialogue with the East an opportunity to attend to a "fundamental tonality" different from the West's regarding the rapport between Being and Nothingness: "To us, emptiness is the loftiest name for what you mean to say with the word 'being,'"[61] his Japanese respondent states. Asia had also drawn a singular *topography* between nothingness, nothing, and emptiness that was foreign to the grammar that Nietzsche feared would long determine our belief in God. That the most powerful antidote to nihilism was to conceive Being not in terms of substance, nor even as Will to Power, but as "place" could well be the unsaid in Heidegger's "argument" with Nietzsche and the transition point toward the unlocatable *topos* that is Buddhist emptiness (*śūnyatā*), in which Nishitani Keiji, taking up the Nietzschean discussion in relation to the Westernization of Japan, saw the only "position" capable of overcoming Western nihilism: "a kind of spiritual ascent through descent into radical finitude," as James Heisig states.[62]

The "Realization" of Nihility

Nietzsche and his two heirs of the East and the West undoubtedly share the train of thought outlined here, roughly speaking, along with the drafting of a kind of "dialectic" specific to European nihilism: the philosophical course is no longer set by surprised wonderment, whether or not followed by doubt, but by a confrontation with nothingness, emptiness, and the absurd, whether or not accompanied by recovery and new wonderment. However, when Nishitani states that "the overcoming of nihilism through nihilism" has been the fundamental problem of his life, he says it for other reasons and from a different point of view than Heidegger's and Nietzsche's;[63] nihilism is so intimately bound to the destiny of the West that its self-overcoming seems not to concern Japan or any other Asian country where neither Christianity nor metaphysics have created the conditions for its appearance. From the Asian point of view, nihilism remains an export product, at least to the extent that the causes that generated it are foreign to the Asian world. For Japan, then, why speak of the "meaning" of nihilism? Is the emergence of a meaning not the sign that an appropriation has taken place, converting the nihilist nonmeaning into significance? Such is indeed the central point in Nishitani's presentation, which demonstrates that the Westernization intended by Japan during the Meiji era (1868–1912), inevitably bearing the deleterious seeds that had weakened Europe, would have had only a minor impact if Japan hadn't lost its traditional and spiritual bearings. But for this weakening, nihilism would have remained a foreign body to be fought or tamed but not to be overcome at the cost of an appropriation whose historical nihility would risk overdetermining the existential trial every human being must experience in facing his or her own nothingness.

Less imbued with the pathos Heidegger felt in his distress over the lack of distress over forgetfulness of Being, Nishitani also emphasizes the fact that this spiritual emptiness prevents recognition of the situation for what it is and delays one's escape from nihilism's vicious circle: "The essential thing is to overcome our inner void, and here European nihilism is of critical relevance in that it can impart a radical twist to our present situation and thereby point a way toward overcoming the spiritual hollowness."[64] Choosing to Westernize at a time when European nihilism was devaluing the heritage that would shape it, Japan was entering a complex game: without the threat to its integrity, Japan would not have felt the need to unearth its buried spiritual foundations and to question the Buddhist tradition by which it had been formed, beyond references to God's ex nihilo creation of the world and man, in which Nishitani claims to see one of the causes of European nihilism: "This nihility stands like a great iron wall that absolutely separates all things from God."[65] Influenced at once by Nietzsche's genealogical method and Heidegger's "step back," Nishitani considers the return/recourse to tradition for only one purpose: "to recover the creativity that mediates the past to the future and the future to the past (but not to restore a bygone era). The (third) significance of European nihilism for us is that it makes these things possible."[66] It was also to recognize, after Nietzsche and Heidegger, that nihilism's self-overcoming would inevitably come with that of modernity, which had consummated the rupture between present and past, accelerating nihilism's progression on a global scale.

Nishitani first notes that the Nietzschean experience, as destructive as it was rejuvenating, reflected the singularity of European nihilism, whose self-overcoming required that it resonate in those rare individuals capable of enduring its purifying fire without succumbing. Did Nietzsche not think of himself as the instrument of destiny, in whom "the supreme act of humanity's return to itself [*Selbstbesinnung*]" announced by nihilism was made "flesh and genius"?[67] Less of an elitist, as he was educated in a culture little inclined to glorify individualism, Nishitani took note of the heroic and eremitic nature of the Nietzschean *Übermensch*, while primarily concerning himself with what the existential experience of nihility revealed in all human beings. If nihilism is not merely a kind of metaphysical question that everyone in search of awakening comes eventually to ponder, it is that it forces subjects to adhere to a historical movement by which one is devalued along with all the suprasensible ideals of which one had thus far been a proponent, while leading to an interrogation of one's own foundation—*in vivo*, one might say—at various levels (psychological, existential, spiritual). Exacerbating the weight of human finitude, nihilism offers a horizon and a way out, on condition that it be transformed into a Lesson from Hell, at the cost of what Nishitani calls "the realization of nihility."

"Realizing" the precariousness of man's situation, subject to impermanence and death, cannot of itself bring about the self-overcoming of a historical and all but ordinary nihilism. At most, the acute awareness of finitude may accelerate the revelation of a foundational absence, still more abyssal for touching the subject's very "being"; realizing his own nihility, he may then "get in touch" with reality "as it is," without objectifying it, and not as represented by an egocentric subject. Insisting on the mysterious "turning point" from which doubt, be it as methodical as Descartes's, gives way to a Great Doubt, purifying and transformative, Nishitani, quite Zen-like in his approach, believes he has exhumed "the 'home-ground' of religion, where religion emerges from man himself, as a subject, as a self living in the present."[68] This "home-ground" cannot be discovered without the subject's prior confrontation with his own abyssal nihility, which dissolves one's egocentric pretensions and restores the only personal-impersonal "position" worthy of being called "religious."

Thus only the *religious quest* enables us to understand what religion is; Nishitani, following his master Nishida Kitarō, could have said of religion that "it regards the nature of our self," to the extent at least that it "encounters its existence in its own negation."[69] While religion brings ready-made answers to man's existential anxieties, the religious quest leads one to empty still more the "abyss of nihility" as it unfolds before us: "Our existence is an existence at one with nonexistence, swinging back and forth over nihility, ceaselessly passing away and ceaselessly regaining its existence. This is what is called the 'incessant becoming' of existence."[70] Reborn from the nihilist fire by which it was "nullified" but not "annihilated," the subject, liberated from the "citadel of self," can testify that religion thus understood is neither a secondary matter in the order of existential priorities nor an abstract personal option of variable dimensions but the only honorable answer to a nihilist challenge that makes it impossible to dissociate the existential and the historical, thus compelling the subject to "realize" his or her own nihility. One can see how nihilism, leveling cultural differences, brings to light the "infinitely abyssal" foundation of religious experience, in the East even more so than in the West, an experience that Nishida had already said "demands that one never forget that dimension where the human being is established within himself."[71] That is why an a-theistic religion like Buddhism, oblivious to the "death of God" but familiar with a nothingness that is anything but nihilistic, can help the West rediscover the apophatic dimension of its own tradition: "All things find their receptacle in the nothingness from which they originate and that is their place. . . . All is thus on a backdrop of nothingness: the fullness is in the void, being rests on non-being, received within it as in a place."[72]

Nihilism, however, could not have had precisely the same impact on a European subject, who has been grappling nervously with personal identity for centuries and with God's—no less—personal identity, as it had on the subject of a Buddhist culture long since familiar with a phenomenally intrinsic absence of substantiality. And while this cultural difference barely comes into play in Nishitani's faithful reconstruction of

Nietzsche's and Heidegger's thought, it nonetheless explains how Asia, in his view, has a good head start on Europe: "Still, the East has achieved a conversion from the standpoint of nihility to the standpoint of *śūnyatā*."[73] Is this to say that Europe, undermined by nihilism and hampered by its cultural heritage, is only now gingerly discovering the "position of vacuity" that has been Asia's from the beginning? Let's rather say that nihilism, having become historically common to one and the other, makes this "awakening to self" (Nishida) equally vital to both, though in a mode that allows nihilism's self-overcoming within and outside of self. It is no coincidence, then, if deconstructing the subject was at the heart of Nietzsche's preoccupations; if its repositioning as *Dasein*, "experienced as place, that is, as the field [*Stelle*] of the truth of Being,"[74] figures as a refounding act in Heidegger; and if the subject, in Nishitani's eyes, is but an empty shell, pulverized as much by the ordinary experience of suffering as by the nihilism that reveals more starkly still the absence of foundation:

If nihilism is anything, it is first of all a problem of the self. And it becomes such a problem only when the self becomes a problem, when the ground of the existence called "self" becomes a problem for itself. When the problem of nihilism is posed apart from the self, or as a problem of society in general, it loses the special genuineness that distinguishes it from other problems.[75]

Free of any interpretative debt to Heidegger, despite the latter's undeniable influence on him, what Nishitani sketches out in the three chapters devoted to Nietzsche in *The Self-Overcoming of Nihilism* (1949) he later expands upon in *Religion and Nothingness* (1961), where he discusses self-overcoming as though Nietzsche's breakthrough, insightful and decisive though it be, called for further investigation and required that one now turn to Buddhism, in particular, in order to grasp why only a "position of vacuity" can attest to nihilism's actual overcoming. More attentive to the continuity between the two thinkers than to Heidegger's analyses of Nietzsche's "metaphysics," Nishitani could not, in 1949, have taken into account the totality of Nietzsche's writings, published only the same year as *Religion and Nothingness*, in 1961. Aware that an entire work would be required to deal with the evolution of Heidegger's thought regarding nihilism, Nishitani preferred to leave unaltered the single chapter dedicated to him in *The Self-Overcoming of Nihilism*, in which Heidegger himself figures as the last metaphysician, elaborating an ontology "within which nihilism becomes a philosophy. By disclosing the nothing at the ground of all beings and summoning it forth, nihilism becomes the basis of a new metaphysics."[76]

Contrary to Heidegger, though, who consigned Nietzsche to the pen of metaphysics, Nishitani recognizes in him the intrepid adventurer and prophetic spirit who took full cognizance of nihilism, traversed it through and through, and overcame it from within, without feeling obligated to suggest his inability to conceive its essence: "At the very end, at the North Pole within Nietzsche himself, nihilism consummates itself and is sloughed off. It swells to a round ripeness within him, and then drops like a fruit from a tree. For Nietzsche, to live through nihilism is to produce an interpretation of it [*auslegen*] in this way."⁷⁷ Characterizing this Nietzschean nihilism as "hyperborean," Nishitani brings to light the extreme and indeed "polar" fulcrum where interpretation, in a perspectivist sense, is transmuted into a "position," of which it remains nonetheless to be seen if it transcends all antagonisms or cancels them out in the manner of Buddhist vacuity (*śūnyatā*). Essentially commenting on *Zarathustra*—his bedside book from a very young age—and *The Will to Power* (edited by Kröner), Nishitani both restores its basic tone with exceptional insightfulness and opens up some suggestive avenues toward Zen Buddhism and Christian negative theology, as if to show that the weakened subject, confronted with its own nihility, is the price to pay for those, Western or Asian, who wish to touch a more fundamental ground and attain what Nishida Kitarō had called "pure experience" and himself "elemental subjectivity." Emphasizing the connection between *amor fati* and the Eternal Return rather than the relationship between Will to Power and the Return as Heidegger had done, Nishitani goes to the extent of recognizing in the Nietzschean vision of the Return an ecstatic experience comparable to the *satori*: "The difficult and improbable moment when the *fatum*'s weight and distress becomes the lightness and freedom of *amor fati* is the moment of crisis when nihilism changes into its own self-overcoming," writes Bernard Stevens.⁷⁸ Returning to this question in *Religion and Nothingness*, Nishitani confirms this interpretation, thus conveying Nietzsche's strongest intuitions regarding a possible encounter between his own philosophy and the force of acquiescence in Buddhism.

Is it faithfulness to Nietzsche that prevents Nishitani from making explicit the obvious discrepancy between this positioning and the meaning—by reference to the *Mahâyâna* (Great Vehicle)—of the expression "standpoint of *śūnyatā*"? Nishitani strives to show that the transition from nihility to vacuity (*śūnyatā*) may occur only if one forsakes any subjective or rational point of view, and thus any perspectivism: "The emptiness of *śūnyatā* is not an emptiness represented as some 'thing' outside of being and other than being. It is not simply an 'empty thing,' but rather an absolute emptiness, emptied even of these representations of emptiness. And for that reason, it is at bottom one with being, even as being is at bottom with emptiness."⁷⁹ Yet the very succession of these points of view in Nietzsche—great nihilist negation, followed by joyous Dionysian affirmation—attests to the fact that nihilism has been simultaneously transformed in time and very briefly overcome outside of time, breaking the cycle of becoming and liberating it from its closure. If liberation it be—and there is no reason to doubt it in Nietzsche—it is the fruit of a "dialectic" foreign to the Buddhist Middle Way (*Mâdhyamika*)⁸⁰ to which Nishitani explicitly refers, revealing the "position" of vacuity, and, shortly afterward, substituting the notion of "field" for that of "standpoint," as if to underscore the fact that *śūnyatā* is indeed anything but a point of view: "Vacuity is the position of wisdom in which the opposition isn't overcome so much as revealed to be an illusion," Heisig recalls.⁸¹ Heidegger underestimated the fact that Dionysian acquiescence transforms the perspectivism of the Will to Power into a "position" that breaks through the closed circuit of the will to will and justifies one's talking about nihilism's self-overcoming. Nishitani, on the contrary, seems to credit Nietzsche with a liberating positioning, too close in fact to Buddhist nonduality to truly take into account a Nietzschean "beyond" that transcends all antagonisms.

At first glance, one may be surprised not to find more references to Heidegger in *Religion and Nothingness*; Heidegger, who had conceived the cobelonging of Being and Nothingness and had been aware that only a "point of view freed of any point of view"[82] would liberate man's *humanitas* from nihilism, was undeniably tending toward Buddhist thinking. But one should not forget that Nishitani's objective was not comparative, in the Western sense of the term. His ultimate aim is evident in his brief reflections (1966) on two lectures given by Heidegger on the "homelessness" of contemporary man now facing a global nihilism. Recalling that Buddhism "also knew, from its beginning, this homelessness," and that Christ didn't know where to lay his head, Nishitani sees in this wandering and statelessness the very foundation of the religious quest and a painful laying bare that heralded the advent of the new world prophesied by Nietzsche: "It calls upon us to return to the most basic plane where man is solely man or is merely a son of man, no more, no less, where he is thoroughly bare, bare-headed, bare-backed, bare-handed and bare-footed, but where he can bare his innermost heart as well."[83] In short, it is a radical Kenosis, whether Christian or Buddhist, which brings back to an original simplicity the historical man while he had been wandering among beings, and which contributes, more than any discourse, to the encounter between East and West: "The encounter of East and West cannot be ultimate as long as it does not plumb that region where resides the marrow of the mind of men."[84]

If nihilism is inevitable, it is also an opportunity for humanity to engage in the most decisive reversal in its history. Nietzsche had to come first, though, exposing himself to its fatal rays so that others after him, both European and Asian, could show that before the nihilist wave threatening to overwhelm the world, neither methodical doubt nor the somewhat incantatory evocation of a purifying tabula rasa would suffice to hold back Nothingness, which, if not recognized for what it is, would threaten Being at every moment. Despite their good intentions, neither comparative philosophy nor interreligious dialogue[85] can measure up to the nihilism that has ambushed an uprooted humanity, forcing crucial choices upon it, which only it can make, to restore the right "measure" with which to save itself. Removing their worth from things of value and afflicting the spirit with asthenia, nihilism may make us forget that within it is unleashed an unprecedented excessiveness that Heraclitus called upon us to extinguish more urgently still than fire.[86]

Notes

This essay was translated from the French by Ron Ross.

1. The idea that the Platonic metaphor of the Battle of Giants over Being and Nothingness (*Sophist*) may also pertain to the philosophical relations between East and West is borrowed from Stevens, *Topologie du néant*.

2. Heidegger, *Nietzsche, vol. IV: Nihilism*, 27; *Nietzsche I (1936-1939), Gesamtausgabe* vol. 6.1, 50 (hereafter GA 6.1).

3. Heidegger, *Achèvement de la métaphysique et poésie*, 97; *Nietzsches Metaphysik*, 125. [My translation.—Trans.]

4. Heidegger, *What Is called Thinking?*, 77; *Was heißt denken?* (1951-52), *Gesamtausgabe* vol. 8, 83 (hereafter GA 8).

5. Haar, "La lecture heideggérienne de Nietzsche," 165. [My translation.—Trans.]

6. Nietzsche, *Sämtliche Werke: Kritische Studienausgabe*, 12, 9 [164], 432 (hereafter KSA). [My translation.—Trans.]

7. Heidegger, *Nietzsche, vol. IV: Nihilism*, 148; *Nietzsche II (1939-1946), Gesamtausgabe* vol. 6.2, 179 (hereafter GA 6.2).

8. Heidegger, *What Is called Thinking?*, 51; GA 8, 55.

9. Nietzsche, *Beyond Good and Evil*, §56, 50 (hereafter BGE); KSA 5, 74.

10. Heidegger, "On the Question of Being," in *Pathmarks*, 321; *Wegmarken (1919-61), Gesamtausgabe* vol. 9, 424 (hereafter GA 9).

11. See Krell, "Heidegger/Nietzsche," 161-66.

12. de Waelhens, *La philosophie de Martin Heidegger*, 353. [My translation.—Trans.]

13. See Benoist, "Nietzsche est-il phénoménologue?," 196-208.

14. Ricoeur "Sur la phénoménologie," 821. [My translation.—Trans.]

15. Heidegger, "Phénoménologie et pensée de l'être," 336; *Zur Sache des Denkens*, 101.

16. Heidegger, "A Dialogue on Language: Between a Japanese and an Inquirer," in *On the Way to Language*, 39; *Unterwegs zur Sprache* (1950-1959), *Gesamtausgabe* vol. 12, 127 (hereafter GA 12).

17. Heidegger, *Nietzsche, vol. IV: Nihilism*, 151; GA 6.2, 182.

18. Nietzsche, KSA 11, 35 [68], 540.

19. Nietzsche, "The Convalescent," in *Thus Spoke Zarathustra*, 329 (hereafter TSZ); KSA 4, 272-273.

20. Heidegger, *Nietzsche, vol. IV: Nihilism*, 195; GA 6.2, 228.

21. Heidegger, "Overcoming Metaphysics," §3, 86; *Vorträge und Aufsätze (1936-53), Gesamtausgabe* vol. 7, 70 (hereafter GA 7).

22. Heidegger, *Metaphysik und Nihilismus*, 22.

23. Jünger, *Sämtliche Werke*, vol. 7, 269 (§18); *Passage de la Ligne*, 70.

24. Nietzsche, *On the Genealogy of Morality*, 67 (hereafter GM); KSA 5, 329.

25. Present throughout Bataille's work, particularly in *La souveraineté*, this distinction originates with Nietzsche, of whom Bataille writes, "As for the sovereign humanity whose brilliance he wanted to shine forth: in contradictory ways he saw the new humankind sometimes as wealthy, sometimes as poorer than the workers, sometimes as powerful, sometimes as tracked down by enemies. . . . Still, he distinguished this humanity on principle from men in possession of power" (*On Nietzsche*, 162).

26. Heidegger, *Nietzsche, vol. IV: Nihilism*, 81; GA 6. 2, 109.

27. Nietzsche, GM, §13, 27; KSA 5, 282.

28. Heidegger, "Letter on Humanism," in *Pathmarks*, 250; GA 9, 328.

29. Nietzsche, KSA 12, 2 [204], 166.

30. Nietzsche, KSA 13, 16 [43], 501. See also Bonardel, *Philosophie de l'alchimie*, 285-312. The significance of the alchemical metaphor has been pointed out by Martin in "Deconstruction and Breakthrough in Nietzsche and Nâgârjuna," 91-111.

31. Heidegger, *Nietzsche, Volume II: The Eternal Recurrence of the Same*, 207; GA 6.1, 422.

32. Heidegger, "Remembrance of the Poet," 265; *Erläuterungen zu Hölderlins Dichtung*, 28.

33. Nietzsche, KSA 10, [432], 105. [My translation.—Trans.]

34. Nietzsche, KSA 7, 5 [115], 125. [My translation.—Trans.]

35. Heidegger, "Aufzeichnungen aus der werkstatt" (1959), in *Aus der Erfahrung des denkens*, 154: "Dies sagt für das sinnende Denken: Der Gott als Wert gedacht, und sei er der höchste, ist kein Gott. Also ist Gott nicht tot. Denn seine Gottheit lebt. Sie ist sogar dem Denken naher als dem Glauben, wenn anders die Gottheit als Wesendes seine Herkunft aus der Wahrheit des Seins empfangt und das Sein als ereignender Anfang Anderes 'ist' den Grund und Ursache des Seienden." [My translation.—Trans.]

36. Nietzsche, BGE, §§55, 50; KSA 5, 74.

37. Nietzsche, KSA 9, 12 [77], 590. [My translation.—Trans.]

38. Nietzsche, KSA 13, 14 [66], 251. [My translation.—Trans.]

39. Heidegger, *Nietzsche, vol. IV: Nihilism*, 337; GA 6.2, 337.

40. Heidegger, *Nietzsche, vol. IV: Nihilism*, 21; GA 6.2, 43.

41. Heidegger, "Metaphysics as History of Being," 1; GA 6.2, 363.

42. Heidegger, *Nietzsche, Volume III: The Will to Power as Knowledge and as Metaphysics*, 209; GA 6.2, 255.

43. Heidegger, *Nietzsche, Volume II: The Eternal Recurrence of the Same*, 19; GA 6.1, 413.

44. Heidegger, *Introduction to Metaphysics*, 217–18; *Einführung in die Metaphysik*, 212.

45. Heidegger, "Postscript to 'What Is Metaphysics?,'" in *Pathmarks*, 233; GA 9, 386.

46. Heidegger, *Nietzsche, Volume II: The Eternal Recurrence of the Same*, 95; GA 6.1, 315.

47. Nietzsche, KSA 13, 24 [1], 622.

48. Nietzsche, KSA 9, 12 [9], 577. [My translation.—Trans.]

49. Heidegger, "The Word of Nietzsche: 'God Is Dead,'" 92; *Nietzsches Wort "Gott ist tot,"* 247.

50. Heidegger, "Overcoming Metaphysics," §16, 97; GA 7, 83.

51. Nietzsche, KSA 8, 11 [38], 229. [My translation.—Trans.]

52. Nietzsche, *Daybreak*, §22, 19; KSA 3, 30.

53. Nietzsche, KSA 9, 6 [359], 288. [My translation.—Trans.]

54. Nietzsche, *The Will to Power*, §1038, quoted in Lingis, "The Will to Power," 61; KSA 13, 525–26.

55. Heidegger, *Contributions to Philosophy (From Enowning)*, §256, 288–93; "Der letzte Gott," in *Beiträge zur Philosophie (Vom Ereignis)*, 409–17.

56. Nietzsche, KSA 11, 34 [199], 112.

57. Nietzsche, KSA 12, 9 [8], 343; KSA 12, 10 [203], 581: "God, conceived as degree of liberation." The Japanese philosopher Nishida Kitarō (1870–1945) would likewise say that religious values "are values denying values. And it is by transcending them that one meets the sacred" (*Logique du lieu et vision religieuse du monde*, 46).

58. Nietzsche, KSA 13, 11 [72], 34.

59. Nietzsche, KSA 10, 1 [77], 30. [My translation.—Trans.]

60. Nietzsche, "The Anti-Christ," §20, 16; KSA 6, 186.

61. Heidegger, "A Dialogue on Language: Between a Japanese and an Inquirer," in *On the Way to Language*, 19; GA 12, 103.

62. Heisig, *Philosophers of Nothingness*, 219.

63. Cited in ibid., 335.

64. Nishitani, *The Self-Overcoming of Nihilism*, 178.

65. Nishitani, *Religion and Nothingness*, 37–38.

66. Ibid. 179.

67. Nietzsche, *Ecce Homo*, 144; KSA 6, 365.

68. Nishitani, *Religion and Nothingness*, xviii.

69. Nishida, *Logique du lieu et vision religieuse du monde*, 45–46.

70. Nishitani, *Religion and Nothingness*, 4.

71. Nishida, *Logique du lieu et vision religieuse du monde*, 83.

72. de Bovelles, *Le Livre du Néant* (1510), 85.

73. Nishitani, *Religion and Nothingness*, 168.

74. Heidegger, "Introduction to 'What Is Metaphysics?,'" 283; GA 9, 373.

75. Nishitani, *The Self-Overcoming of Nihilism*, 1.

76. Ibid. 157.

77. Ibid., 42.

78. Stevens, *Le Néant évidé*, 114.

79. Ibid., 123.

80. See Murti, *The Central Philosophy of Buddhism*.

81. Heisig, *Philosophers of Nothingness*, 224.

82. Heidegger, *Nietzsche, Volume II: The Eternal Recurrence of the Same*, 118; GA 6.1, 339. See also Regvald, *Heidegger et le problème du néant*.

83. Nishitani, "Reflections on two Addresses by Martin Heidegger," 146–47. Wandering being the essence of man, from a Buddhist perspective, Nishida concluded, "Wandering in the religious sense is not to oscillate in one's goals, but to wonder in search of a place where the self may authentically be" (*Logique du lieu et vision religieuse du monde*, 38).

84. Nishida, *Logique du lieu et vision religieuse du monde*, 146.

85. See, for instance, Saviani, "La tradizione filosofica occidentale del pensiero di Nishitani Keiji"; Waldenfels, *Absolute Nothingness*.

86. Héraclite, *Fragments*, 187: fr. 48 (D. K. 43).

Bibliography

Bataille, Georges. *On Nietzsche*. Translated by Bruce Boone. London: Continuum International, 2004.

Benoist, Jocelyn. "Nietzsche est-il phénoménologue?" In *Cahier de l'Herne Nietzsche*. Paris: Éd. de l'Herne, 2000.

Bonardel, Françoise. *Philosophie de l'alchimie: Grand Œuvre et modernité*. Paris: PUF, 1993.

de Bovelles, Charles. *Le Livre du Néant*. 1510. Translated by P. Magnard. Paris: Vrin, 1983.

de Waelhens, Alphonse. *La philosophie de Martin Heidegger*. Louvain: Éditions de l'Institut supérieur de Philosophie, 1942.

Eliot, T. S. *Burnt Norton*. In *Four Quartets*. London: Faber & Faber, 1959.

Haar, Michel. "La lecture heideggérienne de Nietzsche." In *Cahiers de l'Herne: Nietzsche*. Paris: Éd. de l'Herne, 2000.

Heidegger, Martin. *Achèvement de la métaphysique et poésie*. Translated into French by A. Froidecourt. Paris: Gallimard, 2005.

———. "Aufzeichnungen aus der Werkstatt" (1959). In *Aus der Erfahrung des denkens, 1910–1976. Gesamtausgabe* vol. 13. Frankfurt-am-Main: Klostermann, 1983.

———. *Beiträge zur Philosophie (Vom Ereignis). Gesamtausgabe* vol. 65. Frankfurt am Main: Vittorio Klostermann, 1987.

———. *Contributions to Philosophy (From Enowning)*. Translated by Parvis Emad and Kenneth Maly. Bloomington: Indiana University Press, 1999.

———. *Einführung in die Metaphysik* (SS 1935). *Gesamtausgabe* vol. 40. Frankfurt am Main: Vittorio Klostermann, 1983.

———. *Erläuterungen zu Hölderlins Dichtung (1936–1968). Gesamtausgabe* vol. 4. Frankfurt am Main: Vittorio Klostermann, 1981.

———. *Gesamtausgabe*. Frankfurt am Main: Klostermann 1975–.

———. *Introduction to Metaphysics*. Translated by Gregory Fried and Richard Polt. New Haven: Yale University Press, 2000.

———. *Metaphysik und Nihilismus: Die Überwindung der Metaphysik* (1938–39). In *Das Wesen des Nihilismus* (1946–48). *Gesamtausgabe* vol. 67. Frankfurt am Main: Vittorio Klostermann, 1999.

———. *Nietzsche I (1936–1939)*. *Gesamtausgabe* vol. 6.1. Frankfurt am Main: Vittorio Klostermann, 1996.

———. *Nietzsche*, vol. 2: *The Eternal Recurrence of the Same*. Translated by David Farrell Krell. San Francisco: Harper & Row, 1984.

———. *Nietzsche II (1939–1946)*. Gesamtausgabe vol. 6.2. Frankfurt am Main: Vittorio Klostermann, 1996.

———. *Nietzsche*, vol. 3: *The Will to Power as Knowledge and as Metaphysics*. Translated by David Farrell Krell. San Francisco: Harper & Row, 1984.

———. *Nietzsche*, vol. 4: *Nihilism*. Translated by Frank A. Capuzzi. New York: Harper & Row, 1982.

———. *Nietzsches Metaphysik* (WS 1941–42). In *Einleitung in die Philosophie—Denken und Dichten* (WS 1944–45). *Gesammtausgabe* vol. 50. Frankfurt am Main: Klostermann, 1990.

———. *Nietzsches Wort "Gott ist tot"* (1943). In *Holzwege* (1935–46). *Gesamtausgabe* vol. 5. Frankfurt am Main: Klostermann, 1977.

———. *On the Way to Language*. Translated by Peter D. Hertz. New York: Harper & Row, 1971.

———. "Overcoming Metaphysics" and "Metaphysics as History of Being." Translated by Joan Stambaugh. In *The End of Philosophy*. Chicago: University of Chicago Press, 2003.

———. *Pathmarks*. Translated by Frank. A. Capuzzi. Edited by William McNeill. Cambridge: Cambridge University Press, 1998.

———. *Questions IV*. Translated into French by J. Lauxerois and Cl. Roëls. Paris: Gallimard, 1976.

———. "Remembrance of the Poet." Translated by Douglas Scott. In *Existence and Being*. Chicago: H. Regnery, 1949.

———. *Unterwegs zur Sprache* (1950–59). *Gesamtausgabe* vol. 12. Frankfurt am Main: Klostermann, 1985.

———. *Vorträge und Aufsätze* (1936–53). *Gesamtausgabe* vol. 7. Frankfurt am Main: Vittorio Klostermann, 2000.

———. *Was heißt denken?* (1951–52). *Gesamtausgabe* vol. 8. Frankfurt am Main: Klostermann, 2002.

———. *Wegmarken* (1919–61). *Gesamtausgabe* vol. 9. Frankfurt am Main: Vittorio Klostermann, 1976.

———. *What Is called Thinking?* Translated by Fred D. Wieck and J. Glenn Gray. New York: Harper & Row, 1968.

———. "The Word of Nietzsche: 'God Is Dead.'" Translated by William Lovitt. In *The Question Concerning Technology and Other Essays*. New York: Garland, 1977.

———. *Zur Sache des Denkens* (1962–64). *Gesamtausgabe* vol. 14. Frankfurt am Main: Klostermann, 2007. Heisig, James W. *Philosophers of Nothingness*. Hawaii: University of Hawaii Press, 2001.

———. *Les philosophes du néant*. Translated into French by. S. Isaac, B. Stevens, and J. Tremblay. Paris: Cerf, 2008.

Héraclite. *Fragments*. Translated into French by Marcel Conche. Paris: PUF, 1986.

Jünger, Ernst. *Passage de la Ligne*. Translated into French by J. Hervier. Nantes: Le Passeur, 1993.

———. *Sämtliche Werke*, vol. 7. Stuttgart: Klett-Cotta, 2002.

Krell, David Farell. "Heidegger/Nietzsche." In *Cahiers de l'Herne Heidegger*. Paris: Éd. de l'Herne, 1983.

Lingis, Alphonso. "The Will to Power." In *The New Nietzsche: Contemporary Styles of Interpretation,* edited by David B. Allison. New York: Dell, 1977.

Martin, Glen T. "Deconstruction and Breakthrough in Nietzsche and Nâgârjuna." In *Nietzsche and Asian Thought,* edited by G. Parkes. Chicago: University of Chicago Press, 1991.

Murti, T. R. V. *The Central Philosophy of Buddhism: A Study of the Mâdhyamika System.* London: Unwin Paperbacks, 1980.

Nietzsche, Friedrich. *The Anti-Christ, Ecce Homo, Twilight of the Idols and Other Writings.* Translated by Judith Norman. Edited by Aaron Ridley and Judith Norman. Cambridge: Cambridge University Press, 2005.

———. *Beyond Good and Evil: Prelude to a Philosophy of the Future.* Translated by Judith Norman. Edited by Rolf-Peter Horstmann and Judith Norman. Cambridge: Cambridge University Press, 2001.

———. *Daybreak: Thoughts on the Prejudices of Morality.* Translated by R. J. Hollingdale. Edited by Maudemarie Clark and Brian Leiter. Cambridge: Cambridge University Press, 1997.

———. *On The Genealogy of Morality.* Translated by Carol Diethe. Edited by Keith Ansell-Pearson. New York: Cambridge: Cambridge University Press.

———. *Sämtliche Werke: Kritische Studienausgabe.* Edited by Giorgio Colli and Mazzino Montinari. Berlin: Walter de Gruyter, 1980.

———. *Thus Spoke Zarathustra.* In *The Portable Nietzsche.* Translated by Walter Kaufmann. New York: Penguin Books, 1976.

———. *The Will to Power.* Translated by Walter Kaufmann and R. J. Hollingdale. Edited by Walter Kaufmann. New York: Random House, 1967.

Nishida Kitarō. *Logique du lieu et vision religieuse du monde.* Translated into French by Y. Sugimura and S. Carbonnel. Paris: Ed. Osiris, 1999.

Nishitani, Keiji. "Reflections on Two Addresses by Martin Heidegger." In *Heidegger and Asian Thought.* Edited by G. Parkes. Honolulu: University of Hawaii Press, 1987.

———. *Religion and Nothingness.* Translated by Jan Van Bragt. Berkeley: University of California Press, 1983.

———. *The Self-Overcoming of Nihilism.* Translated by G. Parkes and S. Aihara. Albany: State University of New York Press, 1990.

Regvald, Richard. *Heidegger et le problème du neant.* Dordrecht: Springer, 1986.

Ricoeur, Paul. "Sur la phénoménologie." *Revue Esprit,* no. 12 (1953): 821–39.

Saviani, C. "La tradizione filosofica occidentale del pensiero di Nishitani Keiji." In *Comparatismi et filosofia,* edited by M. Donzelli. Napoli: Liguori Editore, 2006.

Stevens, Bernard. *Le Néant évidé.* Louvain-Paris: Éditions Peeters, 2003.

———. *Topologie du néant.* Louvain: Peeters, 2000.

Waldenfels, H. *Absolute Nothingness: Foundations for a Buddhist-Christian Dialogue.* Translated by J. W. Heisig. New York: Paulist Press, 1980.

6 Fink, Reading Nietzsche

On Overcoming Metaphysics

Françoise Dastur

NIETZSCHE'S ROLE IN European thought has been preponderant for at least fifty years. First relegated to literary studies, then, with Hitler's rise to power, to the domain of ideology (by Alfred Baümler, in particular),[1] his work only begins to be considered as philosophy with the publication of Jaspers's monograph in 1936[2] and the lectures Heidegger gave from 1936 to 1940 but did not publish until 1961. The following decade saw the flowering of what may be called "French Nietzscheism" with the publication in 1962 of Deleuze's *Nietzsche et la philosophie*, which, in some sense, had set the pattern. This period is also marked by the decline of phenomenology, which, after the passing of its most eminent representative, Merleau-Ponty, in 1961, was crushed in the structuralist tidal wave that swept through French academe in the 1960s and 1970s. One might have had the impression that the Husserlian maxim of going back to the things themselves, as it was presented in 1901 (that is, tracing the "merely symbolic understanding of words"[3] back to the expressive acts on which they are founded), had given way to the idea expressed by Foucault in a now landmark lecture, that "everything is already interpretation" and that, consequently, "there is nothing absolutely primary to interpret."[4] Foucault was taking up Nietzsche's famous statement, "There is no fact in itself. What happens is a group phenomenon—chosen and collected by the being who interprets them."[5]

Nietzsche's and Husserl's philosophical positions would thus appear to be diametrically opposed. Yet it is on the basis of their respective conceptions of interpretation that the phenomenologist Rudolf Boehm (who attended Foucault's lecture in 1964)[6] attempts to reconcile them in an article published in 1962.[7] He founds his argument on the interpretation Heidegger had given of Nietzsche's doctrine of the will to power in "Nietzsche's Word: 'God Is Dead,'" a text based on his lectures on Nietzsche in 1939–40 and published in 1950 in a collection titled *Holzwege (Off the Beaten Track)*.[8] In this text, as in his courses between 1936 and 1940, Heidegger pointed out that the Nietzschean doctrine of the will to power was not based on a "so-called biologism"[9] but was of metaphysical origin; this meant that it should be considered in relation to modern metaphysics, as the latter had developed in such essential works as Leibniz's *Monadology*, Hegel's *Phenomenology of Spirit*, and Schelling's *Philosophical Inquiries into the Nature of Freedom*.[10] In this regard, Heidegger observed that, within modern metaphysics, it is Leibniz who first thought the volitional essence of the Being of beings, defining the subjectum as *ens percipiens ac appetens*.[11] In his article, Boehm is particularly concerned with the tones, references, and monadological and Leibnizian ramifications that one can find in the posthumous writings published as "The Will to Power." He convincingly demonstrates that Nietzsche had developed from Leibniz's monadological metaphysics a conception of beings as "centres of forces" that exist only to the extent that they unfold and are thus forms of the "will to power," that is, of overarching power, domination, and expansion, and that Husserl, in his research devoted to transcendental phenomenology, had likewise ultimately found it necessary to return to a Leibnizian form of metaphysics. Clearly what had first impressed Husserl was not the Cartesian theory of solipsist subjectivity but the Leibnizian model of monadology, a transcendental theory of the communication of consciousnesses, which prompted him to affirm, as Boehm recalls, that "phenomenology leads to the *Monadology* that Leibniz had brilliantly and insightfully foreseen."[12]

This demonstrates that what Husserl understood by an object's "constitution" by consciousness must not be taken as its "creation"—a word Eugen Fink used, however, in a now famous article—nor as its "unveiling," precisely because being can only be an *interpreted-being*, that is, correlative to the concept we formulate about it and inseparable from our experience of it. In his article, Fink affirms the "productive" nature of transcendental intentionality and states that "the constitutive interpretation of transcendental life identifies it as *creation*."[13] One should note, however, that Fink tempers the importance given such "huge" words[14] by immediately adding:

> No matter how harsh and doctrinal the determination of the essence of constitution as productive creation may appear, it at least counterbalances the receptive character (calling for a being-in-itself) of life based on ontico-mundane (psychological) experience. (We cannot precisely demonstrate here why "constituting" means a relation, neither receptive nor productive, that ontical concepts cannot reach and that only the achievement of constitutive investigations can indicate.)[15]

To speak of constituting therefore refers to the becoming-object of all things, since everything is constituted as object for us in cognition, as a correlate of consciousness. To understand the constitutive act as an interpretation, as Husserl does in the first edition of *Logical Investigations*, in the sense that any perception of the object is reduced to an interpretation of sensory content, is to understand it neither as discovery—for the object does not preexist but is the "result" of interpretation—nor as creation, for constituting does not summon the object ex nihilo but simply gives it meaning. And as Boehm demonstrates, when Husserl broaches the crucial question of the constitution of the perceiving subject itself (in his renowned *Phenomenology of Internal Time Consciousness*), he comes to recognize that at this originary level of constitution there is no preexisting "content" to be "interpreted" but only the flux of an absolute subjectivity, appearing to itself and constituting itself. Such that, with an overlap of the constituted and the constituting, Being in its entirety has thus passed to the sphere of the appearing. There is no object here for one to then interpret.

One finds a similar conception in Nietzsche. Boehm mentions a fragment dating from 1887 in which Nietzsche states, "We have created the concept of a thing" and wonders whether "the only real thing is not the activity that posits things"; he then concludes that "only the subject is demonstrable" and hypothesizes that "there would be only subjects—the 'object' is only a kind of effect of one subject upon another . . . a mode of the *subject*."[16] We do know that Nietzsche criticized the modern notion of the subject, whose Cartesian form assumes a permanent and substantial substrate, and its Kantian the formal identity of "I think." But he has nonetheless allowed for the reality of a subjectivity that appears to meld with the subjectless process of interpretation, as evinced in the following 1887 fragment:

> That things have properties *in themselves*, independent of interpretation and subjectivity, is a completely idle hypothesis: it would presuppose that interpretation and subjectivity are not essential, that a thing abstracted from every relation would still be a thing. Inversely, could the seemingly objective nature of a thing not simply point to a *difference of degree* within the subjective—such that things that change slowly would appear to be "objective," durable, permanent, "in itself"—and objectivity constitute a false category, a false antinomy *within* the subjective?[17]

In light of these texts, Heidegger's association of Nietzsche with the modern metaphysics of subjectivity and his description of Nietzsche as the "last metaphysician" no longer seems as questionable, since, with Nietzsche, we see the disappearance of that vis-à-vis which constitutes the object. Heidegger believes this association with modern metaphysics also characterizes Husserl's phenomenology. After his "transcendental" turn in the years 1905–7, Husserl comes to join the philosophical position of Descartes, Kant, and Fichte, as Heidegger states, for instance, in his "Letter to Richardson" in 1962.[18] While Boehm may well be in line with such an interpretation,[19] at least in part, it is rather significant that Fink—one of the major figures in the "phenomenological movement," and the closest to Heidegger—is not entirely in agreement. At the end of *Nietzsche's Philosophy*, Fink declares that Heidegger's interpretation, which consists of "[seeing] in the will to power Nietzsche's basic ontological formula" and of reading it as the "extreme position of contemporary subjective metaphysics," remains "partial."[20] In Fink's view, far from being the ultimate figure of Western metaphysics, Nietzsche, before Husserl, "heralds" a new "ontological experience."[21]

We know that Fink had been Husserl's private assistant in the last ten years of his life, from 1928 to 1938, a time during which he had wholly dedicated himself to the work of phenomenology's founder. Under Husserl's supervision, he drafted new versions of the lectures given in 1929, the *Cartesian Meditations*, even adding a lengthy *Sixth Meditation*, which remained in project form until it was published in 1988 along with re-editions of the previous Meditations. More than an assistant, then, Fink had coauthored Husserl's later work, as evinced in Husserl's preface to an article Fink wrote titled "Husserl's Phenomenological Philosophy and Contemporary Criticisms," published in the *Kant-Studien* in 1933; Husserl declares, "I am happy to say that there is no sentence in this text that I cannot fully accept as expressing my own conviction."[22] Yet in tones redolent of Heidegger more than Husserl, Fink states in this article that "while dogmatic metaphysics may posit its fundamental driving problem as a question about the origin of *beings*, phenomenology enquires into the origin of the *world*."[23] Indeed he begins to distance himself from Husserl, as evinced in Dorion Cairns's *Conversations with Husserl and Fink*, which took place in 1931 and 1932 and in which he suggests that Husserlian phenomenology was too exclusively focused on the question of the object.[24] He expresses the same criticism in his last lectures on Husserl nearly forty years later, where he says, "For us, the questions that remain open in Husserl's phenomenology point to the problem of the world," while nonetheless recognizing in him "this fatal inclination of the human mind to try to think Being from beings."[25] In this regard, he said of phenomenological reduction that "one cannot set aside the irritating problematic of the concept of Being by shifting the focus of one's thought back from things in the world to a subject for the world."[26]

For in this period, Fink is also under the influence of Heidegger, whose courses he attended as soon as Heidegger returned to Freiburg, where he took up the position left vacant when Husserl retired in 1928. Fink was likely most influenced by the lecture Heidegger gave on *The Fundamental Concepts of Metaphysics* in the 1929–30 winter semester, for that course, which Heidegger dedicated to him upon his death on July 26, 1975,[27] essentially deals with the question of the world, a question that would become the connecting thread in all his later work. In a footnote concerning his 1949 course plan titled "World and Finitude," which is reprinted with an afterword by Franz-Anton Schwarz (who edited the 1966 course text that bears the same title), Fink explained that this course—the first that he would devote to presenting the problem of the world—"will bring to light the problem that remains concealed in Heidegger's works."[28] Indeed rather than merely situate himself in the Heideggerian field, he develops a line of inquiry all his own, what he calls "cosmological difference,"[29] in contrast to and in continuity with Heidegger's ontological difference. Yet the cosmological question is inseparable from that of play, as evinced in the first course Heidegger gave on his return to Freiburg in 1928 and that we know Fink attended.[30] In §36 of this course,

titled "The World as 'Play of Life,'" Heidegger, basing his thought on Kant's definition of the world as "game of life" in *Anthropology*, states that "the world is the name
given to the game played by transcendence,"[31] for transcendence—that is, being in the
world—"is always, in terms of transcendental play, a configuration of the world."[32] The
word *play*, he explains, must not be understood in its usual sense, as a way of relating
to beings, but as that which opens up a space within which we may encounter beings.[33]
Here we see a theme that he develops the following year in his course on *The Fundamental Concepts of Metaphysics*, where man is defined in contrast to the animal, as
"world-forming." This was undoubtedly a passage of particular importance to Fink,
in whose personal notes, as early as 1934, one finds "metaphysics of play" topping a list
of themes to explore.[34] It is in Nietzsche, whom he read beginning at an early age, that
he sees the great thinker of play; he acknowledged as much in his conversations with
one of Husserl's former assistants, Ludwig Landgrebe in 1936 and, in 1946, with Robert
Heiss, dean of philosophy at Freiburg and the reporter for Fink's thesis on the *Sixth
Meditation*, which he was defending that year.[35]

The concept of play opens up the ontological dimension proper, a dimension that
one can reach only through enthusiasm, described by Heidegger, at the end of his 1929–
30 course, as the "breath of all philosophizing" and attested to by the last of the great
philosophers, Nietzsche, in Zarathustra's *Drunken Song*, where he says, "The world is
deep, deeper than day can comprehend."[36] Significantly, one of Fink's initial lectures,
in Leuven in 1940, bore on the "essence of enthusiasm," where enthusiasm is defined
as the means by which human beings go beyond themselves toward the nonhuman. In
his notes of 1937, he defined enthusiasm more precisely still as that which constitutes
the very essence of play.[37] But it is in the lecture he gave in Argentina in 1949, "Zum
Problem der ontologischen Erfahrung" (On the problem of ontological experience),
that he clearly explains that it is through what he calls "ontological reflection"—not to
be confused with the self-reflection of the knowing subject—that the human being is
torn away from that "sleep" which is his natural and obligatory attitude and is sum-
moned to take his own condition as "mediator" seriously, that condition of the human
being who is at once a finite being among finite things and one in whose thoughts
Being itself comes to be manifest.[38] Being is indeed not "given" in the sense that things
are given, nor can it be "made"; it can only be the result of a "project" of thought, an
originary projection that Heidegger said was "the fundamental structure of world-for-
mation."[39] Which prompts Fink to again point out that "the creative nature of thought
that conceives of being does not coincide with the opposition between 'making' and
'finding,'"[40] thus taking up, on an ontological level, the definition he had given in 1933
to Husserlian constitution.

In his 1955 lecture on *Fundamental Phenomena of the Human Dasein*, an essay
of philosophical anthropology from a cosmological point of view, Fink elaborated
at length on the idea that play, along with work, the struggle for domination, love,
and death, were distinct characteristics of man's humanity.[41] He put forward the idea

that these "fundamental phenomena" determined corresponding "ontological models" that informed man's understanding of nonhuman things, for "human existence's relationship with the world closely binds our finite understanding of ourselves with our understanding of beings different from us, closely binds anthropology with ontology."[42] Yet it raises the question as to which of these phenomena is the most fundamental characteristic of this "world-relation," this *Weltverhältnis* that we are—with the exception of death, which one might say is its most privative form. In Fink's view, play, more than work, struggle, or love, provides the "operative model" most conducive to revealing the mundanity of the world; the other characteristics are no less originary than play, from an existential point of view, precisely because, in play, the human being deals not with another, equally real being but with the unreal, such that play is thus always more than mere intramundane behavior. Gadamer, that other "disciple" of Heidegger's, has shown that, as an ontic phenomenon, play has an existence independent of the consciousness of those playing, and it isn't the players who are the subjects of the game: it is play itself that becomes manifest through the players and thus gains representation.[43] Gadamer lays great emphasis on the view that the primary meaning of play is a mean, in the sense that one grammatically defines the mean voice as neither passive nor active.[44] It is this mean sense that attests to the primacy of play in relation to the consciousness of the player, who is absorbed by the game and lacks the initiative. "Human play gives rise to an ekstasis of the Dasein toward the world," says Fink in *Play as Symbol of the World* (*Spiel als Weltsymbol*),[45] which means that in playing intramundane games, the human Dasein has always already to do with something more than at the mere ontic level of finite things. He is always already open to nonbeing, such that the exclusively human sphere can no longer withdraw into itself, as is still the case in work, which opposes man to matter, or in struggle and love, which confront him with his alter ego. It is then indeed the unreality of play that gives us access to the ontological infiniteness of the world, for in the appearance of the game, everything is in some sense manifest within itself, and the world is reflected, so to speak, in a particular setting of the intramundane.[46] The imaginary "scenery" of play—which is at once more and less than sensory reality (more from the ontological point of view precisely because it is less from the ontic)—thus has the distinction of operating on this "breach" in the fabric of the ultramundane. This "window onto the absolute," which Fink, citing Hegel, had already mentioned in his 1929 dissertation on the phenomenology of the nonreal, *Representation and Image* (*Vergegenwärtigung und Bild*),[47] is a breach and window through which an ontic surrogacy of the ontological, a finite image of the infinite, a symbolism of the world become possible.[48]

Two of Fink's most important works, *Spiel als Weltsymbol* and *Nietzsches Philosophie*, appeared the same year, in 1960. The first, an essay on the interpretation of play through philosophy, metaphysics, and mythology, ends with an emphasis on what Fink calls the "mundanity of play." For this play, as opposed to prior interpretations, can only be understood as a relation to the world, that is, to that which is not itself a being, such that a theory of the world, a cosmology, can then no longer be considered part of ontology. At the same time, though, Fink admits that such a "cosmological" thought has yet to be achieved and that it requires that metaphysical tradition, so hostile to play, be brought to its conclusion. The last word is given to Nietzsche's Zarathustra, who, in the dithyrambic "Seven Seals" chapter, celebrates the state of one who, while playing, stands within the boundless, experiences the lightness of a bird that knows neither high nor low.[49] Thus it is this conception of play as symbol of the world, of which he later says that it runs "a subterranean course through philosophy, from Heraclitus to Nietzsche,"[50] that he will strive to articulate in his reading of Nietzsche's work.

A thorough analysis of this book, in which Fink, picking up on the classes he devoted to Nietzsche in the late 1940s,[51] undertakes a chronological survey of Nietzsche's work from the writings of his youth to his posthumous publications, lies outside the scope of this essay. One may simply observe that the chapter devoted to *Thus Spoke Zarathustra*, evocatively titled "The Annunciation," is central to the work, for it begins with the statement that this text opens the way to "the third, definite phase of Nietzsche's philosophy," which "introduces the noon of his thinking," establishing a language all his own to express his particular thoughts.[52] The following chapter, "The Destruction of the Western Tradition," covering Nietzsche's last and posthumous works, begins with the following observation: "Nietzsche did not venture beyond Zarathustra."[53] Nietzsche had himself said of *Ecce Homo* that it constituted "the yes-saying aspect of his task," and according to Fink, subsequent works, including the posthumous work titled "The Will to Power," are its destructive aspects, in which Nietzsche battles traditional notions of religion, morality, and philosophy with a vehemence whose psychological nature remains highly problematic.[54] Fink believes Nietzsche's main objective is indeed "the psychological destruction of metaphysics,"[55] as is already emphatically the case in his early text of the *Aufklärung* period, *Human, All-Too-Human*. But the psychological critique of idealism remains superficial because it questions metaphysical truths while failing to analyze them from a philosophical point of view, which prompts Fink to declare that in works of his later period, such as *Beyond Good and Evil*, "Nietzsche's project is mainly rhetorical."[56]

Fink states early on that "no other philosopher conceals his philosophy behind so much sophistry," such that one has difficulty making out the philosopher in him, "the genuine Nietzsche" nonetheless.[57] Fink does not clearly define what he means by "sophistry" here, but one may say that the term refers to the Protagorean theory of man as the measure of all things; subjectivism, anthropologism, and psychologism may be considered its modern analogues.[58] He states that Nietzsche's basic thesis is that "the so-called 'super-human' . . . is in truth only an all-too-human illusion."[59] But it is precisely because his "anthropological approach" is to understand Pre-Socratic thinkers as personalities that he "remained infinitely distant from the Pre-Socratics."[60] His sophistry does not consist in the rhetorical art of debate, but in what Fink calls an "existential sophistry" that sees in ideas only the vital symptoms and signs by which a way of existing is expressed.[61] His books are written in a confessional style, for Nietzsche, ever the seducer, wishes to draw the reader toward himself. Fink describes his way of speaking of himself as "almost unbearable" and his style as replete with "affectation . . . seduction and magic," similar in this respect to Wagnerian music; Fink recognizes, however, that one finds much "brilliance" in Nietzsche's thought when it approaches the poetic.[62]

He concludes that Nietzsche, Janus-like, must be considered "two-headed: he is a philosopher and a sophist."[63] But he adds that while "Nietzsche's project is mainly sophistic . . . its considerable quality makes it more dangerous,"[64] for the sophistry mingles indistinctly with the philosophy. Indeed Fink convincingly argues that Nietzsche considered man from two points of view: as one who must be freed of his subjugation to transcendent ideals of morality, religion, and metaphysics, stripped down to his vital instincts, to a purely animal level—and this is the sophistic view; and as one who has become a stranger to himself, forgetting that he is the source of those very ideals and that he was thus fully capable of going beyond himself, thus lending real grandeur to human existence—and that is the philosophical view of man.[65] Nietzsche is equally ambiguous with respect to the will to power: on the one hand, he conceives it as an ontological model and understands it as the fundamental inclination of any finite being—in this sense, everything is will to power, the overman's tragic atheism as much as Christian moralism; on the other, he gives it a merely ontic meaning and deems strength to lie in recognizing the will to power and weakness in turning away from it.[66] Thus we can either say that all moralities are configurations of power or that there are moralities of power and moralities of powerlessness.[67] This ambiguity dominates all Nietzsche's writings after *Zarathustra*. One must therefore return to this essential work, even if it falls short of Nietzsche's poetical ambitions, laden as it is with stylistic effects, wordplay, and purple prose, in a style sometimes verging on bad taste and insufferably imitative of the Bible. But one also finds "sections of impeccable beauty" therein and insights that strike us like a flash of lightning, like a revelation, for this work broaches the question of "an emerging new conception of the cosmos."[68]

The crux and pinnacle of this work, in Fink's view, is the third part, the essential idea of which is a "new and secret knowledge of the essence of time," which compels one to rethink the relationship between time and the will to power.[69] In the will to power, he conceives *Wesen* in its verbal sense as beings, following the later Heidegger's understanding of the term, not in its nominal sense as essence or quiddity, nor as an expression of permanence or timeless *eidos*, but in the old sense of the verb *wesen*, as the temporal deployment of the being of a thing.[70] The will to power, on which is founded the possibility of the overman (anchored as well in the death of God), is itself founded on the passage of time. Nietzsche thus goes from thinking about intramundane being (man and God) to thinking about the "embracing and circumscribing world"; he reaches back to the "totality of the cosmos" by way of thinking about the eternal return of the same, an indication that he is breaking away from metaphysical tradition.[71] For the idea of the eternal return negates the opposition between past and future, and time loses its clear direction. Eternity and temporality are therefore not two different things, as in the metaphysical tradition, but one and the same. What this means for Fink is that Nietzsche managed to see finite things in light of that infinite that is the world, but in so doing, he reaches the limits of the expressible, as evinced in "his inability to develop the doctrine of the eternal return conceptually," which "is no individual shortcoming but that of the philosophical tradition to which Nietzsche is bound."[72] One discovers here the idea that Nietzsche, like Janus, is a twin-faced figure, opposing metaphysical tradition but remaining bound to it in his opposition: the reversal of a metaphysical proposition remains a metaphysical proposition, as Heidegger pointed out regarding Sartre.[73] Nietzsche, who seeks to grasp the world by bounding *over* all things, is yet "trapped" in the intramundane that he wants to overcome, for here the world is not seen in itself but from things.[74]

Fink situates the true apex of the work in the chapter titled "On the Great Longing," for this great *Sehnsucht*, this nostalgic yearning, is what induces "human exposure to space and time or his openness to the world," and the overman "is nothing but the human being in the mode of the great yearning."[75] The eternal return is not in itself ultimate, then, for Dionysus is "the answer to the great human yearning," and though Nietzsche does not mention him here, he is indeed "Nietzsche's last word."[76] What is announced in this work and, in accord with the biblical connotation of the word *annunciation,* what it promises in the dancing song and in the final chapter on "the seven seals" is "the advent of Dionysius rather than his actual presence," the arrival of this "formless creator" who causes the appearance and disappearance of all beings, governs all change, and is none other than the very play of the world itself.[77]

What Fink discovers in Nietzsche, then, is what he calls the "cosmological difference," as given in Nietzsche's very last publications and posthumous works. Here indeed is where Nietzsche manages to develop the Apollo-Dionysus duality of the "metaphysics of the artist" discussed in his first book, *The Birth of Tragedy*, by combining both faces of Janus—the will to power and the eternal return—in his conception of Dionysus, the name he gives to Being, "creative and destructive being itself."[78] Still fragmentary in his last work, *Ecce Homo*, is the "hesitant revelation of a new God," not the one defined by metaphysics as *summun ens* but "the inconceivable God of being and of the existing cosmos. It is 'open like the heavens' in whose light all things appear and it is immediate like the sealed earth to whom all created being returns."[79] It is with this "holiness of being itself" that Nietzsche opposes the crucified Christian, which locates saintly being beyond the world, for "only when we succeed to understand Dionysos as the God of play can the divine play of the cosmos in the realm between heaven and earth be understood profoundly."[80]

We can now address the fundamental question as to whether Nietzsche truly managed to overcome metaphysics. The answer given by Fink consists in showing that the Nietzschean figure remains ambiguous and that his relationship with metaphysics is at once one of "captivity" and of "liberation." On the one hand, it proves Heidegger right: Nietzsche is simply overturning the being-becoming opposition,[81] and one may suppose that in the fourfold structure of his investigation (will to power, eternal return, death of God, overman) he remains dependent on the fourfold problematic of metaphysics(*ens, unum, bonum, verum*) as it refers to questions of beings as such, to the totality of beings, to the differentiation of Being-appearance, and to the relationship between Being and truth.[82] One may then conclude:

> Nietzsche's questions correspond to the structure of western metaphysics. He thinks the beingness of being as the will to power, being in its entirety as the eternal return of the same, the highest being on the one hand negatively as the death of God and then again positively as the Apollonian-Dionysian play which creates all things as products of appearance like an artist and the work of art. Finally he grasps the truth of all this in so far as it is human through the overman.[83]

Nevertheless it remains to be seen whether Nietzsche is as completely dependent on metaphysics as Heidegger suggests, or if he doesn't overcome it in some way. For Fink, the Heideggerian interpretation of Nietzsche derives from Heidegger's conception of metaphysics in modern times; it therefore remains closed to indications of a postmetaphysical cosmological philosophy in Nietzsche's work. In the conclusion to his book, Fink states, "Where Nietzsche conceives being and becoming as play he no longer remains within the boundaries of metaphysics."[84] The will to power would thus have another aspect than the one through which, by way of representational thought, an objectification of beings takes place, a will to power having a creative Apollonian character: "The halcyon aspect of the vision of the overman refers to the player not to the violent aggressor or the technical giant."[85] To this underlying message of peace and tranquility, symbolized by the mythic Greek bird Halcyon, Heidegger had remained deaf.

Yet one may also wonder if Fink does not read this message from the standpoint of his own problematic, that of cosmological thought, which he largely developed on the basis of Husserl's transcendental phenomenology, Heideggerian "ontology," and Nietzschean "intuitions" and "visions." To interpret a work or a thought, must we not first project a horizon of comprehension that is itself necessarily partial and finite? In a famous 1957 text that he devoted to "operative concepts in Husserl's phenomenology" (*Operative Begriffe in Husserl's phänomenologie*), Fink concluded with the statement, "Shading is an essential trait of finite philosophizing. The more originary the force that brings to light, the deeper the shadows in its fundamental thought. Only God knows without shadow."[86] And in his last lecture on Husserl, in 1971, he reaffirmed that "one who reveals so many things, also uncovers abysses," in which he sees "moving evidence of the 'human condition,'" which consists in "remaining perplexed before the riddle of Being, exposed to the maze of the world, and transfixed by our finitude."[87] No thinker can leap over his shadow, for human existence is never fully illuminated; at the very noon of our thought, at that hour of the smallest shadow that Nietzsche sang of, life can never escape its primary attachment, that Earth-bound relationship, that opacity that Plato and Husserl both termed *doxa*, belief or opinion, from which thought, like a bird, may well rise, but only for a moment.

Notes

This essay was translated by Ron Ross.

1. Bäumler, "Nietzsche und der National-Sozialismus."
2. Jaspers, *Nietzsche*.
3. Husserl, *Logical Investigations*, vol. 2, pt. 1, §2, 168.
4. Foucault, "Nietzsche, Freud, Marx," 189; English translation: "Nietzsche, Freud, Marx," 64.
5. Nietzsche, *Kritische Studienausgabe*, 12, 1 [115], 38 (hereafter KSA). [All quotations from KSA 12 are translated by the editors.]
6. Rudolf Boehm was the first one to ask a question in the discussion following Foucault's lecture. Cf. Foucault, "Nietzsche, Freud, Marx," 193.
7. Boehm, "Deux points de vue : Husserl et Nietzsche," 167–81. We refer to the author's own German translation, "Husserl und Nietzsche," 217–36. See English translation in this volume, chapter 1 [insert pages later].
8. Heidegger, *Holzwege*, 193–247; *Off the Beaten Track*, 157–99.
9. Heidegger, "Nietzsches angeblicher Biologismus," 517 ff. [Translated by the editors.]
10. Heidegger, *Holzwege*, 233; *Off the Beaten Track*, 189. Boehm, *Vom Geschichtspunkt der Phänomenologie I*, 229.
11. Heidegger, *Holzwege*, 226; *Off the Beaten Track*, 183.
12. Boehm, "Husserl und Nietzsche," 234. On this topic, see Dastur, "Réduction et intersubjectivité," 83–99.
13. Fink, "Die Phänomenologische Philosophie Edmund Husserls," in *Studien zur Phänomenologie 1930–1939*, 143. [Except for quotations from *Nietzsches Philosophie*, all quotations from Fink have been translated by the editors.]
14. In Paul Ricoeur's judgment, who, in the preface to his French translation of the *Ideen I* (xxx), recalls that these words had been countersigned by Husserl.
15. Fink, "Die Phänomenologische Philosophie Edmund Husserls," 143.
16. KSA 12, 9 [106], 396.
17. KSA 12, 9 [40], 353.
18. Heidegger, "Letter to Richardson," viii.
19. Cf. Boehm, "Husserl und Nietzsche," 229 [cross-references to be inserted later Boehm §18], where Boehm expresses his "conviction" that one must "adhere" to the Heideggerian theory that the theory of the Will to Power is a metaphysical one.
20. Fink, *Nietzsches Philosophie*, 178; *Nietzsche's Philosophy*, 162.
21. Fink, *Nähe und Distanz*, 128.
22. Fink, *Studien zur Phänomenologie 1930–1939*, vol. 8.
23. Fink, "Die phänomenologische Philosophie Edmund Husserls," 102.
24. Cairns, *Conversations with Husserl and Fink*, especially 80, 98.
25. Fink, "Bewusstseinanalytik und Weltproblem," in *Nähe und Distanz*, 297–98.
26. Fink, "Reflexionen zu Husserls Phänomenologischer Reduktion (1971)," in *Nähe und Distanz*, 320.
27. Cf. Heidegger, *Die Grundbegriffe der Metaphysik*, v; *The Fundamental Concepts of Metaphysics*, 5. There one finds Heidegger's dedication, "In memory of Eugen Fink," accompanied by these words: "He listened to this lecture course with thoughtful reticence, and in so doing, experienced something unthought of his own that determined his path."

28. Fink, *Welt und Endlichkeit*, 213, 214.

29. Ibid., 19: "I call the distinction between the world and inter-mundane beings the cosmological difference."

30. See Bruzina, *Edmund Husserl and Eugen Fink*, 134.

31. Heidegger, *Einleitung in die Philosophie*, 312 (hereafter GA 27).

32. GA 27, 314.

33. GA 27, 316.

34. Bruzina, *Edmund Husserl and Eugen Fink*, 67.

35. Ibid., 314, 532.

36. Heidegger, *Die Grundbegriffe der Metaphysik*, 531–32; *The Fundamental Concepts of Metaphysics*, 366.

37. Bruzina, *Edmund Husserl and Eugen Fink*, 462.

38. Fink, *Nähe und Distanz*, 137–38.

39. Heidegger, *Die Grundbegriffe der Metaphysik*, 526–27; *The Fundamental Concepts of Metaphysics*, 362.

40. Fink, *Nähe und Distanz*, 136.

41. Cf. Fink, *Grundphänomen des menschlichen Daseins*, 445: "Man, in his quality as man, is distinguished by the fact that he is the only being in the universe who, open to death, exists in work, play, love, and the struggle for domination. Neither God, nor the animal take part in that."

42. Ibid., 450.

43. Gadamer, *Wahrheit und Methode*, 108; *Truth and Method*, 92.

44. Gadamer, *Wahrheit und Methode*, 109; *Truth and Method*, 93–94. Recall that the mean expresses the subject's interest in the action or his part in it, and thus the mean voice is the voice of participation.

45. Fink, *Spiel als Weltsymbol*, 231.

46. Ibid., 232.

47. Fink, *Studien zur Phänomenologie*, 18.

48. Fink, *Spiel als Weltsymbol*, 234.

49. Ibid., 242.

50. Cf. Fink, "Weltbezug und Seinsverständnis" ["World-Relation and Understanding of Being," lecture given in 1968—Eds.], in *Nähe und Distanz*, 275.

51. In a letter dated 1875, Jan Patočka, a friend of Fink's, reminds him of having read excerpts of his lectures on Nietzsche in 1947. Cf. Fink and Patočka, *Briefe und Dokumente 1933–1977*, 123.

52. Fink, *Nietzsches Philosophie*, 59–60; *Nietzsche's Philosophy*, 51.

53. Fink, *Nietzsches Philosophie*, 119; *Nietzsche's Philosophy*, 107.

54. Fink, *Nietzsches Philosophie*, 119–20; *Nietzsche's Philosophy*, 107.

55. Fink, *Nietzsches Philosophie*, 47; *Nietzsche's Philosophy*, 38.

56. Fink, *Nietzsches Philosophie*, 120; *Nietzsche's Philosophy*, 108. In the English translation, Fink's reference to sophistry proper is more explicit in the subsequent passage: "His sophistry, that is his psychological analysis, is based on a psychological transformation of all ontological questions into questions of value" (108).

57. Fink, *Nietzsches Philosophie*, 10; *Nietzsche's Philosophy*, 3.

58. This, however, is not the opinion of Heidegger, who stated that "sophism is only possible on the basis of sophia, i.e., on the basis of the Greek interpretation of being as presence" and that "every subjectivism is impossible within Greek Sophism since man can never, here, become subiectum," such that Protagoras's man as measure must not be considered an isolated ego, but as one who "[restrains] his apprehension to the sphere of unconcealment of what presences at his time" (Heidegger, *Holzwege*, 97–98; *Off the Beaten Track*, 80–83).

59. Fink, *Nietzsches Philosophie*, 46; *Nietzsche's Philosophy*, 38.

60. Fink, *Nietzsches Philosophie*, 43; *Nietzsche's Philosophy*, 35.
61. Fink, *Nietzsches Philosophie*, 44; *Nietzsche's Philosophy*, 36.
62. Fink, *Nietzsches Philosophie* 10–11; *Nietzsche's Philosophy*, 4.
63. Fink, *Nietzsches Philosophie*, 43; *Nietzsche's Philosophy*, 35.
64. Fink, *Nietzsches Philosophie*, 120; *Nietzsche's Philosophy*, 108. [Translation modified.—Eds.]
65. Fink, *Nietzsches Philosophie*, 55–56; *Nietzsche's Philosophy*, 46–47.
66. Fink, *Nietzsches Philosophie*, 122; *Nietzsche's Philosophy*, 90–91.
67. Fink, *Nietzsches Philosophie*, 128; *Nietzsche's Philosophy*, 115–16.
68. Fink, *Nietzsches Philosophie*, 62–63; *Nietzsche's Philosophy*, 53–54.
69. Fink, *Nietzsches Philosophie*, 82; *Nietzsche's Philosophy*, 72.
70. Heidegger, "The Question Concerning Technology," 30–31; Heidegger, "Science and Reflection," 156. Heidegger recalls that *wesen* is the same word as *währen*, "to endure, to remain."
71. Fink, *Nietzsches Philosophie*, 83–84; *Nietzsche's Philosophy*, 74.
72. Fink, *Nietzsches Philosophie*, 91–92; *Nietzsche's Philosophy*, 72.
73. Cf. Heidegger, "Brief über den 'Humanismus,'" in *Wegmarken*, 159; "Letter on 'Humanism,'" in *Pathmarks*, 250.
74. Fink, *Nietzsches Philosophie*, 92; *Nietzsche's Philosophy*, 81.
75. Fink, *Nietzsches Philosophie*, 104, 106; *Nietzsche's Philosophy*, 92, 94.
76. Fink, *Nietzsches Philosophie*, 108; *Nietzsche's Philosophy*, 96.
77. Fink, *Nietzsches Philosophie*, 108; *Nietzsche's Philosophy*, 96–97. [Translation modified.—Eds.]
78. Fink, *Nietzsches Philosophie*, 173; *Nietzsche's Philosophy*, 157–58.
79. Fink, *Nietzsches Philosophie*, 176; *Nietzsche's Philosophy*, 160. "Manifest as the sky" is a line from one of Hölderlin's last poems, "In lieblicher Bläue" ("In Lovely Blue"), which also heralds an entirely new conception of the divine.
80. Fink, *Nietzsches Philosophie*, 176; *Nietzsche's Philosophy*, 160.
81. Fink, *Nietzsches Philosophie*, 140, 182; *Nietzsche's Philosophy* 126, 165.
82. Fink, *Nietzsches Philosophie*, 183–84; *Nietzsche's Philosophy*, 165–67.
83. Fink, *Nietzsches Philosophie*, 184; *Nietzsche's Philosophy*, 169.
84. Fink, *Nietzsches Philosophie*, 188; *Nietzsche's Philosophy*, 172.
85. Fink, *Nietzsches Philosophie*, 188; *Nietzsche's Philosophy*, 172.
86. Fink, *Nähe und Distanz*, 203.
87. Ibid., 322.

Bibliography

Bäumler, Alfred. "Nietzsche und der National-Sozialismus" (1934). In *Studien zur deutschen Geistesgeschichte*. Berlin: Jünken & Dünnhaupt, 1937.
Boehm, Rudolf. "Deux points de vue: Husserl et Nietzsche." *Archivio di Filosofia* 3 (1962): 167–81.
———. *Vom Gesichtspunkt der Phänomenologie I: Husserl-Studien*. Den Haag: Nijhoff, 1968.
Bruzina, Ronald. *Edmund Husserl and Eugen Fink: Beginnings and Ends of Phenomenology 1928–1938*. New Haven: Yale University Press, 2004.
Cairns, Dorion. *Conversations with Husserl and Fink*. Dordrecht: Kluwer, 1976.
Dastur, Françoise. "Réduction et Intersubjectivité." In *La phénoménologie en questions*. Paris: Vrin, 2004.
Fink, Eugen. *Grundphänomen des menschlichen Daseins*. Freiburg: Alber, 1979.
———. *Nähe und Distanz*. Freiburg: Alber, 1976.
———.*Nietzsche's Philosophy*. Translated by Goetz Richter. London: Continuum, 2003.
———. *Nietzsches Philosophie*. Stuttgart: Kohlhammer, 1960.

———. *Spiel als Weltsymbol.* Stuttgart: Kohlhammer, 1960.

———. *Studien zur Phänomenologie 1930–1939.* Den Haag: Nijhoff, 1966.

———. *Welt und Endlichkeit.* Würzburg: Königshausen & Neumann, 1990.

Fink, Eugen, and Jan Patočka. *Briefe und Dokumente 1933–1977.* Freiburg: Alber, 1999.

Foucault, Michel. "Nietzsche, Freud, Marx." Intervention au Colloque de Royaumont de 1964. In *Nietzsche,* Cahiers de Royaumont Philosophie no. VI. Paris: Editions de Minuit, 1967.

———. "Nietzsche, Freud, Marx." Translated by Alan D. Schrift. In *Transforming the Hermeneutic Context: From Nietzsche to Nancy,* edited by Gayle L. Ormiston and Alan D. Schrift. Albany: State University of New York Press, 1990.

Franck, Didier. *De la phénoménologie.* Paris: Editions de Minuit, 1974.

Gadamer, Hans-Georg. *Truth and Method.* Translated by Joel Weinsheimer and Donald G. Marshall. New York: Crossroad, 1985.

———. *Vérité et methode.* Translated by P. Fruchon, J. Grondin, and G. Merlio. Paris: Seuil, 1996.

———. *Wahrheit und Methode.* Tübingen: Mohr (Siebeck), 1990.

Heidegger, Martin. *Les concepts fondamentaux de la métaphysique.* Translated by D. Panis. Paris: Gallimard, 1992.

———. *Einleitung in die Philosophie. Gesamtausgabe* vol. 27. Frankfurt am Main: Vittorio Klostermann, 1996.

———. *The Fundamental Concepts of Metaphysics: World, Finitude, Solitude.* Translated by William McNeill and Nicholas Walker. Bloomington: Indiana University Press, 1995.

———. *Die Grundbegriffe der Metaphysik. Gesamtausgabe* vols. 29/30. Frankfurt am Main: Klostermann, 1983.

———. *Holzwege.* Frankfurt am Main: Klostermann, 1950.

———. "Letter to Richardson." In William J. Richardson, *Heidegger: Through Phenomenology to Thought.* New York: Fordham University Press, 2003.

———. *Nietzsche I.* Pfullingen: Neske, 1961.

———. *Off the Beaten Track.* Translated and edited by Julian Young and Kenneth Haynes. Cambridge: Cambridge University Press, 2002.

———. *Pathmarks.* Translated by Frank A. Capuzzi. Edited by William McNeill. Cambridge: Cambridge University Press, 1998.

———. "The Question Concerning Technology" and "Science and Reflection." In *The Question Concerning Technology and Other Essays.* Translated by William Lovitt. New York: Garland, 1977.

———. *Questions IV.* Translated by J. Lauxerois and C. Roëls. Paris: Gallimard, 1976.

———. *Wegmarken. Gesamtausgabe* vol. 9. Frankfurt am Main: Vittorio Klostermann, 1967.

———. *Zur Sache des Denkens (1962–64). Gesamtausgabe* vol. 14. Frankfurt am Main: Klostermann, 2007.

Husserl, Edmund. *Logical Investigations.* Translated by J. N. Findlay. London: Routledge, 2001.

Jaspers, Karl. *Nietzsche: Einführung in das Verständnis seines Philosophierens.* Berlin: 1936.

Nietzsche, Friedrich. *Kritische Studienausgabe.* Edited by Giorgio Colli and Mazzino Montinari. Berlin: de Gruyter, 1980.

Ricoeur, Paul. *Préface aux Ideen I.* In *Idées directrices pour une phénoménologie.* Paris: Gallimard, 1950.

PART II

POWER AND EXPRESSION

7 Nietzsche's Performative Phenomenology

Philology and Music

Babette Babich

Phenomenological Kinds

Like the manifold significations of Being, phenomenology can be and has been articulated in several ways. To say this is also to underscore that when we choose for one expression of phenomenology, even, say, the most canonic expression, such as Husserl's, we also tend to choose *against* other approaches. This can go so far as to exclude the late in favor of the early Husserl; in other instances this may include favoring analytic readings and opposing classically continental readings of Husserl's phenomenology and can entail excluding Heidegger's or Sartre's or Merleau-Ponty's or Günther Anders' or others' approaches to phenomenology.[1] To the extent that a number of distinctive contributions may be argued as constituting the phenomenological orientations of a range of thinkers, including Theodor Adorno, Michel de Certeau, Michel Henry, Pierre Bourdieu, Jean Baudrillard, and indeed Georges Bataille, as well as and by his own assertion, Jacques Derrida,[2] the problem of articulating the *meaning of phenomenology* is in every sense a multifarious affair. Nor, as we shall see, is this observation new.

As corollary, any definition of phenomenology situates the text in line with one or another approach: a definition—to vary Heidegger, who is for his part already varying Nietzsche—is already an interpretation.[3] Tell me what you think of phenomenology, and I will tell you who you are.[4]

Phenomenology arguably begins with Parmenides (patent if one reads Parmenides as Heidegger does in his own *Introduction to Metaphysics*) as a tradition emphasizing the distinction between appearance and reality, a noetic distinction Hume insists upon as much as Kant, a distinction Nietzsche never relinquished, as the neo-Kantian Nietzsche scholars Abel Rey, Hans Vaihinger, and Walter del Negro recognized long ago. But although dating back to the Greeks and although a tradition that often includes the term as such throughout philosophy, especially in the nineteenth century, phenomenology tends to be used today with specific reference not to Hume or Kant or Hegel but to Husserl—who, very relevantly, did not favor the historical contextualizing of his phenomenology.

For Descartes and the entire Enlightenment order of philosophizing about cognition and perception (Locke, Berkeley, Hume), what the mind knows is the mind. Thus thought must be submitted to logical analysis to gain any sure knowledge of thought. This cognitive division of labor, however, installs unbridgeable chasms between mind and world, thought and object. Husserl's account of intentionality, following Aristotle and Franz Brentano, sidesteps such a separation: "The intentional object of a presentation is the same as its actual object."[5] What is known by any intentional act is the very thing qua intended, that is, the intentional object, that is, the noematic correlate. This is the direction of Husserl's classic cry, *zu den Sachen selbst—to the things themselves.*

What is at stake is the locus and disposition of phenomenological judgment. Thus Husserl proposes, contra Descartes, a new method. The new method is the phenomenological method of *epochē*: suspending or holding in abeyance what Husserl called the "natural attitude," an approach different from the Cartesian project of doubt in that Husserl's more properly Kantian aim was to be the secure knowledge not of things (mental or material) but of the conditions for the possibility of thought as such. This critique does not subvert either Kant or Hume but, and in accord with their original critical intentions, provides a new foundation for the consummation of philosophic insight. By means of the *epochē*, or phenomenological reduction, as a kind of Husserlian "critique," we are able to engage in properly philosophical (and not merely linguistic or scientific) reflection for the first time, enabling, in effect—that is the revolutionary aspect to Husserl and to Kant and of course to Nietzsche—a newly Copernican critique of reason.

What we notice in such rigorously philosophical reflection is an already given engagement of knower and known, which for Husserl circumscribes the givenness of things to consciousness. Heidegger will speak of this coordination as a correspondence between Being and the human way of finding itself in being. Husserl's account of *intentionality*, like his teacher Brentano's, recovers the scholastic and Aristotelian insight into the ideational essence of mental phenomena: the eidetic heart of consciousness as object to itself. For his own part, Nietzsche seeks neither the correspondence between Being and Dasein (like Heidegger) nor indeed noetic insight (like Husserl and, for some, like the Canadian Thomist Bernard Lonergan) but rather poses a radical critique of the knowing subject qua knowing, which epistemological critique is phenomenologically, if also hermeneutically articulated.

For Merleau-Ponty, in a diachronic fusion of synchrony, expressing the primacy of the diachronic characteristic of the different structuralist tradition, phenomenology preexisted its Husserlian impetus and could be found in Marx, as in Nietzsche and Freud as well as Hegel and Kierkegaard. Given such a broadly syncretistic history, for Merleau-Ponty "we shall find in ourselves and nowhere else, the unity and the meaning of phenomenology."[6] This retrospective ubiquity defines phenomenology "as a problem to be solved," and with this experimental definition of phenomenology, Merleau-Ponty captures the continuing appeal of phenomenology as a return to the "things themselves," said otherwise in this context: a return to lived experience.

And if Merleau-Ponty does not take this return to life experience—as does Sartre in his own way and de Beauvoir in hers—to a full-blooded existentialism, it is because, like Husserl before him and Michel Serres afterward, Merleau-Ponty remains true to the rigorously scientific ideal of philosophy in its own domain *as philosophy*, in terms of what accrues to it as a rigorous science—not *natural* science, not *social* science, and not art. In *Signs*, Merleau-Ponty writes of such a rigorous (scientific) conception of philosophy, "Philosophy is irreplaceable because it reveals to us both the movement by which lives become truths, and the circularity of that singular being who in a certain sense already is everything *he happens to think*."[7]

Irretrievably embodied and bound to a lived world of human meaning and possibility, the systematic character of embodied being in the world constitutes Merleau-Ponty's unique contribution to phenomenology: "Our own body is in the world as the heart is in the organism."[8] This constitutive embodiment conceives phenomenology as a dialectics of ambiguity. If both Husserl and Heidegger, along with a long and large German tradition, advert to the importance of a philosophic reflection on existence and world, and if Sartre and de Beauvoir focus important perspectives on the body, Merleau-Ponty offers a phenomenology of gesture or style, projected via the weightiness of movement and the cast of interpretive constitution.

At the end of this essay, we will see that Nietzsche, who thinks through the body in order to understand the body—this is the meaning of his phenomenological critique of the subject, the "who" of causality—offers a phenomenology of his own programmatic "science" of ancient philology, in this case, the "birth" of tragedy out of the spirit of music, meaning the folk festival and the folk dance, realizing or making phenomenology bodily present, as Merleau-Ponty does, for instance, when Nietzsche reminds us to attend to our bodily response to a thought, an idea, a style of music (his famous/infamous choice of Bizet over Wagner, or Beethoven, as I argue).

Science, Perception, and Phenomenology

Nietzsche's thinking on science and the problem of causality parallels Hume's critique and goes beyond Kant, and modern cognitive science stands with Nietzsche on the level of our perception of causality, though it is also true that today's cognitive science would not use the terms Nietzsche uses. He observes, "We learn how to describe ourselves more and more precisely. . . . The suddenness with which many effects stand out misleads us; actually it is sudden only for us. In this moment of suddenness there is an infinite number of processes that elude us." For Nietzsche, this description of the knowing subject is essential to the extent that science is inevitably a humanization; thus he writes, "We operate only with things that do not exist: lines, planes, bodies, atoms, divisible time spans, divisible spaces—, how should explanations be at all possible when we first turn everything into an *image*, our image!"⁹ For those who require an overtly Husserlian parallel in the way of imprimatur, we might *read Nietzsche into* the phenomenological tradition, perhaps in the way Husserl reads Descartes or, still more plausibly, Hume, given Husserl's detailing of Hume's theory of knowledge as so many "fictions"¹⁰ and as the neo-Kantians and as Nietzsche himself also speaks of fictions,¹¹ especially in his theory of knowledge.

Nietzsche's critique of science and knowledge is his phenomenology. One may, though I will argue that one need not, follow certain phenomenological conventions and identify Nietzsche's philological explorations as genetic, his epistemological concerns as constitutional, and his performative explorations and invitations as an instantiation of phenomenological *Vergegenwärtigung* or rendering present, as we have this perhaps most elegantly in Heidegger but also in Merleau-Ponty and, among contemporary phenomenologists, most marvelously in Alphonso Lingis. This approach to and conception of phenomenology will not make chapter-and-verse thumping Husserlians any happier than similarly thumping Hegelians, but it may advance our understanding of both the possibilities of phenomenology and of Nietzsche.

For we need to ask what it is that we mean by phenomenology in every case. And if Merleau-Ponty begins his own *Phenomenology of Perception* with this question, asking, "What is phenomenology?," he himself also found the necessity of the question at once imperative and disconcerting: "It may seem strange that this question has still to be asked half a century after the first works of Husserl."¹² As one scholar observed in English in the mid-1960s, "There was a time when people considered themselves entitled to laugh at phenomenology because, so they said, there were as many phenomenologies as there were phenomenologists."¹³

In *The Idea of Phenomenology*, Husserl distinguishes the natural and the phenomenological attitude, highlighting what has endeared phenomenology to cognitive science with his observation that "*natural thinking* in science and everyday life is untroubled by the difficulties concerning the possibility of cognition."¹⁴ An attention to such "difficulties" is what characterizes the phenomenological attitude and makes phenomenology what it is, now varying Quine's quip that mathematics was "philosophy enough." As Merleau-Ponty observes in this spirit, many readers can have the "impression, on reading Husserl or Heidegger, not so much of encountering a new philosophy as of recognizing what they had been waiting for."¹⁵ Husserl's phenomenological reduction, as Fink puts it, is "the fundamental reflective realization that establishes the possibility of philosophy."¹⁶

When we undertake to read Nietzsche as a phenomenologist, we are also reading him as sharing the concerns of phenomenology—emphasizing, in other words, as Heidegger said to his students, "that Nietzsche knew what philosophy is."[17] As Sokolowski explains, to adopt the "phenomenological attitude is not to become a specialist in one form of knowledge or another, but to become a philosopher. From the phenomenological viewpoint we look at, and describe analytically, all the particular intentionalities and their correlates, and world belief as well, with the world as its correlative."[18]

On Nietzsche's Philology: Toward a Musical Phenomenology

Nietzsche can be shown to have been concerned with such a "phenomenological viewpoint," bracketing our contemporary relationship to stress emphases in today's European languages, and attending instead to the musical pitch and the measure of the tragic music drama as such, the rhythm and meter of the words themselves, as it were, in the context of the work of tragic art, in order to raise the question of the sound of speech itself, thus elaborated very specifically in the guise of a phenomenological philology and including nothing less than a *Vergegenwärtigung* of ancient music drama both in terms of the words themselves and as spoken (i.e., as sung) and in terms of sense experience, which is to say in terms of what Nietzsche calls "aesthetic science" at the beginning of his first book, *The Birth of Tragedy*.[19] This same phenomenological philology also finds expression in Nietzsche's *critical* philosophy, including his reflections on logic and mathematics.[20] At the same time as Nietzsche's project might be read into Husserl's phenomenology, and as both must be distinguished from Hegel's phenomenology or indeed from Schopenhauer's own phenomenology of the world will, it is also important to distinguish Nietzsche and Husserl. I have not emphasized this just because it is, for the most part, both point of departure and terminus.

I began by emphasizing Merleau-Ponty's approach to phenomenology as it has affinities with Nietzsche's philosophy. Thus regarded, Nietzsche offers astonishingly developed elements of a "phenomenology of perception," attending, as many scholars have noted, to what one sees, unpacking in good phenomenological fashion the elements that freight our everyday perception. Thus he writes, "That cloud there! What is 'real' in that?" (GS §57) to criticize what we take to be real in our most realist sensibility (he is here speaking of the Stoics), while emphasizing that, failing the supposed "prejudices" or "convictions" of perception and judgment, we could not perceive at all.[21] This includes his very phenomenological reflections on the senses, on consciousness, and on the unconscious as such, as well as on the body, along with detailed physiological reflections, including a phenomenology of sickness, of health, including the dialectic between sickness and health that is convalescence, but also youth and senescence, observations on men and women and sexuality.[22] He also includes specifically phenomenological reflections on psychology, physics, chemistry, biology, and more. One can also make similar arguments regarding his observations of the human sciences, in theory and practice, including anthropology, sociology, history, and politics.

I argue that Nietzsche's *Birth of Tragedy* can be seen as phenomenological even to the extent of including a kind of "reduction" of traditional assumptions and theories regarding the history of the tragic art form, as well as the history and function of the tragic chorus as a musically poetic performance that can be understood, so he was at pains to argue, only in the life-world of Greek antiquity. Similarly phenomenological, we might argue, are Nietzsche's genetic reflections in his *Untimely Meditations* (on religion, history, education, culture, and politics, and including, well beyond Wagner, his own contemporary musical cultural world), in addition to his critical reflections on logic, perception, and indeed science, as he claims he is the "first" to raise the question of science as such—and here we should think of Heidegger as well as Husserl. And he claims that he is the first to suggest that science itself is worth questioning (BT §ii). In this respect, still too often unadverted to, even by well-established Nietzsche scholars, I have emphasized what ought to be regarded as Nietzsche's most routinely scientific discovery, which he made with respect to establishing the pronunciation or intonation of ancient Greek,[23] a discovery that served as the basis for his own very literal emphasis on the importance of beautiful speech for the Greeks and the centrality of "music" in *The Birth of Tragedy*. This did not mean that his readers attended to what he said there, any more than we do today. Yet it is for this same reason that we find Nietzsche's Zarathustra seemingly compelled to cry out in frustration, "They do not understand me; I am not the mouth for these ears. Must one smash their ears before they learn to listen with their eyes?" (*Thus Spoke Zarathustra*, prologue, §5). Indeed the prelude to *Thus Spoke Zarathustra*, that is, Nietzsche's *The Gay Science*, includes a reprise of Nietzsche's denigration of Aristotle's telic theory of tragic catharsis in *The Birth of Tragedy*, thus emphasizing that what was at stake for the ancients was anything but an all-too-nineteenth-century "attempt to overwhelm the spectator with emotion" (GS §80). Rather, as Nietzsche emphasizes, "The Athenian went to the theater *in order to hear beautiful speeches*. And beautiful speeches were what concerned Sophocles: pardon this heresy!" (GS §80).

I thus argue that Nietzsche's phenomenological philology drove his discoveries regarding the ictus, or in this case the absence of the dramatically emphatic resources of stress,[24] as making all the difference for contemporary theater, music drama, and opera in his studies of ancient Greek rhythm and meter. I have also noted elsewhere that he used commonly conventional, specifically musical notation for the sake of the same. And at the conclusion of *The Birth of Tragedy*, so important is the composer's musical conventionality that he would invoke the technical musical notion of dissonance (referring in particular to Beethoven, and here it matters in this regard that he studied musical composition technique on his own, where it was not less important for his own musical sensibility that he played piano so well that he impressed everyone who heard him, including Wagner).[25]

Thus Nietzsche could contrast the achievement of Greek poetics with the modern ideal of freedom of expression:

> With every Greek artist, poet and writer one has to ask what is the new constraint he has imposed upon himself and through which he charms his contemporaries (so that he finds imitators)? For that which we call "invention" (in metrics, for example) is always such a self-imposed fetter. "Dancing in chains," making things difficult for oneself and then spreading over it the illusion of ease and facility—that is the artifice they want to demonstrate for us. (*Human, All Too Human*, KSA 2 [hereafter HH], *The Wanderer and His Shadow*, §140)

And yet, and this makes it hard for many of us to read him, Nietzsche nearly always *mixes* his concerns. Thus he uses the metaphor of musical dissonance to speak of the themes of tragedy as so many variants on "that which is ugly and disharmonic" as "part of an artistic game," in order to claim that both "music and tragic myth . . . transfigure a region in whose pleasing chords dissonance as well as the horrific image of the world fade away alluringly" (BT §25).

In this sense—and perhaps this is why scholars have tended not to have understood it until now—the conclusion of *The Birth of Tragedy* is a phenomenology of music, or otherwise more precisely said, a phenomenology of Greek tragedy-as-music, heard through Hölderlin's beautifully provocative reflections on Sophocles,[26] and understanding the tragic art form as a resonant expression of the spirit of music, as Nietzsche says in his original subtitle. As he expresses this "spirit of music" at the end, he refers to the very musical possibility of "playing," as he claims that Beethoven plays, with the "thorn of displeasure [*Stachel der Unlust*]," thereby instantiating nothing other than the ancient art of "transfiguring illusion [*Verklärungschein*]." Thus Nietzsche reminds us that "dissonance" only works in a musical tension,[27] suggesting that if one were to imagine "dissonance become human—and what else is human?—this dissonance, in order to live, would thus have need of a magnificent illusion that would cover dissonance with a veil of beauty" (BT §25).

Perspective and *Epochē*

Nietzsche's scholarly practice in classical philology led to a now standardized discovery (nothing less indeed than the conventional pronunciation of ancient Greek),[28] as well as to some very radical insights into ancient Greek music drama, but also politics and life, a methodology including philology as a phenomenology of the text, the word as written for the sake of the performance, which is another way to understand the phonetic achievement that was ancient Greek.

Why call this a phenomenology? It will always strike us, as noted at the outset, that unlike Heidegger or Sartre or Merleau-Ponty or Sokolowski, Nietzsche cannot inscribe himself into the phenomenological tradition by claiming inspiration from Husserl. This is important where one might, to vary Adorno, speak of the fetish character of phenomenology. Husserl tends to be regarded as the standard, as if there were no other phenomenology than his and as if anything that did not replicate his method and his focus ought not be counted as phenomenological. Thus it was necessary to underline that some Husserlians exclude Heidegger (and many other thinkers) as inadequately phenomenological in Husserl's sense. But if it is to Husserl that we owe the important and key phenomenological motto, it is also relevant to note that even this is itself not original to Husserl, as it glosses the Stoic practice of *epochē, to the things themselves*. This Stoic legacy, as indeed for Descartes and for Kant, was of the essence for Husserl as for Nietzsche and any philosopher.

In this sense, we may recall Nietzsche's adumbration of what can seem to be the phenomenological method itself, up to and including the notion of profiles and variations, reminding us of this ancient use of εποχή: "*Fundamental theorem*: No retrogressive hypotheses! Much rather a state of εποχή! And as many individual observations as possible!"[29] Nietzsche's phenomenological methodology beyond his phenomenological terminology thus opposes *both* anthropomorphic and nonanthropomorphic presumptions, where he challenges us and at the same time explains his own programmatic return to things themselves, as it were: "Task: *to see* things as they are! Means: to look at them through a hundred eyes, through many persons!" (KSA 9, 11 [65], 466; cf. *Genealogy of Morals* [hereafter GM], III: 12).

It is as a classical philologist that Nietzsche recommends, in the spirit of the Stoic legacy of phenomenology and not unlike Epictetus or Marcus Aurelius, that we are to adopt a "cosmological perspective" (KSA 12, 6 [26], 244).[30] But Nietzsche's recommended cosmological sensibility, given the history of European nihilism as well as its overcoming (so to speak) in neo-Kantianism and positivism, including the contemporary orientation of analytic philosophy, is neither an impersonal nor an objective perspective. As Nietzsche argues, what is required is the thought "of an eye that simply cannot be thought, an eye which is to have no direction at all" (GM III: 12). In contrast to this absurd and prima facie impossible demand, Nietzsche distinguishes and defines "objectivity" as he speaks of it, "not in the sense of 'disinterested contemplation [*interesselose Anschauung*],'" which disinterested contemplation is itself, again, inconceivable nonsense, but as the capability of *having power* over one's positive and negative arguments and of raising them and disposing of them so that one knows how to make the very *variety* of perspectives and interpretations of emotions useful for knowledge" (GM III: 12). Serially, indeed cumulatively, perspectivally, Nietzsche's "objectivity" is a kind of profiling or "shading," as he emphasizes this in advance of Husserl's own very different *Abschattungen*, not as a means to a neutral perspective to be sure, but "perspectivally," that is, in order to collect a variety of viewpoints, as all viewpoints contribute to what is seen. For Nietzsche, what is taken as objective perception includes active, interpretive powers in its scope, and it is through such active interpretation that he very hermeneutically and phenomenologically emphasizes that "seeing" first becomes a *seeing as*. Later he will write, "Never to observe in order to observe! That gives a false perspective, leads to squinting and something forced and exaggerated. Experience as the wish to experience does not succeed" (*Twilight of the Idols*, KSA 6 [hereafter TI], "Skirmishes of an Untimely Man," 7). In this way his perspectivalism offers a preliminary or pre-phenomenological account of what can, if one takes a sympathetic view, be seen to become Husserl's *epochē*.

Husserl sought to reach the essence of things in his phenomenological investigations. For this he employed a method of "free" or "imaginative variation," leading to eidetic intuition of the *eidos* or essence of the intended object as indeed of the forms of intentionality (perception, memory, etc.). The eidetic analysis of intentionality, betraying Husserl's unswerving focus on truth, yields necessary or apodictic truths.

Like Husserl and Heidegger and indeed Merleau-Ponty, Nietzsche raises the question of what Husserl calls the critique of cognition. Reflecting on this critique genetically, some will suppose, will be the obvious part, but also constitutively or constitutionally, almost and even in accord with what Husserl called "the general doctrine of essences, within which the science of the essences of cognition finds its place."[31] Hence Husserl poses the same question as part and parcel of the "theory of science"[32] precisely as such a theory articulates and maintains in view nothing less Nietzschean, as we have already noted, than the very idea of "science as a problem and as an accomplishment."[33] Indeed Husserl contends:

> No one ever thinks about the predications and truths which precede science, about the "logic" which provides norms within this sphere of relativity, or about the possibility, even in the case of these logical structures conforming purely descriptively to the life-world, of inquiring into the system of principles that give them their norms a priori. As a matter of course, traditional objective logic is substituted as the a priori norm even for this subjective-relative sphere of truth.[34]

But, of course, Nietzsche was concerned to do just this, and we can see this not by tacking between a certain account of Nietzsche's reflections on method and a certain account of Husserlian methodology, but precisely in terms of a common project to present what both Nietzsche and Husserl invoke as "the problem of science" as such and "as a problem" (BT §ii). One might go so far as to call this Nietzsche's "reduction" inasmuch as it can seem that he undertakes, avant la lettre, what is for Husserl imperative "before everything else," namely "the *epochē* in respect to all objective sciences."[35]

Toward a Critical Phenomenology: The Question of Science

Nietzsche puts the truths of science in question. Yet his interest was in the very possibility of knowledge and indeed in the very possibility of science qua science as such and in the first place, and he was very conscientious in emphasizing his priority as the first to put the very idea, the sheer notion of science as science in question (BT §ii). If reading Nietzsche as a phenomenologist does not make him a proto-Husserl, it does mean that both share an emphasis on the role of the phenomenon. Thus

Nietzsche concludes his "short history of an illusion" reflecting that with our new and modern and positivistic inattention to the metaphysical world of ideal truths, such as beauty and the good, it transpires that while we have certainly "abolished" the "true world" of this kind, the achievement gains us less than we think: "What world has remained? The apparent one perhaps? But no! *With the true world we have also abolished the apparent one*" (TI, "How the 'True World' Finally Became a Fable: History of an Error").[36] It is Nietzsche's critical perspective that serves him here. Thus the *cogito, qua* subject, *qua* I that thinks, is for him as problematic as the thought *thought*. "The 'I' (which with the singularizing sovereignty of our essence is not one!) is to be sure no more than a conceptual synthesis—."[37]

"Phenomenalism" must be opposed, by contrast, to Nietzsche's more properly "phenomenological" psychology, as Nietzsche understands psychology much as Husserl does, namely as a "psychology" for psychologists under way to science or phenomenology and as opposed to the more conventionally impressionistic and very moral (in Nietzsche's words) "psychologism" of the brothers Goncourt (to use his own example here): "One lies in wait for reality, as it were, and every evening one brings home a handful of curiosities. But note what finally comes of all this: a heap of splotches, a mosaic at best, but in any case something patched together, something restless, a mess of screaming colors" (KGW VIII/1, 1 [87], 28). In this sense, Nietzsche's project qua fundamentally epistemological, is also a *critically* phenomenological project. In this critically phenomenological sense, what Nietzsche called "interpretation" characterizes his phenomenology, as he expresses the world itself as so much "will to power," arguing that "the world of experience is only a qualitative world, [and] that in consequence logic and applied logic (like mathematics) belong to the artifices of ordering, overwhelming, simplifying, abbreviating power" (KSA 12, 6 [14], 238; cf. TI, "'Reason' in Philosophy," §3). In this sense, Nietzsche writes, "It will do to consider science as an attempt to humanize things as faithfully as possible; as we describe things and their after-one-another, we learn how to describe ourselves more and more precisely" (GS §112). As already emphasized, it is in the same phenomenological sense that he also explains mathematics itself as a means of "humanization" (GS §246).[38]

Nietzsche takes this to his famous critique of phenomena as such, both externally as well as internally, or contra Schopenhauer's analysis of consciousness, arguing, again as Husserl himself recognizes this critique of succession, in terms of Hume's original critique of causality as this famously "woke" Kant from his self-described "dogmatic slumber":

> Nothing is more phenomenal (or, more clearly:) nothing is so much *deception* as this inner world which we observe with the famous "inner sense." We have believed in the will as cause to such an extent that we have from our personal experience introduced a cause into events in general (i.e., intention as cause of events—).
>
> We believe that thoughts as they succeed one another in our minds stand in some kind of causal relation: the logician especially, who actually speaks of nothing

but instances which never occur in reality, has grown accustomed to the prejudice that thoughts *cause* thoughts,—he calls that—thinking. . . .

In summa: everything of which we become conscious is a terminal phenomenon [*Enderscheinung*], an end—and causes nothing—every successive phenomenon in consciousness is completely atomistic. And we have sought to understand the world through the *reverse* conception,—as if nothing were active and real but thinking, feeling, willing! (KSA 13, 14 [152], 335)

It is with reference to logic and to its foundations in grammar, as Nietzsche emphasizes, here reflecting on Descartes's *Meditations* (along with Spir's assessment of Descartes), that Nietzsche is able to remind us, like Husserl, that one inevitably assumes one knows "what 'being' is in order to draw an 'I am' out of the 'I think,'" adding yet more radically than Husserl that "the question concerning the worth of logic must be decided in advance of the question of 'Being'" (KSA 11, 40 [23], 640).

As Nietzsche observes, very hermeneutically, very philologically (and these are all words for phenomenologically investigative kinds), "hidden in the *cogito* of the *cogitat* and the *cogitator* is 'believing' and 'meaning,'" and that one thereby "begins with belief in logic—in the ego above all!—and not merely from the establishment of a fact!" (KSA 11, 40 [23], 640). Logic, Nietzsche now declares, has long stood in need of just the very philological analysis that we have been describing as phenomenological: "Just as mathematics and mechanics were for a long time regarded as sciences with absolute validity and only now risk the suspicion that they are nothing more nor less than applied logic on the basis of the determinate and provable assumption, that there are 'identical cases'" (KSA 11, [40] 27, 643). By contrast, Nietzsche argues, and not only as a result of his own critique but also as a result of the empirical psychology of his day and Husserl's day, "The belief in the immediate certainty of thinking is no longer a belief, and no longer a certainty!" (KSA 11, 40 [25], 641). Opposing Descartes's "dogmatic thoughtlessness," Nietzsche declares as the new watchword of philosophy, "It must be more fundamentally doubted than Descartes!" (KSA 11, 40 [25], 641).

Going beyond Descartes's doubt, Nietzsche also takes Kant's Hume-inspired project of critique further than Kant himself had done, following, as can be seen in the current context, Husserl's methodological constraints, at least in spirit. To say this is not to claim that Nietzsche undertook his inquiry just as Husserl does but indeed for related reasons, and thus we may profit from reading both together. And saying this, it will also follow that reading Nietzsche may help in reading Husserl,[39] especially as we recall not only the conclusion of Husserl's 1935 Vienna lecture, "Philosophy and the Crisis of European Humanity,"[40] with its obvious citation of Nietzsche's "good Europeans,"[41] but also its initial discussion of the "crisis" using the Nietzschean metaphors of decadence and illness.

Questioning, as we have seen, the viability of doubt as foundation for the thinking subject, Nietzsche contends, "Descartes is not radical enough for me. Regarding his demand for certainty and his 'I will not be deceived' it is necessary to ask 'Why not?'" (KSA 11 40 [10], 632). Not unlike Hume's critique of objectivity, and including Hume's critique of causality, the *"propter hoc,* the necessity of succession,"[42] Nietzsche from early to late raises a methodological challenge emphasizing the circularity of the idea of reason as its own self-founding foundation, against Descartes but also contra Kant, as Nietzsche had originally reflected in the context of his first book, *The Birth of Tragedy,* and going on to ask in *Daybreak,* "Was it not rather strange to demand that an instrument should criticize its own value and effectiveness? that the intellect itself should 'recognize' its own worth, power, and limits? was it not even just a little ridiculous?"[43]

Nietzsche's critical phenomenology of knowledge includes a critical phenomenology of perception as well as of logical reflection, taking the culture of scientific reason to its utmost *logical* consequences. By means of "the paraphernalia of science itself" (BT §18)— this would be the critique of scientific reason as Nietzsche reads between both Kant and Schopenhauer—the critical philosopher now qua reflective phenomenologist inevitably outlines "the limits and the relativity of knowledge generally," ultimately denying "decisively the claims of science to universal validity and universal aims" (BT §18).

From the beginning, then, Nietzsche emphasizes that Kant's philosophic legacy signaled the effective and not less *logically significant* destruction of "scientific Socratism's complacent delight in existence by establishing its limits" (BT §19). By contrast, Husserl seeks to ground the possibility of knowledge, whereby "the chief gain from phenomenology," here conceived once again in Merleau-Ponty's terminology, "is to have united extreme subjectivism and extreme objectivism in its notion of the world or of rationality."[44] Nietzsche's own reflections refuse the legitimacy of synthetic a priori judgments—not just some but *all* such judgments. Strictly speaking, as Nietzsche put it, judgments such as Kant's synthetic a priori judgments ought to be impossible for human beings; we have, he says, "no right to them," and hence and "in our mouths, they are plainly false judgments" (*Beyond Good and Evil,* KSA 5 [hereafter BGE] §4; cf. §11).

Synthetic a priori judgments are indispensable not because they are true; rather,

> the falsest judgments (to which synthetic judgments *a priori* belong) are the most indispensable to us, that without granting as true the fictions of logic, without measuring reality against the purely invented world of the unconditional and self-identical, without a continual falsification of the world by means of numbers, humanity could not live. (BGE §4)

These reflections are directly concerned with what Husserl called "the difficulties concerning the possibility of cognition."[45] Here we recognize the quandary and challenge of axiomatic foundations in mathematics and logic and of the conditions of the possibility of human cognition: "We behold all things through the human head and cannot cut off this head; while the question nonetheless remains what of the world would still be there if one had cut it off" (HH §9).

If, as Nietzsche explicitly argues, the nineteenth-century victory of *method* over science challenges even science itself and per se,[46] his own critical undertaking sought not only to extend Kant's critique beyond Kant but to raise the fundamentally *phenomenological* and *philosophical* question of the very possibility of *any* knowledge of the philosophic (epistemic) foundations of science (as art) conceived in the light of what he speaks of as "life." For science qua *techne* is itself not other than art, that is to say, a means for constructing or constituting what is held to be scientific, what is taken to be true.

As Nietzsche infamously accuses the physicists who seek to uncover "nature's conformity to law" (BGE §22) with following a *circular* project on the conviction that, and to begin with, "nature" both has and follows "laws," which conviction, as Nietzsche reminds his physicist colleagues, is drawn not from empirical observation—this would be Hume's problem with causality as Husserl characterizes this critique, and indeed Nietzsche's more sustained and very phenomenological development of that same problematic as what he calls the "four great errors of philosophy," errors concerning causality (and indeed the directionality of succession), arguing that the physicist's vision of lawfulness instead simply extends or projects the nineteenth-century social ideal of democratic politics.[47] Nietzsche's point here is that so far from "fact" (BGE §22), the scientist's belief in "nature's conformity to law" is a *posit*, part of what Husserl names the scientist's own naïve attitude (for there is "the world" of the scientist, as we recall), that is for Nietzsche in any case a convention for Husserl unquestioned as a convention, an assumption trusted as such and thus called the given.

As an art or *techne*, as a theoretical technique and practice, modern science is a means for extracting and certifying what counts as scientific truth. For Nietzsche, the drive to know depends upon the humanizing or anthropomorphic inclination or direction of ego-logocentric engagement with the world. "Ultimately," he writes, "every law of nature is a sum of anthropomorphic relations," and he goes on to emphasize "especially number" (KSA 7, 19 [237], 494), a point reprised in *The Gay Science* and again in *Beyond Good and Evil* and *Twilight of the Idols* (and again we note here, as suggested at the outset, the durability of his epistemological concerns) contra the modern scientific ideal of quantificational, that is, mathematical objectivity. This critically reflexive insight may be regarded as Nietzsche's Protagorean or even Procrustean and certainly Delphic principle: "The basic thought of science is that man is the measure of all things" (KSA 7, 19 [237], 494; cf. BGE §3). Or, as he also writes, "All natural science is nothing but an attempt to understand man and what is anthropological; more correctly, it is an attempt to return continuously to man via the longest and most roundabout ways" (KSA 7, 19 [91], 449).

Nietzsche's epistemological meditations intensify Descartes's doubt and radicalize Kant's critique and thus go beyond Husserl's phenomenological project at least to Heidegger's hermeneutic phenomenology and to the extent that Nietzsche makes questioning central to his philosophy. This distinction is crucial where, as Sokolowski reminds us, the *epochē* is indeed drawn from Greek skepticism just where, for Husserl's phenomenology, the same traditionally "skeptical overtone of the term is not kept."[48]

By contrast, Nietzsche's own quite classically skeptical[49] reflections on truth and lie return again and again to the problem of logic in the wake of Socrates' transformation of the philosophic enterprise, just because, with Socrates, the ideal of truth and "truthfulness gains possession of logic" (KSA 7, 19 [216], 487). By the time we get to Aristotle, the challenge of "the infinite difficulty of classification" (KSA 7, 19 [216], 487) finds its determinative resolution in the principle of noncontradiction, as Aristotle underscores this first principle as an axiomatic assumption apart from any necessity for (or indeed any possibility of) demonstration (*Meta.* 1005b 15–25). This same principle sets the terms for what Nietzsche calls the conflict between art and knowledge.[50]

Phenomenology, however, is all about providing foundations, and reading Nietzsche as a phenomenologist entails that one read him as an epistemologist and above all as a philosopher of science. Husserl shared Nietzsche's project, as he too sought to provide a foundation for science as such. For Husserl, as for David Hilbert and Ernst Mach and Nietzsche, beyond what Kant had supposed in all his Newtonian innocence, the natural sciences, including physics along with chemistry and biology but also mathematics and logic, were very much in crisis.[51] Thus the sciences themselves were not only actively searching from discipline to discipline for such foundations but also absorbing paradigm shock after paradigm shock, as we recall the context for Husserl's own foundational project and just to the extent that the nineteenth century might be characterized as a century of foundational crises, crises to be sure that have yet to be resolved. In mathematics, the urgency of crisis is articulated in Hilbert's address to the 1900 World Congress of mathematicians in Paris, reminding them that, so far from Kant's ideal confidence, *mathematics* had yet to become a science and thus required its own foundational program for the imperative sake of grounding the possibility of mathematical as of scientific knowing.[52] Like Hume and Schopenhauer before him and like Husserl and Heidegger after him, Nietzsche raised the question of foundations, which in his case entailed that he question these very foundations, which he also named "prejudices," "convictions," and "values."

Giving Blood to the Ghosts: *The Birth of Tragedy* as Phenomenology of the Musical Spirit of Language, with Satyrs and the Dance

Nietzsche's phenomenological investigations run from his explorations of the musical character of the Greek language as he began his readerly reflections on Greek music drama and dance (replete with little illustrations: *arsis/thesis*),[53] an exploration that is all about dance and drama, but ultimately and above all about the very literal music of the poem itself, which precisely phenomenological hermeneutic depends upon his discovery of the musical resonances of ancient Greek.[54] The role of the practitioner of the science of classical philology corresponds to neither that of the artist or the composer but rather is akin to that of the performer, as *Vergegenwärtigung* of the kind one can perform by articulating ancient Greek in the constraints, that is to say the "chains" of rhythm and time—out of the spirit of music.

To understand this notion of "performance" in philology, regarding the philologist as a reflective practitioner (Nietzsche's word for this reflectivity was "philosophical," as Erwin Rohde was alone able to see), Nietzsche was as much a student of Otto Jahn's archaeological or "monumental" philology as of Friedrich Ritschl's text-critical approach.[55] Indeed in his public Basel lectures, Nietzsche invoked such archaeological discoveries to frame his discussion of Greek music drama, reminding his listeners of the difference it makes to know that ancient Greek statues had originally been painted in vibrant, today we might even think garish colors.[56] Thus in his inaugural lecture, Nietzsche underscores a phenomenological practice: representing an ideal project for a scientific philology as a kind of playing with variants. In this same sense, he inverted the classicist's motto borrowed from Seneca, arguing, to conclude his lecture, for the imperative value of philosophy for philology, a claim corresponding to his call for a very phenomenological questioning of philology as a science and above all as a practice.

If the philologist cannot hope, as Nietzsche argues, to match antiquity with the genius of the poet or composer, the philologist can aspire to call upon the ingeniousness of performance or *practice*. By recalling the music of the tragic art form, Nietzsche was thus able to explain how the tragic poet plays with the "thorn of suffering." As noted earlier, the essential metaphor was musically technical.[57] Musical dissonance, Nietzsche argued, was the operative key to ancient tragedy inasmuch as sound as such was the heart of the ancient art form: "speaking well," as we have seen. Intoning the tragic poems one, as it were, *plays*—this is Nietzsche's tragic *Vergegenwärtigung*—the past. Hence as early as his inaugural lecture in Basel Nietzsche suggested that the philologist disposes over a very scientific "art." The philologist is a virtuoso capable of singing the "music" of antiquity to life and thus, as he says there, as if "for the first time to let it sound again." At this juncture, Nietzsche offers a first articulation of the musical dynamic and radical insights[58] of his first book, *The Birth of Tragedy out of the Spirit of Music*.

Nietzsche's resolution of the question of tragedy was literally musical (BT §22), taken with phenomenological reference to philological practice as referring, as it were, to the words themselves, to Greek, but not less with reference to the paradoxical question that for Nietzsche illuminates the problem of pleasure *and* pain in the ancient Greek tragedy. And Nietzsche holds to the significance of this musical insight throughout his life. Thus his concluding reflections on "What I Owe the Ancients" in *Ecce Homo* reprise his allusion to the phenomenon of "musical dissonance" (BT §24), including his description of the "becoming human" (BT §25) of such dissonance. The notion of musical dissonance is here understood in a classically nineteenth-century context (as we may read in Beethoven's writing on compositional style)[59] in terms of the play or interaction of consonance and dissonance, given Nietzsche's own notes on harmony and which some argue as under way in a nineteenth-century context to what came to be called the "emancipation of dissonance"[60] in studies of early twentieth-century atonal music. A visual metaphor for this "emancipation" with reference to Beethoven is already evident in Nietzsche's commissioned woodcut illustrating the liberation of Prometheus, which he set as the frontispiece for his first book.

Drawing on nineteenth-century musical theory to make his case, David Allison has shown that Nietzsche invokes the then-current resources of what (this is my emphasis) he called "psychology" and we would call cognitive science as well as musical theory, using the findings of psychology to make his case with regard to the phenomenon of Greek music, in word and culture, emphasizing that Nietzsche draws upon his own experience of the Dionysian as an experience of "a dizzying state of transfiguring ecstasy."[61] As Allison notes, Nietzsche reflects upon his own experience not of music as inchoate or as beyond words but rather in the individually dynamic *experience* of musical dissonance, which same experience, as Allison cites Nietzsche's reflections at the end of *The Birth of Tragedy out of the Spirit of Music* (and here we see how much we need Nietzsche's initial, first full title, a title he changed in response to the book's lack of success), as it is music as Nietzsche understood it here, gives us "an idea of what is meant by the justification of the world as an aesthetic phenomenon."[62] Inasmuch as Nietzsche also specifically invokes the "joyous sensation of dissonance in music" (BT §24), he is indeed referring (as he also refers in his first section) to Beethoven's Ninth Symphony in order to raise, as noted above, a quite specific question about the nature of the tragic work of art. Here Allison reminds us that this is not only a musicological conception, as I have already noted is also on offer in Beethoven's own writings, which were influential for both Nietzsche and Wagner, but again we need to reflect that Nietzsche also represented his discovery of the ictus using musical illustrations. In *The Birth of Tragedy* and related lectures, he sought as much as possible to explore the physical and psychological experience. "The 'phenomenon,'" as Allison emphasizes it, "of 'musical dissonance' is the Dionysian state of ecstasy."[63]

For Allison—and, one might argue, for Bataille as well—what is at stake involves a phenomenology of musical experience:

> In addressing exactly what the object of music is (i.e., the theoretical model of its subject matter), Nietzsche realizes that its object (*Gegenstand*) is given to us as the content (*Inhalt*) of our own intensely undergone aesthetic experience, our ecstatic states of dispossession. This musically charged state of ecstatic disposition is precisely what he terms "the Dionysian state," and such a state is effectively the entire *field* of experience, shorn of simple subject-object relations.[64]

Allison connects this focus with Nietzsche's further explorations of the "Dionysian" in terms of "the most natural and extreme states of intoxication and frenzy"[65] and emphasizes that modern studies of musical cognition support the phenomenological insights of Nietzsche's "focus on dissonance as 'the primordial phenomenon of Dionysian Art.'"[66]

For some of us, to discover here that Nietzsche deploys a kind of phenomenology avant la lettre, as also and of course of a hermeneutic kind, may inspire a version of the anxiety of influence, and it turns out—this is the point that Herbert Butterfield made the center of his historical reflection—that this can work backward from the present as well.[67]

I have shown that Nietzsche's earliest lectures and his first book, as well as his reflections on history as on natural science, on the one hand, and on politics as on morality, on the other, all include important phenomenological elements. Although I have limited myself to only a few examples, I have also indicated that one can find phenomenological elements throughout his work.

Beyond this, one might go on to demonstrate that what I call Nietzsche's *perspectivalism*, including perhaps the terminological distinction between perspectivalism and perspectivism, comes into sharpest relief only in a phenomenological context. Like relativism, perspectivism holds with many perspectives, contending that everything is a matter of perspective, everything is relative: a matter of interpretation. *Perspectivalism* is a higher order reflection, taking as its point of departure a reflection on the significance of such perspectives. The locus classicus for this is the seeming retraction Nietzsche offers at the conclusion of his "ancient philologist's" remonstration to the physicists who go on about "laws of nature," as they suppose that the human conventionality of law extends beyond the human realm of nature. "Assuming that this also is only an interpretation—and you will be eager enough to make this objection?—well, all the better" (BGE §22). Thus as noted above, Sokolowski could emphasize Boehm's emphasis on interpretation (*Auffassung*) with reference to Nietzsche: "Intentionality interprets sensations."[68]

Sokolowski's point regarding Boehm is the point Nietzsche makes with regard to the correlevance of the apparent and true worlds in his "History of an Error." For Sokolowski, the "major problem with phenomena is to see them as true principles. That is, they are not 'merely' appearances behind which a hidden reality exists, but they are the appearing reality itself with nothing behind it."[69] And, as Boehm argues, it "is the phenomenon of an interpretation of a sensible content in and through a 'perception' that forms the crux of the Husserlian problem of the constitution of the object."[70]

I have chosen to approach such a reading in Heidegger's hermeneutic spirit. Thus Nietzsche's pespectivalist or phenomenological philology in *The Birth of Tragedy* recurs in *The Gay Science,* and we have seen that this takes us to Nietzsche's performative practice of *Vergegenwärtigung,* an enthusiast's science for enthusiasts, in the sense that Heidegger himself borrows from both Nietzsche and Hölderlin, of what Nietzsche called the "joyous perhaps." To the same degree, I also argued that in order to tack between the different seas of Nietzsche's thinking and those of the various contributions to phenomenology, we will need to know Nietzsche as well as we can, and at the same time we need to know not just Husserl but the phenomenological tradition in its breadth, including Brentano and also Carl Stumpf, especially on the perception or judgment of tones, where these latter empirical reflections also relate to concerns that, as we have seen, mattered to Nietzsche.[71] Where we inevitably go beyond both Nietzsche and Husserl or Heidegger is where we attempt—and Nietzsche always emphasized such attempts as temptations—to bring them together. We fall short of rigor, and never so much as when we suppose that we can simply begin where we find ourselves without needing a step back, that is, without reflection.

To conclude: Although I note genetic and constitutive elements in Nietzsche's phenomenological investigations, I am most intrigued by the performative, embodied, physically phenomenological and archaeological modality of *Vergegenwärtigung* just to the extent that Nietzsche himself—so we are told—practiced the same. Thus a physically phenomenological investigation illuminates the apocryphal report that has Nietzsche dancing naked in his upstairs room in Turin—fully aroused, to add the detail of the eyewitness who tells us this—playing a flute.[72] It is not the nakedness, it is not Nietzsche's erotico-ecstatic condition, much rather what we "should" be wondering about is Nietzsche's dancing and Nietzsche's flute playing.

I read this dancing-while-playing-a-flute as a scientific investigation of a phenomenological kind. Scientific research and modeling practice involve, as we know, both theory and technique; thus physical scientists use experimental models, and even in the realm of practical theory, architects and engineers make mock-ups of their designs. But there are always limitations, and models ought to be subject to experimental feedback or testing (although in practice they are not always). Given this need for feedback, and the liability of science to fall into convention, often unquestioned, a state that is also the end of science, science remains and must remain inherently unfinished. It is for this reason too that philosophy, for Husserl as he concludes his *Encyclopedia Britannica* article, is also and only the modest affair of a *"philosophia perennis."*[73]

So we ask, to keep questioning alive, what was Nietzsche doing with his flute, and what was he doing while dancing naked? Was he perhaps dancing in celebration of Dionysus? Was he not perhaps playing at being a Deleuzian avant la lettre? Why the flute? Because there was no MTV? Because he had no piano in his room? Maybe. But from the start to the end of his life Nietzsche regarded himself as a scientist, and just as a physical anthropologist or archaeologist might undertake to test a hypothesis by fashioning tools using local stones and materials to see how a fire, for example, might be made, so Nietzsche was perhaps testing a hypothesis. What is actual, what can be enacted, is also—and this is the whole point of the inquiry—*possible*. Nietzsche himself, in Jahn's rather than Ritschl's spirit, similarly approached his own science of classical philology, testing the question of music drama as he had raised this question in his first book, as part of the cultic festival of the tragic work of art.

So perhaps, just one very small perhaps and not even the *many* that Nietzsche said we would need, just perhaps, Nietzsche danced, playing the satyr's pipe as he did, just the way ithyphallic satyrs play.

Notes

1. Thus Natalie Depraz orients her introductory *Comprendre la phénoménologie* by detailing Husserl, Heidegger, Fink, Sartre, Levinas, Merleau-Ponty, Derrida, and Marion. I have added the

usually unnoticed name of Günther Anders, just as I also add Theodor Adorno, who quite explicitly names his analysis of radio in his *The Current of Music* as "phenomenological." (I have a chapter on "Adorno's Phenomenology" in Babich, *The Hallelujah Effect*.) I could also add the well-known Schütz and the less well-known F. Joseph Smith, the well-known Roman Ingarden and the less well-known Ludwig Landgrebe, among numerous other names.

2. For just one example, see the opening pages of Derrida and Vattimo, *Religion*.

3. Heidegger, "Jede Übersetzung ist aber schon Auslegung," 107.

4. Heidegger, *Hölderlin's Hymn "The Ister,"* 63, 65; *Hölderlins Hymne "Der Ister,"* 76. For further discussion, see Babich, "The *Ister*."

5. Husserl, *Cartesian Meditations*, 595.

6. Merleau-Ponty, *Phenomenology of Perception*, viii.

7. Merleau-Ponty, *Signs*, 113.

8. Merleau-Ponty, *Phenomenology of Perception*, 203.

9. Nietzsche, *The Gay Science* §112, KSA 3 (hereafter GS). See my discussion of Nietzsche, including a connection with Husserl's phenomenology, in "Towards a Critical Philosophy of Science." I also include a discussion of Nietzsche and the anthropocentric critique of science and mathematics of the neo-Kantian topologist Felix Hausdorff, who wrote on Nietzsche under the pseudonym of Paul Mongré.

10. Husserl, *Crisis*, 86ff., especially 87. On Hume and Husserl, see Sokolowski, "Fiction and Illusion in David Hume's Philosophy."

11. I discuss this in Babich, *Nietzsche's Philosophy of Science*, including further references to Hans Vaihinger in this same context.

12. Merleau-Ponty, *Phenomenology of Perception*, vii.

13. Luijpen, *Phenomenology and Metaphysics*, 1.

14. Husserl, *The Idea of Phenomenology*, 1.

15. Merleau-Ponty, *Phenomenology of Perception*, vii.

16. Fink, *Sixth Cartesian Meditation*, 10.

17. Heidegger, *Nietzsche, Volume 1*, 4.

18. Sokolowski, *Introduction to Phenomenology*, 47.

19. Nietzsche, *The Birth of Tragedy* §1, KSA 1 (hereafter BT). I discuss this further in Babich, "Nietzsches hermeneutische, phänomenologische Wissenschafts-philosophie."

20. I discuss Nietzsche's critical philosophy in Babich, "Towards a Critical Philosophy of Science."

21. For a specific discussion of this point, see Babich, "Nietzsche's Critique of Scientific Reason and Scientific Culture," 147f.

22. See, for example, one account of these reflections in Babich, "Nietzsche and Eros between the Devil and God's Deep Blue Sea," 159–88.

23. See Babich, "The Science of Words or Philology."

24. See ibid., and for further detail here, see Günther, *Rhythmus beim frühen Nietzsche*.

25. Janz, *Friedrich Nietzsche Biographie*, is invaluable here, as Janz notes that Nietzsche studied piano as a youth, playing Beethoven's sonata's and transcriptions of his symphonies. Nietzsche's ability to improvise at the piano stayed with him even after his breakdown. For a contentious discussion of improvisation, with important historical elements, see Durant, "Improvisation in the Political Economy of Music," especially 263. See also the final chapter on Nietzsche and Beethoven in Babich, *The Hallelujah Effect*.

26. I refer, of course, to Hölderlin's "Sophokles": "Viele versuchten umsonst das Freudigste freudig zu sagen / Hier spricht endlich es mir, hier in der Trauer sich aus."

27. I have called this Nietzsche's *concinnity*, arguing that the reader is inherently implicated in and involved with the reading of Nietzsche's text. It should be added that the same metaphor of

musical dissonance presupposes Nietzsche's theory of composition, which he very musically called "style."

28. See the references to be found in the texts cited in notes 21 and 22 above.

29. Nietzsche, *Kritische Studienausgabe*, 11, 26 [82], 170 (hereafter KSA). All English translations are mine.

30. See Hadot, *Philosophy as a Way of Life*.

31. Husserl, *The Idea of Phenomenology*, 1.

32. Ibid. Husserl's term here is, it should be noted, the usual German term for the "philosophy of science."

33. Husserl, *Crisis*, §34, 135. For Nietzsche, see Babich, *Nietzsche's Philosophy of Science*. For a discussion of both Nietzsche and Husserl in these terms, see Babich, "Towards a Critical Philosophy of Science," particularly the first few sections.

34. Husserl, *Crisis*, §34, 135.

35. Ibid.

36. There is an important connection with Mach's *Erkenntnis und Irrthum*.

37. Nietzsche, *Kritische Gesamtausgabe*, VIII/1, 1 [87], 28 (hereafter KGW).

38. See Babich, "Towards a Critical Philosophy of Science."

39. Thus when Erazim Kohák concludes his essay on the experiential foundations of good and evil by referring to Nietzsche (if his title had not already done this), he intended this allusion as an advance—as well as a qualification, inasmuch as Kohák is one of those who is not sure of the distinction to be made between moral or social phenomenology and pragmatism. See Kohák, "Knowing Good and Evil." In addition to phenomenology and ethics, we may also consider aesthetics. For a general discussion of phenomenology and aesthetics, albeit without focusing on Nietzsche, see Barbaras, "Sentir et faire." See Rampley, *Nietzsche, Aesthetics and Modernity*.

40. Husserl, *Crisis*, 269ff.

41. Ibid., 299.

42. Ibid., 87.

43. Nietzsche, *Daybreak*, §iii, KSA 3. Nietzsche continues: "But logical judgments are not the deepest and most fundamental to which the daring of our suspicion descends" (§iv).

44. Merleau-Ponty, *Phenomenology of Perception*, xix.

45. Husserl, *The Idea of Phenomenology*, 1.

46. See Babich, "Towards a Critical Philosophy of Science."

47. Babich, "*Ex aliquo nihil*," 231–56.

48. Sokolowski, *Introduction to Phenomenology*, 49.

49. For a discussion of this older tradition with reference to skepticism, see Sommer, "Nihilism and Skepticism," especially 262–63; Sloterdijk, *A Critique of Cynical Reason*. In an explicitly critical context, a review of Nietzsche and skepticism will also take us to Nietzsche and Montaigne and indeed to Hume and Kant, and so on.

50. Thus Nietzsche's early *Nachlaß* listing of the key notions of ancient Greek philosophy terminates with the Latin expression that becomes the dominant instrument of philosophy in its scholastic efflorescence: 'Quid quid est est: quid quid non est, non est' (KSA 7, 26 [1], 572).

51. For a discussion of this crisis of foundations, including a range of references, see Babich, "Early Continental Philosophy of Science."

52. For a discussion of Husserl and Hilbert and indeed Gödel in this context, see Ryckman, *The Reign of Relativity*. For further references, see Babich, "Early Continental Philosophy of Science."

53. For a discussion, see Babich, "Wort und Musik in der Antiken Tragödie." In a footnote to this essay, I replicate Nietzsche's own diagrammatic illustration; see 235.

54. See Günther, *Rhythmus beim frühen Nietzsche;* Babich, "Nietzsche's Philology and Nietzsche's Science " and "The Science of Words or Philology."

55. For an overview, including further references, see Bosco, *"Das furchtbar-schöne Gorgonen-haupt des Klassischen,"* 301ff. I discuss this as well in a number of places, most recently in Babich, "Towards a Critical Philosophy of Science."

56. For citations and discussion, see Babich, "Zu Nietzsches Statuen." Nietzsche's point here is almost Kuhnian in advance of Kuhn, for paradigms persist, and despite new discoveries, we tend to retain the older, inaccurate colorless image of classical Greece.

57. See Babich, *"Mousike techne,"* nn200–205. I take this up as well in the final chapters of Bab-ich, *The Hallelujah Effect.*

58. And to date, if we have yet to begin to engage his claim as philosophers, the classical phi-lologists are further still from such an engagement. See, however, Babich, "The Science of Words or Philology."

59. See, for example, Beethoven's notes from his studies with Albrechtsberger as we may read these and as Nietzsche would have known them, in the notes edited by Henry Hugo Pierson on the basis of Ignaz Xaver von Seyfried collection, *Ludwig van Beethovens Studien im Generalbass, Contrapunkt und in der Compositionslehre aus dessen Handschriftlichen Nachlass gesammelt und herausgegeben von Ignaz Xaver von Seyfried,* throughout but especially 130. Cf. Johann Georg Albrechtsberger's *Gründli-che Anweisung zur Composition mit deutlichen und ausführlichen Exempeln, zum Selbstunterrichte, erläutert, und mit einem Anhange.* And see too Pierson, *Ludwig van Beethovens Studien,* 316, where it is perhaps of interest to Nietzsche's own writings on dissonance and harmony and the differences between Greek musical forms and lyric convention, as we read, "Keine Dissonanz soll eher resolvieren, als bis der Sinn der Worte völlig geendet ist—Wo man sich verweilet: lange Noten; wo man wegeilet: kurze Noten." For a contextual discussion of what the author calls the "symphonic monument that towered over the nineteenth century," see Chua, *Absolute Music and the Construction of Meaning,* 235f. For further references and discussion, see the concluding chapters of Babich, *The Hallelujah Effect.*

60. This is the subtitle of Thomas Harrison's *1910: The Emancipation of Dissonance.* The term is usually attributed to Arnold Schoenberg, who uses it in his 1926 essay "Gesinnung oder Erken-ntnis?," 211. For a discussion of the origination of Schönberg's "Emanzipation der Dissonanz" in August Halme's 1900 *Harmonielehre,* as "Befreiung der Dissonanz," see Köhler, *Natur und Geist,* 230ff. Of course, the claims in this regard go even further back in the nineteenth century (see, among others, Barry, *The Philosopher's Stone*), a circumstance to be expected given the dynamic between consonance and dissonance, as Beethoven, via Albrechtsberger to be sure, discusses just this tension in his notes on composition.

61. Allison, *Reading the New Nietzsche,* 64.

62. Ibid.

63. Ibid.

64. Ibid., 65.

65. Ibid., 66.

66. Ibid., 67.

67. At the same time, there are many who insist that phenomenology itself is passé or postdated. For Nietzsche's own part, his laments tended to work in the other direction, as he argued that such claims often betrayed what he called a "lack" of philology, lamenting the pointlessness of his own discipline—not the likely limits of his own readership—as effectively in vain: "all of it *in usum Del-phinorum*" (GS §102). For a discussion of this last reference, see Babich, "On Classical Texts ," 50ff.

68. Sokolowski, *The Formation of Husserl's Concept of Constitution,* 56. See Boehm in this vol-ume. First published in 1962, this version appears in the first of two volumes on Husserl.

69. Sokolowski, "Review of Boehm," 136–37.

70. "This phenomenon of interpreting sensuous content by and through perception is at the core of Husserl's problem of the constitution of objects" (Boehm, "Husserl und Nietzsche"). See translation in the present volume, chapter 1.

71. See Stumpf, *Tonsychologie* ; Smith, *The Experiencing of Musical Sound.*

72. See Lissarrague, "The Sexual Life of Satyrs," and for a preliminary discussion of Nietzsche's active phenomenology in this context, see Babich, "Reading David B. Allison's Reading the New Nietzsche."

73. Husserl, *Psychological and Transcendental Phenomenology,* 102.

Bibliography

Adorno, Theodor W. *Current of Music: Elements of a Radio Theory.* Translated by Robert Hullot-Kentor. Frankfurt am Main: Suhrkamp, 2006.

Albrechtsberger, Johann Georg. *Gründliche Anweisung zur Composition mit deutlichen und ausführlichen Exempeln, zum Selbstunterrichte, erläutert, und mit einem Anhange: Von der Beschaffenheit und Anwendung aller jetzt üblichen musikalischen Instrumente.* Leipzig: Breitkopf, 1790.

Allison, David. *Reading the New Nietzsche.* Lanham, MD: Rowman and Littlefield, 2001.

Babich, Babette. "Early Continental Philosophy of Science." In *The New Century,* vol. 3: *Bergsonism, Phenomenology and Responses to Modern Science: History of Continental Philosophy,* edited by Keith Ansell-Pearson and Alan Schrift. Chesham, UK: Acumen Press, 2013.

———. *"Ex aliquo nihil*: Nietzsche on Science and Modern Nihilism." *American Catholic Philosophical Quarterly. Special Issue on Nietzsche* 84, no. 2 (2010): 231–56.

———. *The Hallelujah Effect: Philosophical Reflections on Music, Performance Practice and Technology.* Surrey: Avebury, 2013.

———. "The *Ister*: Between the Documentary and Heidegger's Lecture Course Politics, Geographies, and Rivers." *Divinatio* 24, no. 32 (2010): 7–32.

———. *"Mousike techne*: The Philosophical Praxis of Music in Plato, Nietzsche, Heidegger." In *Gesture and Word: Thinking between Philosophy and Poetry,* edited by Robert Burch and Massimo Verdicchio. London: Continuum, 2002.

———. "Nietzsche and Eros between the Devil and God's Deep Blue Sea: The Erotic Valence of Art and the Artist as Actor—Jew—Woman." *Continental Philosophy Review* 33 (2000): 159–88.

———. "Nietzsche's Critique of Scientific Reason and Scientific Culture: On 'Science as a Problem' and 'Nature as Chaos.'" In *Nietzsche and Science,* edited by Gregory M. Moore and Thomas Brobjer. Aldershot: Ashgate, 2004.

———. *Nietzsche's Philosophy of Science: Reflecting Science on the Ground of Art and Life.* Albany: State University of New York Press, 1994.

———. "Nietzsches hermeneutische, phänomenologische Wissenschafts-philosophie: Unzeitgemäße Betrachtungen zu Altphilologie und Physiologie." In *Nietzsches Wissenschaftsphilosophie: Hintergründe, Wirkungen und Aktualität,* edited by Günter Abel and Helmut Heit. Berlin: Walter de Gruyter, 2011.

———. "Reading David B. Allison's Reading the New Nietzsche." *Symposium* 8, no. 1 (2004): 19–35.

———. "The Science of Words or Philology: Music in *The Birth of Tragedy* and 'The Alchemy of Love' in *The Gay Science.*" In *Revista di estetica* 45, no. 28, edited by Tiziana Andina, 47–78. Turin: Rosenberg & Sellier, 2005.

———. "Towards a Critical Philosophy of Science: Continental Beginnings and Bugbears, Whigs and Waterbears." *International Journal of the Philosophy of Science* 24, no. 4 (2010): 343–91.

———. *Words in Blood, Like Flowers, Philosophy and Poetry, Music and Eros in Hölderlin, Nietzsche and Heidegger.* Albany: State University of New York Press, 2006.

———. "Wort und Musik in der Antiken Tragödie: Nietzsches 'fröhliche' Wissenschaft." *Nietzsche-Studien* 37 (2007): 230–57.

———. "Zu Nietzsches Statuen: Skulptur und das Erhabene." In *Grenzen der Rationalität: Teilband 2: Vorträge 2006–2009,* edited by Beatrix Vogel and Nikolaus Gerdes. München: Allitera, 2011.

Barbaras, Renaud. "Sentir et faire: La phénoménologie et l'unité de l'esthétique." In *Phénoménologie et esthétique,* edited by Renaud Barbaras. Paris: Encre marine, 1998.

Barry, Barbara R. *The Philosopher's Stone: Essays in the Transformation of Musical Structure.* New York: Pendragon Press, 2000.

Boehm, Rudolf. "Husserl and Nietzsche." In *Von Gesichtspunkt der Phänomenologie: Husserl Studien.* Den Haag: Nijhoff, 1968.

Bosco, Lorella. *"Das furchtbar-schöne Gorgonenhaupt des Klassischen": Deutsche Antikebilder (1755–1875).* Würzburg: Königshausen & Neumann, 2004.

Chua, Daniel K. L. *Absolute Music and the Construction of Meaning.* Cambridge: Cambridge University Press, 1999.

Depraz, Natalie. *Comprendre la phénoménologie: Une pratique concrète.* Paris: Armand Colin, 2006.

Derrida, Jacques, and Gianni Vattimo, eds. *Religion.* Stanford: Stanford University Press, 1998.

Durant, Alan. "Improvisation in the Political Economy of Music." in *Music and the Politics of Culture,* edited by Christopher Norris. London: Lawrence and Wishart, 1989.

Fink, Eugen. *Sixth Cartesian Meditation: The Idea of a Transcendental Theory of Method.* Bloomington: Indiana University Press, 1995.

Günther, Friederike Felicitas. *Rhythmus beim frühen Nietzsche.* Berlin: Walter de Gruyter, 2008.

Hadot, Pierre. *Philosophy as a Way of Life: Spiritual Exercises from Socrates to Foucault.* Oxford: Blackwell, 1995.

Harrison, Thomas. *1910: The Emancipation of Dissonance.* Berkeley: University of California Press, 1996.

Heidegger, Martin. *Hölderlin's Hymn "The Ister."* Translated by William McNeill and Julia Davis. Bloomington: Indiana University Press, 1996.

———. *Hölderlins Hymne "Der Ister."* Frankfurt am Main: Vittorio Klosterman, 1984.

———. "Jede Übersetzung ist aber schon Auslegung." In *Was heisst Denken?* Tübingen: Mohr, 1971.

———. *Nietzsche, Volume 1: The Will to Power as Art.* Translated by David Farrell Krell. San Francisco: Harper & Row, 1961.

Husserl, Edmund. *Cartesian Meditations: An Introduction to Phenomenology.* Translated by Dorion Cairns. The Hague: Martinus Nijhoff, 1960.

———. *The Crisis of European Sciences and Transcendental Phenomenology.* Translated by David Carr. Evanston, IL: Northwestern University Press, 1970.

———. *The Idea of Phenomenology.* Translated by William P. Alston and George Nkhnikian. The Hague: Nijhoff, 1973.

———. *Psychological and Transcendental Phenomenology and the Confrontation with Heidegger (1927–1931)*. Translated by Thomas Sheehan and Richard E. Palmer. Frankfurt am Main: Springer, 1997.

Janz, Curt Paul. *Friedrich Nietzsche Biographie*. Munich: Hanser, 1993.

Kohák, Erazim. "'Knowing Good and Evil . . . ' (Genesis 3:5b)." *Husserl Studies* 10 (1993): 31–41.

Köhler, Rafael. *Natur und Geist: Energetische Form in der Musiktheorie*. Stuttgart: Franz Steiner Verlag, 1996.

Lissarrague, François. "The Sexual Life of Satyrs." In *Before Sexuality: The Construction of Erotic Experience in the Ancient Greek World*, edited by David M. Halperin, John J. Winkler, and Froma I. Zeitlin. Princeton: Princeton University Press, 1990.

Luijpen, William A. *Phenomenology and Metaphysics*. Pittsburgh: Duquesne University Press, 1965.

Mach, Ernst. *Erkenntnis und Irrthum: Skizzen zur Psychologie der Forschung*. 1905. Saarbrücken: Vdm Verlag Dr. Müller, 2006.

Merleau-Ponty, Maurice. *Phenomenology of Perception*. Translated by Colin Smith. London: Routledge and Kegan Paul, 1979.

———. *Signs*. Translated by Richard McCleary. Evanston, IL: Northwestern University Press, 1964.

Nietzsche, Friedrich. *Kritische Gesamtausgabe*. Edited by Giorgio Colli and Mazzino Montinari. Berlin: de Gruyter, 1967.

———. *Kritische Studienausgabe*. Edited by Giorgio Colli and Mazzino Montinari. Berlin: de Gruyter, 1980.

Pierson, Henry Hugo, ed. *Ludwig van Beethovens Studien im Generalbass, Contrapunkt und in der Compositionslehre aus dessen Handschriftlichen Nachlass gesammelt und herausgegeben von Ignaz Xaver von Seyfried*. 1832. Leipzig: Schuberth & Comp, 1853.

Rampley, Matthew. *Nietzsche, Aesthetics and Modernity*. Cambridge: Cambridge University Press, 2000.

Ryckman, Thomas. *The Reign of Relativity: Philosophy in Physics 1915–1925*. Oxford: Oxford University Press, 2005.

Schoenberg, Arnold. "Gesinnung oder Erkenntnis?" In *Stil und Gedanke: Aufsätze zur Musik*, edited by Ivan Vojtěch. Frankfurt am Main: Fischer, 1976.

Sloterdijk, Peter. *A Critique of Cynical Reason*. Minneapolis: University of Minnesota Press, 1988.

Smith, F. Joseph. *The Experiencing of Musical Sound: Prelude to a Phenomenology of Music*. New York: Gordon and Breach, 1979.

Sokolowski, Robert. "Fiction and Illusion in David Hume's Philosophy." *Modern Schoolman* 45 (1968): 189–225.

———. *The Formation of Husserl's Concept of Constitution*. The Hague: Nijhoff, 1970.

———. *Introduction to Phenomenology*. Cambridge: Cambridge University Press, 2000.

———. "Review of Boehm, *Vom Gesichtspunkt der Phänomenologie*." *Philosophy and Phenomenological Research* 32, no. 1 (1971): 135–39.

Sommer, Andres Urs. "Nihilism and Skepticism." In *A Companion to Nietzsche*, edited by Keith Ansell-Pearson. Cambridge: Wiley-Blackwell, 2007.

8 Of the Vision and the Riddle

From Nietzsche to Phenomenology

Élodie Boublil

> To you, drunk with riddles, glad of the twilight, whose soul flutes lure astray to every whirlpool, because you do not want to grope along a thread with cowardly hand; and where you can *guess*, you hate to *deduce*—to you alone I tell the riddle that I *saw*, the vision of the loneliest.
>
> —*Thus Spoke Zarathustra*, III, "Of the Vision and the Riddle"

THE CHAPTER TITLED "Of the Vision and the Riddle" in *Thus Spoke Zarathustra* presents the *Nietzschean* test of the Eternal Return. This invitation conveys the premises of the reevaluation to come, since it reverses the traditional connotations associated with riddles, on the one hand, and those related to vision, on the other hand. From the beginning, seeing does not help solve the riddle—as would have been the case within the context of prophetic revelation[1]—but it leads to the riddle's preservation and concealment so that seeing could turn the riddle into the question *par excellence* that would test the will of the individual confronted by modern nihilism. Only the individual who is "delighted in riddles," only the one who agrees to dance on the moving floor of appearances[2] without seeking grounds and justifications, only this courageous individual can hear and see, in the same synesthetic movement, the enigmatic word and stage that stood before Zarathustra's eyes. My essay does not aim to propose another exegesis of the doctrine of the Eternal Return. Rather, I would like to propose that Zarathustra's connection between seeing and saying—between the vision and the riddle—may be interpreted as a *mise en abyme* of a tension structuring Nietzsche's entire corpus. I argue that this tension anticipates the phenomenological method as a singular way of seeing and questioning the world and its modes of givenness "without inferring." Indeed the tension not only prepares and calls for a deconstruction (*Abbau*) of the grounds of Western metaphysics, but it also introduces a manner of looking at things that is properly phenomenological, that is, that tells us something about a given phenomenon. I claim that this vision has to be a "glance into the abyss"[3] so that the riddle that epitomizes my relation to the world can recover its visibility and its meaningfulness beyond the sufficient reasons given by metaphysics and the "thesis of the natural world." Moreover it has to be a particular kind of seeing that needs to go beyond mere presencing in order to differ from the metaphysical reifying gaze.[4]

I shall argue that Nietzsche anticipates what has to be a "phenomenology of the Unapparent," which is a phenomenology that focuses and reflects on the appearing itself and its constitution rather than on appearances themselves. But as Nietzsche explains from the very first pages of *the Birth of Tragedy*, this "glance into the abyss" disrupts the Apollonian individuation and may cause subjectivity's deconstruction.[5] It therefore questions his project as well as phenomenology's possibilities in terms of taking up a coherent interpretation of the world and its constitution, as well as some ethical consequences for the individual. I would like to show that the tension between vision and enigmatic speech could rearticulate the theoretical space and practical interests of subjectivity more generally in Nietzsche, Husserl, Heidegger, and Merleau-Ponty. This relation between the vision and the riddle indicates a new understanding of finitude and of its coming ethical possibilities: either from its paradoxical achievement in a *seeing* that would give access to some kind of transcendence (Nietzsche/Husserl), or from its preservation and concealing thanks to some *telling* (Nietzsche/Heidegger) whose enigmatic feature would point to the new infinity and the closure/disclosure function of the hermeneutic circle. The scope of this essay is more comprehensive than historical, in the sense that I am well aware of the potential anachronisms that such comparisons may involve. But going back to Nietzsche could help rephrase the ambitions of any phenomenological reflection that wants to confront itself to the problematic connections between an ontological story about subjectivity's intentional relation to the world and a way to liberate its power without damaging its life—that is, annihilating its self-constituting *life-world*.[6]

The first part of the essay brings to light this problematic relation between vision and riddle, showing that it is a central theme in Nietzsche's works and that it defines in some sense Nietzsche's picture of individuation. Indeed this glance into the abyss affects the metaphysical grounds of subjectivity and what could be already called the "natural thesis of the world." In other words, I will argue that Nietzsche divests the phenomenological enigma of my relation to the world of its metaphysical residues thanks to a particular way of looking at things. Indeed Nietzsche's perspectivalism rids philosophy of the principles of sufficient reason and identity which are constitutive of the natural thesis of the world and therefore targets classical conceptions of the subject. This movement gives birth to what could be already called a "phenomenological" horizon that calls for a reformulation of our finite condition and a new relation to the world and grounds of subjectivity. This relation would be an experimentation of the enigma which I am as an individuated singularity that incorporates (*Einverleibung*), through its look, living possibilities.

In the second part, I propose that these three steps of the Nietzschean deconstruction echo what could be considered the three paroxysmal moments of the phenomenological enterprise (Husserl, Heidegger, Merleau-Ponty). The deconstruction of subjectivity leads to the constitution of a particular kind of discourse or signification as well as to some sort of ethical vision or intuition, both of which could be traced back—as I will show—to Nietzsche's approach to subjectivity as a concealing/revealing phenomenon. Indeed the Husserlian phenomenological gaze points to the abyss—to the *Urgrund* of subjectivity—which makes sense of the world thanks to the constituting and valuating activity of consciousness. Surely Nietzsche and Husserl expressed opposite judgments when they came to evaluate the relation that intentional consciousness has to truth and rationality.[7] Indeed genealogical and teleological interpretations seem to be irreducible to one another.[8] But their directionality converges with regard to a similar will to make the sight of singularity depend on the enigma of its constitution and of the world's constitution, as well as the same desire to see in this enigma the *resources* of a new philosophical foundation. Following Boehm's interpretation, I center the comparison between Husserl's and Nietzsche's approaches to subjectivity by bringing to light the similarities between what could be called the Nietzschean morphology that describes the different layers of intentionality and Husserl's genetic phenomenology that uncovers the dynamic process initiated by transcendental subjectivity.

Heidegger's late analysis in *The Principle of Reason* (*Satz vom Grund*, 1957) reveals more explicitly a Nietzschean influence with regard to the way Heidegger then conceives of Dasein's finitude by opposition to its treatment in *Sein und Zeit*. The horizon opened up by the question of Being turns the vision into a process of appropriation (*Ereignis*)[9] and enforces its enigmatic character, though this way of seeing may be the only one able to give its speech back to the individual.[10] Comparable to Nietzsche's project as well, the reformulation initiated by Merleau-Ponty in *Eye and Mind* and *The Visible and Invisible* aims to reconnect seeing to the lived body—to the flesh (*chair*) which is its source—in order to consider the enigma of my embodied relation to the world no more as a threat but as a condition of possibility of any ethical perspective.

I shall ultimately claim that the tension thereby underlined between the vision and the riddle—from the Nietzschean genealogy to phenomenology in its three expressions: transcendental, hermeneutic, and perceptive—help gather the ethical possibilities of any thought that, behind Eternal Return, tries to convert the enigma into desire and the vision into a call for the unforeseen.

Perspectivalism and Phenomenological Seeing: Nietzsche's Deconstruction of Metaphysical Grounds

I should start by bringing to light this problematic relation between vision and enigma in Nietzsche's conception of subjectivity and the world. Nietzsche's thought, thanks to a particular way of seeing, liberated the enigma of my relation to the world and made the phenomenological method possible. The perspectival glance is indeed what allows us to reintroduce enigma after the metaphysical domination of the objective gaze. Some conceptions relative to consciousness, knowledge, and self-overcoming confront each other behind every philosophical questioning about vision. Aristotle perfected the Socratic foundation by conceptualizing the essence of *theoria* in contrast with the two other human activities of *poiesis* (production) and *praxis* (self-determined action, undetermined by external ends). *Theoria* is essentially a disinterested contemplation and is constituted by the typical attitude of the Sage. This conception is conveyed by every idealist doctrine that considers the contemplative method as the only valid relation of truth/correspondence between the intellect and the world. That is precisely the doctrine to which Nietzsche is opposed when he frequently seeks "perspectivalism" by using the metaphor of the mirror. The mirror—*speculum* in Latin—conveys and reflects the image of philosophical activity. But far from reflecting the truth, the philosophical or religious speculation, according to Nietzsche, is just a variation on shadows and lights that are projected on the reality of fleeting appearances shaped by will to power's dynamism. Classical ontology would institute the common dichotomy between the subject and the object and would place the look in respect to a will to objectivity. Perspective—according to etymology—is a sight *through* something, a piercing sight, not the contemplation of an infrangible opacity but rather an awakening stimulated by the enlightening activity of the will to power. "A psychologist must turn his eyes from himself to eye anything at all."[11] Reflection must cease to be a withdrawal into oneself—as the etymological meaning points out—in order to completely spread out in an aesthetic and poetic interpretation and to be performed as a reflection of the shimmering world. Perspective thus belongs to an artistic sight that alternates creation with destruction of pictures according to the rhythm of the intensity that sustains singularity. Zarathustra's poetic account of the Eternal Return illustrates such a conception.

Zarathustra encounters two characters: a dwarf and a shepherd. The dwarf deduces without feeling or perceiving, and he is confident using his theoretical eye.[12] The character of the shepherd, which is evoked next, represents revelation and its consequences. The Temptation (*Versuch*) of the Eternal Return confronts the human being with great dangers. Even exposed and sealed by the metaphoric language, this experience could again constitute the "heaviest weight" that is nihilism and which is symbolized by the suffocation caused by the snake.[13] The confrontation with nihilism—the glance at the bottomless abyss of existence—relieves this character of his Arcadian shepherd condition. After that experience, Nietzsche—or rather, Zarathustra—thus describes him: "No longer shepherd, no longer human—one changed, radiant, *laughing*! Never yet on earth has a human being laughed as he laughed!" (TSZ 272). The picture of metamorphosis is set again to express the radical transformation of the individual and the viewpoints he now has on life. The laugh shows the metamorphosis that sustains the way of looking: it is no longer a question of the awareness of an eventual individuated condition, but one that deals with an attitude, a scenic position in front of the surprise of intuition and the fields of possibilities that the attitude opens.

The transfiguration conveyed by the ineffable vision of the riddle further overcomes the fatality of the Oedipean drama. Nietzsche compares the thought of the Eternal Return with the head of Medusa, a myth that is already present in *The Birth of Tragedy* to account for Apollo's attitude before the Dionysian force: "Apollo who stood tall and proud among them and who with the Medusa's head warded off this grotesque barbaric Dionysian force, the most dangerous power it had to encounter" (BT 25). The temptation of petrifaction, hardening of the sight—and thus the incarceration of the human being in a cellular individuation—would remain constantly present. The survival of the singularity is involved in each way of looking, in each perspective and glance. Only "the mirror of beauty" supported by an artistic sight could outsmart the risks of blindness and reification caused by Medusa, that is to say, the experience of the eternal return of everything—a return that holds reflections of Apollo's sight, which is less a life-saver than it is vengeful in its Dionysian and tragic side. The human being must attempt the Dionysian self-removal (*Entaüsserung*) in order to get rid of the theoretical eye and reverse the stakes involved in vision. This is not a matter of "intellect mirror" (*Daybreak* §121) that would reflect the world-show without playing it by smoothing its rough edges. It is rather a question of looking at the world-show through each of its reflections and at every moment, in order to experience and incorporate every chance of suffering and to overcome it.

Only a theatrical conception of the life, the world, and the human being—as actor and seer—allows such an activity. The condition of someone who sees would determine the human being to passivity, which would, in turn, prevent anyone from taking on creative activity that would give back the resources of self-creation by poetizing the world. Nietzsche describes such an exhaustion of the objective man who, like the dwarf, simplifies without bearing and stays confident with the theoretical and spectacular eye: "The objective man is indeed a mirror: he is accustomed to submit before whatever wants to be known, without any other pleasure than that found in knowing and mirroring. . . . His mirror soul, eternally smoothing itself out, no longer knows how to affirm or negate; he does not command, neither does he destroy. . . . For the post part, a man without substance and content, a 'selfless' man."[14] He reduces consciousness to the pure passivity of contemplative sight which neglects the agonistic dimension of life that urges one to bear the Dionysian suffering and to transmute it in Apollo's mirror, which the image refers to: "that freedom from the wild impulses that calm wisdom of the image-creating god. His eye must 'shine like the sun,' in accordance with his origins; eyes when it rages and looks displeased, it remains consecrated by the beauty of appearance" (BT 21). This new approach to vision would achieve a cohesion of opposites: cohesion of the subject and the object, of the actor and the onlooker, of the will to metamorphosis and the individuated entity. So Nietzsche describes the Dionysian vision of the world: "When we add to this horror the blissful rapture which rises up from the innermost depths of man, even of nature, as a result of the very same collapse of the *principium individuationis*, we steal a glimpse into the essence of the Dionysian, with which we will become best acquainted through the analogy to intoxication" (BT 22). To reinforce the plastic possibilities of the individual, the glance has to be sidelong, and thus it could reproduce the movement of the *Urwachsen*, which increases the will to power. The notion of obliquity points out what is pushed back from the vertical, from the perpendicular to the plane. Such a conception of sight leads to the notion of decentering that could be used to describe the inner configuration of the singularity. This sight's game shapes the distribution of space made by the dramatic transfiguration. The veil of the tragic transfiguration permits the oblique unfurling of the singularity upon the world stage—the singularity has no aim until he or she gets it. The individual endowed by an artistic sight is sustained by a plastic force that analogically echoes the forces that sustain the macrocosm.

Nietzsche thus presents and describes his Dionysian world:

> A monster of force, without beginning, without ending, a feast. Here is my Dionysian world: the world of eternal return of creation and destruction, this mysterious world of ambivalent delights, here is my "beyond good and evil"—without purpose. . . . That world is the world of will to power and nothing else.[15]

The thinker presents his world as "reflected in his mirror" and thus projects an artistic and Dionysian sight through the prism of a singularity undergoing its metamorphosis. By transforming the theoretical eye into a visionary and fragmented perspective, the thinker redefines the nature of the philosophical *speculum* by framing it within a dramatic ontology. The mirror, which is the mythological attribute of Dionysus, reproduces the experience of the *Versuch*, of the confrontation. But the perspectivalism that spreads and the aesthetic dimension of life that flashes on from that mirror present the love of life and the game of existence as revealing the same desire for illusion and appearance:

> What is "appearance" to me now! Certainly not the opposite of some essence—what could I say about any essence except name the predicates of its appearance! Certainly not a dead mask that one could put on an unknown X and probably also take off X! To me, appearance is the active and living itself, which goes so far in its self-mockery that it makes me feel that here there is appearance and a will-o'-the-wisp and a dance of spirits and nothing else—that among all these dreamers, even I, the "knower," am dancing my dance. (GS §54, 63–64)

Thus the appearance is lived and significant reality. One does not need to state the invisible and supersensitive "Beyond," because the appearing itself calls for a necessity of illusion which is, in the Nietzschean perspective, a way to bring to light the figures on stage. Similar to the epiphany of Dionysus, world and singularity appear and hide from view, are destroyed and re-created, and thus, from an aesthetic point of view, call for a kind of dialectic of depth and appearance.

This perspectival sight thus discredits the theoretical eye and reaches the ontological and epistemological foundations which have guaranteed the stability of the metaphysical edifice: the principle of sufficient reason and the principles of identity and noncontradiction—principles that aim precisely to prevent any questioning and presentation from falling into some enigmatic becoming. Therefore perspective also has an epistemic function which anticipates the role of the coming phenomenological sight since it helps the genealogical method to reveal the vanity of what Husserl will call the "thesis of the world" and which reflects the primacy—and the evidence—associated with the principle of sufficient reason and the principle of identity. As Fink noted, Nietzsche's conception of enigmatic vision develops a "negative ontology"[16] of things and beings that seems to echo the phenomenological reduction and destruction that brackets any certainty about their independent existences. The perspectival and phenomenological vision is a coming into presence of the enigma, but a presence that does not necessarily carry out a positive ontological claim about beings. Let us now recall what is at stake in Nietzsche's eradication of the metaphysical grounds—and notably of the principle of sufficient reason—in order to show its phenomenological resonance.

Nihil est sine ratione: here is the principle of sufficient reason.[17] Nietzsche sees behind the unconditional nature of this assertion the following fallacy: negating nothingness (*Nihil . . . Sine*)[18] represents the paroxysmal form of reactive nihilism which paradoxically sets the conditions of possibility of any affirmation under the aegis of metaphysical grounds that negate the deeply polemical and nonlogical dimension of reality. Indeed the principle of identity turns the logical principle of noncontradiction into an ontological ground. However, this enterprise contradicts the lived experience of singularity. Nietzsche thus diagnosed the nihilism carried out by such an approach. But, as is well known, he uses this same nihilism to reduce metaphysics to self-contradiction and nothingness. Deconstructing metaphysical grounds does not lead to answers concerning the "reason" of being and the world but rather to the questioning of some kind of reevaluation, to turn any possible answer into a riddle, which would be a new way to test (*Versuch*) the viability and the affective reality of the relation I have with *this* particular practical world I am related to and interested in. The point is then no longer to attempt to find the "reasons" or the origin of the world and subjectivity but to elaborate a method that brings to light the constituting activity of subjectivity, which assesses its values and which could substitute a rehabilitation of irreducible plurality to the reassuring constraint of fixed principles. It is the very reason why one should "negate being" in a move that seems to anticipate the process of phenomenological reduction.[19] By bringing down the supremacy of rationality and questioning its evident nature as well as the alleged evidence of its principles, Nietzsche replaces the metaphysical grounds with the will to power as the new interpretative key of any exegesis. Since there is nothing but a sensitive and apparent world, the will to power has nothing to do with a rational and substantial static ground. It is the interpretation given to the dynamic of affects that feeds and curves singularity's own depth. It is why the Greeks "were superficial—*out of profundity!*" (GS, foreword to second edition, 8).

To operate this intrinsic linking and make legitimate the transformations it carries out, one should substitute the abyss (*Abgrund*) to the ground—an abyss that only a perspectival or phenomenological sight can reveal. This method is that of the loneliest philosopher:

> He will doubt whether a philosopher could *possibly* have "ultimate and real" opinions, whether behind every one of his caves there is not, must not be, another deeper cave—a more comprehensive, stranger, richer world beyond the surface, an abysmally deep ground [*Abgrund*] behind every ground, under every attempt to furnish "foundations [*Begründung*]." Every philosophy is a foreground philosophy. (BGE §289, 229, translation modified)

The Nietzschean declination of the etymological root *Grund* illustrates the unveiling activity that paradoxically calls for a rehabilitation of enigma. *Abgrund* designates the abyss, the precipice. Suppressing the rational principles that illusorily ground the truth of Being, denouncing their vacuity by delving into the *Abgrund*, and looking for this abyss behind any foundation (*Begründung*) are ways to reflect the genealogical and hermeneutic activity of the will to power. *Begründung* (translated as "foundation") indeed means "instauration" but also "justification," "motivation." Replacing causal explanations with the revelation of the abyss helps unveil the plurality of hidden forces that build up the individual, and institute the depth characteristic of the will to power and growth into a constitutive criterion of the free spirit's new look. But getting rid of the principle of sufficient reason and canceling the metaphysical—and even ontotheological—justifications of the existence of the Cartesian subject is clearly dangerous. Such an approach leads us to reconsider the relation between the finite and the infinite and to relinquish transcendence.

This enterprise turns and converts (*Umwerten*) the metaphysical truth into some original and always opened riddle. It also causes a vanishing of the meaning that liberates the vision and subverts it so that it becomes, paradoxically, as petrifying as Medusa's look. Nietzsche is aware of that consequence carried out by the liberation of horizon associated with the irresolution of enigma, and thus he tries to reconsider the relation between finitude and transcendence within singularity itself in order to avoid such a nihilistic consequence. The vision does not aim to be a new worldview (*Weltanschauung*) but rather a kind of showing, presencing, or even "fulfilling" which points to the necessity of assuming our "human all too human" condition. Going back to riddles therefore questions the grounds of subjectivity and consciousness as well as its destination.

Finitude and Transcendence: The Riddle of Transcendence in Nietzsche's Thought

Nietzsche tries to overcome the dichotomy of finite and infinite, the gap enforced throughout history by moral and religious values, in order to conceive according to his own approach to singularity the possibility of measure within the context of infinite possibilities. In the modern perspective inherited from Christianity, finitude confronts the human being with her own limitation and makes that limitation equivalent to privation and distortion. Individuation is thus viewed as self-closure, and with regard to this perception, the human being's revolt can only lose itself in the meandering of a "bad infinite" which makes her think that she could equal the Divine. The infinite sought for by modern individuals is essentially deprivation of the finite, as the etymology suggests. The lack of measure produces a kind of vertigo,[20] which prevents humans from acting since they cannot situate themselves on Earth and define their relation to the world in the absence of transcendence. Nietzsche's approach to finitude thus destroys the foundations of the principle of individuation without denigrating the existential reality of this phenomenon: subjectivity individuates itself through its shaping of the world or, shall we say, through the constitution and vision of the world. Finitude thus becomes the original enigma, the abyss within which the individual would find the meaningfulness of her existence. The well-known paragraph 124 of the *Gay Science*, "The Horizon of the Infinite," also formulates the riddle seen by Zarathustra and anticipates such a challenge:

> But there will be hours when you realize that it is infinite and that there is nothing more awesome than infinity. Oh, the poor bird that has felt free and now strikes against the walls of this cage! Woe, when homesickness for the land overcomes you, as if there had been more *freedom* there—and there is no more land. (GS §124, 118)

Eradicating principles entails an enlargement of the gaze that gives back some sort of enigmatic depth. The fatigue of the last man and his "blinking," described by Zarathustra in his prologue, are due to his nostalgic attitude toward the finite and to his incapacity to experiment with and incorporate the enigma that represents the enlarged vision of its living possibilities.

The Riddle as a Call for Creation and Self-overcoming: Measuring Life

Paragraph 124 in the *Gay Science* describes a Faustian infinite unable to give humans a measure to their lives. Similar to a bird stuck in its cage, this bad infinite is tainted with the Promethean ambition of a human being who wants to equal the gods. It can only lead us to disgust (*Ekel*), and it shows a deep misunderstanding of openness, which should be considered an *openness to* the world—as a phenomenological horizon—and not as the paroxysmal and paralyzing indeterminacy of things. The character of Faust or the Wagnerian hero exemplifies "all the chills and itching of romantic mysticism" (KSA 12, 1 [228], 60). The infinite, the Unlimited, is lived through as immediacy, as repetition, as passion, since the individual is not able to incorporate it, to "get over it" (KSA 9, 7 [13], 319). Led by the Faustian illusion of a freedom that is in fact license, hubris, and servitude, the modern individual—convinced she is the "measure of every thing"—loses herself in a relativism that makes her forget all genuine measure and enforces a feeling of exile that projects the image of a lost paradise. Nietzsche thus writes in paragraph 224 of *Beyond Good and Evil*, "Let us own it; our thrill is the thrill of the infinite, the unmeasured. Like a rider on a steed that flies forward, we drop the reins before the infinite, we modern men, like semi-barbarians—and reach *our* bliss only when we are most—in danger" (BGE §224, 153). This comparison shows human confusion between emancipation, which guarantees life and is allowed infinite openness to possibilities of metamorphosis, and the agitation valued by those who forget to take into account the two aspects (*Gesichter*) of life: the finite and the infinite, which are no more the results of a metaphysical or theological conception of life but rather the two faces of a continuous self-creation and the two plans of a glance that looks at the world while preserving its enigmatic feature.

I have thus exposed the way Nietzsche's thought, answering Zarathustra's call, articulates the notions of vision and enigma. The eradication of the principles of sufficient reason and individuation has carried out a rehabilitation of the "question," as Heidegger would say, a new kind of visibility to the enigma. But this enigma liberates the horizon of subjectivity and confronts it with a lack of ground and anchor that might be dangerous since it makes contingent the initial moral and ethical meanings attached to individual life. I shall argue now that the phenomenological movement also structures these questions around the notions of vision and enigma. Indeed it rethinks—referring implicitly or explicitly to Nietzsche—the necessity of finding a new measure and direction (*Sinn*) to circumscribe the horizon of subjectivity, which is paradoxically open due to its finitude. These three moments of the Nietzschean phenomenological deconstruction (the destruction of grounds due to perspectivalism, the opening of the horizon, and the necessity to create oneself in order to assume the enigma) resonate respectively in the works of Husserl, Heidegger, and Merleau-Ponty much like the three steps that structure the phenomenological project and guide it through the constitution of a word—of an ethical vision whose force and value come precisely from the preservation of a certain tension between vision and enigma.

Intensity and Intentionality: Going Back to the Riddle Itself

As mentioned in the introduction, the Husserlian gaze also points to the abyss, that is, to subjectivity's groundlessness. Husserlian subjectivity gives meaning to the world due to the primordial constituting and valuating (*Umwertung*) activity of consciousness. It is clear that Nietzsche and Husserl have opposing judgments when it comes to evaluating the powers of intentional consciousness with regard to truth and rationality. Nonetheless they seem to start out with a similar question and diagnosis. Specifically they seem to share a willingness to make singularity's gaze rely on the enigma of its constitution and to share a desire to see in this enigma the potential resources for a new philosophical foundation—a new way to articulate seeing and understanding.[21]

I shall first examine more closely the question of whether it is possible to consider the Nietzschean perspectival glance as "phenomenological," that is, this particular vision allowed by its confrontation to the abyss. First we need to compare it to the Husserlian definition of the phenomenological gaze, which results from a similar will to get rid of metaphysical foundations and to account for subjectivity's finitude. This finitude is paradoxically understood as openness, a form of transcendence within immanence itself resulting from the constituting activity of intentional consciousness. The "principle of principles" becomes the look itself (*Ideas I*, §24), which brings to light the dogmatic feature of the natural attitude, effectively forgetting the constituting process from which it takes its origin and significance.

The phenomenological articulation of seeing and understanding considers the metaphysical interpretation of reality and subjectivity as prejudices of the natural attitude. The natural attitude thinks of individuals as mundane beings governed by causality and therefore misunderstands the deeply dynamic nature of subjectivity and its impossible objectification. We can therefore read, for example in paragraphs 30 and 31 of *Ideas I*, a critique of the natural attitude that seems to echo Nietzsche's denunciation of the alleged evidence of the principle of sufficient reason.[22] The very concept of a sufficient reason itself implies that we take the meaning and the existence of the world and its objects as independent from the constituting activity of transcendental consciousness. In the natural attitude, it is obvious that there is something rather than nothing, and there is no room for riddles or enigma. This kind of look in fact equivocates blindness, which exhausts the phenomenon's reality by objectifying its meaning. The metaphysical approach, which underlies the attitude of the natural sciences, does not reveal a particular articulation of vision and enigma but rather quite the opposite: a movement from which certain truths and facts require blindness to dominate. The phenomenological gaze, thanks to reduction, consists in reversing (*umwerten*) the perspectives that subjectivity has on the world and to restore a vision—an intuition of the enigma—which founds my relation to the world and which is nothing but the constituting activity of my consciousness. The phenomenological reduction therefore restores a more fundamental way of seeing which reveals the very facticity of my individuation—that of embodied constituting consciousness—which is considered to be a lived experience irreducible to reification.[23] The phenomenological reduction, like the Nietzschean perspective, leads to a kind of *Umwertung,* as Husserl himself remarks in *Ideas I,* which traces not only the theoretical scope back to consciousness but also the practical interests that give its direction to the gaze:

> It is a matter of indicative designations of a definite, specifically peculiar mode of consciousness which is added to the original positing *simpliciter* (whether this is or not an actional and even a predicative positing of existence), and, likewise in a specifically peculiar manner, changes its value [*Umwerten*]. This changing of value is a matter in which we are perfectly free, and it stands over against all position-takings in the proper sense of the term. (*Ideas I*, §31)

The phenomenological reduction thus reveals the primordial process of evaluation (*Umwertung*) inseparable from an attitude, a particular layout of my individuality,[24] which leads my consciousness to attach a specific meaning to an object in a given situation. The phenomenological look is therefore a vision that identifies world's grounds within the "absolute nature of subjectivity" (Ricoeur), that is, a sort of self-creation or self-grounding that emerges from the originary giving intuition. This new "ground" is, for Husserl, transcendental subjectivity, which is itself a dynamic process that differs from any metaphysical *substance* or *subjectum*. Transcendental subjectivity is the source of every vision and every common visible space, but its enigmatic character resists objectification.[25] Husserl therefore seems to propose a solution to the enigma revealed by genealogical activity: by apprehending the self-constituting process he reveals as teleological. But Nietzschean genealogy and Husserlian phenomenology are both relying on a gaze that liberates the horizon and does not look for resources and legitimacy in the externality of the principle of sufficient reason. To be sure, the random and polemic character of the forces that sustain the Nietzschean Will to Power differ fundamentally from the teleological nature of Husserlian consciousness, which constitutes itself in such a way that it assures—thanks to its own movement—the foundations of its transcendental activity. Nonetheless the development of an enigmatic glance—of asking riddles—which would be produced by transcendental consciousness is at the core of the phenomenological relation to the world. The Heideggerian treatment of this relation seems to be even closer to the Nietzschean diagnosis since it renounces the teleological structure in order to consider more radically the hermeneutic potential of the ground's vanishing and therefore the visions allowed by the enigma's preservation. The phenomenological sight is no more a coming into the presence of the enigma (Husserl) but its preservation and expression (a game of concealing/revealing), due to a new relation between sight and speech.

Ontology and Vision: The Riddle of the Being-in-the World Structure

The Heideggerian answers to Nietzsche's diagnosis on finitude lie in a rather positive comprehension of Dasein's finitude as being the origin of any potential horizon of understanding. The preservation of the enigma—and thereby of finitude—reflects itself, according to Heidegger, in the quest for a look that would be itself enigmatic insofar as it would precisely allow, in some sense, seeing what does not appear. I will now try to bring to light some filiations between Nietzsche and Heidegger regarding this question of the Unapparent. I shall argue that the later works from Heidegger (inspired by his seminars on Nietzsche) seem to show a Nietzschean reorientation in the way that Heidegger conceives of Dasein's finitude. The horizon opened up by the question of Being makes enigmatic the vision—understood thus as free appropriation (*Ereignis*)—involved in the mere fact of being-in-the-world.

In *The Principle of Reason*, Heidegger analyzes the place taken by the principle of sufficient reason within metaphysics and opposes to it a certain "letting-be" of phenomena expressed by the famous words of Angelus Silesius: "The rose is without why, it blooms because it blooms, it pays no attention to itself, asks not whether it is seen."[26]

The first part of Silesius' verses expresses the rejection of final causes to the benefit of the efficiency of a development that perpetuates itself without being initiated by a first impulse. But the sentence makes sense only if we take into account its ending and the fact that denying grounds necessarily implies a consummation ("it pays no attention to itself") and a suspension of significance and interpretation (*Bedeutsamkeit*) sheltered from theoretical looks and their "productive gaze" (*das Ersehen des Wesens*). The enigmatic saying reflected by Silesius's verses is itself a seeing, a figuration of our own pathway to comprehension of the more original enigma that represents the repetition of the question of Being.[27]

In the manner of Nietzsche, who elaborated an image of the underground to thwart the projects of underworld theories, Heidegger thinks of Being as "without grounds," "without reason," "an Abyss" (*Abgrund*), in order to make possible the advent of signification. This lack of reason, of grounds, allows us to display the infinite task proper to the hermeneutic circle, since the enigmatic structure of seeing leads to a reversal (*Umwertung*) of the paradigm of any possible comprehension—of every glance that is already located within a horizon of meaning. Only an enigmatic seeing, that is, a way of seeing that does not try to objectify the interpretation but that assumes the question of Being (for Heidegger) or singularity's becoming (for Nietzsche), can ensure a promising horizon for the individual. As Heidegger wrote in the Zähringen seminar (1973), which notably analyzed the contribution of Husserl's categorical intuition:

> We need to learn to distinguish between *path* and *method*. In philosophy, there are only paths; in the sciences, on the contrary, there are only methods, that is, modes of procedure. Thus understood, phenomenology is a path that leads away to come before, and it lets that before which it is led show itself. This phenomenology is a phenomenology of the Unapparent. Only now can one understand that there were no concepts for the Greeks. Indeed, in conceiving [*Be-greifen*], there is the gesture of taking possession. The Greek *orismos* on the contrary surrounds firmly and delicately that which sight takes into view; it does not con-ceive.[28]

The Greek *orismos* lets the meaning emerge and derives, as Heidegger noted in the *Beiträge*, the *er-eignen*, the fact of appropriating something for oneself, from the *er-aügen*, the calling out of the gaze. But this grasp is ambiguous because this confrontation could easily become a "risk"—"the heaviest load," as Nietzsche would say—because the nihilistic temptation of technical thinking, the temptation that answered the last men's desire for security, always risks annihilating the enigma and missing the meaningfulness of the Unapparent. The phenomenological seeing that Nietzsche already worked out becomes the true measure of an enigmatic speech which opposes the foreseeable answers sought by modernity. Never thinking the nature of the glance without the pattern of enigma, without the question of which it is already an interpretation—that of the meaning of my relation to the world—allows me to elaborate a way of thinking opened to others and to the world which is opposed to the foreseeable and thus guarantees the word's hearing and respect. In the manner of the Nietzschean *amor fati*, the enigma of Being is then also a test for the individual to measure itself against what she cannot foresee. The Nietzschean sovereignty that results from the individual capacity to will the return of everything (including the spider)[29] seems to resonate in the resolution and commitment that Dasein is invited to adopt vis-à-vis Being in Heidegger's later works.[30] This commitment—the very fact of being able to commit oneself to Being—does not belong to calculative thinking. This commitment is a glance able to give the measure and the rhythm of what is to come if we let ourselves be invaded by the "thrill of the infinite" and if we do not understand that the abyss, the *Abgrund*, the unforeseen, is precisely the resource and the very condition of any potential meaning we could give to words and promises.

Concluding Remarks: The Riddle as the Visibility and Living Structure of the Phenomenological Being-There

To conclude, I would like to briefly touch on the third phenomenological path, that of Merleau-Ponty,[31] in order to show that it echoes Nietzsche's option that consisted in reconnecting the hermeneutics of seeing to the lived body—to the flesh from which it originates itself—in order to think the preservation of the enigma of my relation to the world not as a danger but rather as the condition of possibility of any ethical vision opening up a route to concrete freedom.

Merleau-Ponty, like Nietzsche, Husserl, and Heidegger, shares the idea according to which looking for reasons—definite and simple solutions to Being's and subjectivity's enigma—corresponds to being "blind for Being"[32] ("blindness for Being") and to reject what really *is* and which is nothing else than singularity's life captured in its becoming, according to the perceptive evidence itself. For Merleau-Ponty, the enigma is at the same time preservation but also a spreading (*jaillissement*) of the invisible, of Being, within the scope of an enlarged vision understood as perception of the world. As a questioning, the enigma is in itself an answer, a going back to the prereflective Being it has already been close to:

> Reflection must suspend the faith in the world only [so] as to see it, only so as to read in it the route it has followed in becoming a world for us; it must seek in the world itself the secret of our perceptual bond with it. It must use words not according to their pre-established signification, but in order to state this prelogical bond. It must plunge into the world instead of surveying it. . . . It must question the world, it must enter into the forest of references that our interrogation arouses in it, it must make it say, finally, what in its silence it means to say. . . .
>
> We have with our body; our senses, our look, our power to understand speech and to speak, measurants [*mesurants*] for Being, dimensions to which we can refer it, but not a relation of adequation or of immanence.(VI, 103)[33]

Whether they are applied to life in Nietzsche, to consciousness in Husserl, to Being in Heidegger, to the flesh in Merleau-Ponty, these *mesurants* are expressions, *emblems* of the synchronic nature of my relation to the world—of its directness. They invite us not to dissociate the seer from what is seen, the enigmatic speech from its meaning, the individual from its world and from the existence of other possible layouts and perspectives. But not dissociating what is seen from the seer and taking into account the directness of my experience of the world does not necessarily mean considering this experience as an "immediate" one—quite the contrary. These *mesurants* direct our sight to a particular meaning without objectifying it precisely because they strive to maintain the irreducible *écart* and depth from which only a subjectivity free and able to compose herself could emerge: "What is proper to the visible is, we said, to be the surface of an inexhaustible depth: this is what makes it able to be open to visions other than our own" (VI, 143). The ethical possibilities involved here come from the precedence of the enigma and the Invisible (or the unapparent) over the visible pattern of the life-world. By being "absences that count in the world" (to paraphrase Merleau-Ponty) they let always open the aesthetic, ontological, or ethical possibilities of subjectivity whose movement can be phenomenologically described yet never prescribed. This apprehension of what Nietzsche would have called our "new infinite" seems to attest to the open though *silent dialogue* between Nietzsche and phenomenology.

In this essay, I underlined a tension between the vision and the riddle from the Nietzschean genealogy to phenomenology in its three moments: transcendental, hermeneutic, and perceptual. It has led me to affirm that a connection between Nietzsche and phenomenology could help any contemporary thought longing for ethical possibilities and wishing to overcome the dichotomy between irresponsibility and innocence, on the one hand, and calculative thinking, on the other. This essay has shown that between Nietzsche and phenomenology there persists a certain relation between vision and enigma that eventually offers a new path, a new reflection that, beyond the irreducible differences that oppose these thinkers within the details of their philosophical systems, there is a common vision that is expressed throughout their shared inquiries into the human spirit. As Heidegger noted, perhaps unconsciously characterizing his relation to Nietzsche, "It is only when our thinking turns back to what is already thought, that there is still something to be thought."[34] By going back to Nietzsche, phenomenological reflection is pushed precisely to the very nature of the intentionality at stake in the correlational paradigm. It seems to me that interpreting it in terms of the pure *presencing* of beings would miss the enigma and the dynamism that it tries to leave intact and *alive*—whether we call it "Will to Power," "longitudinal intentionality of the flow," "*Ereignis*," or the "flesh."

Notes

1. As Didier Franck noted, the philosopher's relation to prophetic revelation is quite ambiguous, even though he refused to be a founder of religion himself. See *Nietzsche et l'ombre de Dieu*, 86.

2. See Nietzsche, *The Gay Science*, §54 (hereafter GS).

3. "Is not seeing always—seeing abysses?" said Zarathustra in *Thus Spoke Zarathustra*, III, 269 (hereafter TSZ). In this chapter, the vision occurs before the Moment (*Augenblick*) Gateway. The variation on the meaning of *Augenblick* and its relation to metaphysical grounds have been notably explored by Heidegger (see his *Nietzsche I*), Haar (*Nietzsche et la métaphysique*), and more recently

Shapiro in *Archaeologies of Vision*, in which Shapiro suggests that "we can read Zarathustra as a story of the eyes" (20) and "that Nietzsche sets himself the task of rethinking vision along these lines" (21).

4. In *Réduction et Donation*, 31–33, Jean-Luc Marion proposed a comparison between Nietzsche and Husserl that follows Heidegger's interpretation of Nietzsche. Nietzsche's perspectivalism would anticipate Husserl's reduction since they would altogether reflect residues of the metaphysics of presence (*Vorhandenheit*) by wanting to make everything explicit. I would like to argue in this essay that if there is a comparison to be made between Husserl and Nietzsche, it would pertain more to the discovery of a process of constitution that precisely resists the objectifying gaze and that is itself the process and dynamics of will to power as interpretation (Nietzsche) and of originary-giving intuition (Husserl). I therefore think that Marion's analysis of Husserl's *Logical Investigations*—the grounding relation between intuition and signification—(*Réduction et Donation*, 41–63) would be more relevant to and fruitful for an analysis of Nietzsche's phenomenological intuitions about meaning-making.

5. See Nietzsche, *The Birth of Tragedy*, 54 (hereafter BT).

6. As Boehm wrote, "For both Husserl and Nietzsche, this life-world is the 'only real world' and since it constitutes a unique system of subjective relativities, neither will it ever undergo a rational transformation nor will it serve as a ground for the mere theoretical construction of a philosophy or a truly rigorous knowledge. What is real in this life-world is not so depending on whether it is more or less 'true' or 'false': in this world, everything is expression, realization, and efficiency" ("Husserl and Nietzsche," p. 19 in this volume).

7. For example, Husserl maintains the ideal of objectivity and scientificity (see *Philosophy as Rigorous Science*), whereas Nietzsche tries to overcome the subject/object structure in order to consider a more radical philosophy of expression that would therefore be closer, as we shall see in this paper, to the later works of Merleau-Ponty. See Nietzsche, *Kritische Studienausgabe* 10, 3 [1] 98, 65 and 10, 1 [55], 25 (hereafter KSA).

8. On this topic, see Geniusas, chapter 3 in this volume.

9. See Heidegger, *Contributions to Philosophy,* and his analysis of the event (*Ereignis*) as something that comes to our eyes (*er-aügen*).

10. On vision as condition of possibility of overcoming nihilism and renewed forms of expression, see Shapiro, *Archeologies of Vision*, 158ff.

11. Nietzsche, *Twilight of the Idols*, "Maxims and Arrows," §35, 471.

12. "Upward—defying the spirit that drew it downward toward the abyss, the spirit of gravity, my devil and archenemy. Upward—although he sat on me, half dwarf, half mole, lame, making lame, dripping lead into my ear, leaden thoughts into my brain" (TSZ 268).

13. "A young shepherd I saw, writhing, gagging, in spasms, his face distorted, and a heavy black snake hung out of his mouth. . . . *Who* is the shepherd into whose throat the snake crawled thus? *Who* is the man into whose throat all that is heaviest and blackest will crawl thus?" (TSZ, 271–72).

14. Nietzsche, *Beyond Good and Evil*, §207, 127–28 (hereafter BGE).

15. Translated from the German edition: "Und wisst ihr auch, was mir die 'Welt' ist ? . . . Diese Welt: ein Ungeheuer von Kraft, ohne Anfang, ohne Ende, eine Feste. . . . Diese meine dionysische Welt des Ewig-sich-selber-Schaffens, des Ewig-sich-selber-Zerstörens, diese Geheimniss-Welt der doppelten Wollüste, dies mein Jenseits von Gut und Böse, ohne Ziel. . . . Diese Welt ist der Wille zur Macht—und nichts ausserdem!" (KSA 11, 38 [12], 611).

16. "The thing is a human invention of the mind—nothing else. . . . Nietzsche's fictional epistemology which understands the will to power as the deceiving and violating power of the intellect is in its important aspect a negative ontology of things: there are no things. His critique does not target all cognition but only the cognition of being, empirical cognition and particularly a priori cognition, that is the ontological interpretation in accordance with the categories" (Fink, *Nietzsche's Philosophy*, 150).

17. See KSA 12, 7 [3], 255: "The psychological certainty about the principle of sufficient reason lies in the belief we have that intention causes every event." The problem occurs when one considers that

intentionality means causality. Husserl's critique of causality and natural attitude brings to light a new conception of intentionality that seems to be already at stake in Nietzsche. See Husserl, *Ideas I*, §36, where intentionality is explicitly distinguished from external and factual causal relation.

18. On this topic, see Heidegger's analysis in "Nietzsche's Word 'God Is dead.'"

19. On this topic, see Babich, chapter 7 in this volume.

20. "(1) Vision is never totalizing and absolutely comprehensive; (2) there is no absolute foundation or ground to the abyss (*Abgrund*) which is vision; (3) seeing is never simple; it entails the risk of looking into and sometimes teetering on the edge of an abyss; this induces vertigo; (4) vision is through and through perspectival; there is no intrinsically privileged place from which to see things; and (5) every act of vision is framed in a larger context of which we may or may not become aware" (Shapiro, *Archeologies of Vision*, 20).

21. "For seeing is seeing *Abgründe*, that is, looking into areas where there is no ground, where the more intensely we look, the more the ground falls away" (ibid., 176).

22. See Husserl, *Ideas I*, "The Fundamental Reflection of Phenomenology."

23. See Husserl, *Cartesians Meditations*, V, and *Ideas II* , §§4, 5.

24. An interesting question to be explored in this context would be the issue of *habitualities* and their genesis in Nietzsche and Husserl.

25. Another way to phrase this would be to contrast Husserl's approach to longitudinal intentionality (*On the Phenomenology of the Consciousness of Internal Time*, §39) and the invisibility of its constitution (or its *Ur-konstitution*) with Nietzsche's reference to the Abyss as the invisible core where Will to Power develops itself. In both cases, it is the issue of subjectivity's foundation and the possibility to think, in some sense, subject's ipseity without its metaphysical *haecceitas*.

26. Heidegger, *The Principle of Reason*, 69–71.

27. "'Saying' means, when thought in a Greek manner, 'to bring to light,' 'to let something appear in its look,' 'to show the way in which it regards us,' which is why a saying clarifies things for us. But then how come a saying for the Greeks is a *legein*, a logos? Because *legein* means 'to gather, to lay-next-to-each-other.' But such a laying is, as laying that gathers, raises up, keeps and preserves, an allowing-to-lie-present that brings something to shine forth, namely that which lies present" (Heidegger, *The Principle of Reason*, 107).

28. Heidegger, *Four Seminars, Zähringen Seminar*, 80–81.

29. "And this slow spider, which crawls in the moonlight, and this moonlight itself, and I and you in the gateway, whispering together, whispering of eternal things—must not all of us have been there before? And return and walk in that other lane, out there, before us, in this long dreadful lane—must we not eternally return?" (TSZ 270).

30. See, for instance, Heidegger, "Letter on Humanism," 240, where Heidegger—replying to Jean Beaufret—defines thinking as *"l'engagement de l'être pour l'être,"* which has to be Dasein's ontological activity par excellence.

31. For more reflections on the ontological and aesthetic connections between Nietzsche and Merleau-Ponty, see in this volume chapters 9, 10, and 11, which explore in different ways how Nietzsche and Merleau-Ponty approach subjectivity's individuation and its embodied relation to the world.

32. Merleau-Ponty, *The Visible and the Invisible*, 16 (hereafter VI).

33. This movement could be an ontological phrasing of Nietzsche's conception of Will to Power as a hermeneutic force.

34. "Erst Wenn wir uns denkend dem schon Gedachten zuwenden, werden wir verwendet für das noch zu Denkende" (Heidegger, *Identität und Differenz*, 50).

Bibliography

Fink, Eugen. *Nietzsche's Philosophy*. New York: Continuum, 2003.

Franck, Didier. *Nietzsche et l'ombre de Dieu*. Paris: PUF, 1998.

Haar, Michel. *Nietzsche et la métaphysique*. Paris: Gallimard, 1993.

Heidegger, Martin. *Contributions to Philosophy*. Indianapolis: Indiana University Press, 2000.

———. *Four Seminars: Zähringen Seminar*. Indianapolis: Indiana University Press, 2003.

———. *Identität und Differenz*. Edited by Friedrich-Wilhelm von Herrmann. Frankfurt-am-Main: Klostermann, 2006.

———. *Identity and Difference*. Chicago University of Chicago Press, 2002.

———. "Letter on Humanism." In *Pathmarks*. Edited by William McNeill. Cambridge: Cambridge University Press, 1998.

———. *Nietzsche I*. Translated by David Farrell Krell. San Francisco: Harper & Row, 1979.

———. "Nietzsche's Word 'God Is dead.'" In *Off the Beaten Track*. Edited and translated by Julian Young and Kenneth Haynes. Cambridge: Cambridge University Press, 2002.

———. *The Principle of Reason*. Indianapolis: Indiana University Press, 1991.

Husserl, Edmund. *Cartesian Meditations*. Translated by Dorion Cairns. Dordrecht: Kluwer Academic, 1999.

———. *The Crisis of European Sciences and Transcendental Phenomenology*. Translated by David Carr. Evanston, IL: Northwestern University Press, 1970.

———. *Ideas Pertaining to a Pure Phenomenology and to a Phenomenological Philosophy. First Book*. Translated by Frank Kersten. Dordrecht: Kluwer Academic, 1982.

———. *Die Krisis der europäischen Wissenschaften und die transzendentale Phänomenologie: Eine Einleitung in die phänomenologische Philosophie*. Edited by Walter Biemel. The Hague: Martinus Nijhoff, 1976.

———. *On the Phenomenology of the Consciousness of Internal Time (1893–1917)*. Translated by John Barnett Brough. Dordrecht: Kluwer Academic, 1991.

———. *Phenomenology and the Crisis of Philosophy: Philosophy as Rigorous Science, and Philosophy and the Crisis of European Man*. Translated by Quentin Lauer. San Francisco: Harper & Row, 1965.

Marion, Jean-Luc. *Réduction et Donation*. Paris: PUF, 1989.

Merleau-Ponty, Maurice. *The Visible and the Invisible*. Translated by Alphonso Lingis. Evanston, IL: Northwestern University Press, 1968.

Nietzsche, Friedrich. *Beyond Good and Evil*. Translated by Walter Kaufmann. New York: Vintage Books, 1966.

———. *The Birth of Tragedy*. Translated by Douglas Smith. Oxford: Oxford University Press, 2000.

———. *Daybreak: Thoughts on the Prejudices of Morality*. Edited by Maudemarie Clark and Brian Leiter. Cambridge: Cambridge University Press, 1997.

———. *The Gay Science*. Translated by Josefine Nauckhoff. Edited by Bernard Williams. Cambridge: Cambridge University Press, 2001.

———. *Kritische Studienausgabe*. Edited by Girogio Colli and Mazzino Montinari. Berlin: Walter de Gruyter, 1980.

———. *Thus Spoke Zarathustra*. In *The Portable Nietzsche*. Translated by Walter Kaufmann. New York: Penguin Books, 1976.

———. *Twilight of the Idols*. In *The Portable Nietzsche*. Translated by Walter Kaufmann. New York: Penguin Books, 1976.

Shapiro, Gary. *Archaeologies of Vision: Foucault and Nietzsche on Seeing and Saying*. Chicago: University of Chicago Press, 2003.

9   The "Biology" to Come?

Encounter between Husserl, Nietzsche, and Some Contemporaries

Bettina Bergo

THIS ESSAY ADDRESSES two problems whose outcome indicates the site where a dialogue between phenomenology and Nietzsche might begin. The first problem can be posed as a question: What is the "biology" to which Husserl refers in Appendix 23 of the *Crisis* (published in 1936) and which is set forth as the "universal ontology"? The second problem concerns embodied consciousness and its life-world. If phenomenology was to serve as the foundation for all scientific endeavors, how then could biology be equated with ontology, and what relationship other than derivative could biology have to phenomenology?

Let us recall the spirit of the *Crisis of European Sciences* in light of Husserl's overarching project. By the time he published the *Crisis*, transcendental psychology was to lead back to the fundamental science of phenomenology. Not that Husserl had made a psychologistic turn; on the contrary, he was simply asserting the primacy of embodied, constituting consciousness as the foundation from which to derive what he called "regional ontologies." A number of access routes thus opened to transcendental phenomenology, including the critical-historical, that of a fundamental psychology, and perhaps that of the biology to come, grounded in the *Lebenswelt*. Transcendental phenomenology remained the formal foundation of all other inquiries, subjective or objective. Phenomenological consciousness, as meaning-conferral, remained the dynamic correlation of noetic aiming and noematic donation, out of which other domains of positive knowledge implicitly arose. Yet by the 1930s Husserl's investigation into intersubjective *intropathy* (*Einfühlung*), passive syntheses, and association had clearly shown the conundrums of phenomenological consciousness. Thus consciousness was invariably embodied and tied to bodily movements (*kinestheses*). However, the essential ground of consciousness, as spontaneous self-constitution and as the flow of time, proceeded on the basis of now-moments and their retentions, rooted in neurological processes unavailable to phenomenological description. Thus the brief arguments for biology, presented in Appendix 23 (left out of the English translation), had to do with Husserl's efforts to situate life, understood as physiological processes in lived bodies, in relation to the consciousness brought to light by transcendental psychology. Nevertheless if biology was to be universal *ontology*, that meant that the relationship between life and consciousness had come center stage, with life and consciousness, consciousness and the life-world constituting each other dynamically.

> Biology is certainly also—like all positive science—naïve science and "artwork," where the word is understood as a higher analogy for craftsmanship. The higher consists in that [biology] carries in itself an obscure meaning, whose true and authentic ontological significance [*Seinssinn*] it seeks to work out as knowledge [*Erkenntnis*], although it can never reach this [knowledge] in its present form. But biology, above all, could never become a concrete theory of the life-world . . . [although] its proximity to the sources of evidence makes it so near to the depths of things themselves that the way toward transcendental philosophy ought to be easiest for it and with this too, the way to the true a priori.[1]

The argument for a higher level of inquiry in biology rested on a certainty about which Husserl had long been more dogmatic than Heidegger: a *living* being exists coupled at multiple levels with its world. It is never, as transcendental consciousness might be, separable from world or others. Therefore the biology to come, for Husserl, had to have as its object "living," understood as the correlations of organisms and their life-world: "Biology is, for humans, essentially directed by their actual, originally experienceable humanity, because life alone is original, above all, and given in an authentic way in the self-understanding of the biological [*des Biologischen*]" (Hua VI, 482). Moreover, because living is "subjectivated," individuated thanks to the interaction of organisms with their life-world, the biology of that world, as experienced by human consciousness "on Earth," ought to be universal. It should provide concepts for understanding life in *any Lebenswelt*. Rather than overtaking transcendental psychology, the biology to come pointed to a long-standing tension in Husserl's work between lived experience and its physiological conditions of possibility. This tension accompanied his investigations into affects and drives throughout the 1920s and it haunted phenomenology in its *formalist* quality as the science of consciousness.

By 1936 a dual tension was obvious in Husserl, between transcendental consciousness and embodiment, on the one hand, and between subjective embodiment and life broadly construed as worldly, on the other. How could the biology Husserl envisioned as "fundamental" simultaneously elucidate the *living* that qualified the *Lebenswelt* and the "psycho-physics" that underlay the dynamic flow and subjective pull of transcendental consciousness (as inner time and as ownness)? Was it just a thought experiment that led Husserl to argue that "biology is the concrete and authentic psycho-physics" (Hua VI, 484)—and this precisely because it "has the same world generality as physics"? In principle, this was more than an experiment. "Any sense that a biology of Venus could have, if we were to speak of this as a possibility, is thanks to the originary meaning-constitution [*Sinnbildung*] of our life-world, and hence, thanks to the theoretical elaboration of this meaning-constitution through our biology. . . . This task gives it an infinite horizon" (Hua VI, 484). If biology—reconstituted in accord with phenomenology's approach to experience *before* it is divided into objective versus subjective experience—should rival physics through its direct and universal approach to life, then the biology to come should rival the transcendental psychology Husserl presented in the *Crisis*, because biology encompasses life as the dynamic of living, beyond consciousness as intentionality. Was this Husserl's response to the vast appeal of *Lebensphilosophie* in the 1930s? Was it a way into the "world" Heidegger had considered in his hermeneutic of *Dasein*? However we answer these questions, Husserl clearly struggled against Heidegger's approach to animal life, continually refining his conception of *Einfühlung* between 1910 and 1933. As the science of life, then, understood as self-development and self-sensing, biology alone could provide the extraphenomenological "roots" for embodied processes *even as they enabled and came into consciousness* (as instincts, drives, and sensations). In turn, transcendental phenomenology would elucidate the multiple modes by which drives and sensations were synthesized as the conscious experience of life. This claim was elicited and supported by Husserl's investigations into the synthesis of time consciousness, and it takes on real urgency in his 1920s studies of passive association. Yet the claim urges some reconciliation of life (understood as self-affection *and* as other living beings) with consciousness reduced to the transcendental flow and to passive syntheses.[2] In his methodological neutrality, Husserl refused both dualism and monism, but the task of developing a unified frame of description for bodily and mental events grew more manifest in his "genetic" investigations (i.e., those pertaining to the developmental aspects of consciousness, tied to the body). It is here that Nietzsche's meditation on forces in bodies suggests a dialogue with phenomenology.

Husserl's Phenomenology: An Idealism?

Before proceeding to Nietzsche, some remarks must be made about Husserl's idealism. Husserl largely refused the label—especially by the 1930s, when phenomenology was genetic and critical—of psychologistic consciousness and idealist abstractions, ushered in by the loss of the *Lebenswelt* (through Galileo's mathematization of physics). The *Crisis* questioned back, following a genealogy of the scientific worldview, in search of the *Lebenswelt* still present in Aristotle. It criticized Descartes's dualist ontology. The upshot of these fundamental philosophical decisions was, as Husserl argued:

> The natural science of the modern period, establishing itself as physics, has its roots in the consistent abstraction through which it wants to see, in the life-world, only

corporeity [*Körperlichkeit*]. Each "thing" "has" corporeity even though, if it is (say) a human being or a work of art, it is not merely bodily but is "embodied [*verkörpert*]," like everything real. Through such an abstraction, carried out with universal consistency, the world is reduced to abstract-universal nature. (Hua VI, 230)

Following this critical genealogy of modern philosophy, which Husserl carries out with rigor, the very notion of individuation is modified into substantial *rei*, associated with an equivocal, extended *or* a psychical *substance*, and set down as paradigmatic for all subsequent sciences, including physics and psychology.

> Human beings, concretely, in the space-time of the world, have their abstractly distinguished souls distributed among bodies, which make up, when we adopt the purely naturalistic consideration of bodies, a universe to be considered in itself as a totality. The souls themselves are external to one another . . . in their own abstract stratum, [but] *they do not make up a parallel total universe.* (Hua VI, 231)

As against idealism, "souls" in Husserl never constitute a universe *eo ipso*. The separation of individual psyches is analogous to the abstraction performed on life, breaking physical objects and topographies into homogeneous units. It is therefore the work of transcendental psychology to open a path to phenomenology, as the deformalization of consciousness without the spatial prejudice implicit in modernist abstraction (homogeneous units). The *Crisis* thus follows a critical-genealogical route back toward what Husserl had adumbrated already in the 1905–10 lectures on internal time-consciousness: consciousness understood in and as its proper medium, consciousness understood as transcendental and synthetic yet open to description. Husserl was seeking consciousness as subjective but not in all cases individuated. Living time consciousness was "absolute subjectivity" and a dynamic flow. Beyond that, Husserl "lacked names" in 1905.

On the other hand, by 1936 the *Crisis* has staked out more original positions. It argued clearly that the individuation of "souls" is the result of the individuation of bodies, given the ease with which bodies can be separated and counted. It did not deny the significance of embodiment for consciousness. Yet it intimated the possibility of a totalization of consciousness, at least as Fink understood the project. Thus while the early Husserl emphasized embodiment in service to the upwelling of now-moments forming consciousness, the genealogical phenomenology proposed reductions to what could be called metasubjective effectivity, that is, consciousness as pure act and livingness. The *Crisis* aligned psychology and biology by lifting biology out of the realm of positivistic abstraction. What gave rise to this strategy?

The absolute subjectivity as flow in the time-consciousness lectures is not alien to the hypothetical "pan-psychism" of the *Crisis*. The "names lacking" for the description of the originary source-point of the now and its resulting temporal flow also take a new shape in Husserl's passive synthesis investigations. There he confronted the problem of the limits of the flow and the multiple forms of association taking place in a given now-moment. He explored association as a process of contrast, similarity, and identification, through our passive rapprochement of perceptions. In his notes from the 1920s, he thus moved toward a philosophy of becoming, arguing that "the unity of the thing itself is thinkable only as a unity continuously ordered and extended in time." The possibility of association, whether as contrast or similarity, "rests . . . on the most originary continuity of the temporal extension."³ This most originary continuity presupposes "continuous becoming [*kontinuierlichen Werden*] within the temporal order" (Hua XI, 141), and that becoming has its neurological correlate. While many associations appear gratuitous, irrational, or idiosyncratic, this is due to the fact that each sense (sight, hearing, touch, etc.) unfolds around itself a field particular to it, and "the ideal extension to infinity of the fields is a sort of idealization that we can accept" (Hua XI, 148). Of course, *this* idealization is not idealism; it is just a heuristic about time designed to parallel the dynamic permanence of the body. What, however, made possible the overarching synthesis of these perceptual fields? The answer could only be psychophysical.

A more perplexing problem concerned that curious *non*field called affectivity. Certain associations must be the result of an "originary affection," notably contrastive associations: "We must characterize contrast as the most originary condition [*ursprünglichste Bedingung*] of affection" (Hua XI, 149). Affection, or what was once called "passions," opened phenomenological consciousness to the sheer complexity of embodiment and tied consciousness to its complement, forgetting. Affection is also intertwined with sensuous "data," pleasure and pain, and with drives, the "representatives" in consciousness of the instincts.

> From the sphere of affect [*Gemütssphäre*] we must take into account only those feelings [*Gefühle*] originally tied to sensuous data and say: on the one hand, the affection coming into being is functionally codependent on the relative size of the contrast; on the other hand, it is also dependent on privileged sensuous sentiments [*bevorzugenden sinnlichen Gefühlung*] like a sentiment of sensuous pleasure grounded in its unity by that which detaches [from the flow of consciousness in an associative moment]. We must likewise allow for drive-preferences [*triebmässige Bevorzugungen*], [which are] originally instinctive. (Hua XI, 150).

Uniting embodied perception with events in the *Lebenswelt*, along with embodied recollection of "privileged sensuous sentiments" and the surfacing of "drive preferences," Husserl forges a living consciousness. Only "life" carries the spontaneity, even the disorder of *affective* or passional associations. Affects are woven together with sensibility (feelings of pleasure or pain), forming the conditions of possibility of overarching hyletic unities (Hua XI, 152). In the investigations into passive association, the phenomenology of consciousness reaches a descriptive level that accounts for phenomena of forgetting and "repression." Essential in the study of associative phenomena is that so-called forces in the body have their corollary—*not* their epiphenomena—in consciousness understood as an affectivity-sensibility interweave. What psychoanalysis had ventured to describe as unconscious "repression" of painful or conflictual events opened to phenomenological description precisely thanks to emotions and affects (Hua XI, 152).

As the privileged connection between embodiment and "mental" activity, affection and feelings not only allow Husserl to approach intentionality as a spectrum of intensities, but they also provide a glimpse into patterns whereby certain sets of ideas are as if held out of the sphere of associative reactivation. The existence of these patterns is not directly demonstrable, but it proves heuristically precious when we study the seemingly illogical memory associations. These "repressions" belong so intimately to intentional consciousness—which implies consciousness *beyond* the projections of an individual psyche—that Husserl could speak of "a phenomenology of this so-called unconscious" (Hua XI, 154). With the extension of phenomenological description beyond sense perception per se and into sensuous-affective association and recollection, the phenomenological sphere of consciousness came to encompass embodiment in a broad, almost anti-idealistic way. It understood "intentionality" in such a way that critics could no longer object that the formalism intrinsic to Husserl's phenomenology missed the mark on corporeity, and that it could therefore never grasp the broader destiny of biology—that is, beyond what biology inherited from modernity.

Let me summarize: Starting from the genealogy Husserl proposes in the *Crisis*, I inquired whether phenomenology could offer an alternative biology that provided tools for understanding any life-world, including that in places presently unknown to human inquiry. I noted that this biology could stand as fundamental ontology, encompassing "the concrete world in its entirety [and] implicitly, physics itself."[4] It also referred to the "concrete psycho-physics"[5] that necessarily accompanied the phenomenological project as its indispensable supplement. Clearly, as the psychophysics adumbrated in the *Crisis* §66 had already shown, the biology Husserl had in mind was but a corollary to an a priori psychology of consciousness. This was radicalized in the Appendix, where biology became "absolutely universal philosophy."[6] How to parse the tension?

As a complementary psychophysics elucidating the claims of transcendental phenomenology, biology is averred by Fink's proposed completion of the *Crisis* project. Taking Fink's proposal to eliminate the mutual exteriority of *Seele* to each other as the legitimate end-point, I traced what I believe is the legitimate link between the time consciousness lectures of 1905 and the *Crisis*, namely the search for "absolute subjectivity." Because the works spanning the years 1926–36 introduced a genetic and historical-critical (or "generative") element,[7] it is no longer merely absolute subjectivity that is pursued. It is, rather, consciousness understood as the synthesis of life and subjectivation that is at stake. This claim is borne out by many manuscripts, notably those that treat the life of feeling and affectivity. The courage of those notes on passive synthesis, preparing the *Formal and Transcendental Logic*, lies in their extraordinary expansion of the domain of consciousness into the most elusive and ostensibly arbitrary acts from inexplicable forgetting, memory lapses, to equally inexplicable associative connections. On the basis of that expansion, phenomenology could approach even the clinical observations of psychoanalysis. For example, it could understand Freud's observations that repressed suffering spontaneously "associates" with bodily weaknesses, transforming them into symptoms like paralysis or cutaneous insensitivities. However, when pursued in psychotherapy, these associated psychophysical sufferings thrust roots into a past association of *desire* and *conflict*—of emotions and feelings—that could not come to light without description and dialogue. That would be the farthest phenomenological investigation could reach, that is, toward the conditions of meaning, of life as lived sensation and affection, and thus as consciousness coming into being.

Husserl's Biology to Come, Read with Nietzsche's Hermeneutics of Bodily Forces

Nietzsche's projected completion of Kant's critical project entailed corporealizing theoretical reason, historicizing practical reason, and weaving together the affective inscription of history into bodies, utilizing the concept of forces. Speculatively Nietzsche passed behind consciousness to forces in interpretation and conflict. This allowed him to use the body as the red thread of his philosophical project. We know that he read extensively in the materialist physiology of his time. He was familiar with Ernst Haeckel's reception of Darwin and the agonistic physiology of Wilhelm Roux, for whom struggle for survival was the immanent struggle for ascendancy from which the bodily organs themselves evolved. Above all, Nietzsche extended the notion of forces into a hermeneutics without precedent, such that what forces *did* correlationally probatively defined what they *were* ontologically. The concept of *Wille zur Macht* denoted, in condensed form, the fact of forces as interactions; as Deleuze once put it, will "is the *differential* element of force."[8] I will return to this when I discuss Nietzsche's hermeneutics. If, for Nietzsche, consciousness was the epiphenomenon of forces within bodies, it nevertheless maintained a temporary dignity as sovereign awareness. Yet consciousness mirrored patterns already occurring in the nervous system, in tissues, and between cells. Nietzsche's "agnostic monism" of forces, even when translated as "wills to power," was not concerned with mere material things. Force was one term among many with which he sought to explain the fundamental production of value at all levels of embodied existence. He spoke of "judgment," "spiritual event," even "mind," recognizing clearly that these concepts had come to denote what was intelligible to consciousness even though their power to conjoin or dissociate, to intensify or pacify, ameliorate or degrade was *not* limited to the activities of conscious life alone. They were better than metaphors; they were "catachreses," denoting events for which "names are lacking us." Stated otherwise, a trope—judiciously employed for an event, movement, or temporary entity that has no proper name—is not a fiction but a heuristic designed to expand the intelligibility of the things.

Up to now both explanations of organic life have *failed* to work out; neither that from mechanics, *nor that from mind* [*aus dem Geiste*]. I would stress *the latter*. Mind is more superficial than one suspects. The governance of organisms occurs in such a way that the mechanical world, *just as much as the spiritual one*, can only be used symbolically as explanation.[9]

Though he rejected mechanistic thought in the triumphalist form it assumed in his day,[10] Nietzsche urged that the more pernicious error lay in the direction of idealism. "The body [*der Leib*] as teacher: A moral sign language [*Zeichensprache*] of the affects" (KSA 11, Spring 1884, 25 [113], 43). In the following year he wrote:

All movements are to be grasped as behaviors, as a kind of language [*eine Art Sprache*], through which the forces understand each other. . . . Problem of the possibility of "error"? The opposition is not "false" and "true," but rather the "*abbreviations of signs*" in contrast with the signs themselves. The essential [thing for us] is: the construction of forms that *represent* many movements [*welche viele Bewegungen repräsentieren*], the invention of signs [*Zeichen*] for whole types of signs. (KSA 12, Fall 1885–Winter 1886, I [28], 16–17)

Nietzsche interpreted the interactions of forces "semiotically" as the multiple interactions of partial meanings, expressed by "abbreviations of signs" at every level of existence. That was his perspectivalism and his agnostic monism, and we must recall that the term *semiotics*, as the technique of communication and its interpretation, denoted in his time that branch of medicine concerned with interpreting *bodily* symptoms— an *eidetics*. In this way, the distance between thought and bodily processes could be diminished without introducing an idealistic interpretation of "mind" *or* a merely mechanistic approach to the body. Thought is not yet the internal event itself but rather only a language of signs (*Zeichensprache*) for power adjustments (*Machtausgleich*) among affects (KSA 12, Fall 1885–Winter 1886, I [28], 17).

There is neither a positivistic biology nor a mechanics of forces in Nietzsche. The figure of forces unfolds in two basic stages: the critiques of mechanics and idealism, followed by the reconceptualization of communication as sign-interactions and the generalization of force as behavior and "language." Since human language is fundamentally metaphorical, "meaning" depends on the flexibility that tropes introduce into expression. Thus the second stage entails a search for connections between operative signs in bodies and those "abbreviations of signs" that explain the former and "sum up whole types of signs." This requires reading beneath the description of the contents of consciousness, because "thought is not yet the internal event itself, but rather only a language of signs [*Zeichensprache*], a semiotics of power adjustments." Semiotics notwithstanding, the most effective way past the mechanistic reduction of forces would be through a phenomenology of affectivity, as epiphenomena of forces, and through the extension of the interpretive strategy *beyond* human languages to as broad a domain of codes as possible. Here "codes" simply denote momentary stabilizations of force, "metastabilizations." The first step in this paradoxical naturalization of hermeneutics—which Nietzsche calls "humanization . . . according to us" (KSA 12, I [29], 17)—turns on acknowledging that interpretation is locally purposive. That is, what we call "value-judgments [*Werthschätzungen*] abide in all sense-activities [*Sinnes-Thätigkeiten*]" (KSA 11, 26 [72], 167).[11] The concept of judgment must be extended past discursive construction.[12] The ground of an investigation of life is therefore twofold for Nietzsche: it is essentially interpretive dynamics in view of an operational good or growth (for tissues, for an organism, for a species, for a community), and it is the heuristic "unit" of exchange called *Kräfte* (forces). These are fundamentally the same, approached from different perspectives. That is why "the humanization of nature" is unique in Nietzsche and depends on a multilevel dynamics using combinators called *Zeichen* (signs).

Now this is not to say that psychophysics can be phenomenology, at least given the analytic constituents of the phenomenological project: noematic aiming, noetic objects, and beneath these a "flowing field of lived experiences, in the midst of which there is continuously a field of originary impressions . . . and . . . the ego that is affected by [that field] and motivated to action."[13] Yet, again, Nietzsche himself is not so much proposing a psychophysics as he is seeking imbricated languages or signs for what conditions the phenomena but is not phenomenalizable: *Kräfte, Triebe*. But then, what is psychophysics if not a search for the dynamic accompaniment and conditions of possibility of what we call "psychic" life?

A certain conundrum arises: what Husserl knew of Nietzsche likely came to him through Heidegger's ongoing interpretation of Nietzsche, yet nothing leads us to believe that Husserl grasped the radicality of Nietzsche's revaluation of psychophysics. However, if a crucial dimension of Husserl's expanded phenomenology to come was to be biology, as he indicated, then could psychophysics expand, rather than displace, transcendental psychology, say, by recognizing that the material and the laws of the psychophysics operate alongside, but independently of, the phenomenological reduction of consciousness? It is clear that, in psychophysics, mechanistic causality as well as higher-level distinctions between thought, memory, and fantasy invariably stand under the subjective-objective dichotomy rather than under the phenomenological *epochē* that provides us "experience" *before* subjects and objects are parsed out. Could the dichotomy flowing from the *world thesis* intrinsic to positive science be used *critically* rather than being imposed on a phenomenology of fundamental conscious activity? Certainly, and Nietzsche's (de-)humanization of forces opened toward models of self-regulating processes, with some stasis, but not substantification, and the rejection of linear causality. Nietzsche's agnostic monism "materializes" and historicizes Kant's conception of "judgment," using what Klossowski aptly translated as "semiotics" without one single interpretive code. If the problem of a "hermeneutic biology"—one similarly close to what Merleau-Ponty sought in thinking Husserl's *Ineinander* (in-each-other) of phenomena, as the *entrelacs*—is how to overcome the dualism between living (self-affecting) beings and beings observed as alive, then Nietzsche's was the most radical such overcoming in the nineteenth century.

As a perspectival monism, Nietzsche's use of forces as his "common currency" is not uncommon in the history of science, in which force was necessarily something imperceptible and its "effects" reconstructive. In Nietzsche, however, a dynamics of signs opens ultimately to a good—virtually "moral"—albeit expanded beyond any ethics of "good and evil." This dimension of his project is premodern, prior to the regionalization of reason or to types of substances. We ought not to take it, however, as foreign to the phenomenological monism Merleau-Ponty was seeking. Merleau-Ponty's philosophy of nature explored an expanded sense of the interpretation of information in cybernetic models, arguing critically about the latter in light of self-conscious beings, "The positive value of cybernetics [lies in that] it invites us to discover an animality in the subject, an apparatus for organizing perspectives."[14]

Bridging Forces and the Flesh: From Nietzsche to Merleau-Ponty

It is neither possible nor ultimately desirable to synthesize Nietzsche and Husserl. However, something like their "dialogue" is worked out implicitly in subsequent developments of phenomenology. Working from Husserl's explorations of intersubjective constitution, *Einfühlung*, and the flesh (*der Leib*),[15] Merleau-Ponty first extended Husserl's investigations of the "flesh" of language and body into perception very broadly conceived.[16] The tension between *biology* as "universal ontology" and *psychology* as the ladder toward Husserl's final, transcendental philosophy in the *Crisis* could thus be approached as two pillars of phenomenology, not as vacillation on Husserl's part. To be sure, the problem of psychophysics was rather late in coming to Husserl, with, among other things, the phenomenological constitution of "a universal drive-intentionality."[17] There again, hermeneutic biology represented the indispensable supplement, the heuristic ladder leading from a comprehensive psychology to phenomenology itself.

Nevertheless the phenomenological grounding of all sciences may constitute a debate that resists closure, since the relationship between phenomenologically reduced experience and experience objectified by sciences like biology remains to be clarified. The difficulty that emerges from Husserl's search for a reconfigured biology in Appendix XXIII was that it had to elucidate psychology as "psychophysics"[18] *and* form the ground from which one could describe other life-worlds, including those of animals and of worlds foreign to us. This projected biology opened toward *ontologies* presently unknown (*unbekannte Ontologie*), and all of this indicates a quest for a dualism at least sublated or circumscribed by a *hypothetical* monism.

> If we return to the ultimate sources of evidence . . . it appears that biology is not a contingent discipline in relation to an insignificant planet . . . [but that] a general biology has the same world-commonality [*Weltallgemeinheit*] as physics. The entire meaning that a biology of Venus might have, of whose possibility we might speak, is owed to the originary construction of our lived world.[19]

Although Appendix XXIII was a thought experiment, it was utterly representative of the direction Husserl was striving to take. Its precise place in the version we have of the *Crisis* is unclear and may be contested by Fink's proposed completion of the work. However, what is important is that the radicalized approach to life, understood as the *Ineinander* of living beings in humans, runs parallel with the correlation structure of organisms and their worlds, as well as the a priori correlation of noesis and noema. Merleau-Ponty's comments on the Appendix suggest that Husserl is rethinking Heidegger: "Organism: *Ineinander* of subjectivity, I (and finally I, reflecting) and corporeal machines. The organism [as] a variant of *Einfühlung*. I know the [other] organism because I am it [*parce que je le suis*]. Relation Being man cf. Heidegger (All things in man, but because man is all things)."[20] We know that Merleau-Ponty is more indebted to Husserl than it seemed at the time of his death, in 1961. It was Husserl who, by the mid-1930s, had first pondered a multidimensional ontology: world of life, "life of consciousness," and animal and alien life-worlds. It could well be argued that, as universal ontology and as psychophysics, biology momentarily gave Husserl more than a path toward transcendental phenomenology. Indeed the hermeneutic biology or "universal ontology" set forth in Appendix XXIII could even clarify Fink's outline for the completion of the *Crisis* (cf. Appendix XXIX) through the adumbration of a "world-consciousness" in which "the *appearance of the mutual externality of souls [Ausserein-ander der Seelen]*" is decisively contested (Hua XI, Appendix XXIX, 514–16).

If we ponder this extension, then Fink's Husserl is opening a path not readily inferred from his pre-1920s writings: toward a world-consciousness approached simultaneously from transcendental psychology and from a "biology [become] truly universal."[21] That would agree with his investigations into the universal drive-intentionality proper to all living beings. While it does not resolve the problem of life as self-affection versus life as the observed, living alterity of other beings in the world, it does rethink the best elements in the vitalist biology of his time.

Ineinander: Nietzsche and (Neuro)phenomenology

Recent neurophenomenology, indebted to Merleau-Ponty, is developing a dynamic materialism that is hypothetically monist but does not reduce consciousness to mere brain activity. If we acknowledge the impossibility of constructing a bridge between the immanence of pure self-affection and objective, living beings, we do not have to abandon Husserl's *Ineinander* or Merleau-Ponty's *entrelacs* or chiasm. As we examine neurophenomenology we should hold fast to the need for a concept that joins perception and world. And indeed Merleau-Ponty's great merit was to have approached conscious life from both directions: from lived experience (interpretation) and from a philosophy of nature (biology and aspects of *Lebensphilosophie*). That said, Merleau-Ponty had already ventured past Husserl's approach to consciousness by exploiting resources in the psychoanalysis of pathology, by examining "perception" in neuroses (Freud's *Dora*) and "perception" in the delirium staged in Jensen's novel,

Gradiva.[22] Moreover he proposed what he called an "aesthesiology" of the lived body, contrasting the vitalism of Hans Driesch (1921) with the animal behaviorism of von Uexküll.

Influenced by Merleau-Ponty, Bernard Andrieu moves in a similarly monist direction. Although he does not mention him, Andrieu's monism strikingly recalls Nietzsche's experiments. For Andrieu, the neurophilosophical question is less one of finding common units or forces at work in living bodies than one of consolidating an informational model, with its accompanying sign language, with a programming model that takes into account the ongoing influence of exchanges between world, body, and thought. This is clearly one of the recent extensions of Husserl's *Ineinander*. Andrieu's project of a *matérialisme dynamique* is thus based neither on electrical nor hydraulic metaphors, as was traditionally proposed. He argues instead for a "flesh of the brain," integrating Merleau-Ponty's subjectivations through and as perception with Nietzsche's operative forces. On Andrieu's account, the brain proves to be the "progressive incarnation of incorporations [taken from without]."[23] If phenomenology sought to complexify subjectivity, understood as something static, then Andrieu will argue, following Merleau-Ponty and Nietzsche, that "subjectivity is a result of a continuous movement of adaptation and regulation" (CP 560). He means that subjectivity is first a body that itself is, above all, a variable locus of interactions. He reminds us that "nothing entirely objective can be known" (CP 560), arguing that something absolutely objective would be open to no "perception," to no possible interaction with living bodies. This allows him to conclude that "the knowledge of the world [is] relative to each human body. [Moreover the] relativity of each one in no way forbids the establishment . . . of a provisional truth about the human body within the scientific attitude" (CP 560). Following a model of dynamic subjectivation, animal consciousness broadly construed can be defined as adaptive interactions and as a structure of self-interruption (viz., as the possibility or inaugural hesitation intrinsic to reflection). Consistent with Merleau-Ponty's notion of the flesh, Andrieu argues for the body as an interface, in which the brain produces consciousness indirectly as surplus activity. This is thanks to the multiplicity of interactions between environments and bodies, even between tissues. Hence the programming model mentioned earlier, which operates like an in-forming, at multiple levels, in regard to "information" in continuous exchange. The resemblance to Nietzsche is striking.

Like Merleau-Ponty, Andrieu also argues for an aesthesiology that presupposes biology but does not start with it:

> Sensation is felt by means of the nervous structure in the body, such that two human bodies can never experience the same intensity with regard to the same object. Psychometry, modernized by electro-physiology, quantifies the quality of lived experiences of the body. This method establishes an objective knowledge by measuring reaction times and perceptual thresholds. *But the visualization of electrical exchanges will never say anything about the way in which the body feels these in itself.* (CP 560)

Because he is approaching body, consciousness, and thought as part of a single interactive model, Andrieu proposes what I would call an *epochē* of quantity. He holds temporarily out of consideration quantificational models, without denying their significance to particular contexts of explanation, much the way Husserl bracketed the positive sciences without ever denying their applicability. If experienced sensations and affects are continuously transformed from qualities into quantities, then quality must be considered primordial, the first lived *transitivity*. The primacy of biohermeneutics is thus only supplemented by a physicochemical reduction. Aesthesiology points in the direction of a body in the process of (qualitative) subjectivation. As Andrieu emphasizes, "Two human bodies can never feel the same intensity with regard to the same object. This impossible intersubjectivity *keeps bodies outside of themselves and each body in itself*, thereby making difficult any linguistic expression of aesthesiological lived experience" (CP 560, emphasis added). Approached from the perspective of psychophysics, Andrieu's aesthesiology well describes the transitivity of life, understood as the movements of bodies outside themselves, *toward . . .* Recent phenomenology (Renaud Barbaras drawing from Levinas and Deleuze) has characterized this as "transcendental desire."[24] A body outside-itself is a body "toward-the-other," whether this "other" is the world or another person or entity. The advantage of the model proposed here lies in its ability to explain individuation, interaction without reductionism, and a certain "autonomy" of conscious thought relative to neurological activity. "Autonomy" need not mean "independence"; however, the nature of the contents of thoughts—sentences, images—creates the *illusion* of independence. Indeed in this project, which borrows extensively from Gilbert Simondon's "resolute monism" (CP 561), the organization of the body, and with it mental activity, proceeds ongoingly in interactive connections (CP 563). "Psychological individuation comes down to that of the central nervous system in interactive communication with its genetic programming" (CP 563). This programming—in the development of brain-consciousness—takes place at multiple levels, as it did in Nietzsche. One of these is REM sleep, wherein interactions are laid down and stabilized temporarily.

Another possible way through our conundrum is via the enactive approach to consciousness, proposed by the late neurophenomenologist Francisco Varela and expanded in Evan Thompson's *Mind in Life*. The enactive approach "uses phenomenology to explicate mind science and mind science to explicate phenomenology" as reciprocally elucidating (ML 265). According to their account, indebted both to dynamical systems theory and to Merleau-Ponty, an organism and its primitive milieu (*Urwelt*) cannot be separated, including on a conceptual level, without doing violence to their dynamic coupling. The enactive approach proposes that "living is sense-making" (ML 158): the meaning of an "environment," the information that is available *for* an organism about its milieu, is not simply "out there." Rather the organism, as an autonomous and autopoietic system, along with its *Urwelt* to which it is structurally coupled, form a dynamical system in which the organizational and operational closure[25] of the organism confers on it a stable identity while simultaneously giving meaning (i.e., "valence," or value in an almost Nietzschean sense) to its surroundings. This argument is reminiscent of Nietzsche's account of forces that codetermine each other dynamically. It complements the approach to the notion of autonomy that Andrieu proposed, taking it in a mathematical, informational direction.

In both these neurophenomenological models, subjectivity is never a fixed result but an ongoing process. Individuation is similarly not an outcome but a term ingredient to the definition of any milieu, any environment (CP 564). Finally, the life of an animal unfolds progressively, through fragile stabilizations generally open to degrees of modification. As Andrieu puts it, "'We are thus in the presence of a system of progressive nestings [*emboîtements*] of representations and levels of reality, from the genome to the brain, passing through the body.' In re-evaluating the role of the body in the physiological representation that the brain [develops] of its own genome, thought [broadly construed] becomes the site of the living body" (CP 565, citing Prochiantz).[26]

The spirit of aesthesiology is faithful to phenomenology, notably the late phenomenology that reached toward biology as a psychophysics and the authentic ontology. This concern was both Husserl's own, late in life, and Merleau-Ponty's. The paradox of the dual approach I noted is precisely that to reach anything like a hypothetical monism of living being requires a concerted dual path. Nietzsche understood this, elaborating a poetics of living (*Zarathustra*) and a poetics of forces drawn from his reading of nineteenth-century physiology. The *epochē* Andrieu seems to have placed on quantity has, as its goal, to dispense with "metaphysical" units, imported into arguments to measure *quanta* of excitations. Nietzsche, for his part, had long since demonstrated the necessity of deconstructing such units, whether *Reiz*, atoms, or souls. In light of recent work in neuroscience, Andrieu adds:

> Reasoning on pathology has been able to show the connection . . . between this [bodily] matter and these mental forms [sentences, images]. When destroyed or injured, the physico-chemical matter of our sensibility can no longer furnish matter for thinking; or rather, there is a proportional relationship between the quality of sensations and the qualities of mental activities. The body furnishes matter for thinking *even if the way in which thought represents its mental states is perceived by it as if independent.* (CP 565)

To insist on autonomy, but not independence, reopens the thinking of the body-mind imbrications, and in so doing, invites us to reconceive thought as "a surplus of brain activity," or better, as the body thinking itself *through* mental representations. This further implies a necessary "complementarity between the brain and the unconscious and poses the problem of continuity between the two" (CP 567).

As we know, it was Nietzsche's project to reconceptualize Kant's "judgment." His choice of force managed to elude the problem of units of quantity, opting instead for an early dynamics. Nietzsche's dynamics introduced interpretation, accommodation, and domination into the biological model of his time, emphasizing structures of obedience and command in order to preserve the hierarchy intrinsic to value judgments. This simply means that certain organizations of cells, tissues, even living beings "work" better for their growth and flourishing than do others. The problem I noted of a common currency is temporarily suspended with the *epochē* on quantity—displacing for heuristic ends the primacy of quantity and its metaphysical recourse to units of measure. As a number of Husserl's commentators have asked (Ricoeur among them): What are we to make of conscious life when we *remove* the phenomenological brackets? Could not a similar question be posed of the neurophenomenology flowing simultaneously out of Gilbert Simondon and Maurice Merleau-Ponty? To be sure. But what we would have, upon removing the brackets, simply breaks into the objects of psychology and biology, or again, comes down to human experience as the object of multiple sciences or regional ontologies.

Simondon, like Andrieu and others since the publication of his work in the 1960s, attempted to demonstrate the possibility of a monism based on energetic interactions. His work resists summary because of its complexity and the plethora of new concepts he created. Some of these were the direct result of advances in chemistry and geophysics. The formation of crystalline structures provided one image of what he called "systems of potentials," on the basis of which elementary schemas constitute "meta-stable fields."[27] The metastable field comes from the dynamics of liquids but should not be restricted to that domain. It could well be argued that the Nietzschean contribution to a psychophysics lies in its similar refusal of statics and individual substances. And this strikingly anticipates the structural coupling and dynamic codetermination of organism and *Urwelt* in Thompson and von Uexküll. Without denying that beings "individuate" in transitional and ongoing ways, Nietzsche strove to keep his forces within a framework wherein becoming was *not* opposed to being. He might have found a real interest in the innovations of Simondon, Andrieu, Thompson, and Varella.

That does not mean that we can, or should, speak poetically of qualities, as though no difficulties arose in the absence of some theory of energy or energetics. But most of these theories shared the fate of sociopolitical environments through whose lens they were read and adjusted to the ideals of a given cultural politics. Those readings are, of course, as hazardous as Hans Driesch's 1930s vitalism in which the concept of organic totality and a governing principle slid deplorably into an aestheticized, politicized *Führerprinzip*.[28] Such slippages may be unavoidable, and an entire history of nineteenth- and early twentieth-century misappropriations of vitalism and *Lebensphilosophie* could be written. Nevertheless the imperative of bridging body-world and mind-body dualisms must be taken up by a biology in continuous dialogue with psychology and, today, with neurophilosophy. I have argued throughout that that was the direction in which Husserl's biology as the universal ontology was moving.

Notes

1. Husserl, *Die Krisis*, 1, 483 (hereafter Hua VI).
2. In other words, over the twenty years during which he wrote his notes on passive synthesis, Husserl recognized that events like "association" and changes in affects, mirrored life processes whose intelligibility alone could buttress a phenomenology, extended to affectivity and even drives. Biology would provide this support as psychophysics (see *Crisis*, 400). Does this mean that a path different from psychology and phenomenology was necessary for attaining a transcendental foundation? I prefer to say that Husserl was neither a monist nor a dualist. However, his increasing concern with life reflects the vaster question of a unified approach to it.
3. Husserl, *Analysen zur passiven Synthesis*, 141 (hereafter Hua XI).
4. Merleau-Ponty, *Notes de cours*, 387.
5. Ibid., 386.
6. Ibid., 387.
7. See Thompson, *Mind in Life*, 33 (hereafter ML).
8. Deleuze, "Philosophie de la volonté," in *Nietzsche et la philosophie*, 7, my translation.
9. Nietzsche, *Kritische Studienausgabe*, 11, 1884, 26 [68], 166 (hereafter KSA).
10. Cf. KSA 13, Spring 1888, 14 [79], 258. In a late outline for his project on the *Wille zur Macht*, Nietzsche wrote of mechanistic philosophy, "Quanta of power [*Machtquanta*]. *Critique of Mechanism*. Let us set aside [from our project] two popular concepts: 'necessity' and 'law' [*Gesetz*]: the first posits a false compulsion [*Zwang*], the second [inserts] a false freedom into the world. 'Things' do not behave [*betragen sich*] in a regular fashion, not according to a *Rule*: there are no things (—that is our fiction) [and] they behave even less under a compulsion of necessity."
11. Note also KSA 11, Winter 1884, 25 [401], 116: "There must be an *abundance of consciousnesses* and wills in each complex organic being: our uppermost consciousness takes it as habitual [that] the others are closed [*geschlossen*]. The smallest organic creature [*Geschöpf*] must have consciousness and will." As if by implication, value judgments, like needs, had to be sought in "Life." What is life for Nietzsche? It is a dynamics of encounters, interpretations, and "judgments," creating fragile equilibriums. Clearly the Kantian project, centered on the meaning and possibility of judgment, is "biologized" and extended to a multilayered nature.
12. See, for example, KSA 12, 2 [84], 103: "The [act of] judging is our oldest belief, our habitual taking for-true or for-untrue."
13. Husserl, "Manuscript C 7 I," 18, cited in Franck, *Dramatique des Phénomènes*, 112.
14. Merleau-Ponty, *La nature*, 214–19.
15. See, for example, Husserl's notes "Flesh—Thing—Intropathy," 71–96, notably, §§6 and 7: "The Connection of the Body [*Leib*] and the Soul" and "Regulations in the Constitution of the Thing: The Flesh as Index of Psychic Normality and Abnormality." Also see his 1932 notes on "absolute perception" as apperception and association, in the same collection , 188–98.
16. Husserl, *Ideen I*, §124. Also see Merleau-Ponty, *La phénoménologie de la perception*, parts I and II, chapters 3 and 4.
17. Husserl, "Universale Teleologie," in *Zur Phänomenologie der Intersubjectivität*, Texte aus dem Nachlass, Dritter Teil, 594–95. Compare Husserl's notes on individuation from 1922, §2, where he argues, "The system of appearances has a double normativity, on the one hand that of the causality of things among themselves; on the other hand . . . that of the conditional psychophysical possibility *which we make our constant hypothesis*" (*Zur Phänomenologie der Intersubjektivität* II, 252, Hua XIV).
18. Husserl argues, on the first page of the short appendix, "We have naturally, first, a biological *a priori* for man: the *a priori* of the bodily instincts, the originary drives [*Urtriebe*], whose fulfillment (eating, coupling) contains, internally, this *a priori*. Naturally too, we have a biological *a priori* of

animals to the entire degree to which animality is grasped in a real experience through *Einfühlung* [intropathy]. We thus have a generative *a priori.*" See Merleau-Ponty's translation of Appendix XXIII in *Notes de cours*, 383–84.

19. Merleau-Ponty, *Notes de cours*, 386.

20. Ibid., 387. I follow the punctuation, or lack of it, in the *Notes*.

21. Ibid.

22. Merleau-Ponty, *L'institution/la passivité*.

23. Andrieu, "Le corps pensant," 559 (hereafter CP). All translations mine.

24. Barbaras, *Introduction à une phénoménologie de la vie*, 368ff.

25. "*Organizational closure* refers to the self-referential (circular and recursive) network of relations that define the system as a unity, and *operational* closure to the re-entrant and recurrent dynamics of such a system. An autonomous system is always structurally coupled with its environment. . . . 'Structural coupling' refers to the history of recurrent interactions between two or more systems that leads to a structural congruence between them. Thus state changes of an autonomous system result from its operational closure and structural coupling" (ML 45).

26. Prochiantz, *La biologie dans le boudoir.*

27. Simondon, *L'individuation psychique et collective*, 57.

28. Canguilhem, *La connaissance de la vie*, 123 (97 in earlier editions). Canguilhem discusses Driesch's work, *Die Überwindung des Materialismus (The Overcoming of Materialism)*, 59, in which Driesch argues, "A machine as the instrument [*Werkzeug*] for the *Führer*—but the *Führer* is the main thing [*Hauptsache*]." To this Canguilhem adds, "It is certain that Driesch's thought offers for our consideration a typical case of the transplantation of the biological concept of organic totality onto political grounds."

Bibliography

Andrieu, Bernard. "Le corps pensant: Mouvement épistémologique de la philosophie dans la biologie 1950–2000." *Revue internationale de philosophie* 4, no. 222 (2002): 557–82.

Barbaras, Renaud. *Introduction à une phénoménologie de la vie.* Paris: Vrin, 2008.

Canguilhem, Georges. *La connaissance de la vie.* Paris: Vrin, 2003.

Deleuze, Gilles. *Nietzsche et la philosophie.* Paris: PUF, 1962.

Franck, Didier. *Dramatique des Phénomènes.* Paris: PUF, 2001.

Husserl, Edmund. *Analysen zur passiven Synthesis: Aus Vorlesungs- und Forschungsm- anuskripten, 1918–1926.* Edited by Margot Fleischer. The Hague: Martinus Nijhoff, 1966.

———. *The Crisis of European Sciences and Transcendental Phenomenology.* Translated by David Carr. Evanston, IL: Northwestern University Press, 1970.

———. *Ideen I*, in *Husserliana*, Vol. III-2. Edited by Karl Schuhmann. The Hague: Martinus Nijhoff, 1988.

———. *Die Krisis der europäischen Wissenschaften und die transzendentale Phänomenologie: Eine Einleitung in die phänomenologische Philosophie.* Edited by Walter Biemel. The Hague: Martinus Nijhoff, 1976.

———. "Manuscript C 7 I." In *Späte Texte über Zeitkonstitution (1929–1934): Die C-Manuskripte.* Edited by Dieter Lohmar. New York: Springer, 2006.

———. *Sur l'intersubjectivité.* Vol. I. Translated by Natalie Depraz. Paris: PUF, 2001.

———. *Zur Phänomenologie der Intersubjectivität.* Texte aus dem Nachlass. Zweiter Teil. 1921– 28. Edited by Iso Kern. The Hague: Martinus Nijhoff, 1973.

———. *Zur Phänomenologie der Intersubjectivität.* Texte aus dem Nachlass. Dritter Teil. 1929– 35. Edited by Iso Kern. The Hague: Martinus Nijhoff, 1973.

Merleau-Ponty, Maurice. *L'institution/la passivité: Notes de cours au Collège de France, 1954–1955.* Paris: Belin, 2002.

———. *La nature: Notes de cours du Collège de France.* Edited by Dominique Séglard. Paris: Seuil, 1995.

———. *Notes de cours, 1959–1961.* Edited by Claude Lefort. Paris: Gallimard/NRF, 1996.

———. *La phénoménologie de la perception.* Paris: Gallimard, 1945.

Nietzsche, Friedrich. *Kritische Studienausgabe.* Edited by Girogio Colli and Mazzino Montinari. Berlin: Walter de Gruyter, 1980.

Prochiantz, Alain. *La biologie dans le boudoir.* Paris: Odile Jacob, 1995.

Simondon, Gilbert. *L'individuation psychique et collective: À la lumière des notions de forme, information, potentiel et métastabilité.* Paris: Aubier, 1964, 1989.

Thompson, Evan. *Mind in Life: Biology, Phenomenology and the Sciences of Mind.* Cambridge, MA: Harvard University Press, 2010.

10 Originary Dehiscence

*An Invitation to Explore the Resonances
between the Philosophies of Nietzsche
and Merleau-Ponty*

Frank Chouraqui

ONE OF THE most prominent connections between Nietzsche's thought and the entire phenomenological enterprise lies in Husserl's founding postulate that the thing-in-itself is an invalid concept. Although Husserl never formulates it explicitly, the development of phenomenology demonstrates the root of this invalidity: the thing-in-itself is a contradiction insofar as a thing is, by definition and by essence, always an object of perception. This is also, of course, one of Nietzsche's most explicit, best established, and most consistently repeated claims, and perhaps one that has the greater consequence within the overall economy of his thought. Indeed this connection suggests a kinship between Nietzsche's thought and phenomenology that lies beyond the coincidental or the anecdotic, insofar as this basic thesis, first, is radical enough to constitute a reevaluation of the very object of philosophical inquiry, and second, because this reevaluation also happens to constitute the birth certificate of phenomenology.

In a sense, once this kinship is established, the question of the connections between Nietzsche's thought and phenomenology may be taken one step further, to ask about what *sort* of phenomenology Nietzsche's philosophy points toward. In this essay, I wish to establish that there are specificities in Nietzsche's phenomenological accounts that resonate most strongly with some of the specificities of Merleau-Ponty's phenomenology. Roughly speaking, these specificities consist in the emphasis on the claim that the dehiscence that structures our relation to the world is not a lack but, indeed, an originary and essential feature of being. My contention in this essay is that this fundamental agreement is determinant for both thinkers and that, as a result, their resonances also are fundamental.

If we wish to sharpen our focus beyond the fundamental and prima facie agreement between Nietzsche and Husserl on the question of the thing-in-itself, I believe that our attempts to draw a parallel between the two thinkers may find a first obstacle in Husserl's idealistic claim according to which the lesson contained in the contradiction of the thing-in-itself is a reduction to the subject as consciousness. Husserl famously declares:

> In so far as their respective senses are concerned, a veritable abyss yawns between consciousness and reality. Here, an adumbrated being, not capable of ever becoming given absolutely, merely accidental and relative; there, a necessary and absolute being, essentially incapable of becoming given by virtue of adumbration and appearance. (*Ideas I*, §49)

In other words, the terrain lost by the objective world, as a consequence of the critique of the thing-in-itself, passes entirely into the domain of the subject, which alone is absolute. This move, obviously, has determined the future (at least the midterm future) of Husserl's phenomenology by launching it on the path to transcendental idealism. Indeed it is on the basis of the disparity of status between consciousness and the world that Husserl attempts to maintain an essential distinction between the world and consciousness when, in his reflections on time, he seeks to posit the origins of consciousness outside of the material world. This quest for a nonconscious ground that would have engendered consciousness collapses inevitably into Husserl's paradoxical thesis of the "self-constitution of the ego" (*On the Phenomenology of the Consciousness of Internal Time* §39, *Cartesian Meditations*, V).

Like Husserl, Nietzsche draws certain conclusions from the defeat of the thing-in-itself, and these direct him—like Husserl—to the question of the origins of consciousness. His resulting positions, however, are opposite to Husserl's. This is not to say that he places the absolute on the side of the object (this would be an opposite move only in the superficial sense). On the contrary, Nietzsche believes that a consistent opposition to the thing-in-itself necessarily entails a rejection of the bipolar distinction between the subjective and the objective, a distinction that Husserl maintains. "Finally," Nietzsche writes, "the 'thing-in-itself' also falls, because at bottom, it is the concept of a 'subject-in-itself,' yet, we have understood that the subject is fictitious. The antithesis of 'thing-in-itself' and 'appearance' is untenable."[1]

The Primacy of Intentionality

As a result, we shall see that Nietzsche does not attribute any privileged status to consciousness over the outside world. On the contrary, he affirms that consciousness and the world are of the same stuff. It is worth reiterating that, unlike what has been claimed widely by a number of naturalist readers of Nietzsche, this position does not commit him to any reduction of the conscious to the nonconscious in a move mirroring Husserl's reduction of the nonconscious to the conscious. On the contrary, Nietzsche offers a picture in which world and consciousness are horizons of each other and appear as merely the two horizons of being.

The elaboration of this position was triggered by Nietzsche's genealogical investigations of the years 1885 and 1886, during his work on the preface and book 5 of *The Gay Science* and *On the Genealogy of Morals*. In the latter's Second Essay, §16, he addresses the question of the origin of consciousness, in his words, the origin of the "soul," in a way that is more radical than has usually been acknowledged: "The whole inner world, originally stretched thinly as though between two layers of skin, was expanded and extended itself and gained breadth, depth and height" (KSA 5, 321).

To my knowledge, only two authors have addressed (albeit allusively) the enigmatic metaphor of the "layers of skin" in *On the Genealogy of Morals*. Remarkably, both belong to the naturalist school. Mathias Risse writes in a footnote:

> The image of the skins is curious. Clark/Swensen suggest that one may think of two layers of an onion. It is important that Nietzsche assumes that there already is a "small" inner world. For that deprives him of the task to explain how there could be any form of inner life at all, as opposed to explaining how it could be expanded. . . . Plausibly, Nietzsche thought this bit of the development of consciousness happened at a presocial stage. For the development of consciousness under social pressure, cf. also [*The Gay Science*] §354, and see also [*Beyond Good and Evil*] §19.[2]

Alas, *The Gay Science* §354 does not provide any account of this "previous stage," and neither does *Beyond Good and Evil* §19. Instead both of these texts start after the presumed original separation. In fact Nietzsche does not give any such account. As Risse points out, Clark and Swensen devote a footnote to this enigmatic metaphor in their translation of *On the Genealogy of Morals*, but without much philosophical emphasis.[3] Both Risse's and Clark and Swensen's accounts evade difficulties by assuming that Nietzsche was thinking something (namely that consciousness had an origin in nature) that appears nowhere in his writings. Here is why a dismissal will not do: the difference between an origin in self-identity (which is not in Nietzsche's writings) and an origin in self-differentiation (which is) has structural consequences for Nietzsche's entire philosophy. For now, it might suffice to point out that this importance is expressed by Risse's remark that Nietzsche's assumption according to which "there already is a 'small' inner world . . . deprives him of the task to explain how there could be any form of inner life at all, as opposed to explaining how it could be expanded."[4]

This remark contains the essence of the problem of any naturalism and poses a question that Nietzsche asked himself many times: How does one go about explaining the emergence of the different from the identical or, in this case, of the spiritual from the physical? Although it is obvious that it is a question which Nietzsche initially intended to solve positively, it is no less apparent that in his post-Zarathustra years, he acknowledged the impossibility of finding such an origin and instead posited the nonbirth of consciousness at the start of human history. Two years before the affirmation of an inner dehiscence at the heart of the human self, Nietzsche already posited originary consciousness in terms of a "thin" inner division: "I assume that every organic being possesses memory and a sort of spirit: the apparel is so thin that it seems to us that it doesn't exist. . . . One should not let oneself be deceived by the smallness—the organic non-born [*nicht anschanden*]" (KSA 11, 1884, 25 [403], 117).[5]

Although this opposition between Husserl (who searches for an origin—as ground—of consciousness) and Nietzsche (who affirms the absence of such an origin) does not cancel the original agreement concerning the phenomenological critique of the thing-in-itself, it should be noted that this disagreement is precisely what allows Nietzsche to overcome the opposition of materialism and idealism, while it forces Husserl to yield to it. The potentially radical differences implied in this disagreement therefore demand that we look away from Husserl's phenomenology for a phenomenological interlocutor more suited to Nietzsche. It is therefore useful to remark that Nietzsche's disagreement with Husserl, as I have just laid it out, corresponds in striking detail with the criticisms of Husserl formulated by Merleau-Ponty. These criticisms, as it has often been pointed out, are rarely made explicitly by Merleau-Ponty, who favors opposing two Husserlian philosophies or, in his words, Husserl and his "shadow," thereby generously giving credit to Husserl for having come to final positions that solve the questions raised by Merleau-Ponty's own philosophy. However, as early as the famous foreword to *The Phenomenology of Perception*, Merleau-Ponty adjusts the aim of phenomenology on his own terms. In this text, it is no longer absolute consciousness that appears as the discovery offered by the *epoché*; rather, it is the absence of any absolute. For Merleau-Ponty, "the most important lesson that the reduction teaches us is the impossibility of a complete reduction,"[6] that is to say, the absence of any absolute of the type Husserl finds in subjectivity. This does not mean, however, that the reduction only serves to yield negative facts, for Merleau-Ponty sees this impossibility as the expression of a positive structure of being, namely that there is no world without intentionality. Merleau-Ponty's move is subtle, as it affirms the primacy of intentionality even as it rejects the primacy of consciousness. This is because, according to him, consciousness is an unnecessary overdetermination of intentionality insofar as it implies the presence of a subject that intentionality (when considered unattached to a subject) does not require.

Merleau-Ponty's affirmation that no absolute substratum is revealed by the reduction is in complete agreement with Nietzsche's suggestion of a world lying in the interstice between nature and consciousness. His second suggestion however, namely that we should do away with the subject of consciousness, may seem a stretch from Nietzsche's position, at least as exposed in *On the Genealogy of Morals* II, 16. In his notebooks however, beginning in 1885, Nietzsche is progressively seen doing away with both the subjective and the objective poles, leaving only intentionality standing in the form of the will to power, which he defines as neither subjective nor objective. He declares:

Appearance [*der Schein*] as I regard it, is the genuine and unique reality of things [*Realität der Dinge*]. . . . Therefore, I do not place "appearance" in opposition to "reality," but on the contrary, I consider that appearance is reality, that which resists all transformation into some fantastical "true world," a precise term for this reality would be "will to power." (KSA 11, 1885, 40 [53], 654)

The mention of a test for what resists the "real world" of objects is reminiscent of Husserl's own *epochē*, but again, Nietzsche disagrees with Husserl on the question of the primacy of the subject. Consider this remark, addressed to Husserl across the ages:

"Everything is subjective," you say, but that itself is interpretation, for the "subject" is not something given, but a fiction added on, tucked behind.—Is it even necessary to posit the interpreter behind the interpretation? Even that is fiction, hypothesis. (KSA 12, 1886, 7 [60], 315)

So Nietzsche seems to be left with neither subject nor object, only, as he writes here, "interpretation." This is again in complete agreement with Merleau-Ponty, for the removal of any substances from the world, performed by both Nietzsche and Merleau-Ponty, implies that what they consider to be remaining, intentionality for Merleau-Ponty and interpretation for Nietzsche, can be described only in terms of its activity, since describing it in essential terms is now out of the question. Nietzsche characterizes the mode of this activity as "will to power," that is to say, a "creating, logicizing, trimming, falsifying," about which we must ask whether it "is not itself the best-guaranteed reality: in short, whether that which 'posits things' is not the sole reality" (KSA 12, 1887, 9 [106], 395). The positing therefore is the only reality but not the posited or this that does the positing, for Nietzsche repeatedly insists, "One should not ask 'who interprets?' On the contrary, the interpreting itself, as a form of the will to power, possesses existence [*Dasein*] (not however as a being [*Sein*], but as a process, a becoming)" (KSA 12, 1885, 2 [151], 140).

This is because it is the essence of the will to power to posit objects for itself, and as a result, what idealism calls the subject is also an object for the will to power. This is because the will to power is not a polarized force; on the contrary, it constitutes poles that are alternately subject and object of the will to power. Nietzsche describes the will to power in terms of interest, and interest, he adds, is reversible insofar as we have interest both in conquest and in self-preservation (for there is my interest, which threatens the other, and the other's interest, which threatens me): "Aggressive egoism and defensive egoism are not a matter of choice or even a matter of 'free will,' they are the very fatality [*Fatalität*] of life" (14 [192] 1888, XIII, 379). Nietzsche describes self-preservation in terms of "passivity" (or "reactivity") and conquest in terms of "activity." This uncovers the intimate relationships of the subject and the object at a deeper level. For Nietzsche, as for Merleau-Ponty, their relation is chiasmatic: in "passivity" the object of interest is the self and its subject is the outside world as threat. In "activity" it will be the reverse. It is thus through the notions of activity and passivity that we must understand subject and object: "What do active and passive mean? Is it not becoming master and being defeated? And subject and object?" (KSA 12, 1885, 7 [48], 311).

This indicates that the notions of subject and object do not arise from the experience of the separation of self and world; rather they emerge from the experience of their contact. This relationship is therefore reversible insofar as any act of will implies both activity and passivity. Consider the following two contemporaneous claims:

> What is "passive"? Resisting and reacting. Being hindered in one's forward-reaching movement: thus an act of resistance and reaction. . . . What is "active"? Reaching out for power. (KSA 12, 1886, 5 [64], 209)

> The will to power can only express itself against resistances; it seeks what will resist it—this is the original tendency of the protoplasm in sending out pseudopodia and feeling its way. (KSA 12, 1887, 9 [151], 424)

In the experience of reality, the two opposing drives are almost simultaneously subject and object for each other because they resist each other. As a result, we obtain a line of contact across which subject and object of interest indefinitely alternate: the conqueror (subject) is opposed with some resistance and thereby becomes the object of the resistance opposed to it by the resisting object of the conquest. Conversely, this object, by virtue of its own resistance, becomes subject.[7] For Nietzsche, this "line of contact" is the basis upon which we build the concepts of inside and outside and, further, of subject and object. Even though Nietzsche presents this process as essentially a hostile encounter, it also involves and informs the structure of perception. Indeed he regards perception as a function of the drives' resistance-seeking (recall the identity of increase-seeking and perception in the case of the protoplasm).[8]

For Nietzsche, therefore, the will to power is the only primary fact, and it is determined by its bidirectionality. We must take this bidirectionality in the strictest sense. Nietzsche does not, for example, suggest any sort of alternation between the two directions of the will to power; he writes in fact that "pressure and push," which are the subjective forms of the two directions of the will to power, are "something that is unspeakably late, derived and non-originary [*Unursprungliches*]" insofar as "it presupposes something [the subject] which would hold together and would be able to push and press" (KSA 12, 1885, 2 [105], 112). For Nietzsche, therefore, what is truly originary, *ursprungliche* is an activity that becomes polarized only in a "derived form." In its originary form, it stands as the pure principle of the identity of the "push" and the "pull," as elemental bidirectionality.

Of course, such a figuration of perception as chiasmatic and its subsequent extension to the whole of being constitutes the heart of Merleau-Ponty's philosophy. Like Nietzsche, Merleau-Ponty encounters this chiasma and this reversibility between subject and object as the structure of perception and, like him, he holds that this coincidence of perception and the will to increase are correlative to the coincidence of activity and passivity.[9] He even writes, in strikingly Nietzschean terms, "Shouldn't we conceive of essence as the experience of what resists it?"[10]

This quotation is so circular it is difficult to even understand Merleau-Ponty's meaning: for him, essence as "eidos" (NL 329) is the experience of what resists essence itself as "flux" (NL 329); in other words, being is constituted by opposition with itself. In perception, the figure of the chiasma accounts for the fact that perception is always doubled ("lined by") by apperception. It is exemplified most strikingly through the specularity of mirror-like perceptions[11] and the phenomenon of the "touched-touching": if I touch my left hand with my right, I obtain a configuration of four terms, whose relations cross at a point that belongs to none of the four terms and, as a horizon, to all four of them: my left hand as touching encounters my right hand as touched, and my right hand as touching encounters my left hand as touched (VI 253). The center point of this relationship is the surface of both hands taken in a rigorous sense, in the sense of an intensive horizon (since their contact makes a pure surface impossible, one hand leading directly into the other; VI 263; see also VI 148 ff.). For Merleau-Ponty, this experiential simultaneity of perception and apperception is not absolute, however, as it is structured by an essential "*écart*," a "dehiscence" at the heart of perception, which is indeed the very possibility of reflexivity, and therefore of perception. To put it in Nietzsche's own terms: the existence of consciousness signifies that "nothing is immediate." As Merleau-Ponty concludes, this chiasmatic structure projects the poles of intentionality over the horizon and places intentionality, that is to say, the relational principle, at the heart of being: "One cannot account for this double 'chiasma' by the cut of the for-itself and the in-itself. A relation to being is needed that would form itself within being" (VI 215).

This is the structure that underlies Nietzsche's metaphoric conception of the inner world mentioned in *On the Genealogy of Morals* II, 16. It is worth citing again:

> The whole inner world, originally stretched thinly as though between two layers of skin [*zwei Häute*], was expanded and extended itself and gained depth, breadth and height in proportion to the degree that the external discharge of man's instincts was obstructed. (GM II §16; KSA 5, 322)

Consider also this remark made a few months earlier: "Consciousness always contains a double reflexivity—nothing is immediate" (KSA 12, 1885, 1 [54], 23). Here Nietzsche describes the originary inner world as the origin of the reflexivity of interest: because there is a gap (ever so small) within the individual, her drives have the ability to be redirected toward her other "half": the self is structured in such a way that there is a potential object of domination within it. This setup allows for an inner relation of forces of the same type as the external one: there is externality within the self. This is made possible by the gap between the two "layers of skin," allowing for passivity and activity within the self, and thereby allowing for aggression against oneself, which is what Nietzsche describes in the rest of *On the Genealogy of Morals* II, §16. From this point on, Nietzsche's writings consistently maintain that the rules that apply in external relations of power apply internally as well: "I maintain the phenomenality of the inner world too. . . . The 'apparent inner world' is governed by just the same forms and procedures as the 'outer world'" (KSA XIII, 1888, 11 [113], 53). As a result, Nietzsche declares that both the subject and the object are merely interchangeable horizons in a stunning formula: "'Me' 'the subject' as a horizon line [*Horizont-Linie*], reversal [*Umkehrung*] of the perspectival glance" (KSA 12, 1885–86, 2 [67], 91).

Nietzsche affirms that perspectival vision is necessarily always horizonal (see also KSA 12, 5 [3], 185) and offers a striking anticipation of Husserl's own concept of horizon in *Ideen* (254), but unlike Husserl, he adds that this perspectival glance is reversible, and that, if objects are indeed determined only in perspectival terms, so is the subject. He insists:

> If our "I" is the only being according to which we make [*machen*] or understand any being: very good! It is therefore very legitimate to be in doubt: are we not here dealing with some perspectival illusion—the apparent unity where everything joins together as if on a horizon line? (KSA 11, 1885–86, 2 [91], 282)

This concept of horizon, which Nietzsche developed carefully in the Notebooks of 1885 and 1886, therefore differs from Husserl's inasmuch as it posits even the subject as a horizon and therefore places horizonality in place of the absolute. Horizonality therefore comes to characterize all knowledge, and, in a world deprived of in-itself, it comes to characterize the essence of phenomenality as well. Nietzsche writes about "the world that interests us" (i.e., the only world, since interest is the medium of perception):

> [It] is false, that is to say, it is not matter of fact [*ist kein Tatbestand*] but a poetic product [*Ausdichtung*], a rough total of a meager sum of observations [*Beobachtungen*]: it is "in flux" as something in the process of becoming, as an error that constantly shies away [*eine sich immer neu verschiebende Falschheiteine sich immer neu verschiebende Falschheit*] and never catches up on the truth:—for there is no "truth." (KSA 12, 1886, 2 [108], 114)

For Nietzsche, therefore, there is only this constant race after a horizon that keeps withdrawing from our grasp. The world, he writes, is "in flux" because it is nothing but the race of consciousness after a truth that is nowhere to be found. As a result, any totality, any determinate entity is but "poetry," an act of imagination. Once again, as Nietzsche takes a step further away from Husserl, Merleau-Ponty is there to greet him, writing against Husserl:

> The phenomenon of the horizon exists for the noetic side just like it exists for the noematic side. . . . The role of signs [according to Husserl] is to transmit a signification which they do not partake in (this is in contradiction with the definition of poetry) (my idea of presence, or of the Figured World = there is no knowledge of such a world but poetic knowledge). (NL 332)

The kinship with Nietzsche is striking: not only must we turn the subjective pole too into a horizon, but we must also acknowledge that the phenomenological world is made of only some horizonal presence that becomes determined only by way of linguistic signs that always exceed their signification, "imagine" (NL 341) and "round it off" (Nietzsche). That is, signs succeed in bridging the infinite gap between a "horizonal term" and an "enclosing term" (NL 330) by becoming "poetic." Indeed Nietzsche and Merleau-Ponty both regard the constitution of concepts as a poetic act because they both regard it as the overdetermination of language when it projects itself ahead of its object-signified. Nietzsche writes:

> We put words where our ignorance begins—where we cannot see beyond, for example, the word "I," the word "doing," the word "suffering"; they may well be the horizon lines of our knowledge, but not "truths." (KSA 12, 1886, 5 [3], 185)

When, as we saw earlier, he introduces the language of racing and "becoming" in the ever-failing process of determination of consciousness, Nietzsche indicates that he does not conceive horizons as limits whose great distance makes them practically unreachable. On the contrary, he regards horizons as essentially unattainable. This is why he draws from the horizonality of "knowledge" such radical conclusions regarding truth (namely, that in its traditional sense, it doesn't exist). For Merleau-Ponty as well, perspectivism seeks a synoptic view understood as essentially unattainable. As he writes in many instances, the "invisible" is not the "possibly visible" but "an absence that counts in the world" (VI 227).

History and Becoming

For Nietzsche therefore, the horizonal structure of the activity of consciousness informs the structure of all life (insofar as the process toward determinacy is part of the essence of the will to power) as dynamism. For Merleau-Ponty also, this unending race constitutes what he calls the "prospective activity" of perception.[12] In fact the horizonal structure of this prospective activity was always an essential feature of consciousness since Merleau-Ponty famously declared in *The Phenomenology of Perception*, "The absolute positing of a single object is the death of consciousness" (71).[13]

Strikingly, once more, Nietzsche echoes this remark in similar terms: "If one wished to venture outside of the perspectival world, one would perish" (KSA 11, 1884, 27 [41], 285). In the same vein, he identifies indeterminacy with life: "With the organic world begins indeterminacy and appearance" (KSA 11, 1885, 35 [53], 536) and "the smallest organic creature must possess consciousness and will" (KSA 11, 1884, 25 [401], 116). As a result, Nietzsche can pose and answer his "fundamental question":

> Fundamental question: whether the perspectival [*das Perspectivische*] is part of BEING [*WESEN*]. Or is it merely a form of consideration [*Betrachtung*], a relation between different beings [*Wesen*]? Do the different forces stand in relation so that this relation is determined by a perceptual optic [*Wahrnehmungs-optik*]? This would

be possible if every being [*Sein*] were ESSENTIALLY something perceiving [*etwas Wahrnehmendes*]. (KSA 12, 1886, 5 [12], 188)

Indeed Nietzsche's extension of the concept of the will to power to the whole of existence implies no less than that "every being is essentially something perceiving." Consider the many phenomenological implications of his equivalence between "existence," "conditioning," "knowing," and "perceiving":

> This that concerns nobody whatever [*das Niemanden nichts angeht*] is not at all, and therefore cannot be known either.—Knowing signifies "finding oneself in a conditional [*Bedingung*] relation with something [*Etwas*]": feeling oneself conditioned [*Bedingt*] by something. (KSA 12, 1885–86, 2 [154], 142)

and

> One must understand once and for all that existing [*Existent*] and inconditioned [*Unbedingt*] are contradictory predicates. (KSA 11, 1884, 26 [203], 203)[14]

So it seems that Nietzsche, like Merleau-Ponty, describes the horizonal prospective activity of consciousness in terms of life, and that by introducing it within consciousness, he also makes it an essential feature of "being." Indeed, for Nietzsche, both life and being must be reduced to the will to power, which is nothing other than the process of perception (arising from bidirectional interest) and of determination. For Nietzsche affirms that these are the two aspects that constitute the activity of the will to power, which he defines as "incorporation" (*Einverleibung*): "It is inherent to the concept of the living that it must grow—for it extends its power and consequently, it must incorporate alien forces" (KSA 13, 1888, 14 [192], 379).

This process, which is anterior to subject or object, is therefore not attached to any individual; rather it determines the structure of phenomenality itself. Nietzsche believes therefore that it is applicable to all events, which are thereby defined as incorporative events. These include microscopic happenings (one of Nietzsche's favorite examples is the form of life of the amoeba and bacteria), and political and historical events too. Nietzsche continues: "Therefore, this process is directly applicable to an individual, a living body, or a striving society as a whole" (KSA 13, 1888, 14 [192], 379).

Further, the structure of the will to power may be applied equally to the physical and the spiritual realms (whose distinction itself it challenges; see KSA 11, 1885, 40 [33], 645), and it is therefore easy to understand why the will to power, whose basic modus operandi is incorporation, is repeatedly characterized in Nietzsche's notebooks as a principle of the "interpretation of all happenings [*Geschehens*]" (KSA 11, 1885, 39 [1], 619), including those pertaining to "our intelligence, our will, our sensations of displeasure, our perceptions" (KSA 11, 1885, 40 [61], 661).

This constant activity that pervades all happenings becomes incarnated in events that are defined in terms of incorporation, that is, in terms of domination and defeat. These, however, Nietzsche never calls "events" (*Ereignisse*) but rather "happenings"

(*Geschehens*). Indeed he is mindful of the fact that events are themselves brought forward and singled out from the world, which is the element of productivity of events only through an abusive and—as he and Merleau-Ponty write—poetic surdetermination. In fact if the world is the productivity of events, it does not contain events, for once a "happening" is determined as an "event," it automatically escapes the flow of the world. This is because an event and the appearing of an event are both, according to Nietzsche, acts of incorporation, that is to say, horizonal and necessarily incomplete processes of determination. It is only from the fundamental standpoint that formulates the thought of the will to power as a general explicative principle that we can fully grasp the essential incompleteness of this process of determination. It is only from this point of view, therefore, that we can see that "events" are horizonally detached from the flow of history.

This is precisely the same set of problems that motivated Merleau-Ponty's banishing the notion of events and replacing it with Ricoeur's notion of "advent."[15] For Merleau-Ponty, the traditional view of history as a succession of events "leads to skepticism as long as it is objective history because it presents each of its moments as a pure event and locks itself up into the single moment where it [history] is written."[16]

In other words, "objective history" surrenders its historical endeavor to its objective method and squeezes the historical out of history: an objective account of history alienates its very object (continuous becoming), just like a Zenonian account of movement talks of everything but movement. In order to reestablish history in its dynamics, Merleau-Ponty needs to build upon Husserl's idea of a temporal retention allowing for an overlap (*empiètement*) between events, or rather, that turns "events" (*évènements*, which break the temporal chain down to discrete entities) into "advents" (*avènements*, which arise from the general movement of history). Merleau-Ponty writes:

> We propose on the contrary to consider the order of culture or meaning as an original order of advent, which should not be derived from the order of mere events, if it exists, or treated as simply the effect of extraordinary conjunctions. If it is characteristic of the human gesture to signify beyond its simple factual existence, to inaugurate a meaning, it follows that every gesture is comparable to every other and that they all arise from one single syntax, that each is both a beginning and a continuation which, insofar as it is not walled up in its singularity and finished [*révolu*] once and for all like an event, points to a continuation or recommencement. It applies beyond [*il vaut au-delà*] its simple presence, and in this respect it is allied or accomplished in advance of all other efforts of expression. (S 68)

This claim is particularly radical insofar as it involves considering history as an essential link between all events that become "comparable," that is to say, commensurable on the basis of a "unique syntax." Of course, everything I have said so far shows that this syntax is informed by the structure of intentionality. Because it introduces the dynamics of determination into the world, intentionality triggers the dialectical movement of history, but because it introduces the principle of indetermination in the world, it ensures that all events will be contained within the homogeneous milieu of indeterminacy, which is the vital element of consciousness and, further, of history itself. This amounts to saying that the structure of intentionality as chiasmatic self-differentiation (within the self and of the self with the world) imposes its heredity over human history.

We can now understand how Merleau-Ponty's rejection of communism was soon followed by the rejection of Marxism itself as positing an end to history:

> What then is obsolete is not the dialectic, but the pretension of terminating it in an end of history, in a permanent revolution, or in a regime which, being the contestation of itself, would no longer need to be contested from the outside and, in fact, would no longer have anything outside it.[17]

Indeed the warrant of becoming is the margin of negativity, which makes room for movement. An end of history is correctly understood as the eradication of such a "zone," but incorrectly, it takes this zone to be contingent when sedimentation itself and the dialectic that arises from it establish it as necessary. A dialectic with an end is inconceivable (AD 206).

It becomes clear from his critique of the notion of events that Merleau-Ponty has ceased altogether to consider history in successive terms. History is the milieu of becoming insofar as it is the unfinished unfolding of a certain syntax. However, insofar as it is merely the unfolding of a preexisting syntax, it is grounded in being to the point that Merleau-Ponty can affirm, "Perhaps time does not flow from the future or the past" (S 27). In other words, there is an atemporal structure to time, that is, the "syntax" of history. To be sure, this preexisting "syntax" is not to be understood as implying that the adventures of history will not exist.[18] In fact history and sedimentation carry in themselves the atemporal style that informs their being and that lies nowhere outside them; it exists only as their principle, for "there exists a place [*lieu*] where everything that is and will be, is preparing itself for being said" (PM 6).

For both Nietzsche and Merleau-Ponty, therefore, the structure of originary dehiscence, by precluding determinacy, also determines the structure of history as open-ended. Indeed it is the novelty contained in the reworking of the concept of "events" into "advents" (Merleau-Ponty) or "happenings" (Nietzsche) that every single event can never be exhausted by the determining activity of the will to power (incorporation) or the flesh (sedimentation). For Nietzsche, the structure of existence as will to power places difference at the heart of being insofar as all objects, subjects, and events are horizonally constituted as a result of a differentiating activity of the will to power that precedes them, and therefore self-identity, which would be the only possible closure of history, would amount only to a contradiction. Similarly Merleau-Ponty writes repeatedly that history is an endless process of sedimentation: "It is the hypothesis of a consciousness without future and of an end of history that is inconceivable. Forever therefore, as long as there are men, the future shall remain open."[19]

For Merleau-Ponty, therefore, the end of consciousness (that is to say, the end of sedimentation) is identical to the end of history. As a result, he suggests that man, as the locus of consciousness, is the warrant of the openness of the future. For Nietzsche too, the locus of consciousness poses the horizonality of history, even though, as was shown earlier, he expands the realm of consciousness to all life (a move Merleau-Ponty himself performs in his course on nature). As a result, the whole of life opposes any closure to history. Indeed, just as the impossibility to begin history was formulated in *On the Genealogy of Morals* II, 16, the coessentiality of consciousness and world signifies that history was never started. Nietzsche famously writes: "If the motion of the world aimed at a final state, that state would have been reached" (KSA 13, 1888, 11 [72], 34).

A final state cannot lead into becoming, and since becoming is the present form of the world, a state of stability never was. There is indeed no prehistory, in the same way that self-identical nature cannot have led into consciousness, inciting Nietzsche and Merleau-Ponty—against Husserl—to conclude that consciousness was always part of the essence of the world. Merleau-Ponty concurs with a formula whose psychological undertones themselves seem uncannily Nietzschean:

> What is this end of history? One supposes some boundary after which mankind at long last ceases to be a senseless tumult, and returns to the immobility of nature. Such a conception of an absolute purification of history, a regime without any inertia, without chance and without risk, is the inverted reflection of our anguish and loneliness. (AD 12)

Far from a movement toward some fantasized stability, Merleau-Ponty regards history as a wild and tumultuous productivity, a "symbolic matrix" of events (VI 192ff.; see also S 122) that *creates* events by overdetermining advents through a poetic or symbolic process. Similarly Nietzsche views history as a constant creation and solidification of "objects" on the part of the indeterminate but determinative will to power: "The unconditioned cannot be the creative. Only the conditioned can condition.... The world of the unconditioned, if it existed, would be the world of the non-productive" (KSA 11, 1884, 26 [203], 203).

Genealogy and Archaeology toward Indirect Ontology

It seems therefore that both Nietzsche and Merleau-Ponty take the consequences of placing dehiscence at the heart of perception and constitution to similar consequences by affirming the structure of history as horizonal and its essence as a productivity of time defined as the time of "incorporation" (Nietzsche) and "sedimentation" (Merleau-Ponty).

For both Nietzsche and Merleau-Ponty, such a view of the historical development, based on a rejection of the concept of events in favor of "advents" or "happenings," signifies that the relations between points in time are not, to quote Merleau-Ponty, "parte extra partes" but instead that incorporation and sedimentation must be seen as informing a form of historical development in which every present instant puts every past and future instant at play. For Merleau-Ponty, sedimentative history must be seen as cumulative, preserving the past in the present: "Thus I function by construction. I am standing atop a pyramid of time which has been me" (S 14) and "To understand perception as differentiation, forgetting as de-differentiation. The fact that one no longer sees the memory = not a destruction of a psychic material which would be the sensible, but its disarticulation which makes there be no longer any separation [*écart*], any relief" (VI 197).

In other words, and as has been emphasized by a host of Merleau-Ponty readers, forgetting must be conceived in Gestaltic terms, as the memory becomes invisible not as it is destroyed, as the traditional view has it, but it becomes invisible in the sense of indistinguishable from the background. That is to say, the forgetting of a memory indicates not its absence but its full presence.[20] Nietzsche concurs, again, in strikingly similar terms. Explicitly and consistently suggesting some pre-Gestaltic setup, he writes, "Memory [*das Gedächtniss*], everything we have lived through [*erlebt*] is alive [*lebt*], it is being worked over, ordered, and incorporated [*einverleibt*]" (KSA 11, 1884, 25 [409], 119).

> We must reconsider everything we've learnt about memory: it is the mass of the whole of the lived experience of all organic life, which continues to live. . . . There has to be an internal process . . . : the fact of placing relief [*hereausheben*] ever more insistently on the general schema while abandoning the particular features.—As long as something is still susceptible of being recalled as a particular fact, it has not yet been molten [*eingeschmolzen*] into the rest: the most recent of the lived events still float on the surface. (KSA 11, 1884, 26 [94], 175)

Further, Nietzsche defines memory as the result of a restricted instinct for equalization that maintains the necessary Gestaltic distance to make it stand out as a memory: "Recollection [*Erinnerung*], late phenomenon, insofar as the equalizing instinct appears restrained in it: difference [*die Differenz*] is maintained" (KSA 12, 1886, 5 [65], 209). Finally, he adds that those representations that we possess but have lost awareness of "are not destroyed [*vernichtet*], they are only *pushed back* [*zurückgedrangt*] or subordinated. *In the spiritual realm, there is no destruction*" (KSA 12, 1886, 7 [53], 312, Nietzsche's emphases).

Nietzsche and Merleau-Ponty are therefore in full agreement regarding the issue of memory and forgetfulness, in accordance with their shared belief in the indestructibility of the past and its conservation in a present that sits atop a pyramid of past events. This agreement extends to the historical realm as well. Nietzsche writes, "Principle: every lived experience [*Erlebnisse*], traced back to its origins, presupposes the entire past of the world" (KSA 11, 1884, 25 [358], 107). And further: "Principle: no retroactive [*rückläufigen*] hypotheses, rather, a state of epochē!" (KSA 11, 1884, 26 [82], 170).

The state of *epochē*, of course, is the Holy Grail of phenomenology for both Husserl and Merleau-Ponty, as well as their casus belli. In Nietzsche's mind, the recourse to *epochē* is presented as an alternative to "retroactive hypotheses," that is, historical hypotheses about specific acts, events, and facts of the past. In opposition to these, Nietzsche urges us to avoid factual hypotheses and encourages us to access a certain state that will yield knowledge about the past. It seems obvious (under penalty of portraying Nietzsche as proposing some superstitious access to the facts of history) that this knowledge shall not be of the factual sort. On the contrary, the use of *epochē* for Nietzsche is to access the past incorporated into the present. This is precisely Merleau-Ponty's understanding of *epochē* as well, from which he hopes to gain access not to the past but to the very structure of temporality:

> It is a question of finding in the present the flesh of the world (and not in the past) an "ever new" and "always the same"—. . . . The sensible, Nature, transcend the past-present distinction, realize from within a passage from one to the other. Existential eternity. The indestructible. (VI 267)

What is uncovered by epochal archaeology therefore is not any fact of the past but the very structure of the present moment, saturated with past. This moment is indeed more than an event (an event would be fully determinate, therefore invisible); it is a present that is a sample of presence. The accumulative structure of sedimentative becoming therefore gives access to the structure of being as presence, that is, to the structure of the eternal activity of sedimentation itself. For Merleau-Ponty, therefore, it is this full engagement with the present that offers a glimpse into the eternal, leading the way to his "indirect ontology," which "seeks being through the beings" (VI 225). This being, Merleau-Ponty declares, is nothing but the activity of sedimentation that is both exhibited and exemplified in the thickness of each instant. It is therefore a being of structure, a being that, although it is positive, is better expressed negatively, in terms of the possibilities it restricts, for the "essence is a dehiscence [*écart*], not the possession of some positivity," it is "an in-variance, it is a hinge and not a quiddity" (NL 329).

For Merleau-Ponty, the essence that is found is "*écart*," originary dehiscence, just as it was uncovered in the foreword to *The Phenomenology of Perception*, and if our access to it must be negative, we must observe what possibilities it precludes, for, as Merleau-Ponty points out, "the 'open possibility' is not nothing. One need only consider what it excludes to become certain of it" (NL 332). What it "precludes" is precisely any idea of absolute determinacy or self-identity, that is, any closure and any "entirely determined being" (NL 332). For Merleau-Ponty, the ultimate structure of being, once properly uncovered, is nothing but the descent of the originary dehiscence of perception: it is openness.

Similarly, although he refuses to call it "being" out of concern for promoting becoming over it, Nietzsche uncovers the structure of fatum as openness from within the state of *epochē*: "Everything is absolutely necessary [*absolut nothwendig*] and the lot [*Loos*] of mankind has long been decided because it has been there [*dagewesen*] forever" (KSA 11, 1884, 26 [82], 170).

Thanks to the "state of *epochē*," Nietzsche uncovers the eternity of a fate that is altogether future, present, and past. This fate, of course, is accessed in the present moment not as a prediction of factual developments (Nietzsche constantly opposes his own fatalism with what he calls "petty factualism" in GM II, 24 passim); on the contrary, the present offers an insight into the fateful nature of existence, that is, the structure of the will to power as originary differentiation.

Conclusion

In following the descent of the originary dehiscence that both Merleau-Ponty and Nietzsche find at the heart of perception through its structural status for history and, further, for any truly nonobjectivist ontology, my intention was not to offer an exhaustive view of the connections between the two thinkers. The richness of both philosophies, as well as the uncanny connections, whether semantic, philosophic, or both, are too numerous, too complex, and sometimes too ambiguous for such a task to be achieved in the space available. In any case, if this were my ambition, where are the promising and relevant parallels between both thinkers' treatments of the origin of truth, of perceptual faith, of language and concept formation, and of art? It was the aim of this essay to establish the relevance and to offer a glimpse of the promise contained in a joint reading of the two authors.

This promise seems to me to be warranted, beyond the more or less numerous and specific points of agreements between the two philosophers, by the structural parallels that can be drawn between the overall movements of their philosophies. Both thinkers begin with an observation of the human's insertion in the world, which they find best characterized as an ambiguous mix of distance and closeness, a mix that determines, in both cases, the future development of their philosophies through their final ontological considerations, opening up to a nonconventional ground for ontology, which Merleau-Ponty describes as an indirect ontology that seeks being through the beings. There the specific connections between the two thinkers shine brightest as they both reflect each other's originality: for sure, both are aware that such an "indirect ontology" cannot entirely detach itself from metaphysics, insofar as it explicitly grounds being in "the beings," the ontological into the ontic, and in this sense, both of their philosophies are a culmination of metaphysics, albeit, I suggest, not in Heideggerian fashion as a shortcoming. Perhaps the greatest lesson offered by both thinkers is this: that phenomenology is necessarily a search not for "matter, mind or substance" but for the element of phenomenality, an element that must be understood, as Merleau-Ponty writes, "in the sense of a general thing, midway between the spatio-temporal individual and the idea, a sort of incarnate principle that brings a style of being wherever there is a fragment of being" (VI 139). Whether we call it chiasmatic flesh or the will to power, this element is understood by both Nietzsche and Merleau-Ponty as the very structure of an eternal yet originary dehiscence.

Notes

1. Nietzsche, *Kritische Studienausgabe*, 11, 1887, 9 [91], 126 (hereafter KSA). All translations from KSA are mine.

2. Risse, "Origins of Ressentiment," 142.

3. See Clark and Swensen's "Translator's note," 147.

4. Risse, "Origins of Ressentiment," 142.

5. The expression *nicht anschenden* in this note from the *Nachlass* lends itself to different interpretations. Considering that in this passage, Nietzsche also refers to Ernst Häckel's observation of embryos in *Generelle Physiologie* (1866), it may appear more relevant to translate the expression as "unborn," suggesting that Nietzsche was not establishing, as I take him to be doing, that consciousness was not born, but rather, that embryos are "unborn organisms." However, this possibility is ruled out in the next Notebook, where Nietzsche reiterates the point, again with implicit reference to Häckel, but where there is no doubt that Nietzsche's focus is on the question of the birth or nonbirth of consciousness (see KSA XI, 26 [80], 1884, 170).

6. Merleau-Ponty, *Phénoménologie de la perception*, xv.

7. This line is obviously not a place of stability insofar as total conquest is eventually possible. However, any process of subjection is always identical with a resistance. The disparition of a resistance is the end of the process, and the apparition of a new resistance, since the will to power is defined by its discharge, and that discharge can take place only against resistance. See KSA, V, 2 [63], 1885, 27 and KSA, XIII, 14 [78], 1888, 257.

8. See also KSA XIII, 14 [174], 1888, 360.

9. For the identity of perception and passivity, see KSA, X, 24 [23], 1884, 658.

10. Merleau-Ponty, *Notes de Lecture*, 329 (hereafter NL). All translations from NL are mine.

11. See Merleau-Ponty, *Le visible et l'invisible*, 139, 141 (hereafter VI).

12. Merleau-Ponty, *Parcours deux*, 38.

13. Rudolph Bernet understands this claim as affirming the impossibility of individuation: "A thing can only be perceived through and according to the things that surround it." In doing so, Bernet rightly emphasizes that Merleau-Ponty sees objects as impossible to abstract from their context; however, a look at the textual context shows that Merleau-Ponty's point has further reaching consequences. Merleau-Ponty writes, "The absolute positing of a single object is the death of consciousness, since it congeals the whole of existence, as a crystal placed in a solution suddenly crystallizes it." For Merleau-Ponty, as the metaphor of the crystal shows, the necessary indeterminacy of intentional objects establishes becoming: consciousness is a dynamic process. Bernet, "The Subject in Nature," 64.

14. These thoughts, which define things in terms of the boundaries of our perception, were prefigured in the fascinating aphorism 48 of *Daybreak*: "'*Know yourself*' is the whole of science.—Only when he has attained a final knowledge of all things will man have come to know himself. For things are only the boundaries of man" (KSA, III, 49).

15. Merleau-Ponty, *Signes*, 68 (hereafter S).

16. Merleau-Ponty, *La Prose du monde*, 31 (hereafter PM). Admittedly this remark is directed at the history of language; yet we have seen how language, being the prolongation of truth, and truth appearing as the thread that holds all institution together, is not only the privileged archetype of all sedimentation but its most general determination.

17. Merleau-Ponty, *Les aventures de la dialectique*, 206 (hereafter AD).

18. "The difficult and essential point here is to understand that by positing a field distinct from the empirical order of events, we are not positing a Spirit of Painting. . . . Cultural creation [*la création de la culture*] is ineffectual if it does not find a vehicle in external circumstances" (S 68/110).

19. Merleau-Ponty, *Humanisme et Terreur*, 192.

20. Of course, Merleau-Ponty's critique of full presence suggests that absolute forgetting must be viewed only in horizonal terms.

Bibliography

Bernet, Rudolf. "The Subject in Nature." In *Merleau-Ponty in Contemporary Perspective,* edited by Patrick Burke and Jan Van Der Veken. Dordrecht: Kluwer, 1993.

Husserl, Edmund. *Complete Works*. Translated and edited by Richard Rojcewicz and André Schuwer. London: Springer, 1990.

———. *Crisis of European Sciences and Transcendental Phenomenology*. Translated by David Carr. Evanston, IL: Northwestern University Press, 1989.

———. *Ideas I: General Introduction to a Pure Phenomenology*. Translated by W. R. Boyce Gibson. New York: Collier Books, 1972.

Merleau-Ponty, Maurice. *Les Aventures de la Dialectique*. Paris: Gallimard, 1955.

———. *Humanisme et Terreur*. Paris: NRF/Gallimard, 1947.

———. *Husserl at the Limits of Phenomenology*. Edited and translated by Leonard Lawlor and Bettina Bergo. Evanston, IL: Northwestern University Press, 2002.

———. *L'Institution, la Passivité: Notes de Cours au Collège de France (1954–1955)*. Edited by Dominique Darmaillacq, Claude Lefort, and Stéphanie Ménasé. Paris: Belin, 2003.

———. *La Nature: Notes de Cours au Collège de France*. Edited by Dominique Séglard. Paris: Seuil, 1994.

———. *Notes de Cours, 1959–1961*. Edited by Stéphanie Ménasé. Paris: NRF/Gallimard, 1996.

———. "Notes de Lecture et Commentaire sur Théorie du Champ de la Conscience de Aron Gurwitsch," edited by Stéphanie Ménasé. *Revue de Métaphysique et de Morale* 3 (1997): 321–41.

———. *L'Oeil et l'Esprit*. Paris: Gallimard, 1964.

———. *Parcours, 1935–1950*. Edited by Jacques Prunair. Lagrasse: Verdier, 1999.

———. *Parcours deux, 1951–1961*. Edited by Jacques Prunair. Lagrasse: Verdier, 2000.

———. *Phénoménologie de la Perception*. Paris: NRF/Gallimard, 1945.

———. *Le Primat de la Perception*. Grenoble: Cynara, 1989.

———. *La Prose du Monde*. Edited by Claude Lefort. Paris: TEL Gallimard, 1969.

———. *Résumés de Cours* (Collège de France, 1952–60). Edited by Claude Lefort. Paris: TEL Gallimard, 1968.

———. *Sens et Non-Sens*, Paris: NRF Gallimard, 1996.

———. *Signes*. Paris: Folio Gallimard, 1960.

———. *Le Visible et l'Invisible*. Edited by Claude Lefort. Paris: TEL Gallimard, 1964.

Nietzsche, Friedrich. *Kritische Studienausgabe*. Edited by Giorgio Colli and Mazzino Montinari. Berlin: de Gruyter, 1980.

Risse, Matthias. "The Second Treatise in *On the Genealogy of Morality*: Nietzsche on the Origin of the Bad Conscience." *European Journal of Philosophy* 9, no. 1 (2001): 55–81.

———. "Origins of Ressentiment and Sources of Normativity." *Nietzsche-Studien*. 32 (2003): 142–70.

11 Nietzsche and Merleau-Ponty

Art, Sacred Life, and Phenomenology of Flesh

Galen A. Johnson

It has been little remarked that Nietzsche's *Birth of Tragedy*[1] made Raphael's magnificent painting of the transfiguration of Christ the "monogram" of Nietzsche's account of the origin of tragedy and his philosophy of art. Moreover, since that work introduces us to the figure of Dionysus, who plays an increasingly definitive role for Nietzsche's entire philosophy as it unfolds in the later writings, we can add more emphatically that Raphael's *Transfiguration*, as ironic as it may seem, is the monogram of the philosophy of the death of God. The goal of this paper will be to show how this is the case as well as to bring Nietzsche's account into a comparative dialogue with the philosophy of Merleau-Ponty on the meaning of transfiguration and the death of God. This dialogue must necessarily include reflections on the meaning of phenomenology itself, for transfiguration is a problematic event and figure for phenomenological philosophies of the truth of appearances. Transfiguration appears in the same phenomenological topology as magic, dream, miracle, and mystery—and, more ominously, along with error, illusion, hallucination, fantasy, and psychosis—as challenges to the veridicality or "norm" and "normal" of everyday perception and the life-world.

One of the Nietzsche scholars who has written in detail regarding Nietzsche's high regard for Raphael and the *Transfiguration* is Gary Shapiro, who also has written of "Merleau-Ponty's evasion of Nietzsche."[2] Shapiro means this specifically in relation to Merleau-Ponty's "Indirect Language and the Voices of Silence," both that essay's commentary on Malraux and its critique of the museum as the "historicity of death," which Shapiro contends is an unacknowledged "variant of Nietzschean thought"[3] from the *Untimely Meditations*. Though it is the case that Nietzsche does not figure prominently in the surface of Merleau-Ponty's best known texts, such as *Phenomenology of Perception*, yet, at the same time, Nietzsche provides something like bookends to Merleau-Ponty's philosophical itinerary, for Merleau-Ponty's first published article appeared in 1935 in *La Vie intellectuelle*[4] on the subject of Scheler and Nietzsche's typology of *ressentiment,* and his lecture course in the last year of his teaching, 1960–61, *La philosophie et non-philosophie depuis Hegel,* includes commentary on the preface to the second edition of Nietzsche's *The Gay Science.* In the fourth and final chapter of *The Visible and the Invisible* as well as several working notes we also find important Nietzschean influences on themes of truth, time, and the circle.

I will take full advantage of these texts as our thinking unfolds, though it is certainly the case that one wishes for a more direct and sustained engagement by Merleau-Ponty with Nietzsche such as we find for Husserl, Bergson, Sartre, and Marx. Nevertheless much of what has been called "evasion" is a historical contingency, namely that the wave of Nietzsche studies and interpretations in France did not begin until after Merleau-Ponty's death. Heidegger's two-volume *Nietzsche* was published in 1961, the very year of Merleau-Ponty's death, and Deleuze's *Nietzsche et la philosophie* appeared in 1962.[5] In hindsight, historical contingency may appear as aporia or evasion, but in prospect this only leaves us some of the productive work to be done in thinking with, through, and beyond the texts to understand the aesthetic, theological, and ontological views of these two powerful philosophical thinkers.

Let us first turn to *The Birth of Tragedy*, the case of Raphael, and Nietzsche's interpretation of the meaning of transfiguration. Subsequently I will take up Merleau-Ponty's own views on the meaning of "transfiguration" and the death of God, including the questions of phenomenology and the truth of appearances.

Nietzsche, Raphael, and Transfiguration

The Birth of Tragedy introduces us to the celebrated distinction between the "Apollonian" and the "Dionysian," together with Nietzsche's argument that Greek tragedy came into being through the union of Apollonian and Dionysian elements. Likewise Greek tragedy died through elimination of the Dionysian element in the plays of Euripides, written under the rationalistic influence of Socrates: knowledge = virtue = happiness. Euripides reduced the chorus from its dithyrambic musical chanting, swaying, and pathos, evoking a *methexis* or participation with the audience, to a spoken unison voice of moral commentary. The meanings of the Apollonian and Dionysian are not without their complications in Nietzsche's text, including how to understand his dream analogy for the genuine, "naïve" artist who creates a "mere appearance of mere appearance" (BT §4, 45). I will return to this matter, but for now the main outlines of the Apollonian and Dionysian are clear enough and well known. Nietzsche describes Apollo as "the shining one" (*der Scheinende*), the deity of light, the image-making god, and the sculptor of dream-images (BT §1, 35). The work of the Apollonian in Attic tragedy is creating the space and setting the scene for the action, characters, music, and poetry. The Apollonian is imperturbable calm, serenity, and repose, and it is also the *"principium individuationis"* (BT §1, 36), that principle which individuates and separates images and shapes. Onto this serene setting strides the Dionysian impulse in art, which is its opposite but also its necessary counterpart: "Apollo could not live without Dionysus" (BT §4, 46). The Dionysian is body and nature, song and dance, particularly the "symbolic powers" of music in "rhythmics, dynamics, and harmony." The essence of nature expresses itself in a symbolism of the entire body, "not the mere symbolism of the lips, face, and speech but the whole pantomime of dancing, forcing every member into rhythmic movement" (BT §2, 40). The Dionysian is the chanting, singing, and drumbeat of the dithyramb, that urgent and unknown choral music of the cult of Dionysus, and thus the Dionysian disrupts individuation in favor of "oneness as the soul of the race and nature itself" (BT §2, 40). "In song and dance man expresses himself as a member of a higher community; he has forgotten how to walk and speak and is on the way toward flying into the air, dancing. His gestures express enchantment" (BT §1, 37).

"Flying into the air" is precisely what we see in Raphael's painting *Transfiguration* (1516–20), his last painting, left unfinished upon his death in 1520. The work depicts the Christ transfigured in his glory of light and white raiment, talking with Moses and Elijah in the sky, and revealed to three of the apostles. The painting is divided in half; in the lower half we see the demon-possessed boy, the boy's despairing father and companions, and the disciples who are helpless to heal the boy—these are those apostles who have been left behind while Jesus ascended the mountain with the chosen three disciples, Peter, James, and John. In the upper half of the picture, Raphael shows us the transfiguration scene: Moses and Elijah conversing with the Christ and all three figures floating in the air. The three chosen disciples are lying on the ground, apparently dazed and shading their eyes, with the whole scene bathed in a heavenly sky of blue and white. Nietzsche's commentary on the painting describes the transfiguration scene in the upper half of the picture as the realm of the Apollonian, and the lower half, the scene of despair and suffering, as the realm of the Dionysian:

> Here we have presented, in the most sublime artistic symbolism, that Apollonian world of beauty and its substratum, the terrible wisdom of Silenus; and intuitively we comprehend their necessary interdependence. . . . With his sublime gestures, he [Apollo] shows us how necessary is the entire world of suffering, that by means of it the individual may be impelled to realize the redeeming vision, and then, sunk in contemplation of it, sit quietly in his tossing bark amid the waves. (BT §4, 45–46)

Silenus is the companion of Dionysus whose terrible wisdom Nietzsche attributes to an ancient folk story regarding King Midas. To the inquiry from Midas regarding what is best and most desirable in life, Silenus answered with the words of the chorus spoken in *Oedipus at Colonus* after Oedipus has blinded himself for his transgressions. He is now wandering with his two daughters, Antigone and Ismene, outside the city of Thebes at Colonus, about a mile from Athens, and the chorus answers the question of the best and most desirable in these words: "What is best of all is utterly beyond your reach: not to be born, not to *be*, to be *nothing*. But the second best for you is—to die soon" (BT §3, 42).[6]

I want to bring out three problematic but emphatically interesting aspects of Nietzsche's reading of Raphael's *Transfiguration*: first, Nietzsche's claim that the painting demonstrates the interdependence of the Apollonian and Dionysian; second, his selection of Raphael as an "exemplary" or "naïve" artist; and third, what is most startling, his implicit denial that the painting depicts the transfiguration of Christ at all. He claims that the upper half of the painting is Apollonian, not Christian.

To begin, Nietzsche's claim that the *Transfiguration* demonstrates the "necessary interdependence" of the Apollonian and Dionysian raises the debated question of the unity of this painting. The question itself shows the continuing influence of the aesthetic principles of Plato and Aristotle during the Renaissance, for they had required that the parts of a true work of art exhibit a harmony within an overarching unity. On first glance, the work seems binary as Nietzsche describes, divided into two opposed regions, above and below; more modern eyes may see the painting as a split screen showing two different scenes simultaneously. Nevertheless, upon closer examination the structure of the painting is much more complex, and multiple elements of a unified whole emerge. Ultimately Nietzsche is correct about the interdependence of the upper and lower parts of the work, and therefore of the Apollonian and Dionysian, but in ways more complex than he recognized or analyzed.

The lower part of the work is itself strongly divided into two groups of figures separated by a dark, diagonal gap, giving us three parts of the painting, not two. On the lower right are the father and figures huddled around the suffering boy, and on the lower left appear the other apostles. Between the two groups, in the forefront beneath the diagonal gap, appears a kneeling woman of highly classical stylization with braided hair. She looks fiercely toward the apostles and points with force toward the boy, and she is a figure of extraordinary strength and freedom. For the Nietzschean reading, if this lower half of the painting is the Dionysian, her braided hair may reference the Maenad female followers of Dionysus, though her posture is far from wild and mad. Each of the two groups of figures is distinguished by its own character of expression, color, and form. Among the figures on the right, surrounding the child, we see faces tense, foreheads wrinkled, skin pale, clothing clinging tautly to the bodies. The figures of the apostles on the left are more brightly lit, the folds of their clothing more flowing and softer; they are almost all moving forward, and many are gesturing animatedly. Moreover two of the apostles are pointing not toward the boy and the figures of suffering but directly toward the transfiguration scene arising above them, creating a reference from below to above. Repetition of colors below and above also binds the scenes together. The apostle who is likely Matthew, in the forefront at the lower left, holding an open book, is pictured in the same blue tunic and gold robe that is repeated in the blinded apostle in the middle below the Christ, most likely St. Peter. The woman with braided hair wears a robe in the same blue color, though her dress is rose, which is repeated in the robe of the dazed apostle on the right, likely John. The green in the costume of the father holding the suffering boy is repeated in the blinded apostle on the left of the transfiguration scene, as well as in the tunic of the floating Moses and the book held by Elijah. Additional color repetitions are found in the clothing above and below.

In contrast with the darkness and angularity of the two lower groups of figures, the figures of the upper part of the painting form a perfect circle or sphere. In the upper arc of the circle, Moses appears at the left, holding the tablet of the law, and Elijah, on the right, gazes upward in adoration toward the transfigured Christ, who rises in the center above them both. Completing the lower half of the circle or sphere are the blinded apostles, Peter, James, and John, dazzled by the brightness of the scene arising above them. The heavenly blue and the white clouds and shining white of Christ's clothing are in accord with the biblical text of Matthew (17:2): "His face did shine as the sun, and his raiment was white as the light." By creating figures that genuinely appear to be floating in the air, Raphael accomplished the impossible, never achieved previously in painting.[7] The total illumination and radiance required by the literary biblical text would make a visual painting of the scene impossible, for it would eliminate all shadowing and thereby eliminate all depth in the figure of Christ. But Raphael has worked at the limit between light and shade in the folds of Christ's robe, buoyed up and billowing in the full motion of rising into the shining radiance of the sky. The Raphael scholar Konrad Oberhuber expresses the miracle of the event and of Raphael's painting, writing, "We are removed from earthly laws, from the laws of gravitation and three-dimensional space."[8] The gospel writers also report that a voice spoke from out of the cloud: "This is my beloved Son, in whom I am well pleased; hear ye him" (Matthew 17:5). Thus to miracle is added the revelation of divinity. To the far left of the upper part of the painting appear two individuals witnessing the transfiguration scene, not mentioned in the biblical text. Critics take them to be two early Christian deacons and subsequently saints of the Church, identifiable by their vestments and named Justus and Pastor.[9] Their distant, secret witness may be like own silent witness to the miracle.

In addition to unity of structure, colors, lines, and gestures, a narrative continuity between the two main scenes binds the upper and lower parts of the painting into a narrative whole. Three gospels, Matthew, Mark, and Luke, include accounts of the transfiguration of Christ with remarkably similar details,[10] and all three agree that immediately following the transfiguration, Jesus with Peter, James, and John descended from Mount Tabor and were greeted by a multitude, among which were the despairing father and suffering son. The son is variously described as a lunatic, demon-possessed, or suffering from epileptic fits that sometimes cause him to fall into fire to be burned and sometimes into water to be drowned. The father had brought him to the apostles, but they could not cure him, as depicted in the lower scene of Raphael's work. Nevertheless Jesus healed the child and told the apostles they were impotent because of their unbelief: "If ye have faith as a grain of mustard seed . . . nothing is impossible unto you" (Matthew 7:20). Thus the transfiguration and the healing are bound together by a narrative continuity, but they are also a doubling of miracle and repetition of the necessity for faith.

Among the many commentators on the unity of Raphael's work, which include Hegel,[11] Goethe's *Italian Journey* stands out for its multiple references to Raphael. When Goethe confronted the *Transfiguration* in person on his second trip to Rome, he recorded that he found it "odd that anyone should ever have found fault with the grand unity of this conception." He described the unity this way: "How, then, are those upper and lower parts to be separated? The two are one: below, the suffering part, in need of help; above, the effective, helpful part, both of them linked together."[12]

Equally striking as Nietzsche's appropriation of the *Transfiguration* is his selection of Raphael as an "exemplary" artist who contained the "naïve" force of the Dionysian. It is hard to imagine any idea more contrary to Raphael's status as one of the two leading artists of the Catholic Church during the Renaissance, along with Michelangelo, who was often Raphael's competitor for commissions from the Church. The *Transfiguration* is Raphael's last large altarpiece (405 x 278 cm); he received the commission for the work in 1516 from Cardinal Giulio de Medici, who later became Pope Clement VII.[13] When the work was found in Raphael's studio at his death, it was placed at the head of his coffin "as testimony to the spiritual heights that the religious thought of the Catholic tradition could reach in the Renaissance."[14] In a sense, Nietzsche is following Schopenhauer in his admiration for Raphael, for the concluding paragraph of volume 1 of *The World as Will and Representation* refers to a "peace that is higher than all reason, that unshakable confidence and serenity, whose mere reflection in the countenance, as depicted by Raphael and Correggio, is a complete and certain gospel."[15] Moreover Nietzsche's discussion of Raphael in *The Birth of Tragedy* is not an isolated reference, for Raphael appears throughout Nietzsche's works, from *Untimely Meditations* right through to *Twilight of the Idols* and *The Will to Power*. Consistently Raphael is, for Nietzsche, the figure of the heroic artist, but in his altered interpretation, an artist who was *not* and *could not have been* Christian. In the second of the *Untimely Meditations,* titled "On The Uses and Disadvantages of History for Life," Nietzsche objects to philosophers of history who would make the meaning of history into one of rational or moral progress. He argues that such a Hegelian view of history is refuted by the tragically brief life and early death of Raphael: "Morality is offended, for example, by the fact that a Raphael had to die at thirty-six; such a being ought not to die. . . . It is only because you do not know what such a *natura naturans* [creative nature] as Raphael is that you are not incensed to know that it once was but will never be again."[16] This phrase from Spinoza, *natura naturans*, that Spinoza applies to God or Substance, means Nietzsche regards Raphael as a force of nature whose work is aligned with active and free expression, in no way the passive product of natural causes. And this is precisely what we find in Nietzsche's later writings, where he places Raphael alongside Goethe, Shakespeare, and Beethoven as artists who refuse an easy romanticism in favor of the Dionysian dithyramb and apotheosis:

Is art a consequence of *dissatisfaction with reality*? Or an expression of *gratitude for happiness enjoyed*? In the former case, *romanticism*; in the latter, aureole and dithyramb (in short, art of apotheosis): Raphael, too, belongs here; he merely had the falsity to deify what looked like the Christian interpretation of the world. He was grateful for existence where it was *not* specifically Christian.[17]

Several times Nietzsche insists on the point that Raphael, as a creative force of nature and follower of Dionysus, could not have been Christian. "Expeditions of an Untimely Man" in *Twilight of the Idols* could not be more forceful: "A Christian who would at the same time be an artist simply does not occur. One should not be childish and object by naming Raphael. . . . Raphael said Yes, Raphael did Yes; consequently, Raphael was no Christian."[18] *The Will to Power* comments on the necessary strength and physicality of great artists, Raphael among them: "Artists, if they are any good, are (physically as well) strong, full of surplus energy, powerful animals, sensual; without a certain overheating of the sexual system a Raphael is unthinkable" (WP, 800, March–June 1888).

Finally, and most remarkably and most shocking too, we are confronted with Nietzsche's "transfiguration" of the transfiguration scene itself and of the very meaning of transfiguration.[19] It is easy to read right past what Nietzsche is doing in *The Birth of Tragedy* when he says that the upper half of Raphael's *Transfiguration* work is the realm of the Apollonian. A weak and general reading is possible, in which the entire upper half, taken as a totality, is shown to be the realm of Apollonian radiance without focusing specifically on the Christ figure. However, the text supports a stronger reading in which there is a *substitution* of Apollo for Christ. Apollo *replaces* Jesus. Two brief phrases signal Nietzsche's meaning: he says that it is Apollo who "appears to us" in the painting, and "Apollo, as ethical deity, exacts measure of his disciples" (BT §4, 45, 46). According to Nietzsche, Raphael's *Transfiguration* shows us not a Christ but Apollo floating in the sky as the shining deity of beauty, ethical calm, and individuation. What makes this so shocking to Christian sensibility is that the transfiguration scene is the one place in all of the gospels in which Jesus is revealed as divine. This Nietzsche intends to deny with all the force of his philosophical powers.

Thus Nietzsche replaces the theological meaning of transfiguration with the aesthetic meaning of tragic art in which the Dionysian, properly harmonized with the Apollonian, offers the true justification and redemption of life. This altered aesthetic meaning is found at crucial moments in Nietzsche's mature philosophy. *The Birth of Tragedy* speaks of the Dionysian orgies of the Greeks in terms of "world redemption and days of transfiguration" (BT §2, 40). Much later, *Will to Power* speaks of the "blooming" of the Greek body and soul in the creation of Dionysian art, which transfigures existence: "When the Greek body and the Greek soul 'bloomed,' and not in conditions of morbid exaltation and madness, there arose that mysterious symbol of the highest world-affirmation and transfiguration of existence that has yet been attained on earth. Here we have a standard by which everything that has grown up since is found too short, too poor, too narrow" (WP 1051, 1885). From *The Birth of Tragedy* forward, Nietzsche had always recognized a potential within the Dionysian for "morbid exaltation and madness," which *The Birth of Tragedy* had spoken of as a tendency toward excess that converts the Dionysian into "the horrible 'witches brew' of sensuality and cruelty" (BT §2, 40). We know that part 2 of *The Genealogy of Morals* reflects at length on the inherent cruelty found within the origins of punishment and torture in the relationships of creditor and debtor, punishment as the literal exacting of a pound of flesh. But in the very name of Raphael and of transfiguration, *The Gay Science* declares an end to any association between the Dionysian and cruelty: "*No image of torture.*—I want to proceed as Raphael did and never paint another image of torture. There are enough sublime things so that one does not have to look for the sublime where it dwells in sisterly association with cruelty; and my ambition also could never find satisfaction if I became a sublime assistant at torture."[20] In this way, the meaning of the Dionysian is drawn away from its possible excesses in sensuality and cruelty, ironically perhaps, more toward values and virtues normally associated with a "Christian sublime."

At the end of Nietzsche's writings, we find the motif of transfiguration in the heartbreaking letter from Nietzsche to his musician friend, Peter Gast, written from Turin during his first mental breakdown and dated January 4, 1889: "To my Maestro: Sing me a new song: the world is transfigured and all the heavens are full of joy.— [signed] The Crucified."[21] This is Nietzsche's personal variation on Psalm 96, "Oh, sing unto the Lord a new song," but the term *transfiguration* does not appear in the Psalm but only in Nietzsche's own text. It is Nietzsche and not the Psalmist who is singing a song to the transfiguration of the world. Because the letter is signed "The Crucified," there is an ambiguity about whether its meaning is affirmative or satirical. Oftentimes Nietzsche used "The Crucified" in contrast and opposition to "Dionysus" and signed letters as Dionysus, as in the famous letter of the same day, January 4, 1889, addressed to Cosima Wagner: "Ariadne, I love you.—[signed] Dionysus."[22] However, it seems more likely that in the transfiguration letter written to Gast, Nietzsche is identifying himself with "The Crucified" and identifying his philosophy as the true philosophy capable of transfiguring the world, which means rendering life and world as Dionysian works of art. In spite of Nietzsche's own self-criticism of *The Birth of Tragedy* for its Schopenhauerian and Wagnerian influences and excesses, in the end, that work expressed the nascent meaning of his philosophy of transfiguration.

> Yes, my friends, believe with me in Dionysian life and the rebirth of tragedy. The age of the Socratic man is over; put on wreaths of ivy, put the thyrsus into your hand, and do not be surprised when tigers and panthers lie down, fawning, at your feet. Only dare to be tragic men; for you are to be redeemed. . . . Prepare yourselves hard for strife, but believe in the miracles of your god. (BT §20, 124)

Transfiguration, Phenomenology, and the Truth of Appearances

For the phenomenology of Merleau-Ponty, there is attraction and simultaneous resistance to Nietzsche's account of the origin of art from the spirit of musical mood. The phenomenology of Husserl and Heidegger were deeply concerned with the question of origins, which for the arts means the question of the essence of art.[23] Husserl said that were he allotted the span of Methuselah's days, he would in his old age finally reach the ideal of the philosopher as a downright beginner.[24] Indeed metaphors of origin are found throughout Merleau-Ponty's writings, such as pregnancy, labor (of childbearing), birth, cradle, and dehiscence. Nevertheless, from the beginning of his phenomenological writing, Merleau-Ponty contested the possibility of "complete bracketing" and affirmed the cultural and historical situation of perception, which deprived him of methodological access to anything like "pure intuition" or "original perception."[25] Even in Husserl, Merleau-Ponty argued, "essences are destined to bring back all the living relationships of experience, as the fisherman's net draws up from the depths of the ocean quivering fish and seaweed" (PP xvii/x). Essences are given united to historically, culturally situated existence, rendering perception perspectival. Alan Schrift has drawn a link between Merleau-Ponty's account of this partial *epochē* or bracketing and Nietzsche's own account of philology as the "art of reading well" or philology as *ephexis*[26] (or *ephektéon*). This Greek term means "undecidedness" or "suspension of judgment," and *ephexis* is related to *epéko*,[27] the Greek root of the phenomenological term *epochē*. It demands dwelling with a text or experience without imposing a given interpretation, insofar as possible and with recognition of the limits of culture and time. Nietzsche accuses the theologians of "bad philology" incapable of *ephexis*. In *The Antichrist*, he makes note of the theologians' "incapacity for philology": "Philology is to be understood here in a very wide sense as the art of reading well—of being able to read off a fact *without* falsifying it by interpretation, *without* losing caution, patience, subtlety in the desire for understanding. Philology as *ephexis* [undecisiveness] in interpretation."[28] Nietzsche's repeated primary example of bad philology by the Christian theologians is the "gluing" of the New Testament onto the Old Testament: "To have glued this New Testament, a kind of rococo of taste in every respect, to the Old Testament to make *one* book, as the 'Bible,' as 'the book par excellence'—that is perhaps the greatest audacity and 'sin against the spirit' that literary Europe has on its conscience."[29] However much Jewish scholars protested, since the Old Testament was supposed to speak of Christ and his Cross, every Old Testament reference to a piece of wood, a rod, a ladder, a twig, a tree, a willow, a staff was supposed to be a prophetic allusion to the wood of the Cross. For Nietzsche, this was the dishonest and dishonorable "art of reading badly."

With respect to the origin of the work of art, Merleau-Ponty's *Eye and Mind* makes two references to the cave paintings of Lascaux, but the essay makes no strong claims about painting or cave paintings as origin in the sense of a "first artist." Lascaux, Merleau-Ponty writes, like the painting of our own time, figurative and abstract, celebrates "no other enigma than that of visibility."[30] He was interested in painting and the other arts for what they reveal about the visible, visibility, and the invisible, and if he did locate an "origin" of painting in the "primacy of perception," which means the living body of the artist, his account of the body grew more porous and interleaved, more differentiated and less unified, as his philosophy matured. There appears a multiplicity of arts in his thought—painting, sculpture, music, singing, poetry—without any effort to synthesize or create a hierarchy, even in terms of bodily expression. Therefore Nietzsche's proposal of a singular origin and essence of the arts would accord more readily with a phenomenology of art such as that of Heidegger rather than Merleau-Ponty's.[31]

Nevertheless the Apollonian-Dionysian dyad appears in Merleau-Ponty's lecture course from his last year of teaching, 1960–61, titled *La philosophie et non-philosophie depuis Hegel*,[32] and its occurrence comes in the context of a discussion of Nietzsche's preface to the second edition of *The Gay Science* (1886). Merleau-Ponty worked from Nietzsche's German text and translated sections 2, 3, and 4 of Nietzsche's preface into French nearly in their entirety, with certain elisions. In his preface, Nietzsche makes use of the term *transfiguration*, and it is remarkable that Merleau-Ponty singles out the term for his own commentary. The vocabulary of transfiguration in Merleau-Ponty's texts is rare and, one could argue, therefore inconsequential, yet I would argue for the opposite point of view: precisely because the occurrences are rare, they are important. The rarity indicates an intellectual and linguistic searching or reaching beyond the standard repertoire of philosophical vocabulary he had developed over the years. His life-long trajectory was overcoming dualisms wherever they occur—mind and body, reason and experience, inside and outside, silence and language, form and content, line and color—but yet without falling back into monism. Thus it is not surprising that his mature aesthetic and ontological works are filled with terminology formed with the *trans-* prefix, meaning "over," "across," "beyond," and "on or to the other side of."[33] The list of such terms includes *transparent, transform, transposition, translate, transition, transport, transversal, transmit, transitivity, transcendental, transcendence, transubstantiation,* and *transfiguration. Transcendence* is utterly vital due to its frequency and sustenance in Merleau-Ponty's thought from beginning to end, and *transubstantiation* and *transfiguration* are vital for their infrequency: when they occur, they are important.

I will pursue the meaning of transfiguration in the philosophy of Merleau-Ponty in three phases: his assertion of a fraudulent transfiguration in epistemology and morality, his interpretation of transfiguration as an aesthetic phenomenon found in the history of art, and the meaning of the transfiguration of the Flesh. Throughout I will be concerned with Merleau-Ponty's interpretation of the death of God and meaning of true religion.

In his preface to *The Gay Science*, Nietzsche asks himself if philosophy has not been "merely an interpretation of the body and a *misunderstanding* of the body" (GS preface §2, 34–35), leading to two contrasting kinds of philosophy and two motivations for doing philosophy: sickness and health. From the sick body, its suffering and needs, arises a search for the "sunny places of thought" separated from life, where there is stillness, mildness, patience, medicine, balm, and peace. This sick philosophy divorces body from soul, soul from spirit, and philosophy from life. It forgets, Nietzsche writes, that "we have to give birth to our thoughts out of our pain and, like mothers, endow them with all we have of blood, heart, fire, pleasure, passion, agony, conscience, fate, and catastrophe" (GS preface §3, 35–36). The ascetic philosopher "simply *cannot* keep from transposing his states every time in the most spiritual form and distance," and "this art of transfiguration *is* philosophy" (GS preface §3, 35). Nietzsche's use of the term *transfiguration* here introduces us to a negative, critical meaning that is quite the contrary of the transfiguration of life and world created by the Dionysian artist.

Merleau-Ponty translates and cites Nietzsche's passage on the "sunny places of thought" (*les places ensoleillées*), and in his commentary on Nietzsche's text that follows, he repeats the word *transfiguration* twice. He says that true philosophy goes beyond this sort of transfiguration toward an "a-philosophy by fidelity to what we live; which does not culminate in 'all knowledge' (new positivism) nor in despair, but in the will to appearance. . . . Nietzsche holds on to the quality of the 'philosopher': the absolute of appearance" (NC 278).[34] Thus Merleau-Ponty affirms Nietzsche's critique of the majority tradition of philosophy that falsely transfigures the contingencies of life into a kind of sunny thought and abstract philosophy, as we find in Platonism and in Christianity. He further concurs with Nietzsche's praise of the "will to appearance." Let us first take up the thought of the truth of appearances, then the thought of this fraudulent transfiguration and the phenomenology of error, illusion, or delusion.

Merleau-Ponty incorporates the Nietzschean "absolute of appearances" right into the final statement of his ontology in chapter 4 of *The Visible and the Invisible*, titled "The Intertwining—The Chiasm." Here is Merleau-Ponty's text: "What there is then are . . . things we could not dream of seeing 'all naked' because the gaze itself envelops them, clothes them with its own flesh."[35] Nietzsche's text referenced here is included among the passages Merleau-Ponty translated for his lecture course from the preface to *The Gay Science*: "Today we consider it a matter of decency not to wish to see everything naked, or to be present at everything, or to understand and 'know' everything. One should have more respect for the bashfulness with which nature has hidden behind riddles and iridescent uncertainties" (GS preface §4, 38). Nietzsche's text on truth, appearances, and bashfulness ends with praise of the Greeks: "Oh, those Greeks! They knew how to live. What is required for that is to stop courageously at the surface, the fold, the skin, to adore appearance, to believe in forms, tones, words, in the whole Olympus of appearance! These Greeks were superficial—*out of profundity*" (GS preface §4, 38).

When Merleau-Ponty joins Nietzsche in linking truth with appearances, it is necessary to understand that appearance and truth—profundity—are not opposed in Nietzsche's thinking, nor in Merleau-Ponty's. Plato was the philosopher who established and authorized the opposition between truth and appearance in the "Divided Line" and "Allegory of the Cave" in his *Republic*, and what we find in Nietzsche and Merleau-Ponty is the reversal of Platonism in favor of the wisdom of the Greek tragedians, especially Aeschylus and Sophocles. Husserl had stated the phenomenological "principle of principles" in *Ideas* I: "Every originary presentive intuition is a legitimizing source of cognition, that everything originarily (so to speak, in its 'personal' actuality) offered to us in 'intuition' is to be accepted simply as what it is presented as being, but also only within the limits in which it is presented there."[36] Merleau-Ponty argues that this well-known Husserlian call for the "return to the things themselves" must be distinguished from the idealist return to the inner consciousness of a subject such as we find in Descartes and Kant. Moreover, with respect to Husserl's stress on "intuition," Merleau-Ponty argues that for Husserl, "noematic reflection" that remains within the object bringing to light its fundamental unity replaces a "noetic analysis" that bases the world on the synthesizing activity of the subject (PP x/iv). He proclaims a forceful revision of St. Augustine's "inner man" and writes, "Truth does not 'inhabit' only 'the inner man,' or more accurately, there is no inner man, man is in the world, and only in the world does he know himself" (PP xi/v). The "phenomenon" of phenomenology is that which manifests itself in our bodily engagements with the world; it exhibits a structure of form and content that will be largely shared across cultures and times, though not completely so. Truth is a revealing that is also a concealing in the openness of "letting be" (*laisser être*). This accords with Nietzsche's stress in *The Birth of Tragedy* on Apollo and Dionysus as *Schein* or shining. This is sometimes translated as "appearance" or even "semblance," creating the troublesome suggestion of an appearance or semblance of something else that is the original and "causes" the appearance. In *The Genealogy of Morals*, Nietzsche stressed that there is no cause or "substratum" behind events, "no being behind doing, effecting, becoming."[37] Rather, Nietzsche is already thinking phenomenologically, whereby the phenomenon is that which manifests itself and shines forth in itself.[38]

Many years before commenting on *The Gay Science*, Merleau-Ponty had spoken of fraudulent transfiguration and the true meaning of religion in his essay "The Metaphysical in Man" published in *Sense and Non-Sense*. There he wrote that "the contingency of all that exists and all that has value is not a little truth for which we have somehow or other to make room in some nook or cranny of the system; it is the condition of the metaphysical view of the world."[39] Therefore he explicitly identifies this fraudulent transfiguration with "recourse to an absolute foundation," which, in the practical realm of morality, accords my judgments a "sacred character": "I have at my disposal a plan of escape in which *my actions become transfigured*: the suffering I create turns into happiness, ruse becomes reason, and I piously cause my adversaries to perish" (SNS 95/167, my emphasis). Here the ground of truth and morality is placed outside ongoing human experience, and the individual, we might say, transfigures himself or herself into the appearance of the divine. If we ask ourselves how such a false consciousness is revealed, we contend it is known as such by its position standing aside and apart from lived experience. In *Phenomenology of Perception*, Merleau-Ponty argued that error and illusion are marked, stamped, or made manifest as such *within* experience, and we do not need to appeal to an outside measure as a "higher court of appeal." The one who is mad recognizes the madness and its role in keeping a world and relationships at bay: "The madman, the dreamer, or the subject of perception must be taken at their word" (PP 337/335). For the maniac and the schizophrenic, "insanity and perception are not, in so far as they are different, hermetically sealed within themselves; they are not small islands of experience cut off from each other, and from which there is no escape" (PP 340/338). Almost as if he were addressing the manifestation of the *Transfiguration*, Merleau-Ponty writes, "The myth holds the essence within the appearance; the mythical phenomenon is not a representation, but a genuine presence. The *daemon* of rain is present in each drop which falls after the incantation, as the soul is present in each part of the body. Every 'apparition' (*Erscheinung*) is in this case an incarnation" (PP 338/335–36).

According so much integrity to appearance, myth, miracle, and transfiguration, Merleau-Ponty yet argues that the truth of contingency cannot be reconciled with "positing an absolute thinker of the world" (SNS 96/168). This would return us to the problem of a theodicy that has not taken a single step forward since Leibniz. A number of teachings found within Christianity make it "the most resolute negation of the conceived infinite" (SNS 97/169). These include the teaching that the Fall of mankind was fortunate inasmuch as a world without fault would be a world less good. The creation, originally perfect and sufficient, became more valuable with mankind's disobedient transgressions of the Lord's commandment. If these thoughts seem paradoxical, they bring to mind Merleau-Ponty's repeated description of the human condition as "the flaw in the diamond" of the world, in words drawn from Paul Valéry's "Le cimetière marin" (The Cemetery by the Sea).[40] Merleau-Ponty used this phrase not as a negative but as a positive throughout his philosophical works.[41] Finitude and contingency are the very conditions of creativity and transcendence.

Religion, Merleau-Ponty argues, must cease to be a "conceptual construct or an ideology and once more become part of the experience of interhuman life" (SNS 96/168). Here is found the true meaning of Christianity and the death of God: "The originality of Christianity as the religion of the death of God is its rejection of the God of the philosophers and its heralding of a God who takes on the human condition. The role of religion in culture is not that of a dogma or even of a belief, but a cry [*comme cri*]" (SNS 96/169). Such a text rendering true religion a "cry" echoes what Merleau-Ponty had written of Cézanne as his own exemplary artist and also published in *Sense and Non-Sense*: "The artist launches his work just as a man once launched the first word, not knowing whether it will be anything more than a shout [*un cri*]" (SNS 19/32). Thus Merleau-Ponty joins Nietzsche in rendering the true meaning of transfiguration as aesthetic, interhuman, and this-worldly rather than vertical, ethereal, and other-worldly.

In this vein, in his commentary on Nietzsche's preface to *The Gay Science*, Merleau-Ponty takes up explicitly the meaning of the death of God. This proclamation, he says, is the word not only of Nietzsche but also of Hegel, of Marx's theory of ideologies, and of Kierkegaard's "non-Pharisean Christianity" (NC 279). Heidegger is correct, Merleau-Ponty argues: "God is dead means everything, except: there is no God [*Dieu est mort, cela veut tout dire, sauf: il n'y a pas de dieu*]" (NC 279). Thus, though Merleau-Ponty broke with his Catholic upbringing in his twenties and with the Catholic personalism of Emmanuel Mounier and the journal *Esprit* in 1936, we will not find him blithely joining Sartre's proclamation of atheism nor those interpreters of Nietzsche who infer from the death of God a kind of simplistic and theoretical atheism.[42] What the death of God does mean, Merleau-Ponty immediately adds, is that "it is necessary to think the absolute as capable of dying, not in the sense of beings who are merely alive and are uprooted from existence by an external cause, but in the sense of human death prefigured in mankind with *conscience, Er-innerung* (consciousness and moral conscience)" (NC 279).[43] Simultaneously with these lecture commentaries in 1960, Merleau-Ponty stated in his text "Phenomenology and Analytic Philosophy," "The question for a philosopher is not so much to know *if* God exists or does not exist . . . as to know what one understands by God, what one wishes to say in speaking of God."[44] A God who is capable of dying is a God who is vulnerable and finite, a God who requires the creative work of humanity in the task of redeeming the world.

Merleau-Ponty earlier expressed this same thought in "Indirect Language and the Voices of Silence" in commenting on Hegel and the meaning of the dialectic as showing a "grace in events which draws us away from evil toward the good."[45] Christianity, he argues, is "the recognition of a mystery in the relations of man and God," and "the Christian God wants nothing to do with a vertical relation of subordination" (S 70–71/88). "There is a sort of impotence of God without us, and Christ attests that God would not be fully God without becoming fully human. Claudel goes so far as to say that God is not above but beneath us—meaning that we do not find Him as a supra-sensible idea, but as another ourself, who dwells in and authenticates our darkness" (S 71/88).[46] Here in this middle text of Merleau-Ponty's philosophical development, he reinforces the philosophical theology he had outlined near the beginning, in *Sense and Non-Sense,* and near the end, in the lecture course of his last year. God is "another ourself." What we mean by God is found not above us in an other world but before us in the faces, bodies, and lives of those who are most vulnerable—children, the poor, the ragged, the homeless, the sick—and found in nature too, where it is most vulnerable, in animals, forests, canyons, rivers, and oceans.

Merleau-Ponty's Transfiguration of the Flesh

In "Indirect Language and the Voices of Silence," Merleau-Ponty also speaks explicitly of the meaning of transfiguration in art. This has to do with the transfiguration of history. The art of our own modern age is a transfiguration of the art of the primal and classical worlds. The classical and the modern, Merleau-Ponty states, "pertain to the universe of painting conceived of as a single task, from the first sketches on the walls of caves to our 'conscious' painting." Although primal and classical art are linked to experiences very different from our own, yet our painting "transfigures" these former works, and the primal and classical reappear in the modern. Therefore it is also true to say that the former works "prefigure" our own modern art, for their creators "secretly inaugurated another history which is still ours and which makes them present to us" (S 60/75). It would be interesting to be able to pause in more detail over this thought in relation to ancient cave paintings and certain contemporary pictures made by Picasso and Braque, to mention but these resonances. This relationship between prefiguration and transfiguration, of repetition and variation, in the history of painting and other creative expression is possible because history is not only the order of mere events but also the order of "advent" (*avènement*). Advent is "a promise of events to come," Merleau-Ponty writes, for it is the "institution" (*Stiftung*) or birth of a tradition and anticipates a "future humanity not even outlined in our present life" (S 70/87). The meaning of advent is not exhausted in its immediate historical situation. "It opens a field. Sometimes it even institutes a world. In any case it outlines a future" (S 72/91). Thus advent is transcendence, and this concept resides in close proximity to what Heidegger named *Ereignis* and what Lyotard and Nancy have more recently named "event," a rupture or break in time that inaugurates something new and unforetold. This is transcendence within history and within immanence.

We are therefore not surprised to find that transfiguration makes its appearance in the meaning of Flesh itself in Merleau-Ponty's mature philosophy. He is writing in *The Visible and the Invisible* of what he calls "the most difficult point," which is understanding and articulating the bond between the flesh and the idea, that is to say, between the visible and invisible, between experience and ideality. By what "miracle," Merleau-Ponty asks, are generality, culture, and knowledge created? He argues that pure ideality "streams forth along the articulations of the aesthesiological body" and "transfigures horizons it did not open" (VI 152/200). Continuing the metaphor of transfiguration, he writes, "It is as though the visibility that animates the sensible world were to emigrate, not outside of every body, but into another less heavy, more transparent body, as though it were to change flesh, abandoning the flesh of the body for that of language" (VI 153/200). Thus the flesh of the body and Flesh of the world are transfigured into the lighter, less heavy, and more transparent body of language and thought. Language and culture, algorithm and calculus, painting and music are a "second flesh" likened to the "glorified" or "celestial" body described by St. Paul in the Scriptures,[47] still sensible but now a "sensible idea," changed in transparency, color, tone, and precision. Merleau-Ponty writes that these are transfigured horizons we ourselves "did not open" and uses the language of "miracle" because he also argues that culture and knowledge are created and changed not through a process of pure activity that we control but through an activity-passivity: "We do not possess the musical or sensible ideas, precisely because they are negativity or absence circumscribed: they possess us" (VI 151/198–99). Again referencing Valéry, he draws the penultimate line of *The Visible and the Invisible* from *La Pythie*: "And in a sense, as Valéry said, language is everything, since it is the voice of no one, since it is the very voice of the things, the waves, and the forests" (VI 155/203–4).

Language and culture are a second flesh, transfigurations of the body. It is likely that Merleau-Ponty saw a copy of the upper part of Raphael's *Transfiguration* during his time in Tholonet near Aix-en-Provence in the summer of 1960, just before making his commentary on *The Gay Science* and just as he was working on the draft of chapter 4 of *The Visible and the Invisible*.[48] Transfiguration would have been sealed in his philosophical imaginary. For his philosophy, what matters about transfiguration is that glorious painting itself, a second flesh of Raphael, and also that voice that speaks from out of the cloud, the voice of language and thought, both of which are miracle, mystery, and grace (S 73/91).

Notes

1. Nietzsche, *The Birth of Tragedy and The Case of Wagner* (hereafter BT).

2. Cf. Shapiro, *Archeologies of Vision*, "Merleau-Ponty's Evasion of Nietzsche: Misreading Malraux," 217–25.

3. Ibid., 223.

4. Merleau-Ponty, "Christianisme et ressentiment," 278–308; "Christianity and *Ressentiment*," 1–22.

5. The recent history of French philosophical scholarship surrounding Nietzsche is surveyed at length by Schrift, *Nietzsche and the Question of Interpretation*, especially chapter 3, "The French Scene," and chapter 4, "Derrida: Nietzsche Contra Heidegger."

6. Cf. *Oedipus at Colonus*, 134, lines 1224–26.

7. Cf. Shapiro's discussion in *Archeologies of Vision*, "Floating and Shining," 101–6.

8. Oberhuber, *Raphael*, 224.

9. Cf. Talvacchia, *Raphael*, 222. Justus and Pastor are the patron saints of Narbonne, whose festivities fall on August 6, the day of the feast of the Transfiguration in the Catholic, Orthodox, and Anglican churches.

10. Cf. Matthew 17:1–9; Mark 9:2–8; Luke 9:28–36.

11. Hegel emphasizes the unity of the actions in the two scenes through their narrative continuity and doubling of miracles. Cf. Hegel, *Aesthetics*, 2, 860.

12. Goethe, *Italian Journey*, 364.

13. Oberhuber, *Raphael*, 223.

14. Ibid., 229.

15. Schopenhauer, *The World as Will and Representation* I, 411.

16. Nietzsche, *Untimely Meditations*, 105–6.

17. Nietzsche, *The Will to Power*, Fgt 845 [1885–86] (hereafter WP).

18. Nietzsche, *Twilight of the Idols and the Anti-Christ*, §9, 83–84.

19. Cf. Shapiro, "Transfiguring the *Transfiguration*," in *Archeologies of Vision*, 87–101, especially 98–99. Shapiro argues for what I have called the stronger reading in which Apollo replaces the figure of the Christ in the painting.

20. Nietzsche, *The Gay Science*, §313, 250 (hereafter GS).

21. Nietzsche, *Nietzsche: A Self-Portrait from His Letters*, 141. Also see Krell, *Nietzsche*. Krell quotes this letter at the end of part 1, which is fittingly entitled "Transfiguration" and seems to present Nietzsche's own mental breakdown as an instance of transfiguration.

22. Nietzsche, *Nietzsche: A Self-Portrait from His Letters*, 142.

23. Cf. Heidegger, "The Origin of the Work of Art," 17.

24. Husserl, *Ideas I*, author's preface to the first English edition (trans. Gibson), 21.

25. Merleau-Ponty, *Phenomenology of Perception*, xv; *Phénoménologie de la perception*, viii (hereafter PP; citations give the English pagination first, followed by the French pagination after the slash). A possible exception to this interpretation of Merleau-Ponty's denial of "original perception" should be noted. It is found in his distinction between primary and secondary perception in chapter 3 of part 2 of *Phenomenology of Perception*, titled "The Thing and the Natural World." There Merleau-Ponty attributes to a painter such as Cézanne an "antepredicative" perception of the "pre-world" (PP 322/372). In the chapter titled "Space," he makes a similar claim about a kind of "total perception" capable of perceiving a stone in the Tuileries wall as "nothing but this stone entirely without history" (PP 342/39). I have argued that such primary perception in Cézanne is also informed by the history and cultural world of painting, as is the total perception Merleau-Ponty discusses regarding the stone in the wall.

26. Schrift, *Nietzsche and the Question of Interpretation*, 164, 220n12.

27. Cf. Liddell and Scott, *Greek–English Lexicon with a Revised Supplement*, 741.

28. Nietzsche, *The Antichrist*, 52, cited in Schrift, *Nietzsche and the Question of Interpretation*, 164.

29. Nietzsche, *Beyond Good and Evil*, 52 (hereafter BGE).

30. Merleau-Ponty, *Eye and Mind*, 127; *L'Oeil et l'Esprit*, 26.

31. Regarding Nietzsche and Heidegger, parallels have been drawn between the Dionysian and the Apollonian and Heidegger's notions of "earth" and "world" in "The Origin of the Work of Art." Cf. Taminiaux, "Philosophical Heritage in Heidegger's Conception of Art," the third section of "Heidegger, Martin," 238.

In my own *The Retrieval of the Beautiful*, I have drawn parallels between the Apollonian-Dionysian and radiance and rhythm in the aesthetics of Merleau-Ponty. Cf. chapter 7, "A Radiant Image, A Particular Rhythm," 197–208.

32. Merleau-Ponty, *Notes de cours*, 278 (hereafter NC).

33. *The New Shorter Oxford English Dictionary*, 2:3365.

34. My translation of Merleau-Ponty's French text: "Idée qu'il y a une philosophie qui n'interroge pas assez, qui fuit l'interrogation dans 'places ensoleillées'—toute philosophie est 'transfiguration' (cf. Marx); que la vraie philosophie est au-delà: grand soupçon, abîme, a-philosophie par fidélité à ce que nous vivons; que ceci se termine non par 'tout savoir' (nouveau positivisme) et non par désespoir, mais par la volonté de l'apparence.... Nietzsche tient à la qualité du 'philosophe': l'absolu de l'apparence" (NC 278).

35. Merleau-Ponty, *The Visible and the Invisible*, 131; *Le visible et l'invisible*, 173 (hereafter VI; citations give the English pagination first, followed by the French pagination after the slash).

36. Husserl, *Ideas I* (trans. Kersten), chapter 2, §24: "The Principle of All Principles," 44.

37. Nietzsche, On *the Genealogy of Morals*, First Essay, §13, 45.

38. Cf. Shapiro, *Archeologies of Vision*, 97–98.

39. Merleau-Ponty, *Sense and Non-Sense* 96; *Sens et Non-Sens*, 168 (hereafter SNS; citations give the English pagination first, followed by the French pagination after the slash).

40. Paul Valéry's poem contained these lines: "My doubts, my strivings, my repentances, These are the flaw in your great diamond" ("Mes repentirs, mes doutes, mes contraintes, Sont le défaut de ton grand diamant") ("Le cimetière marin," 216, 217).

41. Cf. PP 207/240, where "flaw in the diamond" occurs in relation to perception; SNS 45/79, where it occurs in relation to Sartre; and VI 233/287, where it occurs in relation to the meaning of transcendence and incarnation.

42. Cf. Ricoeur, "Religion, Atheism, and Faith," 57–98.

43. My translation of Merleau-Ponty's French text: "Cela veut dire: il faut penser l'absolu comme capable de mourir; non pas au sens de la mort des êtres seulement vivants, qui ont déracinés de l'existence par cause extérieure, mais au sens de la mort humain, préfigurée dans l'homme parce qu'il est conscience, *Er-innerung*" (NC 279).

44. Merleau-Ponty, "Phenomenology and Analytic Philosophy," 66. The essay originally appeared in French as "Phénoménologie contre 'The Concept of Mind.'"

45. Merleau-Ponty, *Signs*, 73; *Signes*, 91 (hereafter S; citations give the English pagination first, followed by the French pagination after the slash).

46. With respect to the principle of individuation associated with the Apollonian, in this citation of Claudel, Merleau-Ponty also draws the "true meaning" of Christianity away from individuation toward the community of human suffering, thus toward what Nietzsche means by the Dionysian.

47. Cf. I Corinthians 15:35–53.

48. Merleau-Ponty spent part of the summer of 1960 near Aix in Tholonet, and *Eye and Mind* is signed "Le Tholonet, juillet-août, 1960." Tholonet is the small village outside of Aix near where Cézanne's hut or small studio was located. There is on the eastern wall of Aix's *Cathedrale Saint-Sauveur*, a copy of the upper part of Raphael's *Transfiguration* from 1693 by a local painter named André Boisson. Merleau-Ponty would surely have seen it, eager as he was to see the pictorial context of Cézanne, who was famously a churchgoer and was brought up as a child only meters away from the cathedral on Rue Boulegon. I express my thanks to Dr. Frank Chouraqui for conveying to me this information.

Bibliography

Brown, Lesley ed.. *The New Shorter Oxford English Dictionary on Historical Principles*. Volume 2. 1973; Oxford: Clarendon Press, 1993.

Deleuze, Gilles. *Nietzsche et la philosophie*. Paris: PUF, 1962.

Goethe, Johann Wolfgang. *Italian Journey*. Translated by Robert R. Heitner. New York: Suhrkamp, 1989.

Hegel, G. W. F. *Aesthetics*. Translated by T. M. Knox. New York: Oxford University Press, 1975.

Heidegger, Martin. "The Origin of the Work of Art." In *Poetry, Language, Thought*. Translated by Albert Hofstadter. New York: Harper and Row, 1971.

Husserl, Edmund. *Ideas: General Introduction to a Pure Phenomenology*. Translated by W. R. Boyce Gibson. New York: Collier Books, 1972.

———. *Ideas Pertaining to a Pure Phenomenology and to a Phenomenological Philosophy*. First Book: *General Introduction to a Pure Phenomenology*. Translated by F. Kersten. Dordrecht: Kluwer Academic, 1982.

Johnson, Galen A.. *The Retrieval of the Beautiful: Thinking through Merleau-Ponty's Aesthetics*. Evanston, IL: Northwestern University Press, 2010.

Krell, David Farrell. *Nietzsche: A Novel*. Albany: State University of New York Press, 1996.

Liddell, H. G., and R. Scott. *Greek–English Lexicon with a Revised Supplement*. Oxford: Clarendon Press, 1996.

Merleau-Ponty, Maurice. "Christianisme et ressentiment." In *La Vie Intellectuelle*, 7ᵉ année, nouvelle série, 30, no. 6 (1935): 278–308.

———. "Christianity and *Ressentiment*." Translated by Gerald G. Wening. *Review of Existential Psychology and Psychiatry* 9, no. 1 (1968): 1–22.

———. *Eye and Mind*. Translated by Michael B. Smith. In *The Merleau-Ponty Aesthetics Reader: Philosophy and Painting*. Edited by Galen A. Johnson. Evanston, IL: Northwestern University Press, 1993.

———. *Notes de cours, 1959–1961*. Paris: Gallimard, 1996.

———. *L'Oeil et l'Esprit*, Paris: Gallimard, 1964.

———. "Phénoménologie contre 'The Concept of Mind.'" In *La philosophie analytique*. Paris: Minuit, 1960.

———. *Phénoménologie de la perception*. Paris: Gallimard, 1945.

———. "Phenomenology and Analytic Philosophy" (1960). In *Texts and Dialogues: On Philosophy, Politics, and Culture*, edited by Hugh J. Silverman and James Barry. Atlantic Highlands, NJ: Humanities, 1991.

———. *Phenomenology of Perception*. Translated by Colin Smith. Revised edition. London: Routledge and Kegan Paul, 2003.

———. *Sens et Non-Sens*. 1948; Paris: Les Éditions Nagel, 1966.

———. *Sense and Non-Sense*. Translated by Hubert L. Dreyfus and Patricia Allen Dreyfus. Evanston, IL: Northwestern University Press, 1964.

———. *Signes*. Paris: Gallimard, 1960.

———. *Signs*. Translated by Richard C. McCleary Evanston, IL: Northwestern University Press, 1964.

———. *The Visible and the Invisible*. Translated by Alphonso Lingis. Evanston, IL: Northwestern University Press, 1968.

———. *Le Visible et l'invisible*. Edited by Claude Lefort. Paris: Gallimard, 1964.

Nietzsche, Friedrich. *Beyond Good and Evil: Prelude to a Philosophy of the Future*. Translated by W. Kaufmann. New York: Vintage, 1966.

———. *The Birth of Tragedy and The Case of Wagner*. Translated by W. Kaufmann. New York: Random House, 1967.

———. *The Gay Science*. Translated by W. Kaufmann. New York: Random House, 1974.

———. *Nietzsche: A Self-Portrait from His Letters*. Edited by Peter Fuss and Henry Shapiro. Cambridge, MA: Harvard University Press, 1971.

———. *On the Genealogy of Morals*. Translated by W. Kaufmann. New York: Random House, 1967.

———. *Twilight of the Idols and the Anti-Christ*. Translated by R. J. Hollingdale. London: Penguin, 1990.

———. *Untimely Meditations*. Translated by R. J. Hollingdale. Cambridge: Cambridge University Press, 1997.

———*The Will to Power*. Translated by R. J. Hollingdale and W. Kaufmann. New York: Random House, 1967.

Oberhuber, Konrad. *Raphael: The Paintings*. Munich: Prestel Verlag, 1999.

Ricoeur, Paul. "Religion, Atheism, and Faith." In Alasdair McIntyre and Paul Ricoeur, *The Religious Significance of Atheism*. New York: Columbia University Press, 1969.

Schopenhauer, Arthur. *The World as Will and Representation*. Volume 1. Translated by E. F. J. Payne. Indian Hills, CO: Falcon's Wing Press, 1958.

Schrift, Alan D. *Nietzsche and the Question of Interpretation: Between Hermeneutics and Deconstruction*. New York: Routledge, 1990.

Shapiro, Gary. *Archeologies of Vision: Foucault and Nietzsche on Seeing and Saying*. Chicago: University of Chicago Press, 2003.

Sophocles. *Oedipus at Colonus*. in *Sophocles I*. Translated by Robert Fitzgerald. Chicago: University of Chicago Press, 1954.

Talvacchia, Bette. *Raphael*. New York: Phaedon Press, 2007.

Taminiaux, Jacques. "Philosophical Heritage in Heidegger's Conception of Art." In *Encyclopedia of Aesthetics*, vol. 2. Edited by Michael Kelly. Oxford: Oxford University Press, 1998.

Valéry, Paul. "Le cimetière marin." In *Poems*. Translated by David Paul. Vol. 1 of *The Collected Works of Paul Valéry*. Princeton: Princeton University Press, 1971.

PART III
SUBJECTIVITY IN THE WORLD

12 The Philosophy of the Morning

Philosophy and Phenomenology in Nietzsche's Dawn

Keith Ansell-Pearson

I THINK IT IS difficult for any commentator to declare with total conviction that he has got Nietzsche right in terms of identifying him with a single or specific philosophical movement or doctrine. My view is that naturalism, existentialism, phenomenology, and poststructuralism can all, with a degree of plausibility, claim themselves heirs to his thinking.[1] Nietzsche is a thinker whose texts open up "possibilities," and all these modes of thought can be found prefigured and at work in the text I focus on in this paper, *Dawn*.[2] Having said this, however, it is remarkable the extent to which this text anticipates many of the moves and insights of existential phenomenology: not only is there a quest for authentic existence, but there is a new practice of knowledge that places the emphasis on contemplation and description. In this paper I want to suggest that Nietzsche does not represent a break with the history of philosophy—as Foucault has argued, for example[3]—but rather anticipates one of modern philosophy's founding moments, namely, the moment of phenomenology. My claim is that as part of a newfound "passion of knowledge" (D §429), Nietzsche is carrying out in *Dawn* a series of phenomenological analyses, in which the nature of consciousness is probed and illuminated and shown to be fundamentally intentional, directed to the world and in the world. As Rüdiger Safranski has astutely noted, in the text Nietzsche endeavors to "expand consciousness for the more sublime and broadening experiences in which we are already caught up with our bodies and lives."[4] Nietzsche's philosophy is in search of new descriptions of consciousness and world, attending to their phenomenological features, and, as such, they open a door and open out to a boundless expanse of new fields of experimental inquiry.

I begin with a section on the text in question and highlight some of its distinctive features. I then introduce some of the salient features of phenomenology, drawing on Merleau-Ponty for this purpose. This is followed by sections on the philosophical and phenomenological dimensions of Nietzsche's text. I conclude with the suggestion that what brings Nietzsche and phenomenology into rapport is a shared commitment to experimental philosophy.

I

In this opening section I want to illuminate some important aspects of the character of *Dawn* as a book. It can fairly be regarded as a significant turning point in Nietzsche's thinking.

As Duncan Large has noted, in *Dawn* and the subsequent text *The Joyful Science*,[5] its ideal companion in which the journey continues, Nietzsche consolidates the anti-metaphysical stance initiated by *Human, All Too Human* of 1878, completing his meta-morphosis from the Schopenhauer- and Wagner-adulating camel to a combative and exploratory lion, and from the ship of the desert to the ship of the high seas.[6] He is charting new land and new seas, unsure of his final destination, and has the confidence to take risks and conduct experiments, even to suffer shipwreck in search of new trea-sure. In this text we encounter the "free spirit" setting off on a new course and away from the old philosophical world of metaphysical and moral presumptions. However, it is no exaggeration to claim that for the greater part of Nietzsche's reception, *Dawn* has been among the most neglected texts in his corpus, and perhaps for understand-able reasons: it deploys no master concept, it does not seek an ultimate solution to the riddles of existence (indeed it warns against such a strategy), its presentation of themes and problems is highly nonlinear, and it states his case for the future subtly and deli-cately. It has also been overshadowed by the terser and stridently anti-Christian works of the later polemical period. The death of God is presaged and, in fact, announced, but not presented in any dramatic form as we find in the next text *The Joyful Science* (§125). But it is a text that has hidden riches, a text that has to be read between the lines (as Nietzsche disclosed to his sister, Elisabeth, in the case of *Dawn*'s fifth and final book).[7] And, as Nietzsche notes in *Ecce Homo*, although the book mounts a "cam-paign" against the prejudices of morality, the reader should not think it has about it "the slightest whiff of gunpowder"; rather, the reader should "make out quite different and more pleasing scents."[8]

Dawn is a pathbreaking work and an exercise in modern emancipation—from fear, superstition, hatred of the self and the body, the shortcuts of religion, and the pre-sumptions of morality. In *Dawn* Nietzsche is less of the disappointed idealist he was in *Human, All Too Human*, more assertive about the emerging "rights" of new individu-als who have hitherto been decried as freethinkers, criminals, and immoralists, more metaphorically exuberant, and with glimpses of new dawns on the horizon about to break. As Gary Handwerk notes, the texts of Nietzsche's middle period assume more

the form of a method of inquiry than a doctrine. Nietzsche has invented "an experiential and experimental philosophy," one that expresses itself in the form of the
essayistic aphorism: "In these ground- and spirit-breaking works, Nietzsche invents
for himself a form that is non-linear, interruptive, interrogative, recursive, and, above
all, remarkably flexible with regard to scope and span."[9] Moreover, as Daigle has noted,
the style of "aphorisms" that Nietzsche now adopts in his middle period provides a
clear indication of how he conceives human experience, namely, "not as a rationalistic, systematically organized, continuous, linear narrative but rather as a collection of
perspectives gained through experiences."[10] Furthermore, *Dawn* develops what might
be called trains of thought that sometimes lead to decisive insights but also leave much
for the reader to engage with and to complete. Nietzsche wants his readers to develop
an intimate relationship with the text. The text has a sense of the future—that new
dawns are about to break—but much is deliberately left open for the reader's rumi-
nation. Nietzsche therefore wants his reader to share in the adventure of knowledge
undertaken in the book.

Dawn grew out of notebooks Nietzsche kept during 1880, including notes for a
new book to be entitled *L'Ombra di Venezia* (*Kritische Studienausgabe* 9, 3 [1–172],
47–102; hereafter KSA): the title pays homage to the welcome shade he had discovered
for himself in the city of four hundred bridges and numerous dark and narrow streets.
He had been intrigued by the prospect and promise of a new dawn since the time
of his early reflections on the ancient, pre-Platonic philosophers. In one note from
1872–73, he writes that the role of the philosophers was to prepare the way for the Greek
reformer and precede him, "as the dawn precedes the rising sun." Alas, the sun did
not rise in this instance, and the reformer failed, with the dawn remaining "a ghostly
apparition" (KSA 7, 23 [1], 537).[11] *Dawn* (*Morgenröthe*, literally "morning redness"), the
second installment in what was to become the free spirit trilogy, is one of Nietzsche's
"yes-saying" books, a work of enlightenment which, he tells his readers, seeks to pour
out "its life, its love, its tenderness upon bad things alone," giving back to these things
the "supreme right and *prerogative* to exist" (EH III: D1). The Indian motto from the
Rig Veda's "Hymn to Varuna," "There are so many dawns that have not yet broken,"
is inscribed on the door to the book (EH III: D1). Nietzsche's amanuensis Peter Gast
(Heinrich Köselitz) had written the motto on the title page while making a fair copy of
the manuscript, and this in fact inspired Nietzsche to adopt the new title and replace
its original title of "The Ploughshare." In 1888 he speaks of the book as amounting to
a search for the new morning that ushers in a whole series of new days, and he insists
that not a single negative word is to be found in it, and no attack or malice either. In
this book we encounter a thinker who lies in the sun, "like a sea-creature sunning
itself between rocks" (EH III: D1); and the book was largely conceived in the rocks near
Genoa in solitude and where, so Nietzsche discloses, he "had secrets to share with the
sea." *Dawn* is a book that journeys into the future, which for Nietzsche constitutes its
true destination: "Even now," he writes in a letter of March 24, 1881, to his old friend

Erwin Rohde, "there are moments when I walk about on the heights above Genoa hav-ing glimpses and feelings such as Columbus once, perhaps from the very same place, sent out across the sea and into the future" (KGB III: 1, 75). His appeal to Columbus is figurative; he is in fact critical of the real Columbus (D §37). But as a figure of thought, Columbus the seafarer serves *Dawn* well; he denotes "the true experimenter, who may have an idea of where he thinks he is heading but is always prepared to be surprised by the outcome of his experiments."[12]

The book concludes on an enigmatic note, with Nietzsche asking his readers and fellow travelers whether it will be said of them one day that they too, *"steering toward the west, hoped to reach an India,"* but that it was their fate to shipwreck upon infinity (D §575). At this point in his writings, "India" denotes for Nietzsche the path to self-enlightenment. He holds that Europe remains behind Indian culture in terms of the progress it needs to make with respect to religious matters since it has not yet attained the free-minded naïveté of the Brahmins. The priests of India demonstrated "pleasure in thinking," in which observances—prayers, ceremonies, sacrifices, and hymns—are celebrated as the givers of all good things. One step further, he adds, and one also throws aside the gods—"which Europe must also do one day!" (D §96). Europe remains distant, he muses, from the level of culture attained in the appear-ance of the Buddha, the teacher of self-redemption. Nietzsche anticipates an age when all the observances and customs of the old moralities and religions have come to an end. In a reversal of the Christian meaning of the expression *In hoc signo vinces* (In this sign [cross] you will be the victor), which heads *Dawn* §96, Nietzsche is sug-gesting that the conquest will take place under the sign that the redemptive God is dead. Buddha is a significant teacher because his religion is one of self-redemption, and this is a valuable step along the way of ultimate redemption from religion and from God. Instead of speculating on what will then emerge into existence, he calls for a new community of nonbelievers to make their sign and communicate with one another: "There exist today perhaps ten to twenty million people among the differ-ent countries of Europe who no longer 'believe in God'—is it too much to ask that they *give a sign* to one another?" (D §96). He imagines these people constituting a new power in Europe, between nations, classes, rulers, and subjects, and between the unpeaceable and the most peaceable.

Nietzsche is, then, in search of a new kind of community or "people," a free-minded one that has the "passion of knowledge" and the willingness to experiment and is united by a shared commitment to new ways of thinking, feeling, and existing.

II

In this section I want to highlight the essential moves made by phenomenology. I shall rely primarily on Merleau-Ponty since in my view it is his account that captures the subtle moves made by it, moves that are nonidealistic and that stress the fact that phe-nomenology is, above all, an experimental method of philosophy.

Phenomenology is committed to pure description and, through such description, disclosing the world as the subject directly experiences it. It is this move that will return us to "the things themselves." For Husserl, there is always a limit to naturalizing simply because "subjects cannot be dissolved into nature, for in that case what gives nature its sense would be missing."[13] The world of the subject is not a physicalistic one, but a surrounding world, a "thematic world of . . . intentional life."[14] Merleau-Ponty glosses this insight in the preface to the *Phenomenology of Perception* as follows:

> I am not the outcome or the meeting-point of numerous causal agencies which determine my bodily or psychological make-up. I cannot conceive myself as nothing but a bit of the world, a mere object of biological, psychological or sociological investigation. . . . All my knowledge of the world, even my scientific knowledge, is gained from my own particular point of view, or from some experience of the world without which the symbols of science would be meaningless.[15]

As Merleau-Ponty puts it, scientific points of view are both naïve and dishonest simply because they take for granted the perspective of "consciousness" through which, from the beginning, a world forms itself around us and exists for us. He rightly insists that this is not to endorse idealism, in which the subject is detached from the world and renders it into existence: the unity of consciousness (in Kant, for example) is "achieved simultaneously with the world" (PP ix). Moreover, in Husserl the "noematic reflection" does not beget the object but brings to light its fundamental unity. The task, says Merleau-Ponty, is to neither construct nor form the real but to describe it. The world is there before any possible analysis and is not miraculously brought into being by the subject as a constituting power. He writes:

> When I begin to reflect my reflection bears upon an unreflective experience; moreover my reflection cannot be unaware of itself as an event, and so it appears to itself in the light of a truly creative act, of a changed structure of consciousness, and yet it has to recognize, as having priority over its own operations, the world which is given to the subject because the subject is given to himself. (PP x)

He describes the real as a "closely woven fabric" that does not await our judgment; perception therefore is neither a science of the world nor even an act but rather the background from which all our acts stand out and that is presupposed by them. Thus the idea of the "inner human being" is a fiction since "man is in the world, and only in the world does he know himself" (PP xi). The human being, it might be suggested, is not so much a source of intrinsic truth but more a subject destined to the world.

For Merleau-Ponty, it is such a way of thinking that can disclose the true meaning of the famous reduction performed by phenomenology. According to him, the best formulation given of this reduction is Eugen Fink's when he spoke of "wonder" in the face of the world (PP xiii). It is not, then, a matter of withdrawing from the world and toward the unity of consciousness as the basis of the world: "it steps back to watch the forms of transcendence fly up like sparks from a fire; it slackens the intentional threads which attach us to the world and thus brings them to our notice; it alone is consciousness of the world because it reveals the world as strange and paradoxical" (PP xiii). Thus the only way we can become aware of our relationships with the world is to suspend activity, to bracket out the world, and to put it "out of play." Neither is it a matter of simply rejecting common sense and our natural attitude to things, but rather suspension is required precisely because we take things for granted and they go unnoticed; to bring them into view therefore requires that we temporarily suspend them so as to afford a recognition of them. There is, then, for Merleau-Ponty, an "unmotivated surge of the world," and consciousness is the site of this disclosure of the world. He is emphatic that this is a new "transcendental"—concerned with conditions of possibility—and not Kant's transcendental. Kant's Copernican revolution only succeeds in making the world immanent to the subject. The task, however, is to be filled with wonder, in which the subject is conceived as a process of transcendence *toward* the world. As Lawlor notes, for phenomenology in general, "*every* lived experience is a directedness towards."[16] Of course, there can be no complete reduction since we are *not* pure or absolute mind. Philosophy must therefore be "an ever-renewed experiment," one forever making its own beginning. Far from being a procedure of idealistic philosophy, "phenomenological reduction belongs to existential philosophy"; our "being in the world," for example, can appear only against the background of this reduction (PP xiv). Moreover, as the "laying down of being," phenomenological-inspired philosophy "is not the reflection of a pre-existing truth but, like art, the act of bringing truth into being" (PP xx). "True philosophy," then, essentially consists "in relearning to look at the world" (PP xx). It is not in search of a primordial, preexistent Logos except the world itself. Philosophy is not simply possible but is actual or real, like the world of which it is a part. The task, finally, is to take up such an "unfinished world" and complete and conceive it.

III

In this section I want to highlight some key philosophical motifs of Nietzsche's *Dawn*. To date, the focus has largely been on the text as a work in naturalizing ethics, but what this neglects is the kind of commitment to philosophy Nietzsche has at this time and how he envisages it working as an experimental method of free-minded inquiry. Once this has been drawn out, we shall then be in a good position to appreciate the phenomenological aspects of Nietzsche's analysis.

In one of the opening aphorisms of *Dawn* Nietzsche argues, "We must again rid the world of much *false* grandeur [*Grossartigkeit*]" simply because "it offends against the justice which all things may lay claim to from us" (D 4; KSA 3, 20). In other words, a certain purification of value feelings and knowledge is required if we are to relearn the world and view it afresh, free of the presumptions and prejudices of morality and metaphysics (their fictions, their fantasies, their fabrications). As Daigle notes, Nietzsche's call for "historical philosophizing" in the opening of *Human, All Too Human* is an appeal to us to divest things of the beliefs that we have imposed upon them: "He thus wants us to 'go back to the things themselves,' as they were before we first interpreted them."[17] The key is for the human being to relearn what he has forgotten or perhaps not adequately known: that it is the human subject or *Dasein* that interprets and intends the world.[18] We need to renounce interest in the first and last things—the things of a theologically inspired metaphysics—and instead pay attention to the closest things (but which we fail to see or observe). This renunciation includes the very positing of a metaphysical world since all we can ever say of it is that it is an inaccessible and incomprehensible being-other, a "being" we can only endow with the qualities of a negative ontology (HH §9). It is important that we learn to appreciate the extent to which we, as meaning-bestowers, have been and remain the colorists of our experience of the world.[19]

This approach to questions of the self and the world requires a commitment on our part to knowledge, one that aims to be free of presumptions and prejudices: "Perhaps one day, once an alliance for the purpose of knowledge has been established with inhabitants of other planets and one has communicated one's knowledge from star to star for a few millennia: perhaps then enthusiasm for knowledge will swell to such a high tide!" (D §45; KSA 3, 52–53). For Nietzsche, the happiness of those who seek knowledge increases the amount of beauty in the world and makes everything sunnier: "Knowledge does not merely place its beauty around things but, in the long run, into things—may future humanity bear witness to this proposition! . . . What danger for their honesty [*Redlichkeit*] of becoming, through this enjoyment, a panegyrist of things!" (D §550; KSA 3, 320–21).

Nietzsche is in search, therefore, of a fresh approach to the world. It is an approach that, like phenomenology, values contemplation and description of the world, and its overriding concern is, again as in phenomenology, with the world in the dimension of its appearances. For Nietzsche, it is no longer a question of the philosopher estranging himself or herself from sensory perception and exalting the self to abstractions, in which we would then inhabit the palest images of words and things, playing with invisible, intangible, and inaudible beings and out of disdain for the physically palpable. We can no longer have this Platonic admiration for the dialectic as our sole method and as practiced by the good, desensualized person. Rather, we need to appeal to a multiplicity of faculties, methods, and procedures, including the Platonic:

> The thinker needs fantasy, the leap upward, abstraction, desensualization, invention, presentiment, induction, dialectics, deduction, critique, compilation of material, impersonal mode of thought, contemplativeness and comprehensiveness, and not least of all, justice and love towards everything present. (D §43)

Philosophy's love of knowledge—and to be a lover of knowledge is for Nietzsche to be an essentially unrequited lover—now develops as a form of passion that shrinks at no sacrifice. In aphorism 429 he notes that we moderns fear a possible return to barbarism, and not because it would make us unhappier since in all ages barbarians have been happier peoples. Rather, he argues, our drive to knowledge has become so strong for us that we now cannot tolerate the idea of happiness without knowledge: "The restlessness of discovery and divining has become just as appealing and indispensable to us as an unrequited love is to the lover; a love he would never trade at any price for a state of apathy; indeed, perhaps we too are *unhappy* lovers!" (D §429; KSA 3, 264). We now honestly believe, Nietzsche writes, that "under the pressure and suffering of *this* passion the whole of humanity must believe itself to be more sublime [*sich erhabener*] and more consoled than previously, when it had not yet overcome its envy of the cruder pleasure and contentment that result from barbarism" (D §429; KSA 3, 264). He holds that we feel "more consoled," I think, because of our growth in intellectual strength: we have the chance of knowledge and rendering things comprehensible, and with this there comes a new courage, fearlessness, and cheerfulness (*Heiterkeit*). We even entertain the thought that humanity might perish of its newfound passion for knowledge, though clearly Nietzsche is not an advocate of this. As he notes, such a thought can hold no sway over us. Our evolution is now bound up with this passion, however, and the task is to allow ourselves to be ennobled and elevated by it: "If humanity is not destroyed by a *passion* it will be destroyed by a *weakness*: which does one prefer? This is the main question. Do we desire for humanity an end in fire and light or in sand?" (D §429; KSA 3, 265; see also D §435; KSA 3, 267 on perishing as a "*sublime ruin [erhabene Trümmer]*" and not as a "molehill").

In aphorism 449 he appeals to the "spiritually needy" and considers how the new tasks and new modes of knowledge suppose solitude as their condition. He imagines a time for higher festivals, when one freely gives away one's spiritual house and possessions to those in need. In this condition of solitude the satiated spirit lightens the burden of its own soul, both eschewing praise for what it does and avoiding gratitude, which is invasive and fails to respect solitude and silence. This is to speak of a new kind of teacher who, armed with a handful of knowledge and a bag full of experiences, becomes "a doctor of the spirit to the indigent and to aid people here and there whose head *is disturbed by opinions*" (D §449; KSA 3, 272). The aim is not to prove that one is right before such a person but rather "to speak with him in such a way that . . . he himself says what is right and, proud of the fact, walks away!" Such a teacher exists like a beacon of light offering illumination. Nietzsche imagines this teacher existing in the manner of a new kind of Stoic and inspired by a new sublime:

> To have no advantage, neither better food, nor purer air, nor a more joyful spirit— but to share, to give back, to communicate, to grow poorer! To be able to be humble so as to be accessible to many and humiliating to none! To have experienced much injustice and have crawled through the worm-tunnels of every kind of error in order to be able to reach many hidden souls along their secret paths! Always in a type of love and a type of self-interest and self-enjoyment! To be in possession of a dominion and at the same time inconspicuous and renouncing! To lie constantly in the sun and the kindness of grace and yet to know that the paths rising to the sublime [*zum*

Erhabenen] are right at hand!—That would be a life! That would be a reason to live, to live a long time. (D §449; KSA 3, 272)

In this new mode of life we are strengthened and encouraged by the promise of the sublime and with a love that at one and the same time centers on ourselves and yet freely gives to others. Interestingly, in his treatment of the ancient Greeks Nietzsche had viewed tragic art as the means by which a people had conquered a world-weary pessimism (e.g., the wisdom of Silenus), to the point where they loved life to such an extent that they wanted long lives. The pain and suffering of life no longer counted as an objection but became the grounds of a beautifying and sublime transfiguration of existence. In book 5 of *Dawn* he is now envisaging how such comportment toward life can exist for us modern free spirits who have renounced so much (God, religion, the first and last things, romantic music, etc.). In *Dawn* §440 he in fact raises the question whether the philosopher of the morning is really renouncing things or gaining a new cheerfulness or serenity:

> To relinquish the world without knowing it, like a *nun*—that leads to an infertile, perhaps melancholic solitude. This has nothing in common with the solitude of the thinker's *vita contemplativa*: when he elects *it*, he in no way wishes to renounce; on the contrary, it would amount to renunciation, melancholy, downfall of his self for him to have to endure the *vita practica*: he relinquishes the latter because he knows it, knows himself. Thus he leaps into *his* water, thus he attains *his* serenity. (D §440; KSA 3, 269)

For the thinker who now has the new dedication to knowledge and can recognize the extent of its future-oriented character—it is such because the discoveries of knowledge always run ahead of a humanity that in time will seek to become equal to it—existence is lived magnanimously. In aphorism 459, titled "The Thinker's Magnanimity," Nietzsche writes:

> Rousseau and Schopenhauer—both were proud enough to inscribe upon their existence the motto: *vitam impendere vero* ("to dedicate one's life to truth"). And again—how they both must have suffered in their pride that they could not succeed in making *verum impendere vitae*! ("to dedicate truth to life")—*verum*, as each of them understood it—in that their lives tagged along beside their knowledge like a temperamental bass that refuses to stay in tune with the melody! But knowledge would be in a sorry state if it was meted out to every thinker only as it suited his person! And thinkers would be in a sorry state if their vanity were so great that they could only endure this! The great thinker's most beautiful virtue radiates precisely from: the magnanimity with which he, as a person of knowledge [*Erkennender*], undauntedly, often shamed, often with sublime mockery and smiling—offers himself and his life in sacrifice. (D §459; KSA 3, 276)

Neither Rousseau nor Schopenhauer, Nietzsche is arguing, possessed the cognitive maturity that allows for knowledge and life to enter into a new marriage in which knowledge elevates and pulls life up with it: their emotional personalities interfered too much to permit this process to take place.

We can contrast this with the depiction Nietzsche provides of the likes of Plato, Spinoza, and Goethe in aphorism 497, titled "The Purifying Eye."[20] In the genius of these natures we find a spirit that is only loosely bound to character and temperament, "like a winged essence that can separate itself from the latter and soar high above them" (D §497; KSA 3, 292). Nietzsche then contrasts this genius with another kind, those thinkers who boast of genius but who in fact have never escaped from their temperament, and he gives as an example the case of Schopenhauer. Such geniuses are unable to fly above and beyond themselves but encounter only themselves wherever they fly. Nietzsche does not deny that such genius can amount to greatness, but he is keen to point out that what they lack is that which is to be truly prized: "the *pure, purifying eye.*" Such an eye is not restricted in its vision by the partial sightedness created by character and temperament and can gaze at the world "as if it were a god, a god it loves" (D §497; KSA 3, 293). Although these geniuses are teachers of "pure seeing," Nietzsche is keen to stress that such seeing requires apprenticeship and long practice.

It is clear that, for Nietzsche, true genius is something extremely rare simply because so few can free themselves from their temperament and character.[21] Most of us see existence through a veil or cloak; this occupies his attention in aphorism 539. He challenges us to reflect on whether we are in fact suited for knowing what is true or not. Our mind may be too dull and our vision may be too crude to permit us access to such knowledge. He runs through the many subjective elements of our perception and vision of the world, how, for example, we are often on the lookout for something that affects us strongly and at other times for something that calms us because we are tired: "Always full of secret predeterminations as to *how* the truth would have to be constituted if you, precisely you, were able to accept it!" (D §539; KSA 3, 308). To attain objectivity of perception and vision is hard for human beings—to be just toward something requires from us warmth and enthusiasm, and the lovable and hateful ego appears to be always present—and may in fact be attainable only in degrees. We may, then, have good reasons for living in fear of our own ghost: "In the cavern of every type of knowledge, are you not afraid once more of running into your own ghost, the ghost that is the cloak [*verkleidet*] in which truth has disguised itself from you?" (D §539; KSA 3, 308). For Nietzsche, both Goethe and Schopenhauer are geniuses; the difference is that one is more capable than the other of "pure seeing" and hence is more profound.

Book 5 of *Dawn* begins with an aphorism titled "In the Great Silence," which stages an encounter with the sea. The scene Nietzsche depicts is one of stillness and solitude: "Here is the sea, here we can forget the city" (D §423; KSA 3, 259). After the noisy ringing of bells announcing the angelus,[22] which produces the sad and foolish yet sweet noise that divides night and day, all becomes still, and the sea lies pale and shimmering but unable or unwilling to speak; similarly the night sky plays its everlasting evening game with red and yellow and green but chooses not to speak. We are encompassed on all sides by a "tremendous muteness" that is both lovely and dreadful and at which the heart swells. But is there not hypocrisy in this silent beauty? Nietzsche invites us to ask. Would it not speak well and evilly if it so wished? Would it not mock our feeling of sympathy (*Mitgefühl*) with it? A voice, Nietzsche's voice, then interrupts and declares, "So be it! I am not ashamed of being mocked by such powers." This voice pities nature for its silence and on account of the malice that ties its tongue. In this scene the heart, the regulating source of life's blood flow, continues to swell and is startled by "a new truth": "*It too cannot speak*, it too mocks when the mouth calls something into this beauty, it too enjoys its sweet silent malice" (D §423; KSA 3, 259–60). The voice begins to hate speech and even thinking, for behind every word it hears the error of laughter, of imagination, and of delusion. Should one not, then, mock one's pity and one's mockery? What riddle of existence are we caught up in? Has not all become dark for the philosophy of the morning? The aphorism concludes as follows: "O sea! O evening! You are terrible mentors! You teach the human being to *cease* being human! Ought he to sacrifice himself to you? Ought he to become as you are now, pale, shimmering, mute, monstrous [*ungeheuer*], reposing above himself? Sublimely above himself [*Über sich selber erhaben*]?" (D §423; KSA 3, 259–60).

What sublime state is it that the human being might attain here? How can the human being cease being itself? Is this what has really taken place in this experience? The reader has good reason to pause and reflect on what might be expressed in the aphorism. One response might be to suggest that the encounter with the sea challenges us as humans and our sense of scale and measure, confronting us with something immense and monstrous. But here we have to be careful because of the "mockery" that greets us in the experience. All the names we might come up with to describe the mute sea will come back to us: profound, eternal, mysterious. Are we not endowing the sea with our own names and virtues?[23] Do we ever escape the net of language, ever escape the human?[24]

The basic contrast Nietzsche is making in the aphorism is between stillness and noise (sea and city); in our encounter with the sea, it might be suggested, we quiet our being, become calm and contemplative, think about more than the here and now, the merely fleeting and transient. In *Dawn* §485 Nietzsche has "B" state, "It seems I need distant perspectives to think well of things." If in *Human, All Too Human* Nietzsche had urged his readers to renounce the first and last things and devote instead their energy and attentiveness to the closest things (HH 16), the distant things, including distant times, return in *Dawn*, perhaps prompted by an encounter with the sea. *Dawn* §441, titled "Why What Is Closest Becomes Ever More Distant," captures this new sense of perspective: "The more we think about everything that we were and will be, the paler what we are right now becomes. . . . We grow more solitary—and indeed *because* the whole flood of humanity resounds around us" (D §441; KSA 3, 269).

We have reason to pause because of the reference to the "evening." The dawn-philosophy is a philosophy of the morning, and, as such, it has its suspicions about thoughts that come to us in the evening. Several aphorisms in book 5 address this point. In aphorism 539, for example, Nietzsche draws attention to how our "seeing" the world is colored by different emotions and moods and different hours of the day: "Doesn't your morning shine upon things differently from your evening?" Aphorism 542 begins with Nietzsche declaring, "It is not wise to let evening judge the day: for all too often weariness then becomes the judge of energy, success, and good will."[25] For Nietzsche, there are different ways of seeing, some more human than others and some that are superhuman. (This is what he calls "pure seeing"; see also D §426 on the "richer form of seeing.") The encounter with sea and evening serves to inspire us to think about these different ways of seeing; we no longer inhabit only the day, with its ordinary, prosaic consciousness.

In aphorism 547, "Tyrants of the Spirit," Nietzsche suggests that we should no longer feel the need to rush knowledge along to some end point. There is no longer the need, he holds, to approach questions and experiments as if the solutions to them had to correspond to a typical human time span. We are now free to take our time and go slowly:

> To solve everything at one fell swoop, with one single word—that was the secret wish: this was the task one imagined in the image of the Gordian knot or of Columbus' egg; one did not doubt that in the realm of knowledge as well it was possible to reach one's goal after the manner of an Alexander or a Columbus and to solve all questions with *one* answer. (D §547; KSA 3, 317)

The idea evolved that there was a riddle for the philosopher to solve and that the task was to compress the problem of the world into the simplest riddle-form: "The boundless ambition and jubilation of being the 'unriddler of the world' were the stuff of thinker's dreams" (D §547; KSA 3, 318). Under such a schema of the task of thinking, philosophy assumed the guise of being a supreme struggle for the tyrannical rule of spirit reserved for a single individual. (Nietzsche thinks that it is Schopenhauer who has most recently fancied himself as such an individual.) The lesson to be drawn from this inheritance is that the quest for knowledge has been retarded by the moral narrow-mindedness of its disciples; in the future, Nietzsche declares, "it must be pursued with a higher and more magnanimous basic feeling: 'What do I matter!' stands over the door of the future thinker" (D §547; KSA 3, 318).

IV

We have seen the extent to which Nietzsche is in search of a new practice of knowledge and in favor of a new contemplation and description of the world so as to learn it anew. I now want to bring to light more explicitly the phenomenological character of Nietzsche's inquiries in the book.

Nietzsche is an existential phenomenologist in the sense that his focus is on how, through new and refined practices of observation and self-observation, we as human beings largely unknown to ourselves can become our own *experiments*. We are to become strangers to our ordinary and habitual selves, viewing ourselves afresh as experiments of living and feeling and of knowledge. For Nietzsche, *the* "human being" is a bloodless fiction, and "society" is a general concept. We are to resist, then, the conforming demands of society and attempt to deconstruct and reconstruct ourselves as unique individuals. For Nietzsche, freedom as authenticity is thus, above all, a *task* (*Aufgabe*). As he says in the 1886 preface to volume 1 of *Human, All Too Human*, his writings speak to anyone in whom a "task" wishes to become incarnate, or flesh and blood, and who experiences the will *to* freedom of the will: "It is the future that regulates our today" (HH preface §7).

As Rüdiger Safranski has incisively noted, Nietzsche's project in texts such as *Dawn* is a phenomenological one and opens up "a vast field of phenomenological research."[26] The philosopher as peripatetic, as wanderer, "is the phenomenologist Nietzsche."[27] He is such because he demands from a reading of the signs of life a "phenomenological attentiveness" and attitude that clashes with the demands and certainties of everyday life (what phenomenology calls "the natural attitude"). For Nietzsche a new, *vita contemplativa* is to be cultivated in the midst of the speed and rapidity of modern life; we need to slow down, to go slowly, and to create the time necessary to work through our experiences. This surprise and wonder at the world, that it is and that we are what we are, including our potential for becoming what we are and involving the fashioning of "possibilities of life," is what for Safranski constitutes Nietzsche's new philosophy of the morning:

> We are not sufficiently composed to let the world work its magic. We fail to provide it with a stage on which to appear as an epiphany, rich and enigmatic. . . . For this to be possible, we must not have become too established as creatures of habit. Leeway is required to allow consciousness to observe itself, not in an autistic sense, but in such a way that receptivity for the world can be experienced on an individual level. This degree of attention to the way in which the world is "given" to us entails a decided departure from our customary attitude toward the world. We need to undergo a genuine transition in attitude, the kind we experience every morning when we awaken.[28]

As Safranski points out, Nietzsche's philosophy in *Dawn* is one of "observation," and it works as a kind of phenomenological empiricism. He is "setting out to render visible the jumble of the collaborative resonating stimuli and ideas as if under a magnifying glass, by means of heightened attentiveness and the aid of nimble language. He was aiming not at clarifications and constructions but at visualization and contemplation."[29] Far from being a reductive naturalist in his attention to physiological phenomena and the reality of our drives, Nietzsche posits physiology, perception, and consciousness as forming a continuum.[30] The program of research is phenomenological in that the fundamental principle of its method is that the only things we can know are those that are subject to our attentive observation: "Everything accessible to our consciousness is a 'phenomenon.' . . . It neither interprets nor explains, but attempts to describe what the phenomena are and what they indicate of their own accord."[31] Thus attentiveness to the activities and intentionality of consciousness "eliminates the dualism of being and appearance in one fell swoop."[32] It is in fact consciousness that makes this distinction. Moreover essence is not what remains hidden behind a phenomenon but is itself a phenomenon, "to the extent that we think it or the extent that we think that it eludes us."[33]

In *Dawn* Nietzsche seeks to undermine our confidence in naïve realism and with respect to both internal and external worlds. The inner world is "an internalized outer world" and is revealed to us only as a phenomenon.[34] As Nietzsche puts it, "We have expended so much labour on learning that external things are not as they appear to us to be—very well! The case is the same with the inner world!" (D §116). Nietzsche seeks to intensify our awareness and attention, in large part guided by the insight that "our so-called consciousness is a more or less fanciful commentary on an unknown, perhaps unknowable, but felt, text" (D §119; KSA 3, 113). As Safranski points out, consciousness is neither an empty mirror nor an empty container in need of replenishment; it is the being that is conscious of itself. It bears within itself referentiality; indeed it is the "self" of referentiality in which it has no "within" but is always the "outside" of itself, as in the famous dictum of phenomenology, *Consciousness is always consciousness "of" something.* Safranski writes:

> If we dig down deep enough into our consciousness, we suddenly find ourselves back at the things outside; we are actually flung back to them. Nietzsche depicts acts of consciousness as arising from a "hunger" (D §119; [KSA] 3, 112). Phenomenologists, for whom Nietzsche paved the way with his analyses of consciousness, use the terms "intention" or "the intentional structure of consciousness" in this context.[35]

Nietzsche is one of the first thinkers to bring to light and emphasize this feature of an intentional consciousness, in which the object is not simply registered in neutral terms and only "wanted," "loved," "desired," or "appraised" in an auxiliary act; it is, rather, that each of these intentions creates its own reference to an object, and in each act the "object" is quite distinct. This means that the same "object" can differ for consciousness according to the context and manner in which it is grasped.

According to Safranski, Nietzsche was "a master of shading the particular tinge, color, or mood of experience" and someone who used his own solitude and suffering as a springboard to construct a new philosophy, often providing exquisite depictions of the world while racked with pain. For Safranski, "these are model analyses of an intentional design of the world." Moreover Nietzsche is not content with mere expression and self-expression, but rather uses the example of his own experience to probe new and challenging questions. *Dawn* §114 provides us with an excellent example of his method at work. In this long aphorism "on the sufferer's knowledge," Nietzsche seeks to draw out the value for knowledge of the condition of the infirm who are tormented for long periods by their suffering but whose minds remain unclouded. (Perhaps he is writing of himself.) Such experiences and insights into them are of value because they come from profound solitude and release from all duties and customs, including customary habits of seeing the world and being in the world. Nietzsche now writes:

From within this condition the heavy sufferer looks *out* onto things with a terrifying coldness: for him all those little deceitful enchantments in which things usually swim when regarded by the healthy eye disappear. . . . Supposing that until that point he was living in some sort of dangerous fantasy world: this supreme sobering up through pain is the means to tear him out of it. . . . He thinks back with contempt on the warm, cozy, misty world in which the healthy person lives his life without a second thought; he thinks back with contempt on the most noble and cherished illusions in which he used to indulge himself in days gone by. . . . In this state, one resists to the death all pessimism lest it appear to be a *consequence* of our state and humiliates us as one who has been defeated. By the same token, the appeal of exercising justness in judgement has never been greater than now, for now it constitutes a triumph over ourselves and over the most sensitive of all states. . . . We find ourselves in veritable paroxysms of pride. (D §114; KSA 3, 105–6).

For Nietzsche, then, such an altered state of consciousness can bring with it the possibility of a new just "judgement" on the self and world, affording us insights into existence that are simply not available to us in our normal, everyday, and habitual comportment. Of course, he is honest enough with himself to draw attention to the limit of such an experience:

And then comes the first twilight glimmer of alleviation, recovery—and almost the first effect is that we resist the supremacy of our pride; we call it foolish and vain—as if we had experienced anything! Without gratitude, we humble the almighty pride that had just allowed us to endure pain and we vehemently demand antidotal venom for our pride: we want to become estranged from ourselves and depersonalized after the pain has made us *personal* too forcefully and for too long a time. (D §114; KSA 3, 106)

In short, is the pride not just a "malady" like any other? It is, but at the same time we are now returned to life in a new and surprising way, with our senses restored, but their horizon has also been opened up:

We begin to pay attention again to people and to nature—with a more longing eye: smiling ruefully, we remember that we now have come to know certain things about them in a new and different way than before, that a veil has fallen—but it *restores* us so as to view once more the *subdued lights of life* and to step out of the horrible, sober brightness in which, as a sufferer, we saw and saw through things. We don't grow angry when the enchantments of health resume their play—we look on as if transformed, kind and still weary. In this state, one cannot listen to music without weeping. (D §114; KSA 3, 106–7)

Here Nietzsche depicts in a subtle and varied manner the way our consciousness functions, involving an initial detachment of life and a new reattachment to life. We see through the illusions that characterize normal life, but then, having withdrawn from them, we are filled with a new longing for them, and there comes into being a new appreciation of life.

As Safranski astutely notes, Nietzsche is "a passionate singularist" in the sense that for him the world is composed of nothing but details; even the "self" can be approached in such terms, that is, as a detail that is composed of further details. In the analysis of the detail there is no point of completion or termination: "There are only details, and although they are everything, they do not constitute a whole. No whole could encompass the plethora of details."[36] If for Nietzsche the will to system displays a lack of integrity, so does the will to wholeness in analysis.

V

Dawn can be read as an important moment in phenomenology's history. One of Nietzsche's key insights in the book, which clearly anticipates phenomenology, is that consciousness has a referential structure and comportment; it is, as I noted, always outside of itself and directed to the world and to objects. Thus the objects of our memories, fears, longings, hopes, and thoughts all represent "realities" that serve to "inundate the neat divisions of subject and object."[37] Nietzsche's opening up of himself to great currents, oceanic expanses, and departures for new shores is metaphorical imagery by which he intends to explore the vast unknown territory of human consciousness and existence. His philosophy in *Dawn* is therefore radically human-situated and -centered. It dispels the illusions and fantasies of metaphysics, morality, and religion in an effort to return us to the human being and, through the passion of knowledge, seeks to entice us to remain true to the Earth and equal to the event that is our human being in the world.

In aphorism 501, titled "Mortal Souls," Nietzsche suggests that it is a question of relearning both knowledge and the human, including human time as mortal time. He is inviting his readers to replace the sublime dream of immortality with a new sobriety toward existence, as this aphorism from book 5 makes clear:

> With regard to knowledge [*Erkenntniss*] the most useful accomplishment is perhaps: that the belief in the immortality of the soul has been abandoned. Now humanity is allowed to wait; now it no longer needs to rush headlong into things and choke down half-examined ideas as formerly it was forced to do. For in those days the salvation of poor "eternal souls" depended on the extent of their knowledge acquired during a short lifetime; they had to *make a decision* overnight—"knowledge" took on a dreadful importance. (D §501; KSA 3, 294)

Nietzsche argues that we are now in a new situation with regard to knowledge, and as a result we can conquer anew our courage for making mistakes, for experimentation, and for accepting things provisionally. Without the sanction of the old moralities and religions, individuals and entire generations "can now fix their eyes on tasks of a vastness that would to earlier ages have seemed madness" (D §501; KSA 3, 294). Humanity has now earned the right to self-experimentation. Indeed, for Nietzsche, human beings *are* experiments, and the task is to *want* to be them (D §453). This is the principal legacy he bequeaths to modern thinking. The deep affinity between Nietzsche and phenomenology resides, I suggest, in this shared commitment to experimental philosophy.

Notes

1. For Christine Daigle, Nietzsche is to be considered a phenomenologist avant la lettre, "as a philosopher whose inquiry anticipates traditional phenomenology." She sees this in terms of how the human being experiences himself, the presence of others, how the world is encountered, and how the world and its objects appear to the self, in which the focus is very much on an "embodied consciousness." She also sees Nietzsche in the texts of the middle period formulating the concept of intentionality that is "at the heart of any phenomenological inquiry" (Daigle, "Nietzsche's Notion of Embodied Self," 227). In this essay I seek to augment and expand on such insights. I also share her view that the middle-period texts—especially *Dawn,* I would claim—are important because in them we see Nietzsche carrying out a genuine elaboration and *exploration* of his key concepts and methods of inquiry.

2. Nietzsche, *Dawn* (hereafter D). I have previously examined the text as a contribution to philosophical therapy. See Ansell-Pearson, "For Mortal Souls."

3. See especially Foucault, "Truth and Juridical Forms," 8–9.

4. Safranski, *Nietzsche,* 210.

5. Nietzsche, *The Gay Science.*

6. Large, "Nietzsche and the Figure of Columbus," 163.

7. See the letter dated mid-July 1881: "So read the book, if you will pardon my saying so, from an angle I would *counsel* other readers *against,* from an entirely personal point of view (sisters also have privileges, after all). Seek out everything that you guess is *what* might be most useful for your brother and what he might need most, *what* he wants and does not want. In particular you should read the fifth book, where much is written between the lines. *Where all* my efforts lead cannot be said in a word—and if I had that word, I would not utter it" (*Kritische Gesamtausgabe Briefwechsel* III: 1, 108; hereafter KGB).

8. Nietzsche, "Daybreak," §1, in *Ecce Homo* (hereafter EH).

9. Handwerk, "Afterword," 563.

10. Daigle, "Nietzsche's Notion of Embodied Self," 228.

11. See also *Human, All Too Human* §638 on "the mysteries of the dawning day" (hereafter HH).

12. Large, "Nietzsche and the Figure of Columbus," 174.

13. Husserl, *Ideas II,* §64.

14. Ibid., §55.

15. Merleau-Ponty, *Phenomenology of Perception,* viii (hereafter PP).

16. Lawlor, "Phenomenology," 391. In this essay Lawlor provides a good indication of the *limits* of phenomenology, especially when it is construed as a philosophy of "presence" and ensconced in "subjectivism." The key here is how we think immanence, whether as immanent *to* consciousness or immanent to immanence itself, which would be "life" (conceived as deferral, nonpresence, trace, difference, the nonconscious, blindness, and even death). For Lawlor there are three main resources for this post-phenomenological thinking of immanence: Bergson, Deleuze, and Derrida.

17. Daigle, "Nietzsche's Notion of Embodied Self," 230.

18. Ibid.

19. See HH §16; Daigle, "Nietzsche's Notion of Embodied Self," 231–32.

20. See also *Thus Spoke Zarathustra* I: 8 (hereafter Z); KSA 4, 53: "The liberated in spirit must yet purify himself. Much prison and mustiness is in him yet: his eye must yet become pure." Ironically perhaps, Schopenhauer's own insight into Goethe seems to anticipate Nietzsche: "Such a life, therefore, exalts the man and sets him above fate and its fluctuations. It consists in constant thinking, learning, experimenting, and practising, and gradually becomes the chief existence to which the personal is subordinated as the mere means to an end. An example of the independent and separate nature of this intellectual life is furnished by Goethe" (*Parerga and Paralipomena* 2:75).

21. Nietzsche's conception of the genius surely has affinities with Schopenhauer, who defines genius as "the highest degree of the *objectivity* of knowledge" (this knowledge is a synthesis of

perception and imagination and found in a rare state and abnormal individuals; *The World as Will and Representation* 2:292; see also chapter 31).

22. Since the fourteenth century Catholic churches sounded a bell at morning, noon, and evening as reminders to recite the Ave Maria, the prayer that celebrates the annunciation of Christ to Mary by the angel Gabriel. Note by translator of *Dawn*, Brittain Smith.

23. See also Z II "The Dance Song"; KSA 4, 140: "Into your eye I looked of late, O Life! And into the unfathomable I seemed then to be sinking. But you pulled me out with a golden fishing-rod; mockingly you laughed when I called you unfathomable. 'So runs the talk of all fishes,' you said; 'What *they* do not fathom is unfathomable. But changeable am I only and wild in all things, a woman and not a virtuous one.'"

24. See D §117, titled "In Prison," which ends: "We sit within our net, we spiders, and whatever we may catch in it, we catch nothing at all except that which allows itself to be caught precisely in *our* net" (KSA 3, 110). See also, from book 5 of the text, *The Gay Science* §374 on "our new 'infinite.'"

25. Nietzsche may have been inspired in these reflections by Schopenhauer: "For the morning is the youth of the day; everything is bright, fresh, and easy; we feel strong and have at our complete disposal all our faculties. . . . Evening, on the other hand, is the day's old age; at such a time we are dull, garrulous, and frivolous. . . . For night imparts to everything its black colour" (*Parerga and Paralipomena* 1:434–35).

26. Safranski, *Nietzsche*, 213.

27. Ibid., 218.

28. Ibid.

29. Ibid., 207.

30. See also Poellner, "Nietzsche and Phenomenology." He argues that in Nietzsche the approaches of physiology and phenomenology are not mutually exclusive. Both can be profitably drawn upon depending on the nature of our inquiry—and our polemic, one might add.

31. Safranski, *Nietzsche*, 207.

32. Ibid.

33. Ibid.

34. Ibid., 208

35. Ibid.

36. Ibid., 210.

37. Ibid.

Bibliography

Ansell-Pearson, Keith. "For Mortal Souls: Philosophy and Therapeia in Nietzsche's *Dawn*." In *Philosophy and Therapeia*, edited by Jonardon Ganeri and Clare Carlisle. Royal Institute of Philosophy Supplement 66. Cambridge: Cambridge University Press, 2010.

Clark, Maudmarie, and Brian Leiter. Introduction to *Daybreak: Thoughts on the Prejudices of Morality*, by Friedrich Nietzsche. Translated by R. J. Hollingdale. Cambridge: Cambridge University Press, 1997.

Cooper, David E. *Existentialism*. 2nd edition. Oxford: Basil Blackwell, 1999.

Daigle, Christine. "Nietzsche's Notion of Embodied Self: Proto-Phenomenology at Work?"*Nietzsche-Studien* 40 (2011): 226–43.

"Existentialism." *Stanford Encyclopedia of Philosophy*. Plato.stanford.edu, http://plato.stanford.edu/entries/existentialism/ (accessed January 2, 2012).

Foucault, Michel. "Truth and Juridical Forms." In *Power: Essential Works*, vol. 3. Middlesex, UK: Penguin, 2002.

Handwerk, Gary. Afterword to *Human, All Too Human II*, by Friedrich Nietzsche. Stanford: Stanford University Press, 2013.

Husserl, Edmund. *Ideas Pertaining to a Pure Phenomenology and to a Phenomenological Philosophy*. Translated by R. Rojcewicz and A. Schuwer. Dordrecht: Kluwer, 1999.

Large, Duncan. "Nietzsche and the Figure of Columbus." *Nietzsche-Studien* 24 (1995): 162–83.

Lawlor, Leonard. "Phenomenology." In *The Edinburgh Companion to Twentieth Century Philosophies*, edited by Constantin V. Boundas. Edinburgh: Edinburgh University Press, 2007.

Merleau-Ponty, Maurice. *Phenomenology of Perception*. Translated by Colin Smith. London: Routledge, 1962.

Nietzsche, Friedrich. *Dawn*. Translated by Brittain Smith. Stanford: Stanford University Press, 2011.

———. *Ecce Homo*. Translated by Duncan Large. Oxford: Oxford University Press, 2007.

———. *The Gay Science*. Translated by Walter Kaufmann. New York: Random House, 1974.

———. *Kritische Gesamtausgabe Briefwechsel*. Edited by Giorgio Colli and Mazzino Montinari. Berlin: Walter de Gruyter, 1975.

———. *Kritische Studienausgabe*. Edited by Giorgio Colli and Mazzino Montinari. Berlin: Walter de Gruyter, 1980.

———. *Thus Spoke Zarathustra*. Translated by Graham Parkes. Oxford: Oxford University Press, 2005.

Poellner, Peter. "Nietzsche and Phenomenology, Or: How to Get the Relation between Phenomenology, Science, and Metaphysics Right." In *A Companion to Nietzsche*, edited by Keith Ansell-Pearson. Oxford: Blackwell, 2006.

Sachs, Carl B. "Nietzsche's *Daybreak*: Toward a Naturalized Theory of Autonomy." *Epoché* 13, no. 1 (2008): 81–100.

Safranski, Rüdiger. *Nietzsche: A Philosophical Biography*. Translated by Shelley Frisch. New York: Norton, 2002.

Schopenhauer, Arthur. *Parerga and Paralipomena*. 2 vols. Translated by E. F. J. Payne. Vol. 1. Oxford, 1974.

———. *The World as Will and Representation*. 2 vols. Translated by E. F. J. Payne. New York: Dover 1969.

13 Appearance and Values

Nietzsche and an Ethics of Life

Lawrence J. Hatab

I<small>F WE TAKE</small> phenomenology in a general sense to be concerned with "appearance," Nietzsche's philosophy offers a wealth of pertinent material. Yet the meaning of appearance in Nietzsche's texts is not always easy to fathom. In this chapter I want to explore a "phenomenology of values" by coordinating Nietzsche's complex approach to appearance with his critique of morality.[1]

For Heidegger, Nietzsche represents the culmination of Western metaphysics and nihilism, particularly with his thinking on will to power and eternal recurrence. Presumably Nietzsche remains within the orbit of metaphysics by simply reversing metaphysical binaries (e.g., becoming over being, appearance over truth).[2] Nevertheless I believe that Nietzsche's philosophy, and especially his central concept of will to power, cannot be understood in this manner, and that his approach to appearance is not simply a reversal of traditional realism and models of truth. First of all, will to power is conceived specifically as a rejection of binary opposites, because it names a *process* of overcoming something, in which overcoming and otherness are structurally related to each other. Second, the meaning of "appearance" is complicated in Nietzsche's thinking. Often he will use appearance as a rhetorical weapon against metaphysical conceptions, calling them "apparent" rather than "real." At other times he will use appearance in a more positive sense to designate the way a world of becoming is given to us, as an "appearing" flux. He recognizes that a rejection of metaphysical "reality" also dismisses a deficient sense of "mere" appearance.[3] This is the problem: Nietzsche is happy to bank on deficient senses of appearance (error, lie, fiction, etc.) to characterize human thinking as an ungrounded process of interpretation, but these senses cannot be taken in their traditional connotations because there are no "true" conditions by which we could measure them as "false."

Metaphysics and Will to Power

We can begin with Nietzsche's critique of metaphysics. According to Nietzsche, "the fundamental faith of the metaphysicians is *the faith in opposite values*."[4] The Western tradition has operated by dividing reality into a set of binary opposites, such as constancy and change, eternity and time, good and evil, truth and appearance—opposites that can be organized around the concepts of being and becoming. The motivation behind such divisional thinking is as follows: Becoming names the negative and unstable conditions of existence that undermine our interest in grasping, controlling, and preserving life; being, as *opposite* to becoming, permits the governance or exclusion of negative conditions and thus the attainment of various models of stability.

Nietzsche wants to challenge the priority of being in the tradition, so much so that he is often read as simply reversing this scheme by extolling sheer becoming and all its correlates. This is not the case, even though Nietzsche often celebrates negative terms rhetorically to unsettle convictions. In fact he exchanges oppositional exclusion for a sense of *reciprocal tension*, where the differing conditions in question are not exclusive of each other but structurally related. He suggests that "what constitutes the value of these good and revered things is precisely that they are insidiously related, tied to, and involved with these wicked, seemingly opposite things" (BGE §2). Rather than fixed contraries, Nietzsche prefers "differences of degree" and "transitions."[5] Even the idea of sheer becoming cannot be maintained, according to Nietzsche; discernment of such becoming can arise only once an imaginary counterworld of being is placed against it.[6]

Becoming, for Nietzsche, cannot simply be understood as a world of change. Movements are always *related* to other movements, and the relational structure is expressive not simply of differences but also of resistances and tensional conflicts,[7] something captured in his concept of will to power (BGE §36). Will to power depicts in dynamic terms the idea that any affirmation is also a negation, that any condition or assertion of meaning must overcome some "Other," some obstacle or counterforce. Nietzsche also says that "will to power can manifest itself *only* against resistances; therefore it *seeks* that which resists it" (WP §656, my emphasis). A similar formation is declared in *Ecce Homo* in reference to a warlike nature: "It needs objects of resistance; hence it *looks for* what resists."[8] My reading of this is as follows: Since power can involve *only* resistance, then one's power to overcome is essentially related to a counterpower; if resistance were eliminated, if one's counterpower were destroyed or even neutralized by sheer domination, one's power would evaporate, it would no longer *be* power. Power is *overcoming* something, not annihilating it (KSA 12, 7 [53], 312). Overcoming and resistance seem to be related to each other in an intrinsic way: "A power quantum is characterized by the effect it expresses *and* what resists it. It is essentially a will to violation *and* resisting violation" (KSA 13, 14 [79], 258, my emphasis).

Will to power also applies to cognitive questions, such that knowledge cannot rest on secure foundations or purely objective conditions; rather knowledge arises from different takes on the world, which can only be characterized as an open field of interpretations (GS §374). Interpretations unfold out of differing power relations (WP §643) and can only count as "perspectives" on the world.[9] Throughout Nietzsche's texts, the notions of appearance, perspective, interpretation, and will to power all circulate together as indications of a tensional process of becoming, which rules out traditional convictions about being and truth.[10]

Truth

Nietzsche's perspectivism issues a complicated posture on the question of truth.[11] Contrary to some readings of Nietzsche (and some of his own rhetoric), I believe that he accepts and employs certain motifs of truth, as long as they are purged of metaphysical foundationalism and restricted to a more modest, pluralized, and contingent perspectivism. Even if knowledge is variable, historical, and born out of human interests, that does not render it false, arbitrary, or uncritical (see GS §§2, 191, 209, 307). There are also provocative passages where Nietzsche hints at a pluralized "objectivity," wherein the more perspectives one can adopt, the more adequate one's view of the world will be: "The *more* affects we allow to speak about one thing, the *more* eyes, different eyes, we can use to observe one thing, the more complete will our 'concept' of this thing, our 'objectivity' be" (GM III, §12; see also BGE §211).

We can organize the discussion of truth by way of the following distinctions: (1) Nietzsche affirms a global "negative" truth of becoming; (2) he denies the possibility of "positive" foundational standards of truth; and (3) he strikes a balance between these negative and positive poles by advancing a pluralized field of perspectival truths. A brief elaboration follows: (1) Throughout his writings Nietzsche affirms a dark, tragic truth of becoming, in the sense that flux must be recognized as a primal force that renders all forms and structures ultimately groundless.[12] Various passages speak of a difficult, fearsome truth that must be faced to counter our myopic fixation on life-enhancing beliefs (BGE §39; GM I §1; GS §110). In this way he is exploring a negative truth that so far has been forbidden (EH preface §3). (2) Because of Nietzsche's commitment to the tragic truth of becoming, positive doctrines of truth that presuppose foundational conditions of "being" are denied and often designated as "appearances" or "errors" ("On Truth and Lies in a Nonmoral Sense," WP §§616, 708). Our knowledge structures stem from a filtering process, which screens out strange and unusual elements that disturb our need for stability (GS §355). Although such structures are life-enhancing, they must still be unmasked as a "falsification" of experience (BGE §24). (3) Despite the ammunition becoming provides for Nietzsche's charge that traditional truth conditions are appearances or errors, he does notice the trap in sustaining the binary discourse of reality-appearance and truth-error. Falsification is the flip side of verification. Undermining "truth" also destabilizes any designation of "error" because error has always been measured by some governing truth standard: "The true world—we have abolished. What world has remained? The apparent [*scheinbare*] one perhaps? But no! *With the true world we have also abolished the apparent one*" (TI True World, §6).

Appearance

How can we sort out the meaning of appearance in Nietzsche's writings? In *The Birth of Tragedy*, his account of the Dionysian and the Apollonian deployed a reality-appearance distinction seemingly in line with that of Kant and Schopenhauer. Yet Nietzsche came to recognize the misleading way in which he used the term *appearance* (*Schein, Erscheinung*) in *The Birth of Tragedy*, namely in a seeming metaphysical sense contrasted with an underlying "reality" (thus as "mere" appearance). In his "Attempt at Self-Criticism" (1886), he rejected the use of Kantian and Schopenhauerian terminology because he was all along attempting "new valuations" that were utterly at odds with the philosophies of Kant and Schopenhauer (BT §6).[13] In an 1886 note (WP §853), Nietzsche denies that a metaphysical reality-appearance binary was operating in *The Birth of Tragedy*: "truth" (the Dionysian) is a nihilating disintegration; the (Apollonian) will to appearance is a lifesaving construction of meaning for the Greeks, an artistic "lie" that is *more primal* and *more valuable* than the will to truth, and that consequently cannot be called "mere" appearance.[14]

A central theme in Nietzsche's philosophy is that traditional forms of knowledge run up against the limit of radical becoming, and that such forms arose from the "fixing" effects of language and grammar. For instance, the flux of "phenomena" is converted into a series of discrete "facts" because we are misled by the individuated spacing of words (WS §11).[15] In *The Gay Science* §355, he writes that such knowledge claims stem from reducing the unfamiliar to the familiar, a reduction based on *fear* of the strangeness and flux of experience. Yet he often insists that "errors" such as these are necessary for human functioning and survival. Indeed identifying such errors is not on that account an objection (BGE §4). In *Beyond Good and Evil* §268, he calls the communicating character of words "the most powerful of all powers" because of its life-serving value. Even further, in *Will to Power* §522, after outlining the prejudices of language, he adds, "We think *only* in the form of language. . . . We cease to think when we refuse to do so under the constraint of language." The linguistic order of thinking is "a scheme that we cannot throw off." A comparable claim is given in a published work: "We have at any moment only the thought for which we have the words at hand" (*Daybreak* §257). Remarks such as these make it hard to read the "falsification" of experience as fitting any familiar sense of falsehood, especially if one cannot even *think* outside of such errors and if the fluid excess of becoming cannot really count as a "measure" for any kind of discernible truth.[16]

As indicated earlier, once the traditional binary of reality and appearance is rejected, it doesn't make sense to talk of "mere" appearance in a deficient sense. The idea of appearance can be given a positive sense of temporal emergence and showing forth ("She appeared from behind the curtain"), which accords with a phenomenological dismissal of "things in themselves" behind appearances, and which can fit some of Nietzsche's usage. Indeed, in the notebooks, Nietzsche describes appearance as a nonmetaphysical *reality*, which makes possible the constructed forms of meaning that, while ultimately groundless, are necessary for life:

> "Appearance" itself belongs to reality [*Realität*]: it is a form of its being. . . . Appearance is an arranged and simplified world, at which our *practical* instincts have been at work; for *us* it is perfectly real [*recht*]; that is to say, we live, we are able to live in it: *proof* of its truth for *us.* . . . The world, apart from our condition of living in it . . . does *not* exist as a world "in itself," it is essentially a world of relations: possibly it has a different aspect from every point: its being [*Sein*] is essentially otherwise [*anders*] from every point. (WP §568)

> The world of "phenomena" is the adapted world that we *perceive to be real.* . . . The antithesis of this phenomenal world is *not* "the true world," but the formless unformulable world of the chaos of sensations—thus *another kind* of phenomenal world, one "unknowable" for us. (WP §569)

Here Nietzsche posits two levels of appearance: the primal, formless flux of becoming, and the subsequent gathering of this flux into livable forms. Since *both* are designated as appearance, there is no other "reality" against which either one could be called "apparent" in a deficient sense. Indeed what the tradition had called the (merely) apparent world is, for Nietzsche, "the only world" (TI Reason, §2); the traditional distinction between the apparent world and the true world is in fact a distinction between the actual world and *nothing* (WP §567).[17] In *The Gay Science* §54, Nietzsche decisively rejects the distinction between appearance and some opposite "essence" or "thing in itself." And in this text, he clearly identifies *his* understanding of appearance with "that which lives and acts effectively." So appearance, *in life*, can never be *mere* appearance because it names real living events that nonetheless cannot satisfy traditional standards of metaphysical realism or dogmatic certainty.

Appearance and Genealogy

With his rejection of all forms of transcendence, Nietzsche calls for a kind of immanent naturalism, which, however, cannot be restricted to scientific naturalism because it includes all the "irrational" forces of nature, such as violence, strife, instincts, and drives. Moreover the call to "translate humanity back into nature" is linked with the "will to appearance" (BGE §230) and thus with the notions of perspective and interpretation. Nietzsche's naturalism also implies what could be called a "presumption of immanence," understood in the following way: We can think only in terms of how we are *already* existing in the midst of natural forces not of our choosing and not traceable to some "other" realm beyond the lived world. Such forces are "native" to our lives; we are "born" into them. (This sense of nativity is a nonscientific connotation of "nature" shown in both the Latin *natura* and the Greek *phusis*.) Nativistic immanence mandates that we accept as *given* all forces that we can honestly recognize at work in our lives, for instance, reason and passion, cooperation and power, building and destroying, loving and hating (see BGE §36). This includes the historical and continuing *contest* between such forces, which undermines traditional projects that seek to resolve becoming into "being."

Nietzsche's philosophical method follows his naturalism by constantly examining our beliefs with genealogical investigations into their historical sources, which demonstrates the contingency and fluidity of our convictions. Genealogy shows that revered doctrines are not fixed or eternal; they have a history and emerged as a contest with existing counterforces; indeed they could not avoid being caught up in the conditions they were opposing. Such analysis reveals the complexity of cultural beliefs and undermines their presumed stability and purity. Genealogy, then, is a kind of history different from those that presume discrete beginnings, substantive grounds in "original" conditions, or simple lines of development. Such a historical sense is not nostalgia for a bygone condition but critique in the face of hardened convictions (GM preface §6) and a preparation for new ventures (GM II §24). The complexities of historical emergence undermine foundationalist warrants, and the tensions intrinsic to this history tear at the boundaries of conceptual categories.

Nietzsche claims that genealogical investigations verify the centrality of will to power and interpretation in human culture. In a discussion of punishment (GM II §12), he criticizes other genealogists for identifying "origins" with "purposes." Here he is not utterly rejecting the idea of purposes, because such meanings do come to pass in history; rather he is rejecting the traditional teleological principle of purposes being built into the very manifestation of things from the start. He then elaborates on this critique from the standpoint of will to power. Given a plurality of competing power-complexes, there can be no single coherent "line" of development in temporal movement. The natural competition of power-sites—with no overarching arrangement—gives forth continual breaks and disruptions. Nietzsche offers that *any* emergent condition is "continually interpreted anew, requisitioned anew, transformed, and redirected toward a new purpose by a power superior to it." Surprisingly, he includes "everything in the organic world" in this dynamic of "overcoming and mastering," in which any existing meaning and purpose must be suppressed or destroyed by "new interpretations." Such is the scope of will to power (and interpretation) that it encompasses both natural and cultural phenomena.

Continuing his discussion, Nietzsche claims that any *current* understanding of a phenomenon's "usefulness" cannot be traced back without a break to its original emergence. Here he is not simply considering some particular entity in experience but the history of a general cultural phenomenon that can go by a single name, such as "morality." Genealogical history shows the ruptures and shifts that make for only a *nominal* unity in the word *good*, for example.[18] He says that any particular concept we grasp is not an enduring, substantive essence but an "indication" (*Anzeichen*) of an *emergence* in a field of competitive movements. Moreover his discussion in *On the Genealogy of Morality* II, §12 confirms the reciprocally tensional structure of will to power, because no form of power is immune from being overcome by other forms of power. (That is why master morality was subjected to overcoming by slave morality.) The history of a moral concept, therefore, is "a continuing range of indications, continually revealing new interpretations and adaptations," wherein an instance of "will to power has achieved mastery over something less powerful, and has impressed upon it its own meaning." Therefore the development of a cultural phenomenon cannot be a single "*progressus* toward a goal." Rather such a phenomenon is "a succession of more or less profound, more or less mutually independent processes of overcoming something." Right away, Nietzsche says that *added* to all forms of overcoming are "the resistances used against them every time," the defensive reactions and "the results, too, of successful countermeasures." No form of power, therefore, can ever prevail in complete dominance over time. This is why Nietzsche insists in this text that no form or meaning is ever fixed but is always "fluid" and that the dynamic structure of will to power represents "a major viewpoint of historical method" because it best names the way cultural phenomena unfold, develop, and change in human life.

Values

Nietzsche's thought challenges the standard of objectivity in philosophy, namely that truth should be independent of our interests and desires. For him, all thinking is based in interests; even the notion of "disinterest" stems from certain interests (BGE §220), and the standard of truth independent of desires is something we *desire* (WP §555). Consequently the ideal of disinterested knowledge is a fiction (BGE §207; GM III §§12, 26). There is no such thing as a value-free standpoint. That is why Nietzsche defines human beings as essentially value-creating and meaning-making (Z I, Thousand and One Goals). So "objective explanation" must be exchanged for interpretation, which Nietzsche calls the "introduction of meaning" (KSA 12, 2 [82], 100). Some sense of meaning always precedes and sets up what we call "facts" (WP §556); this is why, in Nietzsche's philosophy, the familiar fact-value or is-ought divide (and the concomitant problems associated with it) can never get off the ground. Value, meaning, and interpretation, then, go all the way down in human life. These conditions are also dynamic processes that Nietzsche identifies with will to power (WP §590; Z I, Thousand and One Goals).

All the notions given in the preceding paragraph connect with Nietzsche's understanding of appearance. The precedence of values shows that there is no "being-in-itself," only "grades of appearance [*Scheinbarkeit*] measured by the strength of *interest* we show in an appearance [*Schein*]" (KSA 12, 7 [49], 311). An 1888 note calls the apparent (*scheinbar*) world "a world viewed according to values," something "ordered, selected according to values" (KSA 13, 14 [184], 370–71). In this same note the appearance of values is connected with perspective, which "decides the character of appearance [*Scheinbarkeit*]." In addition, valuing means the enhancement of power, which entails action and reaction in the apparent world. Indeed the very "world" is "only a word for the total play of these actions." That is why there can be no "true" or "essential" being, because this would mean "a world without action and reaction" and thus no world at all. Continuing, Nietzsche calls the apparent world in this sense *reality* (*Realität*), something we have no right to call "appearance" (*Schein*). In this note it seems that the apparent world is a real "appearing" (*Scheinbarkeit*), as opposed to (mere) appearance (*Schein*)—although, as mentioned earlier, Nietzsche's overall thinking does not consistently operate with this kind of technical distinction.

To sum up thus far: Nietzsche's thought presents a "phenomenology" of human life, understood as the *appearing* of meaning and value in the midst of tensional power relations that can never be reduced to fixed or ahistorical conditions. Interpretation names the way things matter to us and fit our interests in different ways. Since meaning and value go all the way down for Nietzsche, his philosophy can be called "ethical" in the broadest sense, in that it concerns the ubiquity of evaluation, of judging better and worse ways of living. His notorious attack on morality can be understood not as a "reversal" into immorality or amorality but as a critique of a certain *kind* of morality, one that stems from an aversion to the finite and unstable conditions of natural life. There is implied here the possibility of another kind of morality, of valuation more attuned to natural life. The setting for such an alternative ethics can be found in Nietzsche's historical-genealogical analysis of master and slave morality in *Beyond Good and Evil* and *On the Genealogy of Morality*.

History and Moral Values

Nietzsche's examination of morality aims to give an unvarnished look at how moral values have *appeared* in human history. His genealogical treatment of moral ideals aims to disturb the pretense of moral purity and the presumption of moral foundations by suggesting a different look at the historical context out of which certain moral values arose. Ideals such as neighbor love, selflessness, peacefulness, and humility are not universal across history and are not derived from some transcendent source; rather they arose from the interests and needs of particular types of human beings, weaker peoples suffering at the hands of stronger types. Hierarchical domination was the ruling condition of early human societies (BGE §257). What we exclusively call "morality" was originally only a particular kind of morality, one quite different from another kind of morality that reflected the interests of stronger types: "There are *master morality* and *slave morality*. . . . The moral discrimination of values has originated either among a ruling group whose consciousness of its difference from the ruled group was accompanied by delight—or among the ruled, the slaves and dependents of every degree" (BGE §260). Moral evaluations were first located in aristocratic, hierarchical concepts that denoted gradations of superiority and inferiority, nobility and commonness. Nietzsche offers evidence for this historical thesis through an examination of moral language. In *On the Genealogy of Morality* I, §4 he begins an etymological analysis of moral words, which he calls "an *essential* insight into moral genealogy." As opposed to other historical treatments that falsely presume more current meanings of moral terms, he insists that an understanding of ancient words must be our first historical "data," in which is found confirmation for his thesis. The earliest forms of moral language available to us show that "good" and "bad" indeed denoted hierarchical associations of superior and inferior, noble and base, strong and weak, brave and cowardly—which shows "that in these words and roots that denote 'good,' we can often detect the main nuance which made the noble feel they were men of higher rank" (GM I §15). Nietzsche's etymological analysis shows that the earliest recorded senses of "morality" displayed selective grades of performative, social, and psychological *rank*, forms of stratification and power that in many ways are morally questionable, if not immoral, by modern measures.

Nietzsche's account of master and slave morality addresses the question of how and under what conditions an original aristocratic moral sense came to be supplanted by contrary norms. In *On the Genealogy of Morality* I, §§10–11, master and slave morality are distinguished according to two sets of estimation: good and bad in master morality, and good and evil in slave morality. Master types discover what is good out of their own condition of strength; they experience pleasure and exaltation in their victories and their distance from the powerless. Characteristics such as courage, conquest, aggression, and command that produce the feelings of power are deemed "good," while traits of weaker types such as cowardice, passivity, humility, and dependence are deemed "bad." What is important for Nietzsche here is that good and bad are not absolutes. What is good is good only for the master; what is bad in the slave arouses embarrassment and contempt in the master, but not condemnation or denial. In fact the existence of the slave is essential for maintaining the master's sense of distance, rank, and thus "goodness." The condition of the slave is not esteemed, but at the same time it is not annulled, since it provides the master with psychological (and material) benefits. In sum, what is good for the master is something active, immediate, and spontaneous, arising directly out of the master's accomplishment; what is bad is a *secondary* judgment in contrast to an antecedent experience of self-worth.

In relation to master morality, slave morality is constituted by a number of reversals. What the master calls "bad" is deemed good by the slave, and what is good for the master is called "evil" by the slave. The difference between "bad" and "evil" is important for Nietzsche. What is evil is absolutely negative and must be annulled if the good is to endure. (Here is a moral example of the "metaphysical faith" in binary opposites.) Nietzsche traces this different kind of judgment to the existential situation of the slave: the *immediate* condition of the slave is one of powerlessness and subservience; the master is a threat to the very existence and well-being of the slave. In effect the slave lacks agency, and so the initial evaluation is a negative one: the "evil" of the master is in the foreground, while what is "good," the features of the slave's submission, is a reactive, secondary judgment. Moreover because of the slave's immediate powerlessness, the slave's power for revenge cannot be actualized except in an *imaginary* realm of divine punishment (GM I §10).

According to slave morality, anything that opposes, destroys, or conquers is evil and should be eliminated from human relations. In master morality, however, strife, opposition, and danger are essential to the feelings of power and accomplishment that spawn a sense of goodness. (One thinks of the warrior ideals in Homer's *Iliad*.) Harmlessness and security, which are good for the slave, are an embarrassment and encumbrance for the master (GM I §11). Slave morality reverses master morality and recommends humility, selflessness, and kindness as the measure for *all* human beings, but only out of a condition of weakness and as a strategy for self-protection and self-enhancement. Slave morality seeks the simultaneous exaltation of the weak and incapacitation of the strong, but in doing so, slave types find enhancement not through their own agency but through the debilitation of others.

Slave morality is Nietzsche's redescription of Judeo-Christian ideals. The stories and exemplars embodying this moral outlook have promoted the ideal of supplanting worldly power with "justice" and "love." In the context of cultural history, however, Nietzsche sees in this ideal a disguised form of power, in that it is meant to protect and preserve a certain type of life; even more, the images depicting divine punishment of the wicked suggest to Nietzsche that the slave type has simply *deferred* its own interest in conquest (GM I §15). Both master and slave moralities therefore are expressions of will to power, but they are distinguished by "active" and "reactive" attitudes (GM II §11). The slave has no genuine agency and therefore can compensate only by reacting to an external threat and attempting to annul it. For Nietzsche, slave morality is not immediately an affirmation of a good but a denial of something dangerous and fearful, and he grounds this evaluation-by-negation in the psychological category of *ressentiment*:

> The slave revolt in morality begins when *ressentiment* itself turns creative and gives birth to values: the *ressentiment* of those beings who, denied the proper response of action, compensate for it only with an imaginary revenge. Whereas all noble morality grows out of a triumphant Yes-saying to itself, slave morality from the outset says No to what is "outside," what is "different," what is "not itself"; and *this* No is its creative deed. . . . Its action is fundamentally reaction. (GM I §10)

For Nietzsche, it should be said, the difference between active and reactive will to power, between affirmation and resentment, is a fundamental issue that bears on *all* intellectual and cultural topics. The general question is the ability or inability to affirm a finite world of limits, losses, conflicts, and dangers (see Z II, Redemption; TI Socrates, §1)—and thus the ability or inability to affirm the tensional structure of will to power. His analysis of the social arena targets the concrete soil out of which grew a

host of intellectual movements (e.g., epistemological certainty and political egalitari-
anism). He is trying to subvert long-standing values that are animated by notions of
universality, equality, harmony, comfort, protection, and the like—seemingly positive
notions that he insists are connivances of negative attitudes: fear of danger and difference, hatred of suffering, resentment and revenge against excellence, superiority, and
domination. Nietzsche tends to designate this condition of weakness and the perpetu-
ation of the slave attitude as the herd instinct, which is continually seeking to exercise
its own mode of power by enforcing conformity and comfort; in so doing it protects
the self-esteem of ordinary humans by neutralizing differences and denigrating excellence. The overarching problem with reactive will to power is that it undermines the
very conditions of power—reciprocal tensions—by aiming for the elimination of otherness and overcoming.

The Scope of Genealogy

We have noted that genealogy, for Nietzsche, challenges the idea that history moves
in clear lines of development or progress. The same would hold for a "regressive" picture of the move from master to slave morality. I believe that Nietzsche's genealogical
analysis is not meant to reject the slave/herd mentality, but to redescribe the environment of moral values in naturalistic and phenomenological terms, which shows both
the plurality of moral phenomena and the complicated *relationships* between different
kinds of moral values. A careful reading of Nietzsche's texts undermines the idea that
his genealogy is exclusively a defense of crude physical power or overt social control.
Throughout his writings, the meaning of weakness, strength, and power is polymor-
phous and far from clear. For instance, he often calls the values he criticizes necessary
for life. Morality has been essential for human development in its contest with nature
and natural drives (WP §403), and for this it deserves gratitude (WP §404). The exceptional individual is not the only object of honor for Nietzsche; conditions of regulation
are equally important for the species (GS §55). The "weakness" of the herd mentality
turns out to be a practical advantage since it has prevailed over the strong (TI Skirmishes, §14). Indeed the higher types of creative individuals that Nietzsche favors are
more vulnerable and perish more easily because of their complexity, in contrast to the
simplified order of herd conditions (BGE §62).

In *On the Genealogy of Morality* I, §16, Nietzsche claims that the opposition
between good-bad and good-evil has been a "terrible battle" on Earth for thousands of
years. Yet here he discusses an ambiguity in the master-slave opposition. Despite the
victory of slave morality and its enduring power over master morality,

> there is still no lack of places where the battle remains undecided. One might even
> say that meanwhile it has been raised ever higher and because of this it has become
> ever more profound and more spiritual [*geistiger*]: so that there is today perhaps no
> more decisive mark of the "*higher nature*," the spiritual nature, than to be divided in
> this sense and actually be another battleground for these opposites.

This is a very significant passage that can be compared with a remark in *Beyond Good and Evil* §260. There Nietzsche introduced the opposition between master and slave morality. But before he even begins to describe the two standpoints, he interjects, "I add immediately that in all higher and mixed cultures attempts to mediate between the two moralities also appear, yet more often a confusion and mutual misunderstanding of the two, even on occasion their severe, difficult coexistence [*Nebeneinander*]— even in the same person, within a single soul." Such remarks are crucial provisos for coming to understand the meaning and scope of Nietzsche's genealogy. The conflict between master and slave morality is not exclusively a matter of two discrete cultural camps. The conflict can be *mediated* within a culture and even within a single self. This is important because the original sphere of master morality was rather crude, and the slave mentality allowed for more refined and deeper cultural possibilities; it opened up creative pathways that were an advance beyond the limited sphere of the original masters. Moreover Nietzsche believes that such creative pathways can intersect with noble dispositions to generate an advance beyond *both* the original master *and* slave morality by "mediating" their opposition.

Nietzsche connects will to power with creativity, with "spontaneous, aggressive, expansive, form-giving forces that give new interpretations and directions" (GM II §12). Yet creativity, especially in a cultural sense, is not restricted to overt action; it often involves different ways of imagining things. And it seems that the realm of imagination was something cultivated in the outwardly powerless condition of the slave mentality. The slave could exercise will to power only in the inner domain of imagination:

> All instincts that do not discharge themselves outwardly *turn inward*—this is what I call the *internalization* [*Verinnerlichung*] of man: thus it was that man first developed what was later called his "soul." The entire inner world, originally as thin as if it were stretched between two membranes, expanded and extended itself, acquired depth, breadth, and height, in the same measure as outward discharge was *inhibited*. (GM II §16)[19]

For Nietzsche, the inwardness of the slave mentality is the prerequisite for spiritual cultivation (BGE §188); the "weak" represent a positive power of spirit (TI Skirmishes, §14) because their resentment of the strong opens up the possibilities of a higher culture, which is based on *der Vergeistigung und Vertiefung der Grausamkeit*, "the spiritualization and deepening of cruelty" (BGE §229). Such a turn begins to make mankind "an interesting animal" because the most ancient cultural concepts were "incredibly uncouth, coarse, external, narrow, straightforward, and altogether *unsymbolical* in meaning" (GM I §6). Now higher culture is possible since "human history would be altogether too stupid a thing without the spirit that the impotent have introduced into it" (GM I §7).[20]

So the master-slave distinction may have clear delineations at first, but it begins to get complicated in the context of cultural creativity and Nietzsche's brand of higher spiritual types, who are better understood as an "interpenetration" of and tension between master and slave characteristics found in a "single soul" (BGE §260; GM I §16). Consequently the "evil" that designated the destructive threat of the original master is now recapitulated in creative disruptions of established conditions:

> The strongest and most evil spirits have so far done the most to advance humanity. . . . They reawakened again and again . . . the pleasure of what is new, daring, untried. . . . In every teacher and preacher of what is *new* we encounter the same "wickedness" that makes conquerors notorious, even if its expression is subtler and it does not immediately set the muscles in motion. . . . What is new, however, is always *evil*, being that which wants to conquer and overthrow the old boundary markers and the old pieties. (GS §4)

Innovators are the new object of hatred and resentment (Z III, Tablets, §26); they are the new "criminals" (TI Skirmishes §45), the new "cruel ones" (BGE §230), the new perpetrators of "war" (GS §283). In sum, cultural creativity is made possible by a dialectic of master and slave characteristics, so that not everything in the latter is passive and not everything in the former is brute power. In the end, therefore, the creator-herd distinction is *not* equivalent to the master-slave distinction; there are overlaps, but the crude domination found in the original condition of the master cannot be considered the primary focus of Nietzsche's analysis of creative types.

On the Genealogy of Morality I, §17 offers more intimations that Nietzsche's genealogy is not simply a historical account of slave morality's displacement of master morality. He asks if the conflict between these ideals has come to an end, or if there are still possibilities of its being furthered after the ascension of slave morality. He asks if one should not desire and even promote the furtherance of this conflict. He then closes with an indication of his own posture on the question of morality, his own interest in retrieving in some way elements of noble morality as a correction for the dominance of slave morality. He addresses his readers on this matter with the following assumption:

> That it has been sufficiently clear for some time what I *want*, what I actually want with that dangerous slogan which is written on the spine of my last book, *Beyond Good and Evil* . . . at least this does *not* mean "Beyond Good and Bad."— —

Nietzsche not only grants historical importance to the good-bad distinction in noble morality; he also considers this distinction to be a workable alternative to the good-evil distinction for his own thinking on morality, his own recommendations for a moral sense that can overcome traditional versions of slave morality.

Nietzsche and Morality

Although Nietzsche occasionally calls himself an "immoralist" and suggests an overcoming of "morality," it is a *particular* moral system that is being challenged in these maneuvers. If morality refers to values that assess human actions and attitudes in terms of better and worse ways of living, then he is certainly recommending a kind of morality, and so thinking about ethics generally in the light of Nietzsche's thought is quite appropriate.[21] As I have noted, Nietzsche's recommendation to surpass the distinction between good and evil does not mean a refusal to distinguish between good and bad (GM I §17). A note appended to that section in the *Genealogy* reiterates his intention to advocate a *reordering* of values, an "order of rank among values" (*Rankordnung der Werte*), rather than an abandonment of values. Herd morality is only one type of morality among others. It is the *reduction* of "the good" to herd morality that Nietzsche opposes (see BGE §202).

Drawing on life-affirming features implicated in master morality, Nietzsche wants to displace a transcendent, antinatural morality and recommend a naturalized morality that serves, and is measured by, life instincts:

> I bring a principle to formula. Every naturalism in morality—that is, every healthy morality—is ruled by an instinct of life; some command of life is fulfilled by a determinate canon of "should" and "should not"; some inhibition and hostile element on the path of life is thus removed. *Anti-natural* morality—that is, almost every morality that has so far been taught, revered, and preached—turns, conversely, *against* the instincts of life. (TI Morality, §4)

Continuing in this text, Nietzsche reiterates his life-centered philosophy, wherein a *larger* order of life is served by, and therefore not exclusively based in, human life: "When we speak of values, we speak under inspiration, under the perspective of life: life itself forces us to posit values; life itself values through us when we posit values" (TI Morality, §5). What follows from this, he says—echoing a point in the *Genealogy*—is that even an antinatural morality is "a value judgment of [by] life," but one that serves only a particular kind of life, a weakened, declining form of life. And in the next section of this text, Nietzsche connects the idea of "immoralism" with a form of affirmation that is open to all forces in natural life, even counternatural forces:

> We others, we immoralists, have conversely made room in our hearts for every kind of understanding, comprehending, and *approving* [*Gutheissen*]. We do not negate easily; we make it a point of honor to be *affirmers* [*Bejahende*]. More and more our eyes have opened to that economy which needs and knows how to employ everything that is rejected by the holy witlessness of the priest, of the *diseased* reason in the priest—that economy in the law of life which finds an advantage even in the repugnant species of the hypocrites, the priests, the virtuous. (TI Morality, §6)

Given such complexity in Nietzsche's life-affirmative posture, we should not oversimplify or polarize his approach to herd morality. The kinds of moral values that are so problematic for him still find a place in his worldview, and they might even be revamped and rehabilitated in the light of his criticisms. First of all, part of Nietzsche's point is that herd values such as harmony and peacefulness are not entirely misguided, but are harmful when extended to all contexts and all human types; creativity, for example, is a context in which such values can be detrimental. In certain contexts and for certain types, then, herd values can be appropriate. Consequently his attack upon certain moral systems is not meant to erase them or to promote a mere reversal of their values by promoting opposite actions or forms of life. As Nietzsche puts it in the context of religion, refuting God does not mean we are left with the devil (BGE §37). Simply recommending what a moral system finds wrong, its Other, would still be caught up in the measure of that system. To put this in concrete terms, it would be a mistake to interpret Nietzsche's approach as a call for suspending traditional moral prescriptions against killing, stealing, lying, abuse, violence, and so on; nowhere in his texts can we find blanket recommendations for such behaviors. Rather he wants to contextualize and problematize traditional moral values so as to undermine their transcendent isolation from earthly conditions of finitude, their pretense of purity, universality, and stability:

> It goes without saying that I do not deny—unless I am a fool—that many actions called unethical [*unsittlich*] ought to be avoided and resisted, or that many called ethical [*sittlich*] ought to be done and encouraged—but I think they should be encouraged and avoided *for reasons other than hitherto*. We have to *learn to think differently* [*umzulernen*]—in order at last, perhaps very late on, to achieve even more: *to feel differently* [*umzufühlen*]. (*Daybreak* §103)

Nietzsche's destabilization of traditional moral *belief systems* may not imply a renunciation of certain *values* that operate in those systems. Indeed there may be hidden resources in his critique that can open up these values in a more existentially meaningful way. There are passages in his texts that suggest as much—that one might uncover concealed insights and a deeper sense of morality by denying it and unsettling its unambiguous presumptions and comfortable acceptance (see GS §292). A "phenomenology" of values will stress the appearance-character of moral values, their tensional emergence in finite life conditions that will not permit certitude or strict foundations.

Nietzsche's moral criticisms might therefore be called internal in a sense, and this would fit in with the complex meaning of "overcoming" that animates his thought, which is a surpassing without utter negation. Just as one must overcome the sedimented fixations of one's culture, one must also overcome the polar *opposition* to one's culture that marks the initial gesture of independence:

> "Thoughts about moral prejudices," if they are not meant to be prejudices about prejudices, presuppose a position *outside* morality, some point beyond good and evil. . . . One must have liberated oneself from many things that oppress, inhibit, hold down, and make heavy precisely us Europeans today. The human being of such a beyond who wants to behold the supreme measures of value of his time must first of all "overcome" this time in himself—this is the test of his strength—and then not only his time but also his prior aversion and contradiction *against* this time [*seiner bisherigen Widerwillen und Widerspruch gegen diese Zeit*], his suffering from this time. (GS §380)

Consequently we need not segregate certain moral notions that Nietzsche identifies with the "herd" from the rest of his reflections on value and meaning. We need not rest with clear delineations between "Nietzschean" values on the one hand and "traditional" values on the other. We might be able to give a Nietzschean interpretation of familiar moral themes that can *revise* our understanding of ethics rather than overcome, supersede, or marginalize perennial normative concerns. I concede that this would reflect my own hermeneutical moves, but I think they can accord with much of Nietzsche's thinking.

Nietzsche's deconstruction of "good and evil," I believe, is concerned not with denying normative judgments but with supplanting the polar opposition of the good and the nongood. Such categorical segregation generates a number of mistakes and distortions in moral understanding. First of all, it encourages a hyperconfidence in the rectitude of one's sense of the good and in the malignancy of the Other—which can instigate exclusion, oppression, or worse. Second, it ignores or conceals the essential *ambiguity* in values, that no value is "pure" or separable from otherness or immune from complicity with harmful effects. Human existence is enormously complex, and no moral category can be clean enough to sufficiently cover the normative field or to avoid discrepancies, ironies, and unintended detriment in its own operation. In many contexts it is no mystery to recognize the harm in something like murder and violence or the benefit in something like nurturance and kindness. Nietzsche's contribution lies in alerting us to the margins: to contexts in which familiar moral juxtapositions become unsettled. What is called "kind" and "cruel" is not always "good" and "evil." Sometimes what is meant to be kind can be overprotective and inhibiting, and what is perceived as cruel can be a proper challenge to break a debilitating fixation. The "dangerous" is often productive of good results, and the "safe" is often productive of bad results. Any apparently positive value contains an intrinsic capacity for negative effects, and vice versa.

Finally, with whatever is called good, *becoming* good will involve a continual tension with otherness, without which the existential sense of developing and living out the value would evaporate. Without a capacity to be cruel, "being kind" would not have any moral meaning; recommending kindness would be like recommending aging. So becoming kind in an authentic sense would have to involve an existential confrontation with our capacity for cruelty, with an eye toward cultivating its Other. Consequently the existential *field* of kindness includes cruelty, and without such a field-concept, the nature of kindness is distorted or even lost. The moral polarization of kindness and cruelty would attempt to insulate us from our cruelty and view it with disdain, but a moral developmentalism would require that we acknowledge, examine, and orchestrate the tensions between kindness and cruelty in our nature. What is more, polarization can encourage a *repression* of propensities toward cruelty, and we know well that repression can produce pathological effects and even terrible outbursts of cruelty when the force of subliminal drives becomes too great. In these ways, then,

the polarization of values into "good" and "evil" can subvert an existential appropriation of cherished values and can even nourish the fermentation of the most vicious
forces that such values are presumably meant to prevent. Becoming good, therefore,
must include an engagement with contrary forces: "Of all evil I deem you capable:
therefore I want the good from you. Verily, I have often laughed at the weaklings who
thought themselves good because they had no claws" (Z II, Sublime). Such a tensional
engagement with conflicting forces can count as a kind of moral phenomenology that
speaks to the ways ethical bearings emerge and take shape in human life.

If we take a lead from Nietzsche's preference for the good-bad distinction over the
good-evil distinction, we can conclude that moral distinctions and judgments regarding good and bad are possible in the light of his thinking and are preferable to the
traps and distortions that follow from isolating the good from its Other in the manner
of good and evil. One and the same action can be called either "evil" or "bad." In both
cases there is a moral judgment, but the second term is favored from a Nietzschean
perspective, since it allows for the ambiguities and correlations that adhere to normative judgments. With a tensional structure of goodness, there can be no overarching
principle of unambiguous moral purity, or judgments without remainder or regret,
or hopes for the complete rectification of conflicts within the moral field. What is lost
here? Is it certain values that are lost or simply a certain way of interpreting these
values?

It seems to me that we can distinguish Nietzsche's critique of the slave/herd mentality from certain traditional moral values and not assume that his critique exhausts
what can be said of those values. How is it that feeding the hungry is a sign of slavish
weakness and life-denial? Or preventing violence and abuse? Or aiming for honesty
in human relations? Or treating people with kindness and respect? I have no trouble
saying that all these actions are worthy of moral praise and are worth recommending,
and I see nothing of weakness or denial in them as such. Nietzsche is surely right when
he targets a revulsion against suffering and finite life conditions that spawns resentment, exclusions, unhealthy dispositions, and perfectionist hopes. The issue concerns
a certain *attitude toward life* that can be implicated in such values, not necessarily the
values themselves. I prefer to say that such values can be healthy and life-affirming
but that they are complex and always in danger of inciting or valorizing life-denying
attitudes and practices.

We can make some headway here by distinguishing the following: (1) existential
moral commitments, decisions, and judgments that indicate particular estimations
of better and worse ways of living, that reflect particular decisions about a normative
affirmation or denial—choosing one's Yes or No in a certain context—a decisiveness
frequently celebrated and encouraged by Nietzsche;[22] (2) moral theories, formulas, and
metaphysical foundations that have served to ground and guarantee moral judgments,
which in effect decide the issue *for* us—we only have to conform our decisions to such
measures in order to be in the right; (3) moral universalism and perfectionism, which

suggest some transformed condition wherein normative differences and conflicts can be resolved or overcome in the light of a secure concept of the good; and (4) moral judgments that involve a condemnation or vilification of the Other, of that which stands on the other side of the good—which tends toward practices of exclusion or demonization. I think that items 2, 3, and 4—which may interconnect—can be proper targets of a Nietzschean critique. But the first item can be sustained—indeed it can be called an ethical version of the tensional perspectivism championed by Nietzsche—by allowing for existential moral decisions without guarantees, without suppression of conflict, and without casting the Other into oblivion, invisibility, or silence.

Any moral value or virtue, in its appearance-conditions and existential environment, is constituted by a contest with counterforces. When we make a moral decision or act out a moral commitment, when we take a moral stand and are willing to judge better and worse ways of living, we are engaged in specific instances of overcoming, the creation of meaning in the midst of otherness—which is what Nietzsche means by will to power. Indeed moral practice in this sense seems to embody central Nietzschean motifs such as challenge, strife, differentiation, and ranking. Moreover we cannot reduce morality to the herd mentality, since it is often conformist and group forces that work against and inhibit certain moral behaviors; honesty, for example, is often the last thing most people want to hear. In the midst of convention and established power interests, moral action will often require struggle and risk. It is in this sense that egalitarian aversions to harm, offense, difference, and rank that have marked traditional moral rhetoric deconstruct themselves when we consider contexts of moral enactment. *Being* moral often entails disruption, conflict, and gradation.

Applying Nietzsche's phenomenological perspectivism to ethics would certainly disallow any absolute foundation for morality, but we can also intercept a crude intellectual pessimism or facile relativism by noting that perspectivism, for Nietzsche, is not equivalent to radical skepticism or to the notion that differing viewpoints are equally valid. Although Nietzsche considers all knowledge and value to be perspectival, he advocates *commitment* to one's perspective over others; he diagnoses a detached condition or an absence of resolve or a skeptical reserve as forms of weakness. The "objective" person who strives for "disinterested" knowledge is deficient in having no specific stand to take or judgments to make:

> His mirror soul, eternally smoothing itself out, no longer knows how to affirm or negate; he does not command, neither does he destroy.... Neither is he a model man; he does not go before anyone, nor behind; altogether he places himself too far apart to have any reason to take sides for good or evil. (BGE §207)

Our mistake has been "confusing him for so long with the *philosopher*." Likewise we tend to assume a connection between philosophy and skepticism:

> When a philosopher suggests these days that he is not a skeptic——I hope this is clear from the description just given of the objective spirit—everybody is annoyed.... It

is as if at his rejection of skepticism they heard some evil, menacing rumbling in the distance, as if a new explosive were being tried somewhere, a dynamite of the spirit.... For the skeptic, being a delicate creature, is frightened all too easily; his conscience is trained to quiver at every No, indeed even at a Yes that is decisive and hard, and to feel as if it had been bitten. Yes and No—that goes against his morality. (BGE §208)

A phenomenology of commitment and decision would help distinguish a nonfoundationalist ethics from a crude moral relativism, which tends to mean that different moral beliefs simply hold true for those who hold them, that the different beliefs are no better or worse in comparison with each other, simply different. Although some normative areas might properly be called relativistic in this sense, certain moral decisions and commitments would not make existential sense in the light of such thinking. If I believe that political imprisonment and torture are wrong, for example, and I join Amnesty International to make appeals to governments that practice such things, it would seem strange if I were to claim that these governments' "perspectives" on the matter are right "for them" or simply "different" from my perspective. I can be a moral perspectivist who denies the possibility of a global foundation and still commit to my position—which in this instance would have to mean that I think these governments are *wrong* and that my position is *better* than theirs. Such decision and commitment fit in well, I think, with what Nietzsche means by willing in the midst of opposition. From an existential, lived standpoint, one cannot equally affirm one's own values and opposing values; that would make morality so arbitrary as to be blind and meaningless. One must *contend* with other perspectives, both practically and intellectually, and this entails that one find one's "Yes and No," that one argue and work *for* one's own perspective and *against* others, that one think one's own perspective to be the *better* option––all of which would make an attitude of equanimity inappropriate. A tensional perspectivism simply stipulates that one's commitments can not be backed up by some decisive "truth" and that a complete resolution or adjudication of differential strife will not come to pass. We must simply see the ethical field *as* conflicted and *decide* how to live—without allowing *global* undecidability to demoralize us or debilitate our capacity to make local commitments. Nietzsche claims that the desire for certainty is a remnant of religion and that certainty "is not *needed* at all . . . in order to lead a full and excellent human life" (WS §16).

The absence of a ground for moral action will strike some as a threat to moral commitment, but Nietzsche would diagnose this worry as a weakness in the face of the only possible condition for any kind of commitment: a willingness to stand for something that is *not* guaranteed. The search for a decisive ground in ethics can be understood as an attempt to *escape* the existential demands of contention and commitment. For Nietzsche, to act in the world cannot help but be action in the face of obstacles and resistances. To dream of action without differential conflict is actually an unwitting annulment of action. Any assertion of a stable, essential "being" would be "the expression of a world *without* action and reaction" (WP §567). To affirm otherness as constitutive of one's action, then, is to affirm action *as* action, that is to say, an actual move in life amid actual resistances. In this way, ethical action, as a way of *life*, can be seen as an instance of tensional will to power.

In conclusion, I have attempted to show that in the light of Nietzsche's understanding of appearance, ethics can be construed as the *emergence* of valuation in tensional conditions of natural life, in a manner that is neither foundational nor fictional. And a genealogical-historical account shows morality to be a complex range of relations *between* different appearances, which cannot be resolved into one stable framework or one discrete story—whether the story be the traditional kind or the supposed story of Nietzsche's denial of morality.

Notes

1. Portions of this chapter are based on previous work of mine: *Nietzsche's Life Sentence*, and *Nietzsche's* On the Genealogy of Morality.

2. For Heidegger's extensive engagement with Nietzsche, see the four-volume work, *Nietzsche*; see especially vol. 3, pt. 1, and vol. 4, pt. 2.

3. See Nietzsche, *The Gay Science*, §54 (hereafter GS).

4. Nietzsche, *Beyond Good and Evil*, §2 (hereafter BGE).

5. *The Wanderer and His Shadow*, part 2 of *Human, All Too Human*, §67 (hereafter WS).

6. Nietzsche, *Sämtliche Werke: Kritische Studienausgabe*, 503–4 (hereafter KSA).

7. Nietzsche, *The Will to Power*, §568 (hereafter WP).

8. Nietzsche, *Ecce Homo*, "Wise," 7, emphasis in text (hereafter EH).

9. Nietzsche, *On the Genealogy of Morality*, III §12 (hereafter GM).

10. For textual sources of these concurrent indications, see BGE §34; GM II §12; *Twilight of the Idols*, Errors, §5 (hereafter TI); WP §§ 259, 534, 552, 556, 568, 590, 966. The question of the relation between interpretation and perspective is ambiguous in Nietzsche's writings. At times he seems to use the two terms interchangeably. There may be some justification for reserving "perspective" for life forces in general and "interpretation" for articulated meanings. On this question, see Cox, *Nietzsche*, 111–18.

11. For an excellent overview and analysis of the question of truth in Nietzsche, see Anderson, "Nietzsche on Truth, Illusion, and Redemption."

12. See, for example, *The Birth of Tragedy*, §§21–22 (hereafter BT); TI Reason §§2, 6; WP §708.

13. For an account of the difference between *The Birth of Tragedy* and Schopenhauerian metaphysics, see Han-Pile, "Nietzsche's Metaphysics."

14. Throughout his writings, Nietzsche employs different words that can be translated as "appearance" (e.g., *Schein, Erscheinung, Scheinbarkeit*). There does not seem to be a sustained technical distinction between these words in his usage. Whether the meaning is appearance, mere appearance, illusion, deception, or something else can only be discerned in context.

15. See also BGE §34; TI, Reason, §5.

16. To move outside the sphere of epistemological measure, Nietzsche often articulates the meaning of appearance in terms of creativity and art. In an 1887 note, he claims that truth is not "found" in reality, it is *created* as a manifestation of will to power (KSA 12, 9 [91], 385). In GS §58, he insists that "knowledge" of "things" has its origin in historical moments of creativity bequeathed to us by innovative thinkers. Such creations are called *appearances*, yet with familiarity over time such appearances harden into supposed "essences"—only to be replaced by new creations, and so on. The idea of creative appearance is then quite naturally associated with art (BT, "Attempt at Self-Criticism," §5); Nietzsche even calls art "the *good* will to appearance" (GS §107). Since art had traditionally

been excluded from the realm of strict truth, Nietzsche is happy to trade on the idea of "fiction" and to goad a metaphysical faith by celebrating art as "deception" (GS §344), even as "the *will to deception* [that] has good conscience on its side," which is called a basic alternative to the ascetic belief in truth (GM III §25). We should be circumspect in considering such talk of deception replacing truth, because Nietzsche thinks that "artistic deception" is the creative characteristic of "everything that is" in nature and the mark of reality and truth (WP §853).

17. At times Nietzsche exchanges the true-false binary for *degrees* of appearance (BGE §230; WP §560), that is, *how* apparent something is to us.

18. As Nietzsche says elsewhere about the will, willing "is a unity only as a word" (BGE §19).

19. See also GM II §18–19; BGE §51.

20. It might be said that the original masters were more like contemporary action heroes or professional wrestlers. As Nietzsche says, if Homer had been an Achilles, he would not have created an Achilles (GM III §4).

21. See Clark, "Nietzsche's Immoralism," 15–34, which is a helpful treatment of the debate over whether "immoralism" is a rejection of all or only some versions of morality. See also Schacht, "Nietzschean Normativity," which is an impressive attempt to draw from Nietzsche a viable moral philosophy.

22. See, for example, GM III §12.

Bibliography

Anderson, R. Lanier. "Nietzsche on Truth, Illusion, and Redemption." *European Journal of Philosophy* 13, no. 2 (2005): 185–225.

Clark, Maudemarie. "Nietzsche's Immoralism and the Concept of Morality." In *Nietzsche, Genealogy, and Morality: Essays on Nietzsche's* On the Genealogy of Morals, edited by Richard Schacht. Berkeley: University of California Press, 1994.

Cox, Christoph. *Nietzsche: Naturalism and Interpretation.* Berkeley: University of California Press, 1999.

Han-Pile, Béatrice. "Nietzsche's Metaphysics in *The Birth of Tragedy.*" *European Journal of Philosophy* 14, no. 3 (2006): 373–403.

Hatab, Lawrence J. *Nietzsche's Life Sentence: Coming to Terms with Eternal Recurrence.* New York: Routledge, 2005.

———. *Nietzsche's* On the Genealogy of Morality: *An Introduction.* Cambridge: Cambridge University Press, 2008.

Heidegger, Martin. *Nietzsche.* Translated by David F. Krell. New York: Harper Collins, 1991.

Nietzsche, Friedrich. *Beyond Good and Evil.* In *Basic Writings of Nietzsche.* Edited and translated by Walter Kaufmann. New York: Random House, 1966.

———. *The Birth of Tragedy.* In *Basic Writings of Nietzsche.* Edited and Translated by Walter Kaufmann. New York: Random House, 1966.

———. *Daybreak.* Translated by R. J. Hollingdale. Cambridge: Cambridge University Press, 1982.

———. *Ecce Homo.* In *Basic Writings of Nietzsche.* Edited and translated by Walter Kaufmann. New York: Random House, 1966.

———. *The Gay Science.* Translated by Walter Kaufmann. New York: Random House, 1974.

———. *On the Genealogy of Morality.* Edited by Keith Ansell-Pearson. Translated by Carol Diethe. Cambridge: Cambridge University Press, 2007.

———. *Sämtliche Werke: Kritische Studienausgabe.* Edited by G. Colli and M. Montinari. Berlin: Walter de Gruyter, 1967.

———. *Twilight of the Idols*. In *The Portable Nietzsche*. Edited and translated by Walter Kaufmann. New York: Penguin, 1976.

———. *The Will to Power*. Translated by Walter Kaufmann and R. J. Hollingdale. New York: Random House, 1967.

Schacht, Richard. "Nietzschean Normativity." In *Nietzsche's Postmoralism*, edited by Richard Schacht. Cambridge: Cambridge University Press, 2001.

14 The Object of Phenomenology

Didier Franck

> And in a word: it is perhaps, in the entire unfolding of the spirit, a matter of the body.
> —*Kritische Studienausgabe* 10, 24 [16], 655

"This universal *a priori* of correlation between experienced object and manners of givenness," Husserl confided two years before his death, "affected me so deeply that my whole subsequent life-work has been dominated by the task of systematically elaborating on this *a priori* of correlation."[1] The discovery of this universal a priori, which is none other than that of intentionality, signifies that every being, whatever its meaning, points toward a subjective system of lived experiences; that every being, whatever its region of origin, is the object of a consciousness, or again that its objectivity is phenomenality itself. Thus the intentional analysis aligns itself with those objects whose variety it alone can manifest, thanks to its return to their modes of being given.[2] This alignment implies that the object gives itself prior to any clarification of its noetico-noematic structures, which precisely weave together what is given, such that phenomenology, as the absolute science of constituting consciousness, nevertheless takes its point of departure in an object both constituted and relative. Here, once again, the beginning proves to be the outcome, the result.

According to an expression from the *Cartesian Meditations*, the object is thus indeed the guiding thread necessary for exploring the syntheses of intentional life. Phenomenology is the constitutive system of all possible objects of consciousness. In the fashion of constitution itself, this system is stratified. The material ontologies concerned with objects of an eidetically circumscribed and defined region are subordinated to a formal ontology concerned with the object in general. Transcendent objects[3] are nevertheless not the only guiding thread possible, since those immanent acts, by which objects are given up to the gaze, can likewise take on this guiding function as the objects of internal time consciousness, which self-constitutes in an absolutely unique manner. Formal ontology thus presupposes transcendental egology.

If the object, in the expanded sense that Husserl gave it, is indeed a guiding thread, then the guiding thread is always an example, which is to say, a specimen and a model. The choice of exemplary object therefore will not be accidental; it will be commanded by the very meaning of the intentionality to which it opens an access. What, then, is the privileged thread guiding constitutive reflection? Is it the immanent temporal object or the transcendent object? Despite the ultimate character of the investigations devoted to the temporal self-constitution of the *ego*, the pure lived experience could not be the guiding thread of intentional description, as the central problem of phenomenology, that is, the origin of transcendence, cannot be confused with the fundamental problem of the origin of intentionality back to which acts alone can lead us. From the time of his 1907 lectures on *The Idea of Phenomenology*, Husserl endeavored to understand how an absolutely self-enclosed consciousness could emerge from itself and posit something that would be opposed, or counterposed, to it qua object. In other words, constitutive analysis, designed to resolve the enigma of transcendence, is necessarily guided by a transcendent object.

Yet is this object real or ideal? To reach the structures of intentionality, must we follow the constitution of a physical thing or that of an exact essence? The response seems easy enough. From his 1887 thesis, *On the Concept of Number*, up to *The Origin of Geometry* in 1936, the mathematical object would be the permanent theme of phenomenological contemplation. Moreover when, in 1929, Husserl wrote that his 1891 *Philosophy of Arithmetic* was "the first investigation that sought to make 'categorical objectivities' of the first level and of higher levels (sets and cardinal numbers of a higher ordinal level) understandable on the basis of the 'constituting' intentional activities,"[4] did he not tacitly grant that the constitution of formal objects was the paradigm of all constitution in general?

That number would thus have been the initial motif of constitutive analysis does not suffice in making the ideal object into the guiding thread required by and for the study of consciousness. Indeed as long as psychologism is not surmounted—as it will be in the *Logical Investigations*—the authentic meaning of ideality will not be set forth and, in a certain sense, number will remain understood as a reality. The first object of constitutive analysis is therefore not ideal. What, then, is the nature of the objects whose constitution is retraced by the *Logical Investigations*? It is not general objects but rather a box, an inkwell, a book, a house—in short, real, everyday things.[5] Furthermore, with the extension of the concept of intuition to the categorial sphere proceeding in an analogical manner, taking sensuous or "external" intuition for its reference, the constitution of ideal objects is aligned with that of the real objects that are their bedrock. Consequently it is the region of things,[6] to borrow the title of §150 of the *Ideas I*, that serves as the transcendental guiding thread, or clue, in phenomenological investigation.[7] There is nothing arbitrary about this, since it is spatiotemporal and material thingness[8] that forms the fundamental layer of all worldly experience.

If the real object is indeed the principal, regulative structure of intentional syntheses, it remains the case that, for phenomenology, the ideal object is the ideal of the object. Why is this so, and from where does it derive this distinction? Only an analysis of the respective constitution of real objects and of ideal objects can cast light on the phenomenological grounds for the superiority of the latter relative to the former. The constitutive differences between these two types of object are described at length in a chapter of *Experience and Judgment*.[9] I will retain only that which is directly significant for my argument. After having recalled that the apprehension of an object supposes that it is given in advance, Husserl sets forth an initial difference: the objects of receptivity are passively pregiven; they are there before I turn toward them; the objects of understanding are pregiven in predicative spontaneity. This difference in the mode of pregivenness implies a difference in the very essence of the objects. For every sensuous object, "its being apprehended is nonessential," whereas the intelligible object "*can essentially be constituted only in a spontaneous productive activity, therefore, under the condition of the being-there [Dabeisein] of the ego.*"[10] What should this mean if not that the ideal object is an object reduced from the outset to its appearing for a consciousness, an object purely phenomenological, indeed the *phenomeno*-logical object par excellence.

A second—and more profound—difference between these two classes of objects resides in their temporality. Whereas the real object is situated in objective time, dated in some sense, the unreal object, "*at all times* the same,"[11] is supratemporal, and this supratemporality or omnitemporality is a mode of temporality. As a result, the ideal object is the sole object liable to be absolutely true if, on the one hand, "it is the ideality of the truth that constitutes its objectivity"[12] and since, on the other hand, it belongs to all truth in itself,[13] to all truth of reason to be omnitemporal, eternal. The ideal object is, properly speaking, the object of knowledge, essentially designed for truth, relieved of all contingent facticity, the object most purely objective—in short, the object of phenomeno-*logy* as the science of essences.

Is it not strange, then, if by "guiding thread" one understands the exemplary being whose analysis brings to light the being of all beings, that phenomenology, in search of the meaning of objectivity, should choose to align itself on the real object and not on the ideal object, whose objectivity is absolute? Necessarily dictated by intentionality itself, this choice suggests that the true guiding object is neither real nor ideal, and that to reach the being of intentionality and, beyond that, to comprehend the historic signification of Husserl's phenomenology, it will not suffice to start from one or the other of these objects. Thus we will attempt to reach intentionality, taking for our guide—if only on a transitional basis—an object that is neither real nor ideal, because it is both real *and* ideal: the spiritualized object or that "vested with spirit."

These objects form the theme of a paragraph in the *Ideen II*. Let us restore their immediate context. Husserl there describes the mode of being given of the other person. If the living body (*Leib*) of the foreign person is indeed given to me like all the objects of my environment, that does not imply that the other *ego* might be tied to his flesh like a thing. Indeed I do not see a flesh *and* a mind or spirit but rather another man. To perceive the flesh of the other person is to perceive the other himself. A flesh appears to me, which resembles my own. By virtue of this resemblance, the flesh that presents itself is apprehended as pointing toward another psychic life, to which, in principle, I could not have direct access. The neighbor thus forms the object of a presentation interwoven with appresentation. Husserl can thus open section 56*h*, asserting, "The thoroughly intuitive unity presenting itself when we grasp a person *as such* . . . is the unity of the '*expression*' and the '*expressed*' that belongs to the essence of all comprehensive unities."[14] The other person is therefore the primary example of an object vested with spirit or with a unity of comprehension. To what concept of comprehension is Husserl here appealing? Doubtlessly to that defined by Dilthey when he calls comprehension "the process by which we know an interiority starting from signs that are given to us externally in a sensuous fashion."[15] To comprehend is thus to apprehend the relationship between interiority and exteriority as an expression of the one in and through the other. The fleshly movements of an *alter ego* express his spiritual life, and I understand him if I posit this life on the basis of his movements, intuitively grasping the unity of flesh and spirit, of the flesh and the subject of intentionality.

The other person is nevertheless not the sole object vested with spirit, and, in order to reach the essence of these objects, it is fitting that we vary them. The second example Husserl adduces is a book. When I read a book, I see marks on the pages; I see an extended thing. Is it nevertheless toward this that I am oriented when I read? Evidently not. While perceiving a thing, I am turned toward the meaning of the printed sentences; I understand and undergo them in comprehension. How to analyze this situation? We cannot say that, in reading, I would have to deal with two objects, the volume and the sense, set side by side, for to be conscious of a book is not to aim at two objects conjoined in an extrinsic manner but rather to aim at one and the same object in which the corporeal and the spiritual are melded. To be sure, the same book can be the object of two distinct attitudes: I can either pay attention to what is material by considering only its spatial existence or the size of the type, or I can make the text and its ideal contents the center of my interest. Notwithstanding, it is to the book that I have before me that I attribute a meaning; it is this book that is animated by an intention. "The book, with its paper pages, its binding, etc., is a thing. It is not that to this thing would be attached another thing, the meaning, but rather, in a certain way, the latter *crosses through* the physical whole, 'animating' it,"[16] writes Husserl, adding the following observation, which applies to all objects vested with spirit: "The spiritual sense animating the sensuous appearances is, in some way, *fused* with them rather than being simply tied to them through juxtaposition."[17]

Objects vested with spirit are thus essentially characterized by the fusion of the sensuous and the intelligible, the real and the ideal. What does this fusion signify? To

what phenomena does it refer? From whence comes the concept itself? Husserl immediately credits it to Carl Stumpf, who, in his *Tonpsychologie*, responds to the question
of whether a musical chord is perceived as an undifferentiated unity or as a simultaneous plurality by introducing the descriptive notion of fusion, understood as "the
relationship between two contents, especially two contents of sensation, according to
which they do not form a mere sum but rather a whole."[18] For Stumpf, fusion is a mode
of unification of sensuous data preserving their individuality and independent of any
categorial acts. But does it denote the same thing for Husserl, who refers to it in the
Philosophy of Arithmetic at the moment he explains the instantaneous apprehension of
multiplicities? It is a question of understanding, for example, how, in raising my eyes
toward the sky, I can, with a mere glance, judge that there are many stars up there.
The representation of such a multiplicity is not a true representation of multiplicity,
because I do not first apprehend each star in order, only thereupon to apprehend, in
a single higher order act,[19] the ensemble that they form. Husserl thus supposes "that,
in the intuition of a sensuous multiplicity, there are *immediately apprehended indices*
on whose basis one may recognize this character of multiplicity."[20] Given that these
signs could hardly belong to each of the members of the multiplicity, or even to each
of their relations, we must allow that "the complexes of relations that embrace the
global multiplicity fuse, all of them or one by one, into fixed unities that confer to the
global appearance of the multiplicity an *immediately notable, particular character*, so
to say, a sensuous quality of a second order."[21] Experience confirms the existence of
these "quasi-qualitative moments," of these "figural moments": we perceive a row of
soldiers, a bunch of apples, an avenue of trees, a flock of birds, a gaggle of geese. The
expressions *row, bunch, avenue*, and so on do not merely signify the plural, but still
more "a certain *complexion characteristic* of the aggregate intuition of the whole of that
multiplicity."[22] The figural moments are thus unities in which the particularities of the
sensuous contents, or their relations, fuse into a quasi-quality. And Husserl specifies
that "this fusing is precisely analogous to that which Stumpf discovered in the qualities
of simultaneous sensations,"[23] since the elements that fuse into a whole or an all are not
themselves modified by the fusion. This analogy must nevertheless not hide a difference. Indeed from the publication of the *Philosophy of Arithmetic* up to *Experience and
Judgment*, Husserl never ceases expanding the sphere of fusion phenomena beyond
sensuous and simultaneous contents. He will extend this sphere to successive contents
by exhibiting, for example, the continuous fusion to which the object perceived owes
its unity; he will extend it to intentional contents, qualifying the primal intuition as a
fusion of pure sense with incarnate fullness, and finally to the entire field of receptivity
in which he sees a form of passive synthesis.[24] On each occasion the fusion produces
first an "appearance of unity" that is dissipated upon analysis. Consequently it is but a
πρότερον πρός ἡμᾶς (*proteron pròs hēmas*, the prior or initial toward us).[25]

Let us return to objects vested with spirit whose unity is constituted by the
fusion of sensuous appearances and intelligible sense. This determination holds for

everything having to do with comprehension, whether this concerns the other person or a book, an ideal object or a work of art, a usable object or an institution—in short, it concerns all objects of the ambient world of everyday life. However, as we have seen, each of these objects can likewise be apprehended as a simple thing. This implies, conversely, that the ideal sense is in some cases tied to reality, while in others it is without relation to reality. Should we conclude from this that sense itself becomes a reality when it animates the sensuous and fuses with it? Not at all, and we need only vary our examples to show this. Consider the case of a literary work. The sounds and rhythms of a poem come under the jurisdiction of sensibility, even as they remain a part of the ideal unity of sense. They are therefore never the objects of an existence thesis,[26] since the spiritual sense contains the sensuous one, to which it confers an "inner life,"[27] with which it enters into a fusion without losing its ideality. Are there nevertheless not counterexamples? When I take hold of a spoon, is the perception of its real form not necessary to comprehending its sense, and is this sense not adjoined externally to the object perceived? It is not; for to see a spoon as an object of use is to apprehend its form within the horizon of its signification; it is to grasp that the sense requires the sensuous form with which it fuses. Consequently I could not consider, for itself, the real form nor effect a positing of existence without changing attitudes. The spoon is not an enduring physical thing endowed with ontologically distinct, axiological predicates, but an object wherein the sensuous fuses with the intelligible.

Objects vested with spirit thus possess "a sensuous flesh that is not an existent flesh,"[28] some flesh that, in the style of the noema-in-general, is neither real nor imaginary. Description of these objects allows a sensibility peculiar to spirit, to mind, to appear, a kind of spiritual sensibility, a spirituality that contains or conceals the sensuous; it manifests the flesh of the spirit, which is ultimately to say, the flesh of intentionality and of sense. It is not only the a priori forms of sensibility that are ideal but, in a certain way, sensibility itself, and, after having proposed categorial ideality to intuition, Husserl here proposes intuitive sensibility to ideality. This double gesture engages nothing less than a reinterpretation of the *Critique of Pure Reason* and of Kantian thought. I will return to this shortly.

The preceding analysis, which to Husserl's eyes remains highly insufficient, above all raises a fundamental problem. The objects of the everyday world (which world includes everything up to mathematical idealities),[29] are all objects vested with spirit, whose unity is constituted through some fusion. It is in the midst of this surrounding pregiven world that the theoretical attitude arises, having, for its correlate, nature understood as the domain of material realities. Now if the sole objects with which we would first have to do are unities produced by fusions,[30] and if the fusion is a πρότερον πρὸς ἥμᾶς (*proteron pròs hēmas*), then whence do we derive the possibility of considering a book as a simple thing, or sense as purely ideal? How can we dissociate phenomenologically what is given to us in unity, in its unity? Whence arises the fission of sense and the sensuous? What is the source of the operative concepts with which we analyze fused objects?[31] Furthermore, if "the concepts of the *ego* and the surrounding world are inseparably tied the one to the other," then how to distinguish the transcendental *ego* from the worldly *ego* without grasping sense in its pure state by isolating it from the sensuous? The problem raised by the description of objects vested with spirit is therefore that of the motivation for the reduction, the problem of setting the intentional analytic into motion. We cannot attribute the difficulty to some register of "metaphysical assumptions" in Husserlian phenomenology, for recourse to such "assumptions" is never wholly without foundations in the things themselves. It is consequently a matter of knowing whether there is an object vested with spirit and whose essence it is to reveal—in certain phenomenal conditions liable to be repeated or reactivated—a fissioning of sense and the sensuous that could thereupon be extended to all objects of the same type. In other words, is there an object vested with spirit that, implied by all the others, could lead to their common being? The fundamental problem posed by the constitution of objects vested with spirit is accordingly that of the phenomenal origin of phenomenology, the problem of its guiding thread.

Having set forth the ideal sensibility proper to the configurations of "objective mind,"[32] Husserl returns to his first example: the other person. To see another human being is not to perceive the real composition of soul and body. The constitutive apprehension of the other person is not, in effect, simply directed upon the appearing flesh; rather it crosses through it to fuse with it. To have the experience of an *alter ego* and, beyond this, of myself as a human being amounts to intending or aiming at an *ego* to whom this incarnation belongs. I do not grasp a mind stitched into a flesh but a mind in the medium of its flesh. We are thus initially fused wholes, and if "the flesh is, qua flesh, a flesh thoroughly filled with soul," then conversely the soul itself is thoroughly incarnate. In light of this, how and on the basis of what is it possible to distinguish the soul from the flesh, sense from the sensuous,[33] the transcendental *ego* from the human *ego*?

In order to answer this question, we might start by recalling that the flesh is not an object of some kind but "the condition of possibility of all other objects," "the foundation of all objectivity," or, according to the expression in the *Cartesian Meditations*, "the object [that is] first in itself." The animate flesh is thus the sole object vested with spirit whose fission can bring about that of all the others. Now this flesh is also a body, and these two phenomena are at once radically separated and radically conjoined. They are separated because the body, as an extended thing, is not my flesh understood as the support of kinestheses; it is not the organ of the will or the center of orientation. These are tied because my flesh, which is never given outside of a coupling with another flesh, is always and for this reason one body among bodies in the midst of an intersubjective nature. When the flesh is embodied, its sense separates, abstracts itself from the sensuous,[34] and this disjunction extends to all the objects vested with spirit. This concerns the man that I am: in uncoupling my *ego* from the unity it constitutes with its flesh and the surrounding world, embodiment opens access to the transcendental *ego*, and this concerns the other, everyday objects: the fission of the flesh into soul and body yields ideal sense since it liberates it from that which, in a certain way, is equally a reality. Spirit or mind, the subject of intentionality,[35] is therefore no longer anything other than the being external to itself of the flesh; pure subjectivity and the ideality of sense are henceforth but moments of the relationship of the flesh to the body, and the eidetic and phenomenological reductions are effects of the relation of one flesh to another.[36]

We have now reached the object vested with spirit, whose fission commands that of all the others. The animate flesh, the living flesh, is thus the true guiding thread of the intentional analytic. And if the real object and the ideal object have, each in its turn, proved capable of fulfilling this function, then that is because, in light of the mode of donation, the ideality and reality of objects that, starting with the *Logical Investigations*, have an exemplary role are accessible only on the basis of the fission of the flesh. The constitution is thus always a reconstitution. Husserl admits this when, with respect to the other person, he specifies, not without some discomfiture, that the objectivation of the layer of sense is superposed on that of the corporeal layer "in such a way that what is constituted is the unity of an Object, one which in turn (without any kind of binding parts that would presuppose a prior separation) involves Objective strata of lower and higher levels, distinguishable only *after the fact*."[37]

With the guiding thread determined, in other words, that object through which objectivity comes to light or the phenomenon that attests phenomenality, it is possible to elucidate intentionality itself. If it is the flesh that is the support of redoubled sensations,[38] then the being of sensation will lead us to that of intentionality. Husserl generally defines sensation as the nonintentional component of lived experience, as a matter that is subject to the apprehension or grasp that bestows sense and interprets. And yet, negative and relative to intentionality, this definition offers no support when it comes to thinking intentionality itself. It will thus be necessary, first, to characterize sensation in a positive manner in order to arrive thereafter at the principle of phenomenology. At the end of section 15b of the fifth *Investigation*, a paragraph devoted to actions and sensations in the sphere of affectivity, Husserl added a brief note:

> The obvious tendency of our conception is to attribute primary, genuine differences in intensity to underlying sensations, and to concrete acts only in a secondary manner, in so far as their concrete total character involves differences of intensity in their sensational basis. *Act intentions . . . must be without intrinsic intensity.* Deeper analyses are, however, required here.[39]

Sensations are thus intensive. The being of sensation is intensity incarnate: the drive. The flesh is drive-based, and intentionality must be understood as instinctually driven.[40]

Is it nevertheless not contradictory, even absurd to conceive of intentionality starting from what is not intentional by reversing the priority of intention over sensation? From whence does the drive's determination of intentionality gain its legitimacy?

I must first point out that Husserl does not rule out the possibility that the intention might possess an intensity of its own; he speaks of this in the conditional and refers to future analyses. Consequently nothing prevents us from restoring *intention* and *intension* to their common root. I should add, further, that it is precisely at the heart of the pure givenness of sensation that immanent temporality is constituted. Now, at this level—that of the true and ultimate absolute—the subordination of sensuous *hylē* to the intentional *morphē* is inverted, to the benefit of *hylē*, since the proto-impression is the "primal source of all further consciousness and being."[41] Finally, and above all, we should recall that Husserl himself understood intentionality as drive-based. In his 1933 *Universal Teleology*, after having qualified the sphere proper to the system of the drives and the constant flow, he asks, "Shouldn't we or mustn't we posit a universal intentionality of the drive which unifies every original presence as permanence of a temporalization which concretely moves it forward from presence to presence in such a way that all content is the content of the realization of the drives and it is determined by the goal toward which the drive aims?"[42] Thus intentionality indeed has a drive structure and the teleology in which transcendental phenomenology is fulfilled reveals a drive character[43] out of which come the *ego*, other people, and the world.

One difficulty remains. Everything I have just established requires that my flesh (*Leib*) take shape or be embodied by virtue of its essential bond with another flesh. What, however, allows us to assert that the relation to another flesh is a sense-element of my own flesh? What is it that relates my flesh to another one? Abstracting from the question of whether all fleshly drives[44] are or are not sexual, Husserl notes that there in the sexual drive "lies the relation to the other as other and to its correlative drive."[45] Thus sexuality is that by which my own flesh is always related to another. Sexual difference therefore allows us to grasp how and why my flesh is embodied in being associated with that of another person. We could nevertheless not describe this embodiment, nor distinguish flesh from body, without acceding respectively to the one and to the other. Now while the body appears in perception, what is the mode of donation of the flesh itself? Since sexual difference is at once a fleshly or lived bodily (*leiblich*) characteristic and the ground of embodiment (*Verkörperung*),[46] the question must take the following form: Is there a phenomenal situation in which the sexual difference, which constitutes the separation of bodies between the other person and myself, is suspended as the foundation of embodiment without also being suspended in its lived, fleshly characteristic? Or is there a situation in which my drive flesh unites and fuses with that of the other person? After having pointed out that the sexual drive finds its mode of fulfillment in copulation, defined as a *crossing through* one drive intentionality by another, in short, as a fusion, Husserl analyzes the originary mode of drive fulfillment in this way: "In the simple fulfillment of the primary mode [*urmodale Erfüllung*] we never have two separate fulfillments of each drive in the one and in the other primordiality [*Primordialität*], but rather one unity arises through the reciprocal fulfillment [*das Ineinander der Erfüllungen*] of the two primordialities."[47] The copulation that should here be set apart from all corporeal signification is thus that exceptional phenomenal situation in which two intentionalities, coming from respective spheres that in principle are radically separate, are merged in having only a single and common fulfillment. In bringing to light, as if through a reduction, a drive flesh located outside all embodiment, copulation is not a factical event liable not to take place but a pure possibility, constantly opened by the sexuality of the drive, by drive intentionality itself, a possibility without which no other reduction, be it transcendental or eidetic, could be performed.

Let us return, one last time, to section 56*h* of the *Ideas II*. After having described the apprehension of the other person as an apprehension for which the apprehension of the flesh constitutes the bedrock for the apprehension of sense, Husserl continues by observing that the same fusion phenomenon takes place between the word *flesh* and the sense that animates it.[48] Language is thus an object vested with sense, and this determination will be taken up in *Formal and Transcendental Logic*. Not only does Husserl there characterize the ideality of language as that of an object of the world of culture, but he further specifies that "to *the unity of discourse* corresponds a *unity of [intentional] aiming*, to the forms and articulations of discourse correspond the forms and articulations of the aim."[49] The aim, he adds, "does not lie externally beside the words; rather, in speaking we are continuously performing an internal act of meaning, which fuses with the words and, as it were, animates them. The effect of this animation is that the words and the entire locution, *embody* in themselves a meaning, and bear it embodied in them as their sense."[50] Does language not, consequently, raise the same problem as did the other objects vested with spirit? From what phenomenological evidence can Husserl analyze expression according to "the familiar distinction between the sensuous, so to speak, the corporeal side . . . and its nonsensuous, 'mental' side?"[51] How are these two sides given separately if the fusion is a πρότερον πρὸς ἡμᾶς (*proteron pròs hēmas*)? Does the embodiment of the flesh stand at the origin of the fission of language? It is impossible to respond to the latter question without first examining whether the locution *linguistic flesh* is a metaphor or a denomination coming from the things themselves. The examination must be phenomenological and founded on the mode of donation. Husserl justifiably speaks of a "flesh of language" and, more generally, of a "flesh of the mind," because, in every case, it is a question of phenomena to which we would never accede if we were not incarnate subjects, indeed phenomena to which we would never accede if intentionality were not of a drive nature. That which is given solely to and through my flesh can be legitimately named on the basis of the donating instance or entity that shows an affinity of essence. The term *linguistic flesh*[52] denotes a singular phenomenon; it is not metaphoric, and the fission of language indeed comes to pass when the flesh is embodied, giving rise to the separation of sense and the sensuous. Such is no doubt the reason why the phenomenology of language is most often ordered according to the "metaphysical" distinction between soul and body.

Once again, a difficulty remains. Did our interpretation not assume a language whose two sides are merged? In effect, if the scission of the lived bodily and the spiritual sides of language is a consequence of embodiment, then the suspension of embodiment, the reduction of the lived fleshly body, must free the possibility of a language in which sound and sense, even its graphemes, are originally fused. What is this language apt to manifest fleshly subjectivity? At the moment Husserl sets forth the idea of ideal sensibility, as we have seen, he has recourse to the example of the poem. Now poetic language is the language in which sound, sense, and rhythm are from the outset fused together, a language for which significations are not exclusively *objective*, and thus the only language appropriate to an incarnate *subjectivity*. The poem of the flesh is the transcendental logos, and, for the absolute subjectivity of the drive flux, it is only *theoretical* names that we lack.[53]

Let me take up anew my original intention and argument. I sought to identify the guiding object of intentional analysis in order to accede to intentionality itself and to determine the global signification of Husserl's thought. Are we now in a position to accomplish this task? Can we characterize the historical situation of transcendental phenomenology when it comprises the sphere of the flesh and of drive life?[54]

I indicated earlier that the idealization of sensibility and the expansion of intuition into the categorial sphere called for a repetition of the *Critique of Pure Reason*. It is time now to specify what this means. If Husserl considered the first version of the transcendental deduction to be Kant's "approach to a direct grounding, one which descends to the original sources,"[55] this is because he there encountered the problem of the foundation of objectivity, for which the correlational a priori is the true solution. Wherein lies, then, for the community of transcendental philosophy, the difference between Husserl and Kant? The Kantian deduction had judgment for its guiding thread; Husserlian constitution has the object as its guiding thread. What governs this substitution? The discovery of the categorial intuition, which implies that every category is a grounded object[56] that could not, for this reason, prescribe or dictate objectivity as such. In other words, the transcendental deduction is ordered according to judgment because transcendental apperception is a constituted consciousness. Hence the replacement of one guiding thread for another, that of judgment by the object intended, allows us to work back to constituting consciousness. And if, for phenomenology, the object that is first in itself is the flesh, then the transcendental deduction of the categories must give way to what Husserl named, in a text devoted to the constitution of objectivity, a "transcendental deduction of the flesh [*Leib*]."[57] The transcendental deduction of the categories is grounded on the transcendental deduction of the flesh as constituted subjectivity is founded upon constituting subjectivity. And even though the effectuation of the deduction of the flesh overflows the juridical and transcendental framework from which it comes, it will always include—albeit in a subordinate respect—a reinterpretation of the *Critique of Pure Reason*.

"The secret nostalgia of all modern philosophy,"[58] transcendental phenomenology fulfills the absolutization of subjectivity by securing the passage from the constituted, logical subject to the constituting, drive subject. The fact remains that Husserl never interrogated, for itself, this flesh that his intentional analysis ultimately laid bare. Why is there no phenomenology of the flesh? Why did Husserl not thematize this phenomenon that must accompany all phenomena, since it characterizes the originary *datum*? Fleshly drives, the drive flesh, are the object of no description other than oblique mentions because, in a certain sense, Husserl could not see them. He comes to the flesh from subjectivity, within the horizon of unity, identity, and the synthesis in general, a horizon within which the irreducible difference of the drives could not, as a matter of principle, appear. In short, if the flesh is indeed the guiding object of transcendental phenomenology, then Husserl never considered it such, nor did he take it for his point of departure.

The interpretation of the flesh thus requires a change in the orientation of our gaze. Can we define this change? The emergence of the flesh against the grain of consciousness[59] at least signifies that it is subjectively unthinkable. The only path that then opens is that of Nietzsche: to deliberately take the body as one's point of departure and guiding thread. However, this reversal, which can take place only at the end of the absolutization of subjectivity, is not without consequences for phenomenology itself. There results, first, a profound modification of the concept of flesh: it is no longer the support of kinestheses, but a hierarchized plurality of forces or drives. The abrogation of the privilege of the *ego* then follows: it is no longer the apodictic foundation of being and knowing but an effect of the body, an illusion of perspective. Finally, it follows that sense is no longer separable from force: Husserl's constitutive analysis is transformed into a morphology of the will to power, into a genealogy.

Understood in light of the guiding thread of the flesh, phenomenology thus reveals by itself its own historic site: by elucidating the presuppositions of Kantian thought, the constitutive analysis prepares the way for the Nietzschean reversal. But how shall we think the historicity of this situation? Arising neither from a history of the pure reason that is essentially dependent on a constituted subjectivity nor from a universal teleology whose drive foundation remains inconceivable in terms of intentionality, phenomenology can only belong, ultimately, to the history of the body itself. Is this possible without the body being, itself, historical? And has it ever been interpreted in such a way as to be able to be historical? It has, precisely by Nietzsche, who, in 1884–85, wrote this:

Assuming that "the soul" was an attractive and mysterious thought, from which philosophers were right to separate with reluctance—perhaps that which they henceforth learn to accept in exchange is still more attractive, more mysterious. The human body, in which the entire past of organic becoming, from the most distant to the most proximate, lives on and is embodied, through which, over which and beyond which seems to flow an immense inaudible stream: the lived body [*Leib*] is a thought more astonishing than the old "soul."[60]

Notes

This essay was translated by Bettina Bergo. Originally published as "L'objet de la phénoménologie," in *Dramatique des phénomènes*, 57–74.

Franck cites all posthumous notes from the Colli-Montinari edition. The original of the epigraph reads: "Und kurz gesagt: es handelt sich vielleicht bei der ganzen Entwicklung des Geistes um den Leib."—Trans.

1. Husserl, *Die Krisis*, §48, n1, 169 (hereafter Hua VI); *Crisis*, 166.

2. Franck writes *"modes de donnée."*—Trans.

3. In Husserl's terminology, a "transcendent object" is an object identified or constituted as outside, in the world, that is, transcendent relative to a constituting consciousness—Trans.

4. Husserl, *Formale und transzendentale Logik*, §27a, 90–91 (hereafter Hua XVII).

5. Hua XVII, §27a, 90–91; *Formal and Transcendental Logic*, 87.

6. Franck writes *"la région chose."*—Trans.

7. Husserl, *Ideas Pertaining to a Pure Phenomenology*, §150, "Continuation: The Region, Physical Thing, as Transcendental Clue," 359–62 (hereafter *Ideas I*); *Ideen zu einer reinen Phänomenologie und phänomenologischen Philosophie*, 313–16 (hereafter Hua III).

8. Franck writes *"chóséité spatio-temporelle et matérielle."*—Trans.

9. Husserl. *Erfahrung und Urteil; Experience and Judgment*, part II, "Predicative Thought and the Objectivities of Judgment," 197–269.

10. Husserl, *Erfahrung und Urteil*, §63, 300–301; *Experience and Judgment*, 251. [Translation modified for fluency with the French original —Trans.]

11. *Erfahrung und Urteil*, §64c, 311; *Experience and Judgment*, 258–61.

12. Husserl, "Prolegomena zur reinen Logik," in *Logische Untersuchungen*, Erster Teil, §51, 191.

13. Franck writes *"vérité en soi."*—Trans.

14. Husserl, *Ideen II*, 236 (hereafter Hua IV); *Ideas II*, 248. The text of this paragraph comes from a manuscript from 1913, titled *The Constitution of the World of the Spirit*, which the editors, Edith Stein and Ludwig Landgrebe, cut out and inserted between two other manuscripts from 1916. See Walter Biemel's remarks in Hua IV, 397ff, 416 (ad. *Beilage* VI) and 426.

15. Dilthey, *Die Entstehung der Hermeneutik*, 318; "The Rise of Hermeneutics," 235–59. Husserl refers to Dilthey at the beginning of the third section of Hua IV, §48, 181.

16. Husserl, *Ideen II*, §56, in Hua IV, 238 .

17. Hua IV, §56h, 238; *Ideas II*, 249–50. [Translation modified for fluency with the French original. —Trans.]

18. Stumpf, *Tonpsychologie*, 128. Also see 64ff; Gurwitsch, *Théorie du champ de la conscience* and *The Collected Works of Aron Gurwitsch*.

19. Franck writes *"un acte unique de degré supérieur."*—Trans.

20. Husserl, *Philosophie der Arithmetik*, 201 (hereafter Hua XII); *Philosophy of Arithmetic*, 213.

21. Hua XII 201; *Philosophy of Arithmetic*, 213.

22. Hua XII, 204; *Philosophy of Arithmetic*, 216.

23. Hua XII, 206; *Philosophy of Arithmetic*, 218.

24. Hua XVII, III, §§8, 9, VI, §29; *Logical Investigations*, 448–53 (§§8–9), 745–48 (§29); Hua III, §136; *Ideas I*, 326–29; *Erfahrung und Urteil*, §16; *Experience and Judgment*, 72–76.

25. Cf. Hua XII, 201; *Philosophy of arithmetic*, 213.

26. Franck writes *"thèse d'existence."*—Trans.

27. Hua IV, §56h, n1, 239; *Ideas II*, 251.

28. Hua IV, §56h, 243; *Ideas II*, 255.

29. Compare with Hua IV, §51, 193; *Ideas II*, 203.

30. Franck writes *"unités fusionnées."*—Trans.

31. Franck writes *"objets fusionnés."*—Trans.

32. Franck writes, *"esprit objectif."*—Trans.

33. Franck writes, *"le sens du sensible."*—Trans.

34. Franck writes, *"s'abstrait du sensible."*—Trans.

35. Cf. Hua IV, §55, 216, §56, 220; *Ideas* II, 227 (§55), 231 (§56).

36. For a comprehensive explanation of these remarks, see Franck, *Chair et corps.*—Trans.

37. Hua IV, §56h, 244, Franck's emphasis; *Ideas* II, 256.

38. Hua IV, §§36, 37, 152–59.

39. Husserl, *Logische Untersuchungen*, V, §15, 396–97 (the last sentence was added in the second edition); *Logical Investigations*, 575–76.

40. For "drive-based," Franck writes *"pulsionnelle."* For "instinctually driven," he writes *"pulsionnalité."*—Trans.

41. Husserl, *Zur Phänomenologie des inneren Zeitbewusstseins* §31, 67 (hereafter Hua X); *On the Phenomenology of the Consciousness of Internal Time*, 70.

42. Husserl, *Zur Phänomenologie der Intersubjectivität*, 595 (hereafter Hua XV); "Universal Teleology," 335–38.

43. For "drive structure," Franck writes *"structure de pulsion."* For "drive character," he writes *"pulsionnalité."*—Trans.

44. Franck writes *"pulsion charnelle."*—Trans.

45. Hua XV, 593–94; "Universal Teleology," 335.

46. We generally translate Husserl's term *Leib*, which is the lived body, as "flesh," and *leiblich* as "fleshly" to avoid confusion with *Körper*, which denotes objective bodies, bodies as objects of intentional aiming.—Trans.

47. Hua XV, 594.

48. Hua IV, §56h, 240; *Ideas* II, 252.

49. Hua XVII, §3, 26–27; *Formal and Transcendental Logic*, 22. [Translation modified for fluency with the French original. —Trans.]

50. Hua XVII, § 3, 26–27; *Formal and Transcendental Logic*, 22.

51. Hua III, §124, 303–4; *Ideas I*, 294. [Kersten translates *geistig* invariably as "mental"—Trans.] By introducing this difference at the outset of his explication of the noetico-noematic layer of the "logos," Husserl informs us that it is not necessary to proceed to the elucidation of the fleshly side of expression, nor to that of its union with the spiritual side. That being said, he assures us that these are important phenomenological problems. Cf. *Logische Untersuchungen*, I, §§6, 9, V, §19.

52. See Hua XVII, §2, 25.

53. See Hua X, §36, 75; *On the Phenomenology of the Consciousness of Internal Time*, 79.

54. Franck writes *"pulsionnalité."*—Trans.

55. Hua VI, §28, 106; *Crisis*, 104.

56. Franck writes *"objet fondé."*—Trans.

57. Hua XV, 375.

58. Hua III, § 62,148; *Ideas I*, 142. [Franck translates this as "secret aspiration."—Trans.]

59. Franck writes *"à contre-champ de la conscience."*—Trans.

60. Nietzsche, *Kritische Studienausgabe*, 11, 36 [35], 565.

Bibliography

Dilthey, Wilhelm. *Die Entstehung der Hermeneutik* (1900). In *Gesammelte Schriften*, vol. 5. Stuttgart: Teubner, 1974.

———. "The Rise of Hermeneutics." Translated by Rudolf A. Makkreel and Frederic R. Jameson. In *Wilhelm Dilthey: Selected Works*. Vol. 4: *Hermeneutics and the Study of History*.

Translated by Rudolf A. Makkreel and Frithjof Rodi. Princeton: Princeton University Press, 2010.

Franck, Didier. *Chair et corps: Sur la phénoménologie de Husserl.* Paris: Éditions de Minuit, 1981.

Gurwitsch, Aaron. *The Collected Works of Aron Gurwitsch (1901–1973).* Vol. 3: *The Field of Consciousness: Theme, Thematic Field, and Margin.* Edited by Richard Zaner. Dordrecht: Springer, 2010.

———. *Théorie du champ de la conscience.* Translated by Michel Butor. Paris: Desclée de Brouwer, 1957.

Husserl, Edmund. *The Crisis of European Science and Transcendental Phenomenology.* Translated by David Carr. Evanston, IL: Northwestern University Press, 1970.

———. *Erfahrung und Urteil: Untersuchungen zur Genealogie der Logik.* Edited by Ludwig Landgrebe. London: Allen and Unwin, 1939.

———. *Experience and Judgment.* Translated by J. S. Churchill and Karl Ameriks. Evanston, IL: Northwestern University Press, 1973.

———. *Formal and Transcendental Logic.* Translated by Dorion Cairns. The Hague: Martinus Nijhoff, 1969.

———. *Formale und transzendentale Logik, Versuch einer Kritik der logischen Vernunft. Husserliana XVII.* Edited by Paul Janssen. The Hague: Martinus Nijhoff, 1974.

———. *The Idea of Phenomenology.* Translated by L. Hardy. Dordrecht: Kluwer Academic, 1995.

———. *Ideas Pertaining to a Pure Phenomenology and to a Phenomenological Philosophy: First Book.* Translated by Frank Kersten Dordrecht: Kluwer Academic Publishers, 1982.

———. *Ideas II.* Translated by Richard Rojcewicz and André Schuwer Dordrecht: Kluwer Academic, 1990.

———. *Ideen zu einer reinen Phänomenologie und phänomenologischen Philosophie: Ideen I. Husserliana III.* Edited by Karl Schuhmann. The Hague: Martinus Nijhoff, 1977.

———. *Ideen zur einer reinen Phänomenologie und phänomenologischen Philosophie (Ideen II): Phänomenologische Untersuchungen zur Konstitution. Husserliana IV.* Edited by Marly Biemel. The Hague: Martinus Nijhoff, 1952.

———. *Die Krisis der europäischen Wissenschaften und die transzendentale Phänomenologie: Eine Einleitung in die phänomenologische Philosophie. Husserliana VI.* Edited by Walter Biemel. The Hague: Martinus Nijhoff, 1976.

———. *Logical Investigations.* Translated by J. N. Findlay. New York: Humanities Press, 1970.

———. *Logische Untersuchungen I: Prolegomena zur reinen Logik. Husserliana XVIII.* Edited by Elmar Holenstein. The Hague: Martinus Nijhoff, 1975.

———. *Logische Untersuchungen. Zweiter Teil. Untersuchungen zur Phänomenologie und Theorie der Erkenntnis.* 2 vols. *Husserliana XIX.* Edited by Ursula Panzer. The Hague: Martinus Nijhoff, 1984.

———. *Logische Untersuchungen: Ergänzungsband.* Erster Teil. Entwürfe zur Umarbeitung der VI. Untersuchung und zur Vorrede für die Neuauflage der Logischen Untersuchungen (Sommer 1913). *Husserliana XX/I.* Edited by Ulrich Melle. The Hague: Kluwer Academic, 2002.

———. *Logische Untersuchungen. Ergänzungsband.* Zweiter Teil. Texte für die Neufassung der VI. Untersuchung. Zur Phänomenologie des Ausdrucks und der Erkenntnis (1893/94–1921). *Husserliana XX/II.* Edited by Ulrich Melle. The Hague: Kluwer Academic, 2005.

———. *On the Phenomenology of the Consciousness of Internal Time (1893–1917)*. Translated by John Barnett Brough. Dordrecht: Kluwer Academic, 1991.

———. *Philosophie der Arithmetik. Husserliana XII. Mit ergänzenden Texten (1890–1901)*. Edited by Lothar Eley. The Hague: Martinus Nijhoff, 1970.

———. *Philosophy of Arithmetic (1890–1901)*. Translated by Dallas Willard. Dordrecht: Kluwer Academic, 2003.

———. "Universal Teleology." In *Husserl: Shorter Works*. Edited by Peter McCormick and Frederick Elliston. Translated by Marly Biemel. Notre Dame, IN: University of Notre Dame Press, 1981.

———. *Zur Phänomenologie der Intersubjectivität. Husserliana XV, Texte aus dem Nachlass. Dritter Teil. 1929–35*. Edited by Iso Kern. The Hague: Martinus Nijhoff, 1973.

———. *Zur Phänomenologie des inneren Zeitbewusstesens (1893–1917)*. *Husserliana X*. Edited by Rudolf Boehm. The Hague: Martinus Nijhoff, 1969. Nietzsche, Friedrich. *Kritische Studienausgabe*. Edited by Giorgio Colli and Mazzino Montinari. Berlin: DTV/de Gruyter, 1967–77, 1988.

Stumpf, Carl. *Tonpsychologie*. Vol. 2. Nabu Press, 2010, online.

15 Beyond Phenomenology

Didier Franck

"Beyond phenomenology"—what should this expression mean? To begin with, what is phenomenology or what should we understand by the name, whose formation occurred so late? Through what movement, according to what logic, by virtue of what necessity should phenomenology be carried beyond itself? Moreover, what indeed could be the end or destination of such a movement, when phenomenology asserts and maintains that there is nothing to seek beyond the phenomena?

This taboo nevertheless is but the reverse side of an obligation. While the phenomena cannot be surpassed, it is fitting by contrast to determine which ones they are and what they are. In its most general sense, that is the task that philosophy sets itself from the moment it calls itself phenomenology, and which Husserl attempted to honor. Did he succeed at this, and, above all, to what degree did he succeed? As long as this question remains unanswered, as long as we remain, under the circumstances, unaware of the limits of transcendental and constitutive phenomenology, any attempt to exceed it will only give rise to false starts.

In introducing pure phenomenology as the "fundamental science of philosophy"— and to bring out its novelty as much as its exceptional status—Husserl begins by pointing out that the designation "science of the phenomena" applies to all the sciences of reality. It is in this sense that psychology studies psychical phenomena, that physics has as its object natural phenomena, and history historical phenomena. After this, he specifies:

> However different the sense of the word "phenomenon" may be in these expressions, and whatever the significations it may yet have, it is certain that phenomenology

relates equally to all these "phenomena" and according to all the meanings of the term: however it does so in an entirely different attitude, an attitude in virtue of which each of the senses of phenomenon that the sciences present us, with which we are familiar, is modified in a determinate manner.[1]

In what respect does the phenomenological attitude differ from the scientific attitude? Through what modification can the phenomenon, in its scientific understanding, receive a purely phenomenological sense? And, above all, what is the nature of the connection between subjectivity and phenomenality, when the sense of the latter varies in function of the attitudes taken by the first, by subjectivity?

Let us begin by characterizing the scientific attitude in light of which phenomenology distinguishes itself, using the example of psychology. Psychology is an experimental science that concerns real facts or events. What should this mean other than that the "phenomena" with which it is concerned are inscribed in the spatiotemporal world governed by causality? Psychology thus supposes the real existence of the world, to which belongs the totality of phenomena with which psychology has, and will always have, to be concerned, to know. Whatever the degree of its rigor, psychology—and this applies ultimately to all the regional sciences—presupposes the world as the very ground of its activity. But what is meant here by "presuppose"? To presuppose the world is not simply to take it as real, but even more, and above all, to take as clear and distinct the very sense of this reality—in short, and to speak like Descartes, to inscribe existence and reality among those "notions themselves so clear that one obscures them in attempting to define them."[2] From this moment, and indeed as long as the sense of existence of the world to which, one way or another, all scientific disciplines refer, remains obscure, the philosophy that is their ultimate foundation will always stand in the shadow of skepticism. Science's presupposition of the world thus amounts to slackening reason and, if Europe is the geographical name for philosophical rationality, that is, for an absolute foundation of all possible knowledge, then it is true that "weariness is the greatest danger that threatens Europe."[3]

How to surmount this weariness, which Husserl, after Nietzsche, likewise qualified as the "danger of dangers"? Since the danger concerns the very idea of science, only the recovery[4] of science by itself is liable to save us. But what should we understand by this, other than a returning on itself and to itself, a returning of science to what is most proper to it? If what is proper to science, starting from philosophy, is to be methodical, if method alone guarantees in the final analysis philosophy's scientific status, then is it not through the implementation of "the primal method of all philosophical methods"[5] that reason shall rediscover its pure form and overcome its fatigue? Will the method of methods not respond, then, to the "danger of dangers," as "the true philosophy is the same thing as the true method"?[6]

The phenomenological reduction is this true method, which alone can make its way back to true philosophy, that is, to a philosophy that has finally recognized in phenomenology its fundamental science, the science of its foundation. This has to be emphasized from the outset: "beyond phenomenology" cannot fail to mean "beyond philosophy" such as it has been up to now, and if philosophy merges with and is ultimately the same as metaphysics, then surpassing phenomenology comes down to exceeding the metaphysics that phenomenology attempts to reestablish in its originary truth.[7]

What, then, is the phenomenological reduction? The suspension, the setting aside of the world thesis. How should we understand this, how is such a setting out of play possible, and to what determination of the phenomenon does it lead? To presuppose the world is preeminently to posit it as real:

> I find constantly present, as vis-à-vis, a single spatio-temporal reality, to which I myself belong as well as all other men found therein and who relate to it in the same manner. As an awakened I[8] and in a never-interrupted, coherent experience, I find "reality" [*Wirklichkeit*], the word already states it, as pre-*existing* and *I receive it such as it gives itself to me who am likewise existing*. Any placing in doubt or any rejection of the data of the natural world changes nothing in the *general thesis of the natural attitude*. "The" world qua reality is always there; at the very most, it is, here or there, "otherwise" than I presumed and, if it is necessary to cross out this or that ... as an "appearance" or a "hallucination," then this is relative to the world, which, in the sense of the general thesis, is always existent.[9]

The world thesis is evidently not an act of judging that concerns the reality of its existence, but the most general character of empirical consciousness and the givenness of the world.[10] It is therefore not one thesis among others, but the thesis of theses, since consciousness posits there the very ground of every apophantic judgment and utterance. Nevertheless, is this thesis the work of consciousness alone? And if such were to be the case, how then to understand that the reality of the world—which signifies the ontological independence of the latter relative to consciousness—might be but the intentional production of a consciousness that is transcendent with regard to the world? When clearly understood, these questions converge on that of phenomenality, for, if the reality of the world were to be produced by consciousness, then the world, by contrast—that is, the totality of beings—would be none other than the global phenomenon of that consciousness.

Since it is a matter of elucidating real existence as a characteristic proper to the world for consciousness and, consequently, of seeking the sense of what has always already been found in and through the experience of this consciousness, there is no other path or method to follow than that which consists first in closing in on consciousness alone and putting out of play the characteristic of transcendent reality with which the world is naturally present to consciousness. This, in order to examine thereupon whether and how the consciousness thus reached is liable to confer on the world appearing to it that sense of reality with which it appeared to consciousness. Is this possible? The precedent constituted by Cartesian doubt allows us to respond in the affirmative. Nevertheless if doubting means to hold something as *uncertain*, doubt itself implies two distinct moments: the placing in doubt, which is but a suspension of judgment, and the negation of certitude, which assumes the counterpositing[11] of the world in the form[12] of its of nonbeing:

> In the *attempt to doubt* which accompanies a positing that, as we presuppose, is certain and continued, the "excluding" is brought about in and with a modification of the counter-positing, namely the "*supposition*" of—*non-being* which is, therefore, part of the substratum of the attempt to doubt. In Descartes this part is so predominant that one can say that his attempt to doubt universally is properly an attempt to negate universally.[13]

And, in regard to the supposition of nonbeing, Husserl adds straightaway, "Here, we [will] disregard this part."[14] If Husserl retains of the Cartesian doubt only the moment of putting out of play, this is because, in supposing the non*being* or the non*reality* of the world, Descartes continues to hold the meaning of being and of the reality of the world as intelligible, clear, and distinct—to say nothing of the meaning of the negation, although it was precisely a question of ultimately undertaking its elucidation. In certain regards, and already for Husserl, Descartes did not make explicit the meaning of reality, which is to say of the being of the world. The phenomenological reduction is thus indeed the point of departure of a clarification of the meaning of being qua consciousness and reality.

What happens once the putting out of play of the natural position of the world is accomplished? No longer appearing as anything other than the intentional correlate of consciousness, the world becomes a pure phenomenon, and, in its modified phenomenological understanding, it must therefore be defined as the product of the global system of intentional experiences[15] of a transcendental consciousness. Is this determination sufficient, nevertheless, if the intentional experience has a complex originary structure? In other words, does phenomenality arise equally from all the components of the lived experience? How to respond to this question, without proceeding to a description liable to bring out the different moments of the lived experience?[16]

> We see a tree unchanged with respect to color—its color, the color of the tree—while the positions of the eyes and our relative orientations are changing and our regard is incessantly moving over the trunk and branches, and while, at the same time, we come closer and thus, in various ways, bring the mental process of perception[17] into a flow.[18]

What does this description reveal? It shows, first, that one and the same tree gives itself in a multitude of sketches or profiles which are so many contents of sensation. It further shows that the multiplicity of these givens of sensation or these hyletic *data* among which we must not merely inscribe the visual, tactile, and so on *data*, but likewise "the sensuous pleasure, pain, and tickle-sensations, and so forth, and no doubt also sensuous moments belonging to the sphere of the 'drives'"[19]—that this multiplicity comes out of a dimension entirely different from that of the thing's unity. In effect, if the profiles or the contents of sensations are lived experiences and really belong to lived experiences, then this is evidently not the case for the tree itself. In other words, the sensuous contents (or primary contents, according to the terminology used in the *Logical Investigations*) are not phenomena—except in being, in turn, taken for objects—since, although I readily see the tree in the garden, I do not see my sensations. As the lived content is not the perceived object, phenomenality does not arise from the hyletic layer of lived experience. To what other moment of lived experience should we then attribute it? Let us return to the description. In living in a continuous flow of hyletic *data*, I am conscious *of the* same tree, and this consciousness of identity is, likewise, itself lived. There is, then, in lived experience itself—besides the sensuous moment, which, by its nature, has no meaning—a moment effecting unity,[20] a moment that carries and gives meaning, a moment in virtue of which the sensuous multiplicity is apprehended according to *the same meaning*, a properly intentional moment without which I could not have consciousness *of* the tree.

If the presence of the object arises from such a meaning-bestowal, then we must consequently attribute phenomenality solely to that act without which, strictly speaking, nothing appears. The appearing of the object thus resides exclusively in the phenomenological character of an apprehension that animates or interprets sensations, and only those lived experiences that carry intentionality are agents of phenomenality. Husserl gives the name *morphē* to the intentional moment of concrete, lived experience responsible for phenomenality. The totality of relations variously stratified between *hylē* and *morphē* thus defines the domain of the constitution of objectivities, a domain coextensive with phenomenology itself, since Husserl asserts that "every existent is constituted in the subjectivity of consciousness."[21] To the question, What should we understand by the term *phenomenon*?, Husserl ultimately responds that to be a phenomenon is to be constituted by a subjectivity to whose experiences belong the sensuous *hylē* and intentional *morphē*.

This Husserlian definition of phenomenality nevertheless raises a serious problem that Husserl obviously did not fail to recognize. Indeed the general scheme of constitution just described can define phenomenality only as long as it is the sole such scheme. Whereas phenomena are multiple, phenomenality is one. Yet not all constitution follows the relation apprehension/content of apprehension, the hyle-morphic relation. Starting from the section of *Ideas I* dedicated to sensuous *hylē* and intentional *morphē*, Husserl indicates that this distinction loses all relevance when it is a matter of describing "the obscure depths of the ultimate consciousness which constitutes all such temporality as belonging to mental processes [or lived experiences],"[22] that is, when it is a question of the consciousness of time, which "in a certain profound and quite specific sense, constitutes itself and has its primal source in what is ultimately and truly absolute."[23] In short, the distinction loses relevance when it is a matter of the phenomenological absolute. Is this not, by the same token, to subtract phenomenality from constitution?

Husserl never thought so and attempted indefatigably to describe the self-constitution of consciousness, of the *ego*, and of time. What is the essential difficulty to which the analysis of the self-constitution of internal time consciousness is exposed? If constitution must absolutely define phenomenality, then everything must be constituted, up to and including the temporal *hylē* itself. Yet, in a general fashion, the intentional *morphē* applies to a *hylē* in itself lacking meaning, and consequently the latter should precede the former. When it is a matter of describing the constitution of the temporal *morphē*, which is to say the absolute *morphē*—when it is a matter of recovering the originary intentionality and the ultimate origin of intentionality, there is accordingly no other possible point of departure than the absolute temporal *hylē*. In other words, in seeking the constitutive origin of the consciousness of time in *hylē*, Husserl necessarily aims to resolve the opposition between *hylē* and *morphē* constituted in the midst of a primal *hylē*; he attempts to derive *morphē* from the originary *hylē*. But he is thereupon caught up in a double bind since he must simultaneously describe the constitution of the *morphē* on the basis of the *hylē* and that of the originary *hylē* itself; in short, he must reduce the essential lateness[24] of *morphē* relative to *hylē*. He believes he accomplishes this by recognizing in the "primal impression . . . something absolutely unmodified, the primal source of all further consciousness and being."[25]

Is this defensible? Several questions are thus opened. First, is it possible to get out of the circle that Husserl himself formulated when he specified, in a manuscript from 1932, "I need two things; on the one hand, the flowing field of lived experiences in the midst of which there is continuously a field of originary impressions that disappear in retention and forwardly in protention and, on the other hand, the *ego* which is thereby affected and motivated to action. However," he added, "is not the proto-impressional already an apperceptive unity, something noematic [which is to say constituted][26] issuing from the *ego*, and does the question not always lead back to an apperceptive unity?"[27] Second, as every impression has, by essence, an intensive magnitude, must force not belong to intentionality and phenomenality themselves? Indeed if the intentional *morphē* arises from the primal *hylē*, then it is no longer possible to assert—as Husserl did in the *Logical Investigations* after attributing differences of intensity to foundational sensations alone—on this basis that "*act-intentions*, the inseparable aspects which give acts their essential distinctive peculiarities . . . *must be without intrinsic intensity.*"[28] From the moment that the intentional *morphē* comes out of a hyletic flow whose intensity is essentially differentiated, we must either attribute intensity to intentionality or indeed, contrariwise, explain how intentionality levels and equalizes differences of intensity. However, in this latter case, and considering the fact that all constitutive analysis starts from something constituted, access to the differences in intensity proper to sensations would become impossible. It would then remain for us to make the intensity of intentionality constitutively intelligible, something that Husserl, it seems, never did. Third, can one ultimately assimilate phenomenology simply to originary sensation if sensation, as such, is not absolutely separable from the body (*Leib*); in other words, if corporeity lies at the ground of sensation as its very event?[29]

Let us examine each of these questions. Endeavoring to derive form from matter, sense from the sensuous, and manners of signifying from manners of feeling, the analysis of primal constitution[30] finds itself caught in a circle. Nevertheless the circularity depends here on the comprehension of the flowing sensuous *datum* as pure matter and diversity, and on sensation as essentially devoid of thought. Is this determination founded on a sufficient description? To say that sensation possesses an intensive magnitude, a degree, amounts to saying that our sensibility functions within the confines of a determinate quantum range. Whence would this quantum receive its determination, if not from our conditions of existence, since possessing senses more or less considerably acute would no doubt place our existence in peril? In other words, if the intensity of our sensations is dictated by the conditions of our existence, and these conditions dictate, in turn, those general laws in whose parameters we can see and touch what we see and touch as we see and touch it, then this is because it is best, for our own preservation, that we have a given degree or acuity of sensibility rather than another. Our sensations are thus governed by value judgments that thoroughly permeate them, and there is nothing less blind than a sensation. In thus noting that, in "all sensations there are particular *valuations* [*bestimmte Schätzungen*],"[31] Nietzsche contradicts not only Kant, for whom only the intensive quantity of sensation may be known a priori, but also Husserl. He contradicts Kant because if value—or, in other words, the quality of sensation—is indeed reducible to differences of quantity,[32] then through this approach the quality of sensation becomes a priori knowable. And he contradicts Husserl, since sensation, understood as that which is indissociable from valuation, becomes a "moral," an intellectual phenomenon.

The response thus furnished to the first question likewise allows us to respond to the second. For, in effect, if sensation is always already, qua intensive magnitude, a thought,[33] in other words if, in sensation, force never goes without a thought, that is, without a form that commands it by determining a priori its field and the limits of its possible, gradual variations, then it is in turn necessary to allow that this intensity be inseparable from thought, and that intentionality could never go without intensity. Once the concept of pure sensuous matter is given up, once we lift the limitations of the concept of sensibility to the given and to receptivity, there is no longer any obstacle to recognizing the intensity of intentionality, an intensity without which it would be absurd to speak, for example, of something like a weariness of reason, that is, of a reason that is, as we know, "an essential and universal structural form of transcendental subjectivity in general."[34]

But does taking account of the intensity of intentionality not modify the very nature of subjectivity? Can we continue to speak of intentionality? Intentionality is consciousness of . . . , and what is essential therein is the transitivity of the relation to . . . Thus to explain the intensity of intentionality and to resolve the problem of originary constitution without giving up constitution itself for the benefit of a datum that is de jure unconstitutable and to which both subject and thought would be properly and totally subject; to explain the intensity of intentionality without consequently giving up the very principle of phenomenological knowledge (which clearly does not imply that phenomenology would be the last word of all philosophy and all knowledge), two steps would be necessary: (1) to understand this transitivity of intentionality on the basis of intensities alone, and (2) to bring consciousness back to these same intensities. But is that possible, and if so, how? Let us return more directly to Husserl's analysis of temporality, which is none other than an elucidation of the being of intentionality itself.

"We regard sensing as the original consciousness of time."[35] What does this mean, if not that sensation is the modality of the givenness of the now?[36] "A primal impression has as its content that which the word 'now' signifies, insofar as it is taken in the strictest sense."[37] Yet sensation or the pure now can provide access to time only by itself giving access to another sensation, that is to say, to another now. How is that possible? How is it that sensation as such is related to other sensations or, what comes to the same thing, how is it that sensation might be modified? "Sensation is the presenting consciousness of time."[38] By qualifying the originary consciousness of time in temporal terms, this expression, which concentrates in itself the difficulty of the argument, means first that originary sensation could not be sensation of self through self without being presented to oneself, or again, that sensation could not be the originary consciousness of time unless it presented itself to itself. But the expression also allows us to respond to the question of the alteration of sensation. Indeed how could sensation present itself to itself without intending itself, in short, without a certain dislocation of what is felt in relation to feeling, without a lag in sensing, pausing over that which it senses, without a tiny phase difference, or lapse, which is itself another sensation and the gap in which the origin of time and of intentionality simultaneously reside? No doubt this analysis contradicts the very possibility of an originary impression if we thereby mean the absolute simultaneity of the felt and of feeling.[39] But can the primal impression, thus understood, be a phenomenological datum if, to see it and intend it, one must first divide it from itself? As necessary as it may be to the description of the temporal constitution of the data of sensation, the primal impression—"appearance without apprehension,"[40] that is, appearance without any appearing object—nonetheless remains, precisely for want of apprehension, as phenomenologically inaccessible as it is indescribable.

Husserl gave the name "retention" to the modality of the uncoupling of sensation between a feeling and something felt.[41] The intentional aiming of sensation separates from the sensation aimed at by retaining it in such a way that the sensation aimed at can present itself to the aiming of the sensation. "The present is always born from the past,"[42] he says. And this tiny differentiation in which, as Levinas put it, "the intending and the event coincide,"[43] is time and the consciousness of time, the common source of time and of intentionality—in short, phenomenality. Yet this uncoupling, without which phenomenology could simply not exist, presupposes the passage, the transition, from one impression to another, for the retention of just passed sensation is itself a new sensation or impression, if we abstract that which it retains. "But when the consciousness of the tone-now, the primal impression, passes over into retention," says Husserl, "this retention itself is a now in turn, something actually existing."[44] In other words, retention, without which consciousness could not be taken as an object, without which there would be no time, this retention supposes the transitivity of sensation. How, then, to understand this transitivity of sensation on which all phenomenology depends?

The analysis of time consciousness unfolds in the space of transcendental life:

> The waking consciousness, the waking life, is a living-towards, a living that goes from the now towards the new now. . . . But the regard from the now towards the new now, this transition, is something original that first paves the way for future experiential intentions. I said that this belongs to the essence of perception; I would do better to say that it belongs to the essence of impression. It is certainly true of every "primary content," of every sensation.[45]

But of what life is it a question, and, above all, how is it possible to describe it? Indeed here, in regard to the origin of intentionality and of phenomenological time, it is obviously no longer possible to take the mode of donation as the point of departure for description, for to speak of a "mode of donation" is already to suppose intentional aiming and, consequently, intentionality itself. At the level of the phenomenological absolute that makes all description possible, it is impossible to appeal to the resources of intentional description and to set in motion the fundamental principle according to which the mode of what is given reveals the being of that given.[46] We must thus attempt to explain the transitive vivacity of sensation—in other words, phenomenological time—starting from sensation itself.

In order to do this, let us start from one of Husserl's notes. After having asserted that all impressions—whether these be primary contents or lived experiences bearing intentionality—are constituted in originary consciousness, Husserl recalls that there are two fundamental classes of lived experiences: "Experiences in the one class are acts, are 'consciousness of . . . ,' are experiences that 'refer to something'; experiences in the other class are not. The sensed color does not refer to something."[47] And at the end of this sentence, he adds the following note:

> Inasmuch as one has the right to designate the primal consciousness itself—the flow that constitutes immanent time and the experiences belonging to it—as act, or the right to divide according to unities and acts, one could and indeed one would have to say: a primal act or a nexus of primal acts constitutes unities that are themselves either acts or not. But this gives rise to difficulties.[48]

What does this note mean? Above all, what are the difficulties raised? They are tied to the concept of an act. From the *Logical Investigations* on, and with regard to the term *act* that designates the lived experiences of signifying, that is, properly intentional lived experiences,[49] Husserl sought in effect to emphasize, "In talking of 'acts' . . . we must steer clear of the word's original meaning: *all thought of activity must be rigidly excluded.*"[50] However, if this originary sense and this exclusion hold for the constituted intentional experiences, whose constitution the "time consciousness" lectures question, they could not, on the other hand, hold unequivocally and without other consideration for the flow of originary consciousness, for the flow of lived experiences in which precisely those units[51] that are intentional acts are constituted. What, then, is the meaning of the concept of act when it designates lived experiences constitutive of immanent time itself, when it comes to designate the *urhyletic* experiences that have for their direct correlates intentional lived experiences and, for their indirect correlates, those objective units constituted in and through these intentional experiences?

In order to attempt to respond to this question, let us attend to the manner in which Husserl characterizes more than he truly describes the flow of originary impressions, the flow of originary consciousness. "The primal impression," he writes, for example,

> is the absolute beginning of this production, the primal source, that from which everything else is continuously produced. But it itself is not produced; it does not arise as something produced but through *genesis spontanea*; it is primal generation. It does not spring from anything (it has no seed); it is primal creation. If it is said: A new now continuously forms on a now that becomes modified into a not-now, or a source quite suddenly engenders it or originates it, these are metaphors.[52]

Or again:

> We can say nothing other than the following: this flow is something we speak of *in conformity with what is constituted*, but it is not "something in objective time." It is *absolute subjectivity* and has the absolute properties of something to be designated *metaphorically* as "flow"; of something that originates in a point of actuality, in a primal source-point, "the now," and so on. . . . For all this, we lack names.[53]

Not only should nothing keep us from ascribing to originary consciousness, or to the originary impression, a dimension of activity whose exclusion concerns only the constituted units themselves; on the contrary, everything here requires it. Husserl insists, in effect, on the spontaneity and thus the activity of the originary impression; he emphasizes the indefatigable activity, the incessant transitivity of the hyletic flow, of absolute immanent life. Moreover how could originary consciousness go "from one now-moment toward another" and "level off the path of intentions of experience," that is, toward objectifying intentionality, if consciousness were essentially inactive and incapable of deploying force? Or, to put it differently, from the moment that "all experiences are intended through impressions or are impressed,"[54] and every impression or every now-moment is "the living source-point of being,"[55] the primally constituting flow is the incessant renewal of a source, its activity. In short, intentional acts and the intentionality of consciousness owe their constitution to the activity, to the force, to the intensity of the originary impression—in a word, to the energy of absolute transcendental life.

We can therefore take it as given, henceforth, that the transitivity of sensation is a function of its vivacity, and that intentionality draws its constitutive origin from the intensive quality[56] of the transitive sensation. Nevertheless by qualifying the primal impression as originary source and creation, and absolute subjectivity as flow, Husserl took care to specify that he was speaking in images, in metaphors. Is it legitimate, then, to make such claims about intentionality on the basis of images? In admitting that he was compelled to name the absolute constituting, subjective flow on the basis of what is constituted therein, Husserl himself justified the nature of his discourse. Yet what does this constraint mean, if not that there is no properly phenomenological name or concept for the phenomenological absolute and, ultimately, for phenomenality itself? What is this if not the recognition that, in order to state absolute subjectivity, words are lacking us— and does this not necessarily open transcendental phenomenology onto its beyond?[57]

Is it possible, then, to conceive that which Husserl designated by images and metaphors, and under what conditions? If the division between image and concept is specific to any philosophy as such, it remains true that the dividing line is not fixed once and for all, and each philosophy is led to trace it differently. There is thus no princial impossibility[58] in conceiving that which is phenomenologically inconceivable. Notwithstanding, such an enterprise would have no sense, relative to phenomenology, if the latter had not itself suggested, and in a certain fashion opened, its possibility. To be sure, no one can leap over his shadow, other than to leap into the sun, as Hegel did, on Heidegger's account—or better, to leap into *his* sun, like the thinker of eternal recurrence.[59] Yet it always remains possible patiently to recognize the outlines of one's shadow. Indeed Husserl often could and would let possibilities come up that, de jure, could not fail to escape him. Is that the case here, and did he point to the dimension on whose grounds might be thought that "for which words are lacking us"?

Without a doubt. Coming back in 1933 to temporality, Husserl declared:

> In my old theory of the internal consciousness of time, I dealt with the intentionality introduced here precisely as intentionality—set up as protention and retention, self-modifying yet preserving the unity; but I did not talk about the ego, and I have not characterized this intentionality as egological (in the broadest sense of intentionality of the will). Later I introduced the latter as founded in an egoless intentionality ("passivity"). But isn't the same ego of actions and habits deriving from it, a developing ego? Shouldn't we or mustn't we posit a universal intentionality of the drive which unifies every original presence as permanence of a temporalization which concretely moves it forward from presence to presence in such a way that all content is the content of the realization of the drives and it is determined by the goal toward which the drive aims . . . ?[60]

Thus Husserl indeed led the transitivity of originary sensation back to a universal drive intentionality. Nevertheless if one understands time as a passage from one now to the next, then this drive intentionality is not itself strictly temporal, precisely because it assures the transition from one present to another, a transition without which there is no time. In other words, by "drive intentionality" one should not understand here an intentionality that would moreover be driven,[61] but rather the opposite, an instinctual drivenness[62] on the basis of which intentionality itself is constituted. Husserl—let us again recall—had always sought the origin of the consciousness of time and of the time of consciousness, the origin of intentionality, in the hyletic *data* from which also arise the sensuous moments from the sphere of the drives. However, if Husserl found himself compelled to presuppose a pre-intentional and pretemporal drivenness,[63] he never proceeded to an analysis of the drive, let alone explained the way a drive could give rise to intentionality—in short, how sense and phenomenality stem from force.

What, then, is a drive? In a general way, every drive is an impulsion toward something, a force ordered and subordinated to a term or goal at which it aims, toward which it is intensely tensed or extended.[64] In that sense, there is no drive without an intention or, better, the intention is a moment of the drive. Husserl no doubt neutralized the intensive signification of tending-toward . . . , but it is for having initially conceived all intentions on the basis of objectifying, theoretic intentionality, and, there, where it is a matter of recovering the constitution of the latter, we are justified in lifting Husserl's neutralization of the intensity of intentions. The intention that is at the ground or principle of intentionality may thus be brought back to the drive, as to its origin. Nevertheless that does not suffice to bring intentionality itself back to drives. In order to do that, it would also be necessary to show that sensation and sense also belong to drives:[65] sensation, because it is in sensation that Husserl sees the origin of time and of intentionality; sense, because all intentionality carries sense. If every drive is a tending-toward . . . , that toward which the drive propels itself, that is, its goal or end, must be a priori open and appropriate to it, failing which the drive precisely could not tend, a tension toward . . . which is none other than the drive in its very exertion.[66] Now, if to feel is to be open to that which can specifically affect and, in this affection, to open to oneself,[67] then sensation is a moment of the drive, since the latter, which is never a state but rather always an event, comes to itself in tending to its proper goal. The drive is thus not a drive toward something absolutely indeterminate and indifferent but toward something that is good for it. Nietzsche said, "Every 'drive' is a drive toward 'something good' and this, from one point of view or another; there is therein an evaluation that, for this very reason, has been incorporated."[68] An evaluation, that is to say a thought and thus a signification. Thought, and sense, are also moments of every drive. And of these three moments—intention, sensation, and sense—the last is by right the first, for no drive could tend toward a goal without tending to its goal, nor could it tend to its goal without tending toward that which is good for it, to that which has value for it and for it alone—and which, in order to be an evaluation, is that sense to which it owes its being the exertion that it is.

To measure the consequences of leading intentionality back to an instinctual drivenness,[69] it is certainly not useless to take a step backward. If to be a phenomenon is to be constituted by transcendental subjectivity, then the latter—which is unto-itself and for-itself its own phenomenon—must necessarily constitute itself and could only do so on the basis of hyletic life. Yet how can *hylē*, as appearance without apprehension and wherein nothing appears, give rise to a primal apprehension, to a first appearing of something? To attempt to resolve this quite fundamental difficulty and to account for the transitivity of sensation without whose retention there is neither intentionality nor temporality, Husserl ends by appealing to the instinctual drivenness of absolute life.[70] What, then, becomes of subjectivity itself? Must it not be constituted as instinctually driven,[71] that is, as that body for which transitive sensation is its event?[72] There can be no doubt about it. It is thus on condition of being a drive body that subjectivity can be truly constitutive, and it is, consequently, in such a body that we should seek the ultimate source of phenomenality. Moreover if it is not absurd to lead the intentional subjectivity that bestows meaning, back to the drive body, then this is because there is neither sensation nor drives without a foregoing evaluation or, to put it otherwise, because every transcendental aesthetic, whether that of Kant or, more broadly, that of Husserl, supposes a system of value judgments, a "morality."[73] This assertion, we note in passing, does not imply the dissolution of the transcendental aesthetic into a transcendental logic because value judgments do not form a class of apophantic judgments; it means, on the contrary, that transcendental aesthetics and logic rest on these same value judgments, on this same "morality" that is not (indeed, far from it) the only possible morality.[74]

In following the internal movement and logic of the constitutive analysis, we have thus been led beyond phenomenology. Beyond phenomenology, and not toward some in-side of phenomenology, since in the latter case the project of constitution may still preserve its meaning. In fact, do we not ultimately vindicate the intellectual dimension of intentionality by leading sensation back to a drive—and the drive back to a value or a thought, without which it is nothing? The "intellectual dimension" does not necessarily mean the theoretical dimension here. By the same token, does leading sensation back to a drive not amount to holding open the possibility of constitutive investigation? No doubt, the latter gets radically modified or rather, displaced, thereby. In asserting—against that empiricism on which Husserl remains in certain respects dependent—that "the intellect seems to be older than sensation,"[75] Nietzsche formulated the principle of this displacement. For what does this precedence of intellect over sensation signify if not that modes of feeling depend on the modes of signifying or thinking? Or again, what would it mean, if not that the body is a "great reason [*grosse Vernunft*]" whose "lesser reason," subjective reason, is its "instrument"?[76] What would it mean, to conclude, if not that the body can be more powerfully constitutive than the constitutive flow of absolute subjectivity itself?

Notes

This essay was translated by Bettina Bergo. Originally published as "Au-delà de la phénoménologie," in *Dramatique des phénomènes*, 105–23.

1. Husserl, *Ideen zur einer reinen Phänomenologie und phänomenologischen Philosophie, Erstes Buch*, 3 (hereafter Hua III); *Ideas I*, 5. [Didier Franck translates from the German, and we here give priority to his translation—Trans.]

2. Descartes, *Les Principes de la Philosophie*, I, §10; *Principles of Philosophy*, 160–212. [Translation modified for fluency with the French original—Trans.]

3. Husserl, *Die Krisis der europäischen Wissenschaften und die transzendentale Phänomenologie*, "Die Krisis des europäischen Menschentums und die Philosophie," 348 (hereafter, Hua VI); *Crisis*, "The Vienna Lecture," 299.

4. Franck writes *"resaississement."*—Trans.

5. Husserl, "Manuscript C 2 II," 7.

6. Hua VI, 439. [Appendix XIII is not included in the English translation—Trans.]

7. Cf. Husserl, *Cartesianische Meditationen*, §60; *Cartesian Meditations*, 139 (hereafter CM).

8. Franck writes *"ego éveillé."*—Trans.

9. Hua III, §30, 63; *Ideas I*, 57. [Translation modified for fluency with the French original—Trans.]

10. Franck writes *"de la conscience et de la donnée empiriques du monde."*—Trans.

11. Franck writes *"qui suppose l'antithèse."*—Trans.

12. Franck writes *"figure."*—Trans.

13. Hua III, §31, 54; *Ideas I*, 59. [Translation modified for fluency with the French original.—Trans.]

14. Hua III, §3, 55; *Ideas I*, 59. [Translation modified for fluency with the French original.—Trans.]

15. Franck writes *"vécus intentionnels."*—Trans.

16. Franck writes *"différents moments du vécu."*—Trans.

17. Franck writes *"le vécu de perception."*—Trans.

18. Hua III, §9, 203; *Ideas I*, 237.

19. Hua III, §85, 172; *Ideas I*, 203.

20. Franck writes *"moment facteur d'unité."*—Trans.

21. Husserl, *Formale und transzendentale Logik*, §94; *Formal and Transcendental Logic*, §93, 232.

22. Hua III, §85, 171; *Ideas I*, §85, "Sensuous ὕλη, Intentive μορφή," 203.

23. Hua III, §81, 163; *Ideas I*, 193.

24. Franck writes *"retard essentiel."*—Trans.

25. Husserl, *Zur Phänomenologie des inneren Zeitbewusstseins*, §31, 67 (hereafter Hua X); *On the Phenomenology of the Consciousness of Internal Time*, §31, 70 (hereafter PCIT).

26. These brackets are Didier Franck's addition.—Trans.

27. Husserl, "Manuscript C 7 I," 18.

28. Husserl, *Logische Untersuchungen*, V, §15, 396–97; *Logical Investigations*, vol. 2, Investigation V, §15, 576 (hereafter LI).

29. [Franck writes *"événement."*—Trans.] Cf. *Ideen II*, §39, 153; *Ideas II*, §39, 160; Levinas, "Intentionnalité et sensation," 162; *Discovering Existence with Husserl*, 151.

30. Franck writes *"archi-constitution."*—Trans.

31. Nietzsche, *Kritische Studienausgabe*, 11, 1884, 27 [63], 290 (hereafter KSA, with volume, date, notebook, and fragment).

32. Nietzsche, KSA 12, 1887, 6 [14], 238, KSA 13, 1888, 14 [105], 282–83; Franck, *Nietzsche et l'ombre de Dieu*, 184ff.

33. Franck writes *"une pensée."*—Trans.

34. *Cartesianische Meditationen*, §23, 92; CM §23, 57. [Translation modified for fluency with the French original.—Trans.]

35. Hua X, §31; PCIT, Appendix III, 112.

36. Franck writes "*donnée du maintenant.*"—Trans.

37. Hua X, §31, 70; PCIT, 67.

38. Hua X, Appendix III, 112; PCIT 107. By "presenting," Husserl means "making present," making some lived experience present (*gegenwärtigend, Gegenwärtigung*).

39. Franck writes "*du senti et du sentir.*"—Trans.

40. Hua X, Appendix VI, 111; PCIT, 116.

41. Franck writes "*entre un sentir et un senti.*"—Trans.

42. Hua X, 106; PCIT, Appendix III, 111.

43. Levinas, "Intentionnalité et Sensation," 153; *Discovering Existence with Husserl*, 142.

44. Hua X, 29; PCIT §11, 31.

45. Hua X, 106–7; PCIT, Appendix III, 112.

46. Franck writes "*le mode de donnée révèle l'être du donné.*"—Trans.

47. Hua X, §42, 89; PCT, 94.

48. Hua X, §42, 89; PCT, 94.

49. See *Logische Untersuchungen*, V, 344; LI, 2, Investigation V, §3, 540.

50. *Logische Untersuchungen*, §13, 379, §30, 453; LI, 2, Investigation V, §13, 562, §30, 616–18.

51. Franck writes "*ces unités.*"—Trans.

52. Hua X, Appendix I, 100; PCIT, 106.

53. Hua X, §36, 75; PCIT, 79.

54. Hua X, §42, 89; PCIT, 93.

55. Hua X, §31, 69; PCIT, 71.

56. Franck writes "*intensivité.*"—Trans.

57. Franck writes "*sur son au-delà.*"—Trans.

58. Franck writes "*impossibilité de principe.*"—Trans.

59. Cf. Heidegger, *Die Frage nach dem Ding*, 153; *What Is a Thing?*, 150–51. Also see Nietzsche, "Von den Erhabenen" in *Also sprach Zarathustra I-IV*, KSA 4, 151; "Of the Sublime Men," in *Thus Spoke Zarathustra*, 140.

60. Husserl, "Universale Teleologie," in *Zur Phänomenologie der Intersubjectivität*, 594–95; "Universal Teleology," 336.

61. Franck writes "*intentionnalité qui serait par surcroît pulsionnelle.*"—Trans.

62. Franck writes "*pulsionnalité.*"—Trans.

63. Franck writes "*pulsionnalité.*"—Trans.

64. Franck writes "*intensément tendue.*"—Trans.

65. Franck writes "*la pulsion.*"—Trans.

66. Franck writes "*exercice.*"—Trans.

67. Franck writes "*s'ouvrir à soi-même.*"—Trans.

68. Nietzsche, KSA 11, 1884, 26 [72], 167.

69. Franck writes "*pulsionnalité.*"—Trans.

70. Franck writes "*la pulsionnalité de la vie absolue.*"—Trans.

71. Franck writes "*pulsionnelle.*"—Trans.

72. Franck writes "*dont la sensation transitive est l'événement.*"—Trans.

73. Franck writes "*système de jugements de valeur, une 'morale.'*"—Trans.

74. On the relationship between value judgments and predicative judgments, between sensation and evaluation, see Franck, *Nietzsche and the Shadow of God; Nietzsche et l'ombre de Dieu*, 288ff, 299ff.

75. Nietzsche, KSA 8, 1876–77, 23 [186], 470.

76. Nietzsche, "Von den Verächtern des Leibes" in *Also sprach Zarathustra I-IV*, KSA IV, 39; "Of the Despisers of the Body," in *Thus Spoke Zarathustra*, 62. [Translation modified for fluency with the French original —Trans.]

Bibliography

Descartes, René. *Les Principes de la Philosophie.* In *Oeuvres de Descartes.* Edited by Victor Cousin. Paris: F. G. Leuvrault, 1824.
——. "Principles of Philosophy." In *Descartes: Selected Philosophical Writings.* Translated by John Cottingham, Robert Stoothoff, and Dugald Murdoch. Cambridge: Cambridge University Press, 2009.
Franck, Didier. *Nietzsche et l'ombre de Dieu.* Paris: PUF, 1998.
——. *Nietzsche and the Shadow of God.* Translated by Bettina Bergo. Evanston, IL: Northwestern University Press, 2012.
Heidegger, Martin. *Die Frage nach dem Ding (1935).* In *Gesamtausgabe,* vol. 41. Frankfurt am Main: Vittorio Klostermann, 1989.
——. *What Is a Thing?* Translated by W. B. Barton Jr. and Vera Deutsch. Chicago: Henry Regnery, 1967.
Husserl, Edmund. *Cartesian Meditations.* Translated by Dorion Cairns. Dordrecht: Kluwer Academic, 1999.
——. *Cartesianische Meditationen und Pariser Vorträge.* Edited by S. Strasser. The Hague: Martinus Nijhoff, 1973.
——. *The Crisis of European Science and Transcendental Phenomenology.* Translated by David Carr. Evanston, IL: Northwestern University Press, 1970.
——. *Formal and Transcendental Logic.* Translated by Dorion Cairns. The Hague: Martinus Nijhoff, 1969.
——. *Formale und transzendentale Logik: Versuch einer Kritik der logischen Vernunft. Husserliana XVII.* Edited by Paul Janssen. The Hague: Martinus Nijhoff, 1974.
——. *Ideas Pertaining to a Pure Phenomenology and to a Phenomenological Philosophy: First Book.* Translated by Frank Kersten Dordrecht: Kluwer Academic, 1982.
——. *Ideas II.* Dordrecht: Translated by Richard Rojcewicz and André Schuwer. Kluwer Academic, 1990.
——. *Ideen zu einer reinen Phänomenologie und phänomenologischen Philosophie: Ideen I. Husserliana III.* Edited by Karl Schuhmann. The Hague: Martinus Nijhoff, 1977.
——. *Ideen zur einer reinen Phänomenologie und phänomenologischen Philosophie (Ideen II). Phänomenologische Untersuchungen zur Konstitution. Husserliana IV.* Edited by Marly Biemel. The Hague: Martinus Nijhoff, 1952.
——. *Die Krisis der europäischen Wissenschaften und die transzendentale Phänomenologie: Eine Einleitung in die phänomenologische Philosophie. Husserliana VI.* Edited by Walter Biemel. The Hague: Martinus Nijhoff, 1976.
——. "Manuscript C 7 I." In *Späte Texte über Zeitkonstitution (1929–1934): Die C-Manuskripte.* Edited by Dieter Lohmar. New York: Springer, 2006.
——*On the Phenomenology of the Consciousness of Internal Time (1893–1917).* Translated by John Barnett Brough. Dordrecht: Kluwer Academic, 1991.
——. "Universal Teleology." In *Husserl: Shorter Works.* Edited by Peter McCormick and Frederick Elliston. Translated by Marly Biemel. Notre Dame, IN: University of Notre Dame Press, 1981.
——. *Zur Phänomenologie des inneren Zeitbewusstesens (1893–1917). Husserliana X.* Edited by Rudolf Boehm. The Hague: Martinus Nijhoff, 1969.
——. *Zur Phänomenologie der Intersubjectivität, Husserliana XV, Texte aus dem Nachlass. Dritter Teil. 1929–35.* Edited by Iso Kern. The Hague, Netherlands: Martinus Nijhoff, 1973.

Lévinas, Emmanuel. *Discovering Existence with Husserl*. Translated by Richard A. Cohen and Michael B. Smith. Evanston, IL: Northwestern University Press, 1998.

———. "Intentionnalité et sensation." In *En découvrant l'existence avec Husserl et Heidegger*. Paris: Vrin, 1967.

Nietzsche, Friedrich. *Kritische Studienausgabe*. Edited by Giorgio Colli and Mazzino Montinari. Berlin: DTV/ de Gruyter, 1967–77, 1988.

———. *Thus Spoke Zarathustra*. Translated by R. J. Hollingdale. New York: Penguin Books, 1969.

Index

Contributors

Keith Ansell-Pearson is a professor of philosophy at the University of Warwick. He has written monographs on Nietzsche, Bergson, and Deleuze. He serves on the editorial boards of, among others, *Nietzsche-Studien*, *Journal of Nietzsche Studies*, and *Deleuze Studies*. He is the coeditor of *The Nietzsche Reader* (Blackwell, 2006), the editor of *A Companion to Nietzsche* (Blackwell, 2006), and the series editor of *Henri Bergson Centennial Series* (Palgrave Macmillan).

Babette Babich is a professor of philosophy at Fordham University. She is executive director of the Nietzsche-Society in the United States (est. 1978) and executive editor of the journal *New Nietzsche Studies* (which she founded in 1995 and coedits with David B. Allison). She is the author of *Eines Gottes Glück voller Macht und Liebe: Beiträge zu Nietzsche, Hölderlin, Heidegger* (Klassik Stiftung Weimar, Bauhaus-Universität Weimar, 2009) and *Words in Blood, Like Flowers: Philosophy and Poetry, Music and Eros in Hölderlin, Nietzsche, Heidegger* (State University of New York Press, 2006). She is also the editor of *From Phenomenology to Thought, Errancy, and Desire: Essays in Honor of William J. Richardson, S.J.* (Kluwer Academic, 1995).

Bettina Bergo is an associate professor of philosophy at Université de Montréal. She teaches courses on continental philosophy, psychoanalysis, and French postmodern thought. She is the author of *Levinas between Ethics and Politics: For the Beauty That Adorns the Earth* (Phaenomenologica Series 152, Martinus Nijhoff, 1999; paperback edition by Duquesne University Press, 2002) and the coeditor with Jill Stauffer of *Levinas and Nietzsche: After the Death of a Certain God* (Columbia University Press, 2009).

Rudolf Boehm is Professor Emeritus in philosophy. He participated in the edition and publication of Husserl's complete works (*Husserliana*) in Leuven (Husserl-Archives). He is notably the editor of Husserl's *Zur Phänomenologie des inneren Zeitbewusstseins (1893–1917)* (Nijhoff, 1966) and the translator in German of Merleau-Ponty's *Phénoménologie de la perception*. He has written several books and articles dedicated to phenomenology, among them *Vom Gesichtpunkt der Phänomenologie* I and II (Nijhoff, 1968–80).

Françoise Bonardel is a professor of philosophy at Sorbonne University (Paris I). She teaches philosophy of religion and continental philosophy (Nietzsche, Heidegger, Ricoeur). She is the author of several books dedicated to East-West philosophical dialogue, such as *Bouddhisme et philosophie, en quête d'une sagesse commune* (L'harmattan, 2008); she also analyzed the limits of the Western concept of rationality in the light of religious and esoteric traditions in *L'irrationnel* (PUF, 1996) and *La voie hermétique* (Dervy, 2002). She recently published a book on the crisis of European cultural identity, *Des héritiers sans passé—Essai sur la crise de l'identité culturelle européenne* (Les Éditions de la Transparence, 2010), and an essay titled *Triptyque pour Albrecht Dürer* (Editions de la Transparence, 2012).

Élodie Boublil graduated from Sorbonne University (Paris I) and Sciences-Po Paris. She is now a PhD candidate in philosophy at McGill University. Her thesis focuses on the relation between subjectivity's individuation and world's perception within the phenomenological movement (notably via Husserl, Heidegger, and Merleau-Ponty). She teaches philosophy at the United Nations International School (New York). Her article "La notion de *Weltanschauung*, généalogie d'un concept et d'un processus" was published in *PhaenEx* 4, no. 1 (2009), and she has written book chapters dedicated to Husserl, Nietzsche, and Heidegger.

Frank Chouraqui is an assistant professor of philosophy at Koç University in Istanbul. He took a PhD in philosophy from the University of Warwick. His thesis, "A Study in Ambiguity: Nietzsche and Merleau-Ponty on the Question of Truth," focuses on Nietzsche's and Merleau-Ponty's common ontological commitments as expressed in their treatments of truth. He is the translator and editor of Auguste Blanqui's *Eternity by the Stars* (Contra Mundum, forthcoming) and has recently published a chapter titled "Nietzsche and the New Science of Life" (in Vanessa Lemm, ed., *Nietzsche and the Becoming of Life*, Fordham University Press, forthcoming) as well as various journal articles and book chapters on the ontologies of Nietzsche and Merleau-Ponty.

Christine Daigle is a professor of philosophy and Chancellor's Chair for Research Excellence at Brock University. She is the author of *Le nihilisme est-il un humanisme? Étude sur Nietzsche et Sartre* (Presses de l'Université Laval, 2005) and *Routledge Critical Thinkers: Jean-Paul Sartre* (Routledge, 2009). She has edited the book *Existentialist Thinkers and Ethics* (McGill/Queen's University Press, 2006), in which she contributed a chapter on Simone de Beauvoir's ethics. She has also coedited the volume *Beauvoir and Sartre: The Riddle of Influence* (Indiana University Press, 2009) with Jacob Golomb and is the author of papers on Nietzsche, Sartre, and Beauvoir.

Françoise Dastur is Professor Emerita in philosophy. She is associated with the Husserl Archives of Paris and is the honorary president of the Ecole Française of Daseinsanalyse, of which she was the founder in 1993. She has published many articles in French, English, and German on Husserl, Heidegger, Merleau-Ponty, Ricoeur, and Derrida. She is the author of several books in French, of which three have been translated into English: *Heidegger and the Question of Time* (Humanities Press, 1998), *Telling Time: Sketch of a Phenomenological Chrono-logy* (Athlone Press, 2000), and *Death: An Essay on Finitude* (Athlone Press, 1996). She recently published *Daseinsanalyse. Phénoménologie et psychiatrie* with Philippe Cabestan (Vrin, 2011) and *Heidegger et la pensée à venir* (Vrin, 2011).

Didier Franck is a professor of philosophy at University of Nanterre (Paris X) and a member of the Institut Universitaire de France. He teaches courses in phenomenology and the history of German philosophy. He has published books and articles on Husserl, Heidegger, and Nietzsche, including *Chair et Corps, sur la phénoménologie de Husserl* (Editions de Minuit, 1981), *Heidegger et le problème de l'espace* (Editions de Minuit, 1986), *Nietzsche et l'ombre de Dieu* (PUF, 1998; English translation by Bettina Bergo titled *Nietzsche and the Shadow of God*, Northwestern University Press 2011), *Dramatique des phénomènes* (PUF, 2001), *Heidegger et le christianisme* (PUF, 2004), and *L'un-pour-l'autre, Levinas et la signification* (PUF, 2008).

Saulius Geniusas is an assistant professor of philosophy at the Chinese University of Hong Kong. His main research interests lie in continental philosophy, particularly in phenomenology and hermeneutics. His work explores how European philosophy of the past few centuries opens up new avenues for the pursuit of subjectivity and selfhood. He is the author of *The Origins of the Horizon in Husserl's Phenomenology* (Springer, 2012). He has published articles on Husserl and Nietzsche, including "Husserl et la phénoménologie de la donation," trans. Lydia Ardjouni, *Methodos 9: L'Autre Husserl* (2009) and "Nietzsche's Critique of the Subject," *Žmogus ir Žodis* 10, no. 4 (2008).

Kristen Brown Golden is an associate professor of philosophy at Millsaps College. She has published book chapters on trauma theory and on Merleau-Ponty and journal articles on topics in phenomenology, philosophy of body, feminist philosophy, Nietzsche, and Aristotle. She is the coeditor of *The Trauma Controversy: Philosophical and Interdisciplinary Dialogues* (State University of New York Press, 2009) and the author of *Nietzsche and Embodiment: Discerning Bodies and Non-dualism* (State University of New York Press, 2006).

Lawrence J. Hatab is Louis I. Jaffe Professor at Old Dominion University. He teaches courses on nineteenth-century philosophy and twentieth-century continental philosophy, especially Nietzsche and Heidegger. He has published many articles and books on Nietzsche and Heidegger, with emphasis on their relation to ethics and politics. Works include *Nietzsche's Life Sentence: Coming to Terms with Eternal Recurrence* (Routledge, 2005), *A Nietzschean Defense of Democracy: An Experiment in Postmodern Politics* (Open Court Press, 1995), *Ethics and Finitude: Heideggerian Contributions to Moral Philosophy* (Rowman & Littlefield, 2000), and *Nietzsche's On the Genealogy of Morality: An Introduction* (Cambridge University Press, 2008).

Galen A. Johnson is a professor of philosophy at the University of Rhode Island. His research interests are phenomenology, recent French philosophy (especially Merleau-Ponty), aesthetics, and American philosophy. He is the author of numerous articles in contemporary continental philosophy and has held fellowships from the National Endowment for the Humanities, the American Council for Learned Societies, and the American Philosophical Society. He is currently the general secretary of the International Merleau-Ponty Circle and is the director of the URI Center for the Humanities. He is the editor of *Ontology and Alterity in Merleau-Ponty* (Northwestern University Press, 1990) and *The Merleau-Ponty Aesthetics Reader: Philosophy and Painting* (Northwestern University Press, 1993, 2008). He recently published a book dedicated to Merleau-Ponty's aesthetics: *The Retrieval of the Beautiful: Thinking through Merleau-Ponty's Aesthetics* (Northwestern University Press, 2010).

CPSIA information can be obtained at www.ICGtesting.com
Printed in the USA
LVOW07s1948281214

420652LV00001B/364/P